the story of
the Car

the story of
the Car

David Hodges   **David Burgess Wise**

HAMLYN
London · New York · Sydney · Toronto

Published by the Hamlyn Publishing Group Limited
London · New York · Sydney · Toronto
Astronaut House, Feltham, Middlesex, England
Copyright © The Hamlyn Publishing Group Limited, 1974

ISBN 0 600 31307 7

Text set in 11/12 point Bembo 270, captions in
9 point Univers 689
Filmset in Great Britain by Servis Filmsetting Ltd, Manchester
Reproductions by Metric Reproductions, Chelmsford, Essex
Printed and bound in the Canary Islands by
Litografia A. Romero, SA, Santa Cruz de Tenerife,
Canary Islands (Spain)

D. L. TF. 831 - 74

Acknowledgments
The publishers are grateful to the following individuals and organizations for the illustrations in this book: Alfa Romeo; Associated Press; Aston Martin; *Autocar*; Automobile Manufacturers Association; Bertone; Birthplace of Speed Association; Lionel Birnbom; Hugh Bishop; Alice Bixler; BMW; Michael Bowler; Griffith Borgeson; Bristol Cars; British Leyland Motor Corporation; British Petroleum; Neill Bruce; Diana Burnett; Camera Press; Castrol; Central Press Photos; Chevrolet; Chrysler; Citroen; *Custom Car*; Daimler-Benz; Datsun; Detroit Public Library; Deutsches Museum, Munich; Fiat; Ford; Fuji; General Motors; Geoff Goddard; Greater Ormond Beach Chamber of Commerce; Gulf; Hans Edwards; David Hodges; Jeff Hutchinson; Ray Hutton; IPC Transport Press; Indianapolis Motor Speedway; Jaguar; Jensen; Leigh Jones; Keystone Press Agency; Louis Klemantaski; Lamborghini; Mike Lintern; Giovanni Lurani; Ozzie Lyons; Mansell Collection; T.C. March; Mercedes-Benz; *Motor*; Musée de l'Automobile du Mans; Musée Française de l'Automobile Henri Malartre; National Motor Museum; Opel; Phipps Photographic; Pirelli; John Player Motor Sport; Charles Pocklington; Porsche; Cyril Posthumus; Press Association Photos; Radio Times Hulton Picture Library; Renault; Rolls-Royce; Stanley Rosenthal; Rover; Royal Automobile Club; Shell; Nigel Snowdon; F. David Stone; STP; de Tomaso; Toyota; United Press International; Vauxhall; H. Roger Viollet; Volkswagen; David Burgess Wise.

Pierce Arrow V-12, 1934

Contents

Swedish Grand Prix, 1973

Odd Notions
the first century

'Carriages without horses shall go,' said that garrulous and inaccurate prophetess Mother Shipton: but though the good mother flourished in the 16th century, technology was not up to the production of a true motorcar in her day.

Certainly some of the rich men of the era had complex carriages built, powered by springs, cogs or strong men hidden inside the bodywork, but these were novelties brought out to impress the crowds at holiday parades, quite impracticable as a means of transport.

It was not until the dawn of the Industrial Revolution that the right power, steam, and accurate standards of engineering could be combined to produce a self-moving vehicle–James

John Scott Russell ran a steam carriage service between Glasgow and Paisley in 1834; on July 29 an act of sabotage caused an explosion and five deaths

Watt's condensing stationary engines were built to the accuracy of 'a worn sixpence.'

However, Watt was not interested in steam carriages, and only took out a patent for a road vehicle in 1784 to keep his assistant, William Murdock, from wasting his time on similar projects.

But by then the first road carriages, built by the French engineer Cugnot in 1769 and 1770 had made their first faltering runs. Cugnot's first machine, intended for artillery haulage, had insufficient boiler capacity; the second was tested in the streets of Paris when it 'overbalanced itself on turning a corner and fell over with a crash; after which, its employment being thought dangerous, it was locked up in the arsenal to prevent further mischief.'

That ensured its continued survival (although Napoleon did have it put back in running order for some equally

unsuccessful tests in 1804). It can still be seen today in the Conservatoire des Arts et Métiers in Paris, a unique survivor of the prehistory of motoring and a complete evolutionary dead end.

In 1801, the first successful road engine was built in Cornwall by Richard Trevithick; it climbed Camborne Beacon 'like a little bird.' Four days later it broke down; Trevithick and his cousin (and financial backer) Andrew Vivian left it under a lean-to and adjourned to a neighbouring hotel for 'a roast goose and proper drinks.' The boiler ran dry while they were feasting, and carriage and lean-to went up in flames.

Two years later Trevithick built an improved carriage and took it to London. Although Sir Humphry Davy, who saw the engine, commented: 'I shall soon hope to hear that the roads of England are the haunts of

One of Hancock's most successful steamers was the Autopsy ('see for yourself') which was in service in London in 1833

Captain Trevithick's dragons,' Trevithick failed to develop either this idea (or his other major invention, the railway engine) any further–the atrocious state of the roads was against him, and so was his own mercurial temperament.

But where Trevithick had led, others followed: in 1815 the Czech engineer Josef Bozek built a $\frac{1}{20}$ hp steam carriage which ran in the streets of Prague, its fitful progress punctuated by frequent halts to allow the boiler to build up working pressure, while in 1819 the British inventor Medhurst built the first of two carriages.

This ran successfully in London, and was followed a couple of years later by an improved machine capable of carrying four people at 7 mph.

The 1820s and 1830s saw a tremendous flowering of steam carriages in Britain. Gurney, Hancock, and James were among those who led the field–Hancock built a fleet of buses which ran successfully in London.

In 1835, a correspondent to the *Mechanics' Magazine* described a round trip from London to Marlborough in Hancock's *Erin*, which could average 10 mph (excluding breakdowns), and concluded:

'Mr Hancock started from Marlborough to return to London on Friday at half-past five. The carriage accomplished the ascent of Marlborough Hill–the steepest acclivity on the Bristol road, being full one mile long, and having a rise of about one in twelve–in six minutes, with a stoppage of four minutes. The *Erin* reached Reading by ten, and stayed one hour and a half for breakfast. After running through the town we continued our journey, and reached London by half-past five, being again twelve hours on the road, and having lost nearly about the same time in stoppages as on our journey down.

'Our reception on the road was very cordial; there was scarcely any manifestation of bad feeling throughout the journey–indeed, wherever we stopped to take in water we had every assistance given us by the bystanders. We were particularly well received at Marlborough, where we stayed two days. The carriage made a trip through the town each day, and Mr Hancock astonished the inhabitants by the easy manner in which he could turn, stop, or back his carriage. Two gentlemen of Marlborough most hospitably entertained the steam travellers whilst they remained in that town.'

Hospitality, however, was a rare commodity–the jealousy and blind prejudice of the horse-owning aristocracy drove steam vehicles off the road, first by imposing ridiculously high turnpike tolls on steam carriages, then by restrictive legislation which

Below: early private vehicle attempts in the 1850s included Thomas Rickett's vehicle *(left)* and Richard Dudgeon's light carriage, which survives in a Massachusetts museum.
Following pages: oldest of all self-propelled vehicles, Cugnot's carriage

Leon Serpollet steam cars generally looked like contemporary petrol-driven vehicles; this curious hansom cab of 1898 was delivered to the infamous Harry Lawson's Motor Car Syndicate in London

Serpolet had demonstrated this tricycle, his first successful vehicle, in Paris a decade earlier. It was largely built from scrap and second-hand material, had a coal-fired flash boiler. It achieved a measured speed of almost seven mph

favoured the slow and clumsy traction engine rather than the fast steam carriages, some of which were capable of over 30 mph.

In 1865 the law brought steam carriages down to the speed of a man walking in front. It was not just the hostile legislation which forced the steam carriages off the road, for in France and America, where other steam carriage pioneers were at work—notably the Dietz family, who had vehicles running in Belgium and France

in the 1830s—few such vehicles were built after 1840, mainly, one suspects, because railway travel was faster and less eventful.

Already 'King Steam' had a rival. In 1794 the Englishman, Robert Street, patented a crude gas engine; two years later the Frenchman Lebon d'Humberstein developed a method of distilling gas from wood, followed in 1801 by a design for a three-cylinder, two-stroke power unit. This might have been used in a carriage if d'Humberstein had not been assassinated. . . .

The first internal-combustion vehicle to move under its own power appeared soon after, the work of a Swiss, Isaac de Rivaz. Built around 1805, his machine had a tall vertical cylinder open at the top; gas was admitted below the piston and exploded by an electric spark from a Voltaic battery, forcing the heavy piston up the cylinder. When de Rivaz kicked open the exhaust valve, the piston fell again, pulling a chain attached to a ratchet wheel, which turned the front wheels through a belt and pulleys.

The inventor managed to coax the machine several times across a room, gave it up as a bad job and built a pumping engine instead.

Then, in 1826, one Samuel Brown drove a 40 litre 'gas and vacuum' carriage up Shooters Hill, in Kent, but the machine proved far costlier to run than a steam carriage, and was shelved.

Cost, too, prevented David Gordon from building his compressed-gas carriage of 1824, while plans laid by Medhurst in 1800 and Mann in 1828 to run vehicles on compressed air, proved just as fruitless, though in 1848 Von Rathen tested a compressed-air carriage at Putney, and in 1855 Julienne drove a similar machine through Paris, with three people aboard.

Attempts by the ominously-named Monsieur Popp to revive compressed air for private and public transport in the late 1890s proved short-lived, too. 'Hot air' was the motive power proposed by aviation pioneer Sir George Cayley for the carriage he patented in 1837. Appropriately?

By the middle of the 19th century the internal-combustion engine had become light enough to be seriously considered as a power unit for light carriages. Around 1858 Jean-

Joseph-Etienne Lenior, a Belgian working in Paris, invented a gas engine running on a primitive two-cycle system. A remarkable feature was the ignition, which used a Ruhmkorff coil in conjunction with a platinum and porcelain sparking plug. By mid-1860 Lenoir was confident enough of his engine, which could run either on gas or carburetted oil, to apply it to a car. Trials were not always successful; Lenoir had brief moments of qualified triumph, but his machines never left the experimental stage.

'In 1863,' he recalled, 'I built an automobile carriage on which we went to Joinville-le-Pont in September: an hour-and-a-half getting there, the same for the return journey. The carriage was heavy: the engine, of one-and-a-half horsepower, made a hundred revolutions a minute, with a fairly weighty flywheel.' The entire journey –18 kilometres–was punctuated by halts to repair the vehicle. 'The consumption of water and petrol was considerable.'

News of this machine even reached the ears of the Tsar of Russia, who bought it as a mechanical plaything and had it shipped to St Petersburg. Its fate is unknown.

America's first internal-combustion engined vehicle was built in the 1860s by Reuben H. Plass, whose father was a partner in the firm of Carpenter & Plass, gas engineers and general machinists, on East 29th Street, New York, generally known as the 'Inventors' Emporium'.

Young Reuben was renowned for his 'crazy notions,' one of which was that a practicable and safe engine could be built to utilise the energy contained in an explosive mixture of gasoline and air. His experiments convinced his father, and they set to work on a self-propelled fire engine.

'Ponderous' was the only word to describe its water-cooled four-stroke engine, for the four vertical cylinders were cast like the cannon the company had made during the Civil War. It featured mechanically-operated poppet valves for inlet and exhaust, plus electric ignition developed by 'an ingenious electrician called Chester,' who had a shop on Broadway. Power output was 'nearly twenty horsepower.'

Steered by handlebars, the machine

Independent front suspension, twin engines and geometrically perfect steering were some of the advanced features of Amédée Bollée *père*'s *L'Obeissante* of 1873. This lofty 4½ ton 12-seater is now in the Paris Arts et Metiers museum

had a sliding gear change and an angle-iron chassis. The engine drove through a fifth road wheel.

Soon after the engine had crashed en route to a fire (it had no brakes!), an ordinance from the Mayor of New York forbade its use in the streets of the city, and it was sold to an engineering firm in Cincinatti.

However, young Reuben was still obsessed by his 'crazy notion', for a few years later he built another 'explosive motor.' This only had two cylinders, although it used the same cylinder castings as before. The engine was mounted at the back of an 'English cart', with a double cone and belt infinitely-variable transmission, controlled from the seat, driving the left rear wheel through a chain. Reverse gear was available, though the engine 'would run equally well in either direction.'

This horseless carriage was apparently successful, for on February 27, 1875, Plass was arrested and charged with violating the boiler act. Although Justice Murray of the Fourth Court discharged the case, this arrest was too much for Plass. He had been arrested three times, starting around 1868, and the fines–$5, $10 and $50–had got progressively steeper. So, tiring of surreptitiously operating his machine after dark, he decided to sell it. None of his friends were interested, and in desperation Plass removed the engine and gearing, 'smashed them to fragments with an axe' and sold the cart for $150.

Plass was not the only American pioneer, for in 1878 a twin-cylinder Brayton oil engine was fitted in a bus in Pittsburg. Its specification, with shaft, bevel and chain drive and coil ignition, promised great things, but the 'state legislature' refused to grant a licence to operate a regular service and the project was abandoned.

Around the same time Siegfried Marcus, a Viennese inventor, was experimenting with a motor vehicle. His first attempt, built in 1864, consisted of a simple handcart–cheaper to convert than a horsecarriage, thought the frugal Marcus–which made one brief run in April 1865, covering 150 yards in two minutes. Ten years later, Marcus tried again, with an improved design, and followed this with two more vehicles. The last, dating from the 1880s, was the most successful, and is still in existence.

The police complained about the noise of Marcus' *strassenwagen*, one of which is recorded as having frightened the monks of Klosterneuberg out of their cells, and the dilettante inventor, convinced that no good would come of his 'thundering machine,' turned to a newer enthusiasm, the electric light, but a certain Mr Edison beat him to it. . . .

Other early builders of internal-

combustion-engined cars, like Dela-
marre-Debouteville in France (1883)
and Edward Butler in England (1884–
5) were also quick to lose enthusiasm,
either from lack of success or through
hostile legislation.

Steam was *still* king, although even
a genius like Amédée Bollée failed to
make a commercial success of the self-
propelled vehicle. Bollée was one of a
dynasty of bell-founders from Le
Mans; his 1873 *l'Obéissante* 12-seater
featured twin engines and independent
front suspension, while *La Mancelle* of
1878, first vehicle to go into series
production, pioneered the general layout of motor vehicles for the next 75
years.

No matter what its motive power,
the motor vehicle seemed destined to
remain a temperamental–and pro-
hibitively expensive–novelty. The railway mania had taken passengers away
from the roads and put them on rails,
but the coming of the bicycle in the late
1860s brought renewed interest in
highway travel, gave many young men
their first taste of self-propelled free-

dom from fixed routes and rigid
timetables, and, perhaps most import-
antly, taught engineers how to build
light yet strong vehicles that owed
nothing to the elephantine steam locomotive traditions of the 1830s.

The little de Dion steam tricycle in
the Conservatoire des Arts et Metiers
represents the first successful cars sold
to the public; the Austrian Marcus car
(below), once dated at 1875, is now
thought to have been built sometime in
the late 1880s

14

Petrol Pioneers
a legacy of annoyance and expense

'Without any sign of motive power, such as that generated by steam, and without the aid of any human element, such as is necessary with a velocipede, the vehicle rolled onwards, taking bends in its stride and avoiding all oncoming traffic and pedestrians. It was followed by a crowd of running and breathless youngsters. Those who witnessed this strange spectacle could scarcely believe their own eyes. The surprise was as general as it was great. The gasoline engine, which is its motive power, is located beneath the seat, and all eyewitnesses agree that the trial was highly successful.'

A rare survivor of one of the first motor races—the 1896 Paris-Marseilles-Paris event—is this rear-engined parallel-twin Delahaye with three-speed belt and chain drive

The occasion was one of the earliest public demonstrations of Karl Benz's three-wheeled car, which had originally appeared in 1884.

Benz—the first man to mass-produce petrol cars—might never have built a motor vehicle at all had the 'iron foundry and machine shop' he founded in 1871 in Mannheim, Germany, proved more of a success. Crisis after crisis swamped the little company, and in one last desperate attempt to keep the bailiff from the door, Benz returned to an old obsession, the internal-combustion engine.

At first he built two-strokes, as Nikolaus Otto had attempted to file a master patent on the four-stroke cycle in 1877. Benz's two-stroke gas engines were quite successful, and his company expanded rapidly. When Otto's patent

was ruled invalid in 1886, Benz was already running a four-stroke-engined car on the streets. Unlike the Daimler horseless carriage of the same year, this was designed as a complete entity, a true motor car rather than a powered carriage.

To keep the steering as simple as possible, the Benz had only three wheels; its rear-mounted single-cylinder engine had the flywheel revolving horizontally to prevent gyroscopic action from upsetting the vehicle's directional stability!

By 1888 the Benz was in limited production—but there were no buyers. Even the appointment of a Paris agent, Emile Roger, one of the first people ever to actually buy a car, produced little worthwhile business.

Roger assembled cars from compo-

This elegant vehicle is the 1888 Benz; a similar car was probably the first petrol-engined vehicle to be imported into England. One wonders whether the dog would really have sat so still!

nents shipped from the Benz factory at Mannheim to dodge import duty. He garaged his car at the engineering works of Panhard and Levassor, who were building two-stroke engines under Benz licence. They showed little interest in the machine, for they were already involved with Daimler, and would soon begin building Daimler vee-twin engines under licence.

This arrangement stemmed from Daimler's long-standing business ac-

One of the first Daimler cars built by the Daimler-Motoren-Gesellschaft in 1891. Designer Wilhelm Maybach holds the tiller; beside him sits the portly figure of Gottlieb Daimler

quaintance with Edouard Sarazin, French agent for Otto engines built by the Gasmotoren Fabrik Deutz, where Daimler was manager from 1872–82. When Daimler resigned to develop high-speed petrol engines, Sarazin followed his progress. So impressed was the Frenchman that even on his deathbed he told his wife to continue fostering the company's relationship with Daimler.

'That which he is working on is

unquestionably worthy of confidence and has a future beyond anything we can imagine.'

La Veuve Sarazin followed her late husband's instructions to the letter. She travelled to Daimler's factory at Cannstatt to conclude the arrangements, and drove back in one of the very first Daimler cars (it was claimed that only through the intervention of a 'minister of state', was the car allowed through the French customs).

Among Karl Benz's first customers was the German industrialist Theodore von Liebig (in the light suit), one of the first to go touring by horseless carriage

Sarazin had been collaborating with Panhard and Levassor to develop Daimler engines for the French market; his widow continued the association with considerable success and when she married Emile Levassor in 1890, she brought the very useful dowry of the manufacturing rights to Daimler's power units.

Having seen the total apathy with which both the Daimler and Benz motor cars were received at the 1889 Paris World Fair, Panhard and Levassor were initially not interested in building motor vehicles. They fitted the new power units to their established wood and metal working machines, and passed over the rights to use Daimler engines in cars to the massive Peugeot bicycle company.

Peugeot, established as ironmongers in the late 1700s, had produced steel 'whalebones' for crinolines during the 1850s, which led them into the manu-

facture of corset stays. This was a prelude to cycle manufacture during the high-wheeler boom of the 1880s, when the company's expertise in making thin metal rods was turned to good effect in producing wheel spokes by the thousand.

By 1889 Peugeot had three factories and 2,000 workmen. Then Armand Peugeot, who had studied engineering in Leeds, decided to experiment with a motor car. His company built a three-wheeled steam car to the designs of Léon Serpollet, who had brought his first flash-boilered tricycle to Paris in 1887. This machine was not fully developed, and while fifteen years later the Serpollet was regarded as the *ne plus ultra* of steam cars, the 1889 Peugeot-Serpollet was far too heavy and very prone to break down.

Emile Levassor, hearing that the steamer was not performing as successfully as anticipated, hurried to see Armand Peugeot, convinced him that the days of steam were definitely numbered, and that the Daimler petrol engine was the power unit of the future. Basic agreement reached, the two

discussed the mounting of the engine. Levassor postulated it should be at the rear to protect the occupants of the car from the smell of the machinery. In front, countered Peugeot, so that the car would be better balanced.

Both men must have been convinced by these arguments, for Peugeot's first petrol car of 1890 had the engine at the rear, while Panhard and Levassor, after trying one experimental rear-engined model in 1890–1, plumped firmly for engines in front. . . .

One problem common to all early petrol car builders was the inflexibility of the power unit, which meant that some kind of variable-speed gearing was essential. Benz and Daimler solved this with variable-ratio belt drives which, if prone to slip or break, were at least silent in operation. Daimler's partner and designer, Wilhelm Maybach, tried a four-speed gear transmission on his 1889 'Steel-wheeler' car, but soon returned to the more forgiving belt drive.

The problem was basically that those early power units, based on gas-engine practice, were virtually con-

Benz cars were widely copied. Among the imitations was this Lutzmann motor carriage of the mid-1890s, which was the immediate ancestor of the German Opel car

stant-speed motors. In fact, most of them were governed in some way to prevent any real variation in running and the difficulty of trying to engage gears of varying diameter on shafts running at differing speeds can be imagined.

Nevertheless, Panhard and Levassor used gears from the start, while Peugeot only made a few belt-drive cars before adopting a four-speed sliding gear similar to Panhard's, in which the mechanism operated in the open air, without lubrication.

'C'est brusque et brutale, mais ça marche,' said M. Levassor, hoping that something better might soon come along. But it didn't . . . and for the forty years before syncromesh arrived, the sliding gear was the curse of the learner driver.

In Britain, the Lanchester brothers, who built the first of their highly original cars in 1895, favoured the no-clash epicyclic change; but this never became widely accepted in Europe, where drivers like to boast of their skill in gear changing.

The best technique with those early cars was to slip the clutch gently and bang the gears home as quickly as possible, in the hope that you might catch the cogs unawares. It didn't always work, but at least the brief complaint of the side-grubbing teeth was preferable to the prolonged agony if you took your time and waited for the warring cogs to come into alignment!

Small wonder then that the belt-driven Benz suddenly began to find customers, mainly due to the proselytising zeal of Emile Roger in Paris—by 1895 there were 49 Benz cars running in that city alone. And most of this success dated from 1893, when Benz introduced his first four-wheeler, the 3 hp Viktoria, following it in 1894 with the lighter, cheaper 1½ hp Velo. These were the world's first 'mass-production' cars, with an output of 135 in 1895, rising to 434 in 1898, and by the end of 1899, more than 2,000 Benz cars had been built.

Within their limitations, the early Benz models—and the many copies,

licenced and unlicenced, built by other manufacturers—were simple to drive.

They had electric ignition, not the temperamental system of the Daimler, in which burners kept platinum tubes projecting into the cylinder heads hot enough to ignite the petrol, and which was liable to set the entire vehicle on fire in the event of an accident.

To start the vehicle, you lifted the tailboard, and pulled the flywheel—now vertical, not horizontal—over compression. Provided that the petrol was sufficiently volatile and that the trembler coil ignition was working properly the single-cylinder engine would start, running with a measured hiss-thump tempo. If not, like J. A. Koosen, who imported a Lutzmann (a clumsy Benz imitation) into Britain from Germany in 1895—because his wife had seen an advertisement, and liked the look of the car—you were in trouble.

Poor Mr Koosen—he 'had then never seen a motor-car, and was under the impression that you take your seats, press the button, and the machine does the rest.'

His mechanical ignorance was soon shattered when the car arrived at Portsmouth Town Station on November 21, 1895.

'I had been told in a letter from the maker that to start the engine you had to turn the flywheel towards you, which I did until darkness overtook me. The only result was a pair of worn out gloves.'

And his problems were only just beginning . . .

'**November 23**: *Took train to Lee and tried to make our motor work; wouldn't; came home at five.*

November 24: *Awfully cold; played with our motor—no result.*

November 25: *After luncheon saw to our motor, but didn't get it out of shed.*

November 26: *Drove to Lee and took Smith and Penning (engineers); Penning spent the day on his back without results.*

November 27: *Drove to Lee; first we drove to T. White & Co to see about oil, but they gave us five gallons of the stuff costers burn in their flares over their barrows, which messed up our motor, which of course didn't go.*

November 30: *Motor went with benzoline for first time; awfully pleased.*'

And even when you managed to make your horseless carriage run, your troubles were far from over.

For one thing, there were no garages or service stations; if you were planning on a trip of any distance in Britain, you would have had to carry sufficient fuel with you, or telegraph to chemists *en route* to make sure that they had a stock of petroleum spirit of the correct density—a petrol densimeter was an essential part of the tool kit.

One pioneer motorist, faced with a fuelless car which had just been unloaded from the Cross-Channel ferry,

The first cars marketed by the Coventry Daimler Company were imported Panhards, like the 1896 model *(left)* owned by the English billiards champion J. H. Peall. The following year the first Coventry-built cars appeared, and the Hon. Evelyn Ellis, a Daimler director, drove one to the summit of Malvern Beacon amid much publicity *(below)*

recalled his first motoring experiences:

'I had to search all the chemists in Dover, armed with a little specific gravity meter which had to show 68 on the red line. Benzine, whisky, chloroform and even beer were suggested, but all failed to pass the test until finally I was told that I should have to go to some people in London called Carless, Capel and Leonard, who sold motor spirit. Up I went by train to fetch a two-gallon can, and the con-tents, recording 68 as per instructions, were poured into the tank and off we went to Brighton.'

Nor were there any driving schools—the pioneer motorist had to teach himself by trial and error, often without the least idea of how his machine worked, for instruction books were rare, there was no standardised control layout, and each make had its own idiosyncrasies.

Moreover, experience with an 1898 Georges-Richard (another Benz copy) showed that any misjudgment in changing from low to high speed made this type of rear-engined car rear up on its back wheels like a frightened horse, while the machine could gather momentum alarmingly on down-grades, to a speed far in excess of the steering's meagre capabilities. And since the steering wheel was about the size of a saucer and controlled the front axle through a crude sprocket-

and-chain mechanism, the possibilities of catastrophe were infinite. . . .

Take the case of Edwin Roots Sewell, who, coming down the one in eight slope of Grove Hill, Harrow, on the evening of 25 February 1899, applied the hand and foot brakes of his Daimler waggonette at between 15 and 25 mph to demonstrate their stopping power to his passengers. One of the solid rear tyres tore from the rim and caused the slender wooden spokes of the rear wheel to collapse. Sewell and one of the passengers were killed, victims of Britain's first fatal car accident.

Sermonised *The Autocar*: 'No man should fly a really steep hill, nor should any declivity be taken without the greatest care.'

In addition to his lack of road sense, the mechanical naiveté of the average pioneer motorist was quite unbelievable–most were wealthy men unaccustomed to handling any mechanism more complex than a penknife. (To

Louis Renault, son of a Parisian button-maker, built his first car *(below)* in 1898, in a shed at Billancourt. It had an air-cooled de Dion engine and live axle drive. One of the most powerful cars of 1898 was the Hon. C. S. Roll's 8 hp Panhard racer *(bottom),* with an obvious appetite for tyres. Charles Duryea *(right)* built one of America's first cars in 1893, this one followed in 1895

be fair, the blacksmiths and cycle agents who masqueraded as motor repairers in those days were almost as ignorant of the workings of the internal-combustion engine). But motorists always blamed their breakdowns and accidents on the hapless makers.

Typical was John Hope, an early Benz owner, who complained in 1899:

'We do doubt the wisdom of selling any gentleman a car entailing such a legacy of annoyances and expense as I have experienced. And how are we to know that another car will be different?'

However, it seems that most of his mechanical ailments were self-inflicted. . . .

'I have had to take the front axle from under my car twice in order to have it straightened. The first time I do not know how it was done, but the second time myself and my wife were coming home along a country road at a good pace with all lamps lit, for it was dark, when we hit something with terrific impact. I guessed it to be a big stone, or its equivalent. It was something of a dark colour, or I would have seen it, for I had a good dash-board light. I did not stop to ascertain, but hastened home, as it was beginning to

spurt rain. On examination, I found the front axle badly bent.

'I saw afterwards by the papers that a man had been found dead on that road the next morning, having been repeatedly run over by passing vehicles. I do not know, nor have I been able to ascertain, if that was the object we ran over. . . .'

It was not, perhaps, surprising that these pioneer motorists came into harsh contact with the law, and even less of a surprise that they bitterly resented the situation–the policeman who had politely touched his forelock when the squire rode past in his carriage and pair, was now just as eager to haul his social superior before the local magistrates.

Ever since a misguided bench had applied the workings of the 'Locomotives on Highway Acts of 1865 and 1878' to the light steam tricycle owned by Sir Thomas Parkyns of Greenwich in 1881, all motor cars used on the roads of Britain had been required to have two men in control and one walking in front, usually with a red flag by day and a red lamp at night, though the 1878 Act had removed the legal necessity for this.

This senseless restriction drove some

pioneers off the road, and some to experiment abroad, where the law was less restrictive. Others, like Frederick Bremer, of Walthamstow, who built a tiny petrol carriage in 1892–4, tried running their cars after dark to avoid the law. Even this was not always fruitful, as the Hon T. R. B. Elliott found when he drove to Berwick on Tweed one dark February night in 1896 on his newly-acquired 3½ hp Panhard phaeton:

'Arriving at Berwick at 3 am I proceeded to picnic under the shadow of the Town Hall, and was there soon surrounded by the entire police force on duty–thirteen men in all. The sergeant took my name, but did not think that any action against me would be taken. However, this was not the case, as I was eventually fined the large sum of 6d with 19s 6d costs, for "using a horseless carriage without having a man on foot preceding it." '

Although the Lord Chief Justice of Scotland, Sir J. H. A. Macdonald, was a keen motorist, most magistrates were horsy types who resented the new locomotion, seeing it as a danger to their vested interests. They attempted to put it down with excessive fines: £10 fines–equivalent to around £100 today–for exceeding the speed limit were not uncommon at the turn of the century and police resorted to trumped-up charges, to gain promotion.

American pioneers had entirely different problems to contend with. While the highroads of Europe had merely fallen into disrepair in the mid-19th century, the United States lacked any kind of national road system. The country had been settled first by river and canal traffic, then by railroad. Towns were linked by dirt roads which usually became impassable in winter, with axle deep mud waiting to bog down any vehicle unwise enough to travel outside city limits. But even so, there were visionaries who thought that the motor car had a future.

John W. Lambert of Ohio ran a three-wheeled car in 1891, issued a catalogue offering similar machines for $550, but decided that the market was not profitable enough. He built further experimental models from 1898–1900, finally going into production in 1902.

In 1892 Gottfried Schloemer, a cooper from Milwaukee, and his friend Frank Toepfer, a machinist, built a buggy powered by a Sintz gas engine. It never performed very successfully but proved so durable that it is still in running order, preserved in a Milwaukee museum.

The same year, two brothers, Charles and Frank Duryea, began work on a motor car, which first ran on the road in September 1893; the Duryea Motor Wagon Company, producing an improved version of this machine, was active from 1895 to 1898, and actually exported a handful of cars to England, establishing a sales office near Cannon Street, in London.

Other pioneers were Henry Nadig, whose first car dated from 1891 and was modified in 1893; Elwood Haynes, whose 1894 motor buggy was formerly claimed as America's first car; and Charles Brady King, whose 1896 design was the first car on the streets of Detroit, followed on a bicycle by Henry Ford, whose Quadricycle made its own maiden trip soon after.

Benz, Daimler and the other pioneers had performed the thankless task of establishing the motor car as a marketable proposition; now farsighted engineers in Europe and America, were hard at work independently improving and developing it.

'The motor carriage will never displace the smart trotting pony or the high-stepping team,' wrote one 1896 commentator; but a whole new industry was stirring itself to prove such glib forecasts wrong.

For the Nobility and Gentry
society accepts the car

By the mid-1890s, society was beginning to take to the motorcar. The new locomotion had even become respectable enough for royalty to sample its delights: in 1892, recorded pioneer motoring journalist Paul Meyan, the Prince of Wales (later Edward VII) was driven round the Bois de Boulogne in Paris by M. Mayade, at the tiller of an iron-tyred Panhard. The following year the Prince was a passenger in the Serpollet steam car belonging to millionaire chocolate maker, Gaston Menier. Also in 1893 Kaiser Wilhelm was driven fifteen miles in thirty-five minutes in a Benz, 'built with the greatest attention to precision.'

Of all the nobility and gentry who flocked to the motorcar in the 19th century, probably no-one made a greater impact than the Marquis de Dion, born in 1856 into a family which could trace its ancestry back to the 13th century.

The young Albert de Dion was keenly interested in mechanics, and in 1876, while studying in Munich, he built himself a model steam engine. Once his education was over and he returned to Paris and established himself as a society lion—a dueller, sportsman and gambler for high stakes: 'Hardly a drawing-room in Parisian aristocratic circles was considered complete without the good-natured and popular Albert de Dion.'

One day in December 1881, de Dion visited a novelty shop in the Boulevard des Italiens, run by a certain M. Giroux, who had a beautifully made model engine driven by spirits-of-wine on display.

De Dion picked it up, examined it in detail, bought it, and established that it was made by Georges Bouton, who, with his brother-in-law, Trépardoux,

ran a business in the Passage Léon, Rue de Chapelle, making toy engines for Giroux and more complex showcase models for the Ducretet precision engineering company. The Count found the two middle-aged men slaving away in a ramshackle wooden shed for a joint daily income of 8 francs (then worth around 37½p). He invited them to work for 10 francs a day. Each!

Seduced by the thought of such a vast guaranteed income, the two craftsmen left the shed for a tumbledown house at the junction of the Rue Pergolese and the Avenue Malakoff, and began development of a light steam car, which first ran two years later.

In 1883, the de Dion, Bouton and Trépardoux partnership moved to new premises at Puteaux, and began production of light three- and four-wheeled steam cars.

But at the 1889 Paris Exhibition, de Dion realised that the steam engine would inevitably be replaced by petrol. Trépardoux, a dyed-in-the-wool steam enthusiast—and possibly a more gifted engineer·than his brother-in-law— disagreed, resigning in a huff in 1895. However, he left one legacy to modern automobile engineering, a rear axle design in which unsprung weight was reduced to the minimum by carrying the rear wheels on a 'dead' axle, fastening the differential unit to the chassis and driving the hubs through universally-jointed hubs. Perversely, this arrangement has become known as the de Dion axle, just as the front-engined, rear-driven layout devised by Emile Levassor is called the *Système Panhard*!

De Dion and Bouton continued to build steam tractors for another ten years, but the design changed very

little. Their first petrol engine was a real breakthrough.

'It was,' wrote Baudry de Saunier in 1899, 'the first motor to show the importance of revolutions per minute as a factor in power developed. Lenoir's gas engine turned at 100 rpm, Daimler's at 750: but the de Dion engine ran at 2,000! On the test bench it often reached 3,500 rpm, limited solely by the inadequacies of its gas passages, its inlet valve, and its ignition make-and-break.'

The first of these engines was fitted in a tricycle, driving the rear axle through direct gearing. It developed 0·5 hp; it was soon found that this was not enough, and as production increased, so did the engine size. As a sporting vehicle, the de Dion tricycle was unique, and thousands of early motorists began their careers on one.

The important thing about the de Dion operation was that they began to build their engines in sufficiently large numbers to supply other manufacturers. Spared the problem of developing and building a reliable power unit, dozens of small engineering companies could now enter the motor industry as assemblers.

Of course, building on the scale of the rapidly-expanding de Dion Bouton company entailed many problems, for nobody had mass-produced petrol engines in such numbers.

When the day of the tricycle passed, in 1899–1900, de Dion introduced a range of light cars which were equally successful. But when one early owner wrote to Puteaux for further instructions in driving his new de Dion, the reply, couched in appalling 'Franglais', was hardly enlightening. . . .

'For Making the Mover Walking–Lean on the pointeau of the carburateur

Master and man: the aristocratic figure
of the Comte de Dion and his engineer
Georges Bouton, whose straw hat and
smock seem to have been donned just
for the photograph

until the essence unbordes . . . Push
thoroughly the handle on, and hurl the
mover till his starting. . . . Increase the
advance to the lighter with an eighth
of lathe forward at the right; then take
sensibly back at left backward the
second manette with a fifth of lathe;
just at this moment the mover must
goes regularly with 1,500 lathes. . . .
Raise up again the pedal with $\frac{3}{4}$, and
take completely and progressively back
the crowbar of embrayage to you,
while you keep the direction with your
right hand and the crowbar with your
left hand. . . .

'*For Going Backward*–When you are
at the thoroughly debrayage push the
pedal of backward step with your right
wheel, and push completely forward
the crowbar of embrayage. For the
backward step, take back the crowbar
in little speed, and in debrayage if you
will stopped.'

While de Dion, Bouton, Benz and
Daimler were all genuinely devoted to
the promotion of the motor car, across
the Channel others, less scrupulous,
realised that the horseless carriage trade
offered rich financial pickings.

Among Victorian company pro-
motors the name of Ernest Terah
Hooley stands out. He started with the
financing of reputable and successful
companies and, discovering how easy
it was to persuade people to part with
their money when they believed they
were on to a good thing, floated an
increasing number of dubious ventures,
like the Simpson Lever Chain Company, capitalised for £1 million, which
enjoyed a brief and hectic career from
1895–7, and the Cycle Manufacturers'
Tube Company of 1896, in which
Hooley sold 6 acres of waste land in
Coventry for £250,000 on the strength
of several contracts to supply tubes for
the cycle and motor trades, to be
produced in an as yet unbuilt factory. . . .

Terah Hooley's most adept disciple
was Harry J. Lawson, who, having
dabbled in cycle company promotion,

Oscar Bickford acquired this Voiturette
Parisienne in 1898; the car, which
pioneered front-wheel drive, used a
de Dion tricycle rear end as a front axle

'The doyen of the British court, His Royal Highness the Duke of Cambridge, has not allowed his eighty-two years to prevent him from patronising the motor car,' wrote the *London Magazine* in 1901; the Duke's tricar was an 1897 Bollée

The clothes suggest the early 1900s; the Daimler chars-à-bancs are clearly of the late 1890s, and the occasion is the annual beanfeast of the Mitchell Butlers' Brewery workers. The leading car has gained an auxiliary radiator to cope . . .

saw the potential of the motor car industry at an outdoor display organised at Tunbridge Wells, Kent, in October 1895, by Sir David Salomons.

Public reaction was negative, but Lawson realised that once the archaic law restricting motor cars to 4 mph with a man walking in front was repealed, there would be a growing demand for these vehicles. So he bought up the British rights to the leading Continental designs. Late in 1895 he formed the British Motor Syndicate to exploit the Daimler rights, which had been acquired from Frederick R. Simms, whose Daimler Motor

Henry Ford began work on the internal-combustion engine in 1892, but his first car, the Quadricycle, was not finished until May 1896. It made its first run on June 4, 1896, through Detroit

Syndicate had been operating since May 1893, fitting Daimler engines into launches, in a workshop under Putney railway bridge.

In January 1896 the Daimler Motor Company was incorporated; in April that year, a disused cotton mill at Coventry was acquired, which Daimler shared with the Great Horseless Carriage Company (another Lawson company, which later became the

Motor Manufacturing Company). Production did not start until early in 1897; until then Daimler-engined chassis were imported from the Continent in penny numbers and fitted with English coachwork.

Other Lawson group activities included London's first motor exhibition, at the Imperial Institute in May 1896; the first British motor magazine, *The Autocar*, which soon broke away from its origins; the 1896 Emancipation Day Run from London to Brighton, celebrating the raising of the speed limit to 12 mph and the abolition of the man on foot walking ahead.

Lawson's partner in the Great Horseless Carriage Company venture was the incredible E. J. Pennington, an American charlatan who had devised a number of improbable designs, which he sold to Lawson for £100,000. Perhaps five three-wheeled Torpedos and two motor cycles were built at Coventry by Humber, another tenant of the Motor Mills.

Aided by shrewd publicity, such as the first motor trip from John O' Groats to Land's End, in 1897, Daimler made a much more positive impact on the British market, and the company was strong enough to survive the collapse of the Lawson empire in the early 1900s, and the imprisonment of Harry Lawson for fraud.

Lawson is often called 'the Father of the British Motor Industry:' but his contemporaries had less flattering names for him. . . .

'For the most part of ten years' wrote one 1905 commentator, 'the British motor industry has been swinging on an ebb tide . . . one of the chief factors in prolonging this period of suspense and trial has been the disinclination of the British capitalist or investor to put money into the British motor industry. How much of that distrust was due to the Lawsonian blight which fell with such withering effect some 8 or 9 years ago is largely a matter of opinion. That extremely clever architect of his own fortunes certainly put back the clock of the motor industry and otherwise deranged its working; but he was not the prime cause—he was merely a contributory. There was something of mania in those who followed Lawson. He was their financial Moses who led them to the mountain top and showed

them Canaan smiling—but afar off. He got their money on prospectuses that shouldn't have deceived a child. . . . There was a lot of money lost . . . but the losers were not the only—or indeed the sane or sound—investors of the country. These were content to let others test H. J. Lawson's wildcat schemes and prospectuses formed on patent specifications and imaginative pictures of motor cars flying across chasms and similarly absurd suggestions. They stood aside and have stood there ever since.'

Not only that, but Lawson's much-publicised efforts eclipsed the activities of the British pioneers who were attempting to work outside his monopoly, like Herbert Austin, newly returned from Australia, who was persuading the Wolseley Sheep-Shearing Company that motor vehicle production would be a worthwhile sideline, or the Lanchester Brothers whose elegant, smooth-running cars were so far ahead of the rest of the industry that they failed because of their unorthodoxy.

Lawson and Pennington even tried to extend their operations into the United States with the Anglo-American Rapid Vehicle Company of New

Mr Pennington's Torpedo Autocar, claimed this 1890s publicity photograph, 'with four places, starting with nine people, speed 18 miles per hour, will mount any gradient'

A generation after the Pennington, this Cadillac 8½/10 hp with limousine top of *circa* 1904, has far more of the old-time horse-buggy about it

One of the best American steam cars was the White; this team of three finished in the 1902 Long Island Endurance Contest. The front axles were downswept for maximum clearance on the atrocious roads of the day

York, with a capital of $750,000; it produced as few cars as its English equivalent.

In fact most early American motor manufacturing operations sprang from companies already well established in other fields: Colonel Albert A. Pope established the country's largest bicycle works (at Hartford, Connecticut) before he asked Hiram Percy Maxim to start a horseless carriage factory, initially producing electric vehicles. ('You can't get people to sit over an explosion,' was the Colonel's philosophy). In 1895–7, Pope built 500 electrics and 40 gasoline carriages.

Then came the Stanley brothers, Francis E. and Freelan O., identical twins whose interests ranged from violin making to photographic equipment. With the fortune they had made from their photographic dry plate process, sold to Kodak, they established a factory to build steam buggies, only to be bought out by a consortium which offered $250,000 for their design, subsequently marketed as the Locomobile, America's first successful volume-production car, which accounted for 4,000 of the 8,000 motor vehicles in the USA in 1901.

Other companies early on the market included White and Grout (both progressing from sewing machines), Studebaker (the world's largest carriage builder), Olds (gas engine makers), Buick (bathtubs and plumbing sundries) and Pierce (from birdcages through bicycles to motor vehicles).

Strangest metamorphosis of all was that of Peerless, who started life making, of all things, mangles. The first Peerless was a de Dion-engined runabout, and from that humble start Peerless became one of America's three great luxury makes, along with Packard and Pierce-Arrow. The company foundered in the depression of the early 1930s, only to rise again with the repeal of prohibition, as the Peerless Corporation, brewers of Carlings Ale!

One of the few companies to be formed specially to produce cars, the Detroit Automobile Company had as chief engineer the ex-chief engineer of the Edison Illuminating Company, Henry Ford. But it lasted only a couple of years, from 1899 to 1902, when Ford left and Henry Leland, a distinguished precision engineer was called in to re-organise production under a new name –Cadillac.

Rivalling Locomobile on the volume production front was the little curved-dash Oldsmobile, a one-cylinder petrol buggy, the only design saved from a disastrous fire that destroyed Ransom E. Olds' factory in 1900. It was cheap and popular: 600 were made in 1901, 2,500 in 1902, 4,000 in 1903 and 5,000 in 1904. Then the company's financiers decided that the time had come to drop the buggy in favour of more expensive models. Olds disagreed, and left the company to found Reo.

Already one man was establishing himself as the arch-advocate of the cheap, mass-produced car for everyman–the unlettered, idiosyncratic and quirkishly brilliant Henry Ford, who had attracted sufficient backing, thanks to much-publicised racing victories, to start the Ford Motor Company in 1903.

America was on the road to becoming the world's greatest motor manufacturing country.

Remarkable Reliability
motoring comes of age

'Engines of death' was how turn-of-the-century popular opinion regarded the motor car in Britain. But, reasoned the Automobile Club, formed in 1897, this prejudice was the result of ignorance, for there were still many people in the country who had not seen a car. So they proposed a reliability trial of unprecedented length, which, they hoped, would 'advance the Automobile Movement in the United Kingdom.'

'It is hoped,' pontificated the official programme, 'that the passage of some eighty Motor Vehicles over 1,000 miles of the roads of Great Britain, and their exhibition at big centres of population, may have the effect not only of proving that the best of these vehicles are capable of covering long distances and of mounting steep hills, but also of demonstrating what are the respective capabilities of the various

Officials for the Third Heavy Motor Trials assemble outside the town hall at Warrington, Lancashire, in 1901. Mr Shrapnell Smith's Self-Propelled Traffic Association organised the event

vehicles . . . they have taken every precaution to prevent the passage of the Trial vehicles being a source of annoyance or danger to other users of the road; and they earnestly beg the drivers of vehicles not to exceed the legal limit of speed, and to show the greatest consideration to the drivers of restless horses and other users of the road.'

The Thousand Miles' Trial, which started from Hyde Park Corner, London, on April 23, 1900, was a huge success: of the 67 cars taking part 'with the exception of a few vehicles, most or all of which ought never to have started, all covered the whole or greater part of the Trial.' Even though, as the mechanics of a Marshall dog-cart recalled: 'We were under the cars as much as on them!'

Such tests of reliability helped the car to reach an early maturity. So, too, did the suggestions of wealthy owners like the Austrian Emil Jellinek, who bought a 6 hp Cannstatt-Daimler, found it too slow, and asked the Daimler Motoren Gesellschaft to build him four cars capable of 40 kph (25

mph), a speed the company regarded as only attainable by express trains.

Then he demanded six more powerful cars, with a front-mounted four-cylinder engine, and set about selling them in a distinctly enterprising manner as Baron Henri de Rothschild recalled in 1903:

'In 1899 I was at Nice with one of my Uncles, Baron Arthur de Rothschild. On climbing the Turbie Hill one day with an 8 hp Panhard, we were passed by an enormous motor-car which had more the characteristics of an elephant than of the gazelle, and got to the top of this long gradient some time before us. This easy victory of the elephantine vehicle rather ruffled the equanimity of my Uncle who prided himself on possessing the fastest car turned out at the time. He sought the owner of the car and proposed to buy the vehicle. The bargain was immediately concluded and my Uncle descended La Turbie with the car which had beaten him on the up-grade. The car was of German make and had been constructed at the Daimler Works at

Cannstatt. It had a motor of 12 horse-power and weighed 1½-tons. Its driver was M. Jellinek.

'Scarcely a fortnight afterwards, we were again driving up La Turbie when we heard a loud noise behind us and suddenly another car passed us driven by the same M. Jellinek. My Uncle was exasperated; another cheque was offered to M. Jellinek who accepted it. My Uncle could not bear the idea of another vehicle beating him on the Hill and thus he found himself the owner of two Daimler cars.

'On making better acquaintance with M. Jellinek he told us of the projects of the Daimler Company and asked if we would place an order for the new type of 24 horse-power vehicle which was to entirely eclipse those recently purchased. We decided on giving the order and thus were the two first customers for the new Model. I drove to Stuttgart to take over the car and found it by no means elegant, but the price was certainly proportionate to the weight, its great size creating anything but a favourable impression amongst people who preferred the light carriages of 8–12 horse-power constructed by the French makers. When it came to climbing hills, the Daimler was always leading and the others had difficulty in following. Nothing ever went wrong with its mechanism and we were never in difficulties. I pointed out to M. Jellinek, if the Daimler Works could build motors running with such remarkable reliability, it ought to be possible to put them in lighter frames, giving them a more elegant appearance. In 1899 took place the first Motor Race organized on the Riviera. The Daimler cars participated and were well in at the finish though they were not in such expert hands as those representing the French makes.

'When we came to the year 1900, M. Jellinek and the Stuttgart engineers decided to modify the general dimensions and in a general way lighten the

By the early 1900s, racing and touring design had diverged widely. The 24 hp de Dion phaeton contrasts strangely with the two racing Darracqs practising for the 1905 Gordon Bennett contest

vehicle with a view to bringing it within the weight of 1,000 kilos and, in 1901, appeared on the Promenade des Anglais, at Nice, the first 35 horsepower Mercedes. It was scarcely possible to recognize in this new car the extremely heavy vehicle of previous years.'

The Mercedes, named after Jellinek's daughter, was the work of Wilhelm Maybach–Gottlieb Daimler had died in March 1900, and less than a month later the company he had founded signed an agreement giving Jellinek exclusive sales rights for Austro-Hungary, France, Belgium and Germany. In return, he undertook to buy the first 30 of the new 'car of the day after tomorrow,' an order worth over half-a-million marks.

Though the features of the new car were not unique, the way they were combined was a major breakthrough– with its pressed-steel frame, mechanically-operated inlet valves, low-tension magneto ignition and selective 'gate' for gear changing, the Mercedes

caught the imagination of the motoring world in an unprecedented fashion.

The Mercedes-Simplex of 1902 was a vast improvement over its predecessor, so rapid was the rate of progress in those days, and set a style that was copied all over the world, opening an extravagant era during which the motorcar became, more than at any period before or since, the symbol of wealth and ostentation.

As early as 1902, newspaper magnate Alfred Harmsworth could write: 'I am running at present four cars of French construction, two of American, two of English, and some others which are practically English. Three are driven by petrol, three by steam and two by electricity.'

In 1901 the tyre bill for this modest équipe came to over £500 (equivalent to around £5,000 today) and Harmsworth wondered whether 'the pneumatic tyre craze had been altogether overdone by motor-car owners . . . for some time past I have been increasing the proportion of solid tyres in my stable.'

But pneumatics meant extra speed and extra comfort, and Harmsworth was fighting a futile rearguard action. The next year he made a complete

volte-face and bought the most luxurious tyre-gobbler on the market, a 60 hp Mercedes costing £2,200. This model was the high peak of the collaboration between Mayback and Jellinek, who changed his name to Jellinek-Mercedes in its honour. With a racing body, it made fastest time in the 1903 Nice Speed Trials; even in touring trim it was capable of nearly 80 mph.

Harmsworth, of course, had it fitted with the very latest pattern of coachwork, the *Roi des Belges* body, with deeply buttoned seats like *art nouveau* tulips. The first body of this type was built on a 40 hp Panhard for King Leopold of the Belgians in the spring of 1902, inspired, so it was said, by the shape of the armchairs in the apartment of the King's mistress.

This was the first impact of styling on the motor world, which had hitherto relied on coachwork based on horse-carriage designs: and it created a furore of excitement. As Rothschild of Paris, who had built the first *Roi des Belges*, had not registered the design, the body building firms of England and France were soon busy building replicas.

Most bodies at this period were open

Inside Lillie Hall, the London Panhard
and Mors agency run by Mr Rolls before
he joined with Mr Royce. The monstrous
racing car is Rolls's 1902 11½-litre
Paris-Vienna Mors

and windscreenless—it was not until
Edouard Benedictus discovered safety
glass in 1909 that windscreens became
universal. Until then it was a toss-up
between keeping the weather at bay or
being cut to shreds in the likely event of
a collision, for with no compulsory
driving test, anyone could take a highpowered car on the road without
previous experience, and accidents
were often avoided only by good
fortune—in fact the regulations governing the issuing of driving licences in
Britain were so vague that *The Autocar*
obtained one for a blind beggar without
difficulty, just to prove that it could be
done.

Many early motorists turned a blind
eye to speed limits, in any case, and
displayed a Toad-like obsession with
high velocity that often ended in
disaster.

In 1901, the *Motor Car Journal*
recorded the wreck-strewn progress of
a Parisian scorcher: 'He collided with
a pony and trap, reduced it to a wreck,
scattered its three occupants about the
road, made cat's meat of the pony and
continued his wild career without so
much as a word of apology. Whilst
looking round at the hue and cry
which he had raised, he ran over an
old man who was wheeling a peram-
bulator, fortunately empty. The mad-
man is reported to be still at large. . . .'

Fortunately, such cases were exceptional, but sensational reporting of
this kind created an irrational fear of
the car among non-motorists, and
undid much of the good feeling
created by events such as the Thousand
Miles' Trial.

In a well-publicised petition to
Queen Alexandra, the Cottage Dwel-
lers of the United Kingdom complained: 'We are only poor people,
and the great majority of those who
use motorcars take no account of us.'

Others, as a 1905 newspaper report
bears witness, carried their hatred of
the motoring classes to greater ex-
tremes:

'An extraordinary attack was made
on a Nottingham motorist the other
day. As Dr Tressider, of the Rope-
walk, was driving his car along Lower
Eldon Street, a man named John
Thomas Drewett, a maltster, threw
himself in front of the car and refused
to move, and then attempted to cut the
tyres with a knife. On the doctor and
his chauffeur alighting, he attacked
them with a poker he had concealed
under his coat. Dr Tressider is seriously
injured about the head, and Drewett
stands remanded in custody.'

Colonel Gordon, chairman of the
Market Rasen Magistrates' Court, was
another motorphobe, who declared
that when out with his pony and trap,
he had been 'nearly thrown into
ditches by those motorcars' so often
that for safety he always hoisted a red
flag whenever he saw a car approaching!

In an attempt to introduce some
rationality into the motoring question,
in 1902, the British Conservative Government, headed by A. J. Balfour (a
keen motorist, who owned three
Napiers), proposed that all cars should
be registered and carry number plates.
In return the speed limit would be
raised from 12 mph to 20 mph.

Despite protests from motor owners
against 'being numbered like crim-
inals,' the Motor Car Act came into
force in 1904. It proved a mixed blessing, for the new 20 mph limit was
enforced far more strictly than the old
12 mph one, and police armed with
half-crown stopwatches were deployed
to catch speeding motorists.

Maps of the current trapped roads
were published weekly in *The Autocar*,
and the Automobile Association,
founded in 1905, instituted road patrols
of bicycle-mounted scouts. Members
were requested to stop if a scout failed
to salute and ask the reason, which
more often than not was that there was
a police trap ahead.

Even so, the police in the 'anti-
motorist' counties managed to notch
up an impressive total, none, perhaps,
more spectacularly than Sergeant Jar-
rett of Chertsey, Surrey, who caught
so many motorists in 1904–5 that he
was promoted to Inspector. But motoring was becoming too popular to be
set back for long by such gadfly tactics.

The British motor industry, although
hardly in the mass-production market,
was beginning to make definite progress: 'To my certain knowledge,'

By Napier standards, this 1909 30 hp model was quite a baby: their 1907/8 90 hp six offered 14½ litres at a chassis price of 2,500 gold sovereigns

wrote one 1902 scribe, 'one English firm has at the present moment 183 cars on order at an average price of £1,000 each.'

By the standards of the French industry, admittedly, this was a pretty insignificant order: in 1902 France produced 12,000 cars, and exported well over a million pounds-worth of this total. More than 180,000 people were involved in the industry, earning an average of £72 yearly. America and Germany, too, had thriving indust-

From tiny acorns . . . This little voiturette was the first Rolls-Royce car, shown at the 1904 Paris Salon, where the Delaunay-Belleville was also launched

ries—the Mercedes was in such demand that Jack Hutton, the London agent, had to pay the Daimler-Motoren-Gesellschaft a £600 premium above list price to make sure of the new 18 hp model he had ordered for the 1903 Agricultural Hall Motor Show. Even Italy, where a prohibitive oil tax made motoring disproportionately costly, was producing cars, notably the Fiat.

By mid-1904 there were 40,000 cars and motor cycles in the United Kingdom; between June 1904 and May 1905, 6,000 new cars were registered in London alone. Wolseley, one of Britain's leading makers, expanded their weekly production of nine cars a week in 1903, to thirty a week in 1904. The petrol age was really getting under way.

Many of the technical advances in those days were made empirically. The earliest cars had single- or twin-cylinder engines, with the cylinders cast separately. When customers called for more speed, the makers just doubled the number of cylinders—and motorists often referred to their power unit in the plural: 'The Engines.' Then it was found that a four was far smoother-running than a twin.

At the December 1902 Paris Motor Show, Charron, Girardot and Voigt showed a 40 hp eight-cylinder car which was so powerful and flexible that it needed only one forward speed, giving a top speed of 50 mph at 900 rpm. The American maker Buffum built a few flat-eights a year or so later, but these rarely managed to run on more than seven cylinders—the eight-cylinder Winton racer of 1903

was also a flop—while Clément Ader, who had achieved fame for a brief hop in a steam aeroplane in 1890, built the world's first V-8 for the 1903 Paris-Madrid race.

It was not, however, the eight which captured the imagination of the Edwardian luxury car owner, but the six-in-line engine, pioneered (in a motorboat) in 1889 by the French inventor Ferdinand Forest.

Once the six-cylinder engine had become an established, successful fact, there was no shortage of claimants for the honour of first thinking of the idea—Spyker had built a four-wheel drive six-cylinder racer in Holland in 1903, while in France, a six-cylinder Automotrice took a class award at the Dourdan speed trials of November 1903—but the first man to build sixes commercially was the brilliant but modest Montague Napier whose 18–24 hp model was announced in October 1903 by S. F. Edge, the ebullient Australian who masterminded the Napier sales operation. He was one of the first people to realise that sporting success sells cars, and won the 1902 Gordon-Bennett Race on a 40 hp Napier; he also entered Napiers for reliability and speed trials and carried on a voluminous, and often vitriolic, correspondence with the motoring press for many years.

The power output of those early Napiers was always understated as a matter of policy, for Edge's philosophy was that if a customer got more than he'd bargained for, he had no right to complain!

Their long bonnets gave Napier sixes a nose-heavy look, but they steered and handled like the thoroughbreds they were. Describing a run on a Napier in 1907, an enthusiast summed up the marque's unique appeal.

'As for her petrol consumption, I am afraid it does not worry me. It is the sort of thing which troubles an omnibus company desirous of making a profit, but it does not cause any anxiety to the rich men and women, of whom the supply is seemingly unlimited, who buy Napier six-cylinder cars.' To such people also, the argument, often used, that the extra luxury is not worth the extra money, has no meaning. 'Like the difference between first, and third class in a railway train, it is worth buying for people who like comfort,

The Hon. C. S. Rolls starting from Monte Carlo in 1906 in a successful attempt to beat Charles Jarrott's time of 35½ hours to London by 40 hp Crossley. His car? A Rolls-Royce 20 hp TT Replica

and there are many to whom the cost is a matter of no moment.'

Only one make could hold a candle to Napier–but it was a challenge which eventually prevailed. Born of the commercial union between a perfectionist engineer and a peer's son who was both motor trader and racing driver, the 40/50 hp Rolls-Royce came to epitomise all that was best in motoring, yet it was a car that relied more on painstaking quality of workmanship than on any originality of design.

F. H. Royce, an electrical engineer, bought a 10 hp, two-cylinder, Decauville, one of the best light cars of 1902, and used its general layout as a basis for a vehicle of his own design, although he omitted the Decauville's most original feature, unit construction of engine and gearbox. The little Royce car ran well enough to attract the attention of the Hon C. S. Rolls, who was looking for a quality British vehicle to supplement his agencies for top French cars like Panhard and Mors, and an agreement was signed to produce similar cars under the name of Rolls-Royce. A third partner in the venture was Claude Johnson, ex-secretary of the Automobile Club.

Royce refined the design, 'which combined in one engine the best features of many engines,' still further, and the first two-cylinder Rolls-Royce cars made their public debut on an insignificant little stand at the December 1904 Paris Motor Show.

A British visitor to the show, a man who claimed he had 'never ridden in a bad car or sat beside a driver who was not first-class,' was invited to try the car along the Champs-Elysées.

'It was,' he enthused, 'a revelation. Never before had I been in a car which made so little noise, vibrated so little, ran so smoothly, or could be turned about so easily and readily in a maze of traffic.' Indeed, the conclusion almost reached then and there, was that the car was too silent and ghost-like to be safe.

'That the car could be set running while the car was at rest without any noise or vibration perceptible to the occupants of the car was good; that the

car in motion should overtake numerous wayfarers without their giving any indication that they had heard it, so that the horn had frequently to be called into use, was almost carrying excellence too far!'

Building on eulogies like these, Rolls-Royce introduced a four-cylinder 20 hp model in February 1905, followed by a 30 hp six and the unsuccessful 3½ litre V-8 Legalimit, designed to rival the electric broughams of the day for silence, with a governor on the engine that allowed it to maintain a steady speed of 20 mph–but no more–on any type of road.

The six took part in the 'Battle of the Cylinders', a well-publicised trial in June 1906 against a four-cylinder Martini (built by the Swiss armaments firm) driven by Captain Deasy, and won on points.

But one suspects that the result made little difference to the final choice of the rich purchaser, who judged a car's merits by the length of the bonnet, and whose whole-hearted acceptance of the six was proved by the fact that over thirty companies showed cars of this type at the 1906 Olympia Motor Show, just three years after Napier.

At the Show, Brooke Cars announced that in future they would be following a six-cylinder-only policy and soon Rolls-Royce followed suit, concentrating on their new 40/50 hp model.

On June 21, 1907, a 40/50 Rolls-Royce named the 'Silver Ghost' started on a trial run of 15,000 miles, observed by officials of the Royal Automobile Club (which had received King Edward's accolade in 1907); apart from the ever-present tyre troubles, it made only one involuntary stop, after 629 miles, when the petrol cock vibrated shut, causing a minute's delay. It took part in the Scottish Reliability Trials, then, six days a week, shuttled backwards and forwards between London and Glasgow until August 8.

It spent 40 hours of that time being repaired and overhauled; repairs, replacements and renewals came to £11 11s 5d, the tyre bill, at £12–£13 a tyre came to £187 12s 6d, and the total running cost was £28 8s 4½d–approximately 4½d a mile.

Meanwhile, one of the top Continental models, a 45 hp Hotchkiss, was also put through an RAC 15,000 mile trial, offering an ideal standard for comparison.

It started earlier–on April 29–and finished later–on August 20–which meant that its results were rather overshadowed by those of the Rolls-Royce. It made one major involuntary stop when the leather grease cap on the propellor shaft fell on to the hot exhaust pipe and caught fire. It proved less needy of care and attention, only spending 9 hours 44 minutes in the repair shop, but wore out no fewer

The *dernier cri* in elegance — a 24 hp Mors pullman saloon, *circa* 1905, with ventilated roof to guard against the mid-day sun of the British Raj. Monty Grahame-White and the Maharajah of Cooch Behar only have straw boaters to fend off the heat . . .

Fitzgerald Verity Dalton, Esq. and his family take the road in their 12 hp Darracq, capped, goggled and coated against the dusty roads of 1906. On the back of the car is an anti-dust shield

E 868

V.C.C.
1901
DECAU-
VILLE

RAC
62

34

This little 8½ hp 1901 Decauville *(opposite)* is reputedly the very car which inspired Henry Royce to take up motor car engineering.

Right: Renault's most popular model before the First World War was the 1,100 cc twin-cylinder Type AX. The type achieved immortality as the *Taxi de la Marne* used by General Gallieni to rush Paris garrison troops to the field to halt the German advance in 1914.

Below: Paris Singer, son of the sewing machine magnate, operated the City & Suburban Electric Carriage Company in London, where in 1902 they opened an 800 car garage in a converted skating rink in Westminster. This quaint Columbia Victoriette was supplied to Queen Alexandra by City & Suburban in 1901

Above: massive and handsome, this 1906 de Dietrich was one of the finest cars of its day. Another contender for the title was the Delaunay-Belleville, much favoured by Tsar Nicholas II of All the Russias, seen *(left)* setting out from St Petersburg in a 40 hp Delaunay. Less elegant certainly, but possibly more practicable, was Ransom Eli Olds' tractor-and-trailer Reo outfit *(below)* on Ormond-Daytona Beach, in 1905

than 46 Michelin Non-Skid tyres, at a cost in the region of £600.

The Rolls-Royce test caught the public imagination, even though the observers complained that the rear suspension was too soft and the front footboards became uncomfortably hot, and the 40/50, named the Silver Ghost in honour of the trial car, soon ousted Mercedes from the position of 'The Best Car in the World.'

Admittedly Daimler, with their new Silent Knight sleeve valve engine, ran Rolls close in the snobbery stakes, and could boast that King Edward VII was one of their best customers along with the Prince of Wales, half-a-dozen Oriental potentates and more than eighty Dukes, Earls, Viscounts and Baronets; but their cars could not equal the elegant lines of the Rolls, with its Palladian radiator. Daimler coachwork always seemed ill-matched to the marque's finned radiator–a feature shared only with some makes of truck–and characteristically high scuttle dash.

Daimler did not introduce a six until 1909, by which time the six-cylinder vogue had already produced its most spectacular excesses, built, appropriately, by the two firms which had started it all – Napier, whose 1907–8 90 hp model offered 14·5 litres at a chassis price of £2,500 and Ariel-Simplex, who during the same period offered a 15·9 litre 50/60 hp chassis at a mere £950; the cost differential being, presumably, something to do with the price of fame!

Another fine six-cylinder model was built by Sheffield-Simplex, whose Lon-don depot was only a couple of doors from the Rolls-Royce showrooms. These sixes were built at Tinsley, near Sheffield, from 1907 to 1922; in 1909 the company introduced a 45 hp model which dispensed with the gearbox entirely, and had only one direct speed–'over 150 parts dispensed with; over 300 lb reduction in weight,' they claimed.

In an age which set great store by top gear flexibility it was a remarkable achievement, but it was just a matter of allying a flexible powerful engine with a suitably (but not too) low final-drive ratio. The Sheffield-Simplex also had an accelerator pedal that pivoted sideways, and a single pedal to operate both clutch and brake. Eventually the marque bowed to convention, and fitted a gearbox, but the car was still capable of making the first-ever run from Land's End to John O'Groats using top gear only, and completing a run from London to Edinburgh in top without stopping the engine, a feat also attempted by Napier and Rolls-Royce.

'Strength with lightness' was the watchword at the ultra-modern Sheffield-Simplex factory, and the car incorporated a high proportion of chrome-nickel steel. 'Costs all the world,' said the works manager, 'but it lasts for ever.' Which is more than could be said of the company....

In common with many quality cars of the era, the Sheffield-Simplex featured a circular radiator. Continental makes with this feature included the Delaunay-Belleville, built by a famous firm of boilermakers. In 1905, they pioneered forced lubrication of the crankshaft, rather than the imprecise splash or drip systems common then –and for many years after. The Delaunay was the favourite car of the Tsar of all the Russias (Lenin, on the other hand, was a Rolls-Royce fan).

Hotchkiss, too, had a round radiator. Like other armament firms who had gone into the motor industry–FN in Belgium, Martini in Switzerland, BSA in England–they had discovered that machines which could ream out the barrels of guns could turn out a nice line in cylinder bores....

Other leading French makes included de Dietrich, magnificent cars built by a company which had originally been founded in 1684; the Mors, managed by an engineer called André Citroën; Rochet-Schneider; Brasier; Turcat-Méry.... Even firms which had made their name with light cars moved into the millionaire market, among them de Dion with a V-8, and Panhard with a Knight-engined monster of 7.4 litres, which looked especially handsome clad in Monsieur Labourdette's skiff bodywork–polished mahogany, flared wings and doorhandles disguised as rowlocks.

Italy could boast Fiat, Itala and Züst, while even brave little Belgium could boast of Minerva, Metallurgique and Germain. As for Holland, there was the dustless Spyker, so called because its clean underbody design raised little dust on the dirt roads of the day. Switzerland, of course, had the splendid Piccard-Pictet; Germany was famed for Mercedes, Benz and Opel; Austria built the Austro-Daimler and the Gräf und Stift (in one of which the Archduke Franz Ferdinand was riding when he was shot at Sarajevo); and Spain was producing the Abadal and the Hispano-Suiza, both of which were also built abroad, Abadal in Belgium and Hispano-Suiza in France.

Some very fine luxury cars were built in America in the pre-First World War era–Packard, Pierce-Arrow and Peerless, Lozier, Locombile, Smith & Mabley Simplex, Welch, Pope-Toledo, Coey–the list is virtually endless, composed of cars which for style and engineering were fully the equal of anything to be found on the other side of the Atlantic.

One make which attracted a unique aura of enthusiasm was the Thomas Flyer, from Buffalo, New York, active from 1900 to 1912, which achieved world fame in 1908 when a 60 hp model won the 20,000 mile New York to Paris motor 'race'.

The 1908 Thomas Flyer was a massive, long-striding car, with a T-headed side valve engine of around $9\frac{1}{4}$-litres swept volume with the four cylinders cast separately. After 62 years a Flyer owned by Curtis Blake of Massachussetts was still capable of living up to the 'Flyer' part of its name with a cruising speed of 45–55 mph and a top speed of around 65 mph, at a touring fuel consumption of 11–17 miles per gallon.

It was as fine a representative of the Edwardian luxury car–'a method of travel that is well-nigh ideal'–as you could find, combining, as Filson Young wrote in 1906, 'all the luxury that any reasonable creature can desire, with the advantages of fresh air and safety.'

Before they went in for mass-production, Fiat produced some outstanding quality cars like this elegant little 10/12 hp landaulette of 1906 *(above)*. One of America's leading makes in Edwardian days was the E. R. Thomas Co. of Buffalo, New York. This 1908 60 hp Thomas Flyer is based on the New York-Paris racer

Two of the more powerful veterans in the 1973 Brighton Run were the 1903 Daimler tonneau *(top)*, with characteristic fluted radiator (though the flutes were then at the side) and scuttle dash fitted with drawers and cupboards, and the 1902 de Dietrich *(above)*. This car is said to have been an entry in the 1902 Paris–Vienna race, and was later used by Lord Iveagh for many years.

The delicate Phébus-Aster of 1900 *(opposite)* is in complete contrast. It had a 3½ hp engine and elaborate C-spring rear suspension

Fast and Furious
the dawn of racing

Few people in the Western world had ever seen a horseless carriage when the first motoring competition was proposed in 1887, to stimulate public interest in the new device. On the appointed day, however, only a single vehicle appeared for the meeting in Paris, one of the delicate little de Dion Bouton steam quadricycles. The Comte Albert de Dion duly drove it to complete the course, watched by a large crowd. Private contests between gentlemen doubtless followed, but publicly the pioneers were for a few years content to demonstrate that their rattling contrivances could cover long distances.

The true dawn came in 1894. At the end of 1893 the Paris newspaper *Le Petit Journal* announced a motoring competition, published regulations and invited entries. This was in no way a race: prizes were to be awarded for the machines which 'were without danger, easily managed, and not expensive to run'–regulations which like so many

in the subsequent history of motor sport proved open to varying interpretations at the end of the event!

Just over 100 entries were received, although had anybody recalled some of the absurdities entered for the Rainhill locomotive trials of 1829, when railways were at an almost comparable stage of development, some of them would surely not have been countenanced–among the methods of propulsion specified were gravity, hydraulic, compressed air, the weight of passengers, various systems of levers or pendulums, and mysteriously, 'automatic' and 'self-acting'. In fact, only steam and internal combustion were represented in the 26 vehicles in the elimination trials; 17 actually completed the trials, and subsequently 8 more were admitted to start in the first proper motoring competition on July 22, 1894. They ranged from two–seater cars to buses, 13 of the 25 were petrol-engined.

The contest was over an 80-mile run

from Paris to Rouen, with frequent stops for observers to change vehicles and exchange notes, for lunch at Mantes–and to courteously pick up the occupants of vehicles which fell by the wayside. In fact, only four steamers failed to complete the course, the first retirements being a Serpollet soon after the start and a Scotte bus which burst a boiler tube.

A de Dion steam tractor with a semi-articulated trailer set the pace, averaging about $11\frac{1}{2}$ mph. However, it clearly did not meet the regulations or spirit of the contest, so the first prize was awarded jointly to a Panhard and a Peugeot. Motor sport was born; the next obvious development was a contest in which speed would be the deciding factor. A race.

A committee formed from participants in the Paris-Rouen event devised the first race, from Paris to Bordeaux and back, over the enormous distance of 732 miles. The rules were simple: manufacturers were allowed to enter any number of cars, but no two identical; only tools and spares carried could be used in repairs, but drivers could be changed at will; the first car with more than two seats to finish would win. Team planning for this race would today be considered more appropriate to a rally–teams even issued maps to their crews–while efficiently planned relays of drivers were felt by most to be the key. However, Emile Levassor drove a Panhard single-handed over the whole course to record the fastest time, 48

Best performance in the first-ever competitive motoring event was put in by this de Dion steam tractor. Its compound engine—one high-pressure cylinder, one low-pressure—developed a nominal 20 hp

Emil Levassor's triumphant return to Paris after his epic drive to Bordeaux and back. His Panhard had a twin-cylinder Phénix engine, giving 4 bhp at 800 rpm, and 'a gearbox, so that the gears were protected from dust'

hours 48 minutes (15 mph). Levassor's relief driver was still asleep when he arrived at the pre-arranged take-over point, so he simply drove on, reputedly refreshed at Bordeaux by no more than champagne!

Emile Levassor did not win, for his car was a two-seater. Koechlin in a Peugeot was declared the official winner, in 59 hours 48 minutes–one minute ahead of Doriot on another Peugeot. Nine cars finished, of the 20 which started, and the 6 steamers were completely outclassed by the petrol-engined machines–unlike the Paris-Rouen trial, the qualities required for this *race* were speed and stamina, and while steam may have been able to provide speed over short distances, it was ever to be handicapped on long runs.

At the celebration banquet a speaker proclaimed that a road journey to Bordeaux would eventually be covered at four times Levassor's speed; of that prophesy René Panhard commented that 'always one person makes an ass of himself.' Levassor equalled Panhard in profundity, remarking that air-filled tyres would never be a practical proposition for cars; like most competitors and observers, he had not been impressed by the Michelin brothers'

struggles in the race with their Peugeot *l'Eclair*, which was fitted with their pneumatic tyres.

The pattern for mainstream European racing was set for six years, while in America the sport developed more hesitantly, and along different lines. Although there have been suggestions that parts of the programmes at county fairs in the early 1890s were competitions between horseless carriages (and in fact who is to gainsay that trials between traction engines were not just that?), the first motoring competition in the USA was the Chicago *Times Herald* contest, late in 1894. This comprised a race and a series of laboratory tests for mechanical efficiency. Only two of the entries appeared for the first attempt to run this, a Duryea and a Benz, and only the latter completed the 94-mile course. A re-run of the 'race' was arranged for November 26, when because of snow the course was shortened to 54 miles. Two electric cars did not fare well, while only two of the six petrol-

engined cars completed the race. Frank Duryea drove his high-wheeled Duryea to win in 8 hours 23 minutes, form Muller's Benz.

A Duryea won the next American race, over a 60-mile course in 1896, but it was the only car of the seven starters to finish. This fiasco did not impress America with the potential of the car.

Unconvincing though this race was, the notorious Pennington was quick to see the value of race-success advertising in promoting the automobile, to the extent that he invented the first British race, in 1896: 'The Pennington Motor has proved itself to be the leading Motor in the world. This machine so easily beat all comers in the great Motor Car race which took place in England in May of this year between Coventry and Birmingham. The starters in the above race included the de Dion Steam Carriage (winner of the Motor race from Marseilles to Nice this Spring) and the Panhard-Levassor Vehicle (winner of the great Motor Car race between Paris and Marseilles); also winners of all other important Motor races and competitions hitherto held in the world.' Just whom the Pennington Motor Patents Syndicate thought might swallow this one must remain a puzzle. . . .

One of three 7.7-litre 45 bhp Napiers built for the 1903 Gordon Bennett race, probably the first car to race in 'British racing green' and the oldest surviving British racing car

In mainland Europe the sport moved ahead rapidly. Out of the committee which had organized the Paris-Bordeaux race came the Automobile Club de France, which ran its first race in 1896, a stage event from Paris to Marseilles and back. Foul weather threatened to wreck the event—Amédée Bollée crashed into a fallen tree, many drivers ran into storm debris, the wind blew out the burners of tube ignition—and other natural forces introduced elements of farce. Two cars were charged by bulls, and having pushed their Rossel to the top of a hill, one crew failed to allow for gravity, and watched the car roll back down again, to be sadly damaged. Nevertheless, 15 cars finished, Panhard works foreman Mayade win-

ning at a speed of 14·5 mph for the 1,062 miles. Among those who crashed was Emile Levassor, who was to die in the following year, in part as a result of his injuries.

There were no major long-distance races in 1897, but several short events were notable. The 149-mile Paris-la Turbie saw the only open road race victory for a steam vehicle, Chasseloup Laubat's de Dion; the Paris-Dieppe saw Panhard make the first moves towards a racing car, as distinct from a road car used for racing, with lightened components and a mildly pointed nose, in a 'wind-cutting' essay; the 107-mile Paris-Trouville was the first race to be won at over 25 mph (by Hourgières in a Panhard).

The first racing accident occurred in a race at Perigueux in 1898, when the Marquis de Montaignac rolled his Landry et Beyroux as he overtook a Parisienne; the marquis and his

mechanic were both killed. Later that year came the first mass start, when the organizers of the Paris-Amsterdam essayed what was regarded as a dangerous experimental departure from the normal practice of starting cars at timed intervals. Then came the race from Paris to Amsterdam and back, and trouble with Authority. The start had to be moved to Villiers and the finish to Montgéron, both outside the jurisdiction of the Paris Prefect of Police—to back up his authority to inspect certificates of roadworthiness, that gentleman called out a squadron of cavalry to the official starting point at Champigny! The race was run, and won at 26·9 mph by Panhard driver Charron.

Races became more numerous, longer (the 1899 Tour de France stage event was run over 1,350 miles), and faster—the last race of the 19th Century, from Bordeaux to Biarritz, was won by

Levegh on a Mors at 37 mph.

By the end of the century distinct racing cars had emerged. Generally, Panhards had been the outstanding cars, although their challengers were gaining strength (immediately, Mors threatened Panhard domination). The 1895–97 Panhards had two-cylinder in-line engines, of 1·2 to 1·6 litres. By 1898 an in-line four was used, and in the cars which took the first four places in the 1899 Paris-Bordeaux the capacity of these was increased to 3·3 litres. Doubling the number of cylinders had enforced a longer wheelbase, which brought handling benefits, for the early cars had been short and high. Pneumatic tyres were used from 1897, when the characteristic Panhard radiator also appeared, and steering wheels were fitted in 1898 (tillers, with very direct steering, were at least partly responsible for Levassor's accident, and almost entirely to blame for Montignac's).

The easy way to increased speed in the new century was through sheer power, through larger and ever-larger engines. Chassis were flimsy, made of wood or 'armoured wood' until Mercedes introduced the pressed-steel frame in 1901. Axles were rigid, shock absorbers as such unknown, wooden-spoked wheels were universal, and tyres were notoriously prone to failure (for the first ten years of racing they had to be replaced with the wheel still mounted on the car). These qualities meant herculean work for drivers on the poor roads of the day, and the lot of the riding mechanic was no easier—as well as attending to his duties such as engine lubrication, he had to stay on the bucking brute. Crews were seated high, with virtually no protection from wind, rain or dust, and the stones thrown up from unsealed surfaces.

There were signs of the sophistication that was to come in little more than a decade in the voiturettes, where tubular frames appeared and engine efficiency was more important, and in many events these light cars came close to matching the heavy cars in performance. (Classes were defined in 1901, simply by weight: voiturettes, up to 250 kg (551 lb); voitures légères, 250–400 kg (551–882 lb) and 'heavy cars', over 650 kg (1,432 lb): in the following year a maximum limit of 1,000 kg (2,204 lb) was imposed, and this led to liberal drilling of main members and minor components).

In an attempt to broaden racing, the Gordon-Bennett Trophy series was inaugurated in 1900, as an event where national teams were to compete for a trophy presented by *New York Herald* proprietor James Gordon-Bennett, an enthusiastic follower of motor sport since the 1894 Paris-Rouen event. For the first time, national racing colours were allotted—blue for France, white for Germany and yellow for Belgium, which were permanently adopted, and red for the USA. Only one team started in the first Gordon Bennett, from Paris to Lyon, three French Panhards (two finished), while single entries of a Belgian Bolide and an American Winton failed to complete the 353 mile course. The great event of the year was the Paris-Toulon-Paris race, won at 40·2 mph by Levegh, driving a Mors.

Speeds in the marathons down the highways of Europe went up and up, passing the 50 mph milestone when Fournier won the 1901 Paris to Bordeaux race at 53 mph (even more impressively, he won the 687 mile Paris–Berlin race at 44·1 mph).

The Gordon Bennett struggled through a farcial stage. In 1901 it was run concurrently with the Paris-Bordeaux, when the only contestant to finish was Girardot, in tenth place overall. In 1902 it was run as an event within the Paris-Vienna, and the Trophy went to the crew which finished 16th overall. Fastest car over the 615 miles was a Renault voiturette driven by Marcel Renault, who averaged 38·9 mph. In bringing his Napier to the finish, at 31·9 mph, Selwyn Francis Edge won the Gordon Bennett and gained the first international race victory for a British car.

That year saw one of the odder events in racing history, and a notable drive by another Englishman, Charles Jar-

rott. He distinguished himself by finishing second, knocking down a senior police official as he did so. The consequences he feared did not materialize, he surmised because the event was government sponsored. The event was the Circuit du Nord, dubbed the 'Concours du Ministre' as it was sponsored to promote the use of a home produced fuel–alcohol. 'The fumes emitted from the exhaust were exceedingly nauseous' commented Jarrott. Few competitors tuned their engines to thrive on this diet, most consequently complained of erratic running and loss of power. The two-day event was run in almost continual rain through the dreariest regions of northern France, to the almost total disinterest of the populace, and won by

The crude Benz *rennwagen* of 1900 gained a bad reputation, and is very obviously a badly balanced car compared with the 1901 Panhard *(below)*. The Benz had a twin-cylinder 16 hp engine—with a most generous radiator!

Léonce Girardot poses on the 40 hp Panhard which he drove to win the 1901 Gordon Bennett, in the main because he was the only competitor to complete the course! His speed of 37 mph was good enough for only 10th place overall in the concurrent Paris–Bordeaux race

Renault most clearly demonstrated
that sheer power was not essential
in road racing when Marcel Renault
drove this 3.7-litre *voiture legère*
to win the 615-mile Paris–Vienna race
outright, in 1902

The Chevalier René de Knyff was a
flamboyant but talented driver who
later became a motor sport
administrator and President of the CSI.
Here he waits on his Panhard to start
in the 1901 Paris–Berlin race

Maurice Farman, driving a Panhard. The French did not run another 'alcohol race', but an Italian event on similar lines was more successful.

Public opinion had been hardening against open-road races since 1900, when two cars had crashed into spectators during the Paris–Roubaix. Crowd control was usually ineffectual, and few of those who lined the edges of courses had any real conception of the speeds at which cars travelled, or the imprecision of control which their drivers had. Safety margins were very very narrow.

The end to the first heroic age of motor racing came in 1903, in the tragic Paris–Madrid race, which the French government permitted only with great reluctance, and was to cut short at Bordeaux.

Very early in the morning of May

Top: Charles Jarrott before the start of the ill-fated Paris–Madrid race. He placed his 9.9-litre de Dietrich fourth.
Left: Madame du Gast with her smaller 5.8-litre de Dietrich, which appropriately has a shapelier tail (the gallant lady is 'Inspecting the examining control officer's letter box'). She finished in 77th place.
Below: winner of the last city-to-city race, Fernand Gabriel, bringing his Mors into the last control at Bordeaux, where the race was abandoned

24, 1903 'all Paris seemed to be moving out along the Versailles road,' to watch the 275 starters set off one by one: as the leader on the road (Louis Renault) reached Tours, the last competitor was starting at Versailles, 135 miles away. Speeds down the dusty highway to the south-west were unprecedented. In moving past the first starters, Jarrott and de Knyff, to take the lead, Louis Renault was reputedly timed at almost 90 mph in his light car—at that time the official Land Speed Record was just over 80 mph. Many cars fell out in the early stages, when there were remarkably few accidents. But, inevitably, these came.

Renault arrived at Bordeaux first, Jarrott second, having started third and first respectively. Forty minutes passed before another car arrived; Gabriel's Mors, with the start number 168. Apprehension turned to alarm as stories of carnage began to circulate.

Marcel Renault died when his car rolled after he had put a wheel in the gutter when attempting to pass Théry; when Barrow swerved to avoid a dog, and hit a tree, his mechanic was killed; Porter's mechanic died when their Wolseley hit a house and burst into flames; Brouhot driver Tourand tried to avoid a soldier who dashed after a child into the road—his mechanic, the soldier and the child died. As the catalogue of disaster built up the government stopped the race at Bordeaux, even requiring that the cars were returned to Paris by train. Charles Jarrott later marvelled 'not that several had been killed, but that so many had escaped.' Gabriel was declared the winner, having *averaged* 65·3 mph over the 342 miles from Paris.

This put an end to the primitive age of open-road racing. Generally, the future of racing was to be on circuits or tracks, although there were to be exceptions. There were the Tours of Sicily, and there were two St Petersburg-Moscow races, in 1907 and 1908, when Victor Héméry won in a GP Benz at 51·4 mph—a remarkable speed on the abominable Russian roads. Even worse going was experienced by the competitors in the trans-continental marathons; races only in title, these were in fact extraordinarily challenging

trials, run when much of Europe was hardly opened up to cars. Five cars started in a race from Pekin to Paris in 1907; four finished, Prince Scipione Borghese completing the journey in 60 days to win with a 7·4 litre Itala. An even more ambitious 'race' was run from New York to Paris in 1908; a Protos completed the run in 166 days, but was disqualified, so the Thomas Flyer which reached the French capital four days later was declared the winner. In 1909 two stripped Model Ts were assisted across North America by the Ford dealership network to win the

New York-Seattle race.

A quarter of a century after the Paris-Madrid the greatest of all open-road races, the Mille Miglia, was first run. The first city to city race in South America, from Buenos Aires to Cordoba, was run in 1910, and the later *turismo carretera* races which reached their peak in the 1940s were wholly to the pattern of the earliest of all races. As late as 1950 the *Carrera Panamericana* was inaugurated in Mexico–an event which would have seemed right and proper to the first great racing driver, Emile Levassor.

The monument to Emil Levassor, winner of the first motor race, at the Porte Maillot in Paris

Against the Clock
the first speed records

It was inevitable that speeds claimed for the horseless carriage should be put to the test against the watch, and perhaps surprising that this did not 'officially' happen before the end of 1898, when the car had been in existence for years, and long-distance races had already been run. The first recognized speed record was a by-product of a hill climb meeting, a motoring activity which was to be completely over-shadowed by record-breaking.

Soon subsidiary record classes were to be created, for classes by engine capacities, over distances, or durations, while innumerable spurious 'records'—coast-to-coast across America, 'beating the Blue Train', and so on—were to inspire yards of advertising copy down the years.

Until the 1960s, the Land Speed Record was the record which captured public imagination; after 1964 it became the property of devices far removed from cars, and in an age when in any case men were rocketing into space it lost much of its one-time magic.

That first speed record was set on December 18, 1898 by the Comte de Chasseloup-Laubat in the Achères park at St Germain near Paris. Driving an electric Jeantaud, he achieved 39·24 mph, over a 'flying kilometre' (the second of two measured kilometres, the first being covered from a standing start). In the following year a series of challenges and counter-challenges between Camille Jenatzy and Chasseloup-Laubat ended with the former pushing the record to 65·79 mph, the Belgian thus becoming the first driver to exceed 60 mph and 100 kmh. His car was the remarkable *La Jamais Contente*, which had a cigar-shaped body atop tiny wood-spoked wheels—the fact that Jenatzy sat almost on top of it spoiled this early essay in automobile aerodynamics! It proved to be the last electrically-powered car to take the premier speed record.

Jenatzy's record stood until 1902, when on the Promenade des Anglais at

Electric power, steam power. *Left:* Camille Jenatzy starting a record run on *Le Jamais Contente* in 1899. The more effectively streamlined Baker Electric Torpedo of 1902 *(left)* failed to make any impression on the record. This fell twice to a steam car, to Serpollet in 1902 and to Frank Marriott *(below)* with a Stanley at Daytona in 1906

Above: Henry Ford about to set off on his wild record attempt on Lake St Claire, with mechanic Spider Huff clinging to the side of 999. The Gobron-Brillié *(right)* with which Rigolly first set the record above 100 mph was an unconventional car, with tubular chassis and opposed-piston engine. It is seen here at a Gaillon hill-climb in 1904

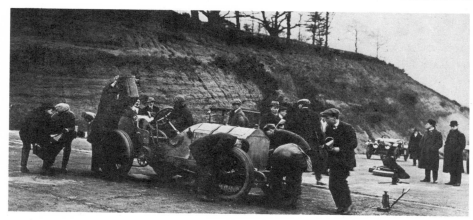

Nice during the speed week, Léon Serpollet achieved 75·06 mph, in his own steam car. Four years later the record was broken by a steam car for the second and last time, when Fred Marriott set it at 121·57 mph at Daytona in the Stanley *Rocket*.

Between those two steam highlights the record fell to internal-combustion engined cars 13 times, albeit three of those 'records' were not officially recognized, and nor were several other improvements on previous best times. A major problem was that the autocratic Automobile Club de France, until 1909 the controlling authority, refused to recognize some attempts, on occasion showing the partisan attitude not entirely absent from its handling of other branches of the sport. Thus Rolls' 82·84 mph in 1903 was disallowed (the ACF did not approve the timing methods) and to Arthur Duray with a Gobron-Brillié stands the honour of being the first man to raise the record above 80 mph (83·47 mph). Similarly, Henry Ford's incredibly heroic 90 mph record on the frozen Lake St Clair in Michigan early in 1904 received only AAA recognition (his speed in the crude 16·7 litre '999' was 91·37 mph).

Later that year the record was edged up by W. K. Vanderbilt Jr, whose 92·30 mph set in a Mercedes 90 at Ormond-Daytona, was the first universally-recognized record set on US soil (or sand, to be strictly accurate!), by Rigolly and de Caters. Then in July, Louis Rigolly achieved the magic 100 mph (103·55 mph) during the Ostend speed trials, driving a Gobron-Brillié.

Centre: record meets were a feature of early motor sport. This trio at Daytona in 1905 are Vanderbilt's 90 hp Mercedes, the 90 hp Napier driven by McDonald, and E. R. Thomas' Mercedes

Above: the speed record was broken on a track for the first time at Brooklands in 1909, by Victor Hémery with a Benz. Here the car is made ready in a flurry of activity

Fred Marriott's 1906 record at Daytona convincingly smashed Victor Hémery's 109·65 mph set in 1905 (accepted by the chauvinistic French, despite the fact that Herbert Bowden had already recorded 109·75 mph at Daytona in his twin-engined Mercedes *Flying Dutchman*). However, there was no disputing Hémery's 1909 record of 125·95 mph, set in the 21½ litre Blitzen Benz at Brooklands–the first outright

record to be set on a banked track. The same car was then used by two flamboyant Americans, Barney Oldfield and Bob Burman, to 'improve' on the record. Neither speed was accepted outside the USA, however, and there was in any case, considerable doubt about the length of the Daytona 'mile' used by Burman.

The last Land Speed Record set before the First World War was 124·10

ing took place in 1899; in 1902 a meeting at Bexhill—of all staid places!—was the first of any type to see top-line Continental drivers in action in England; in 1904 the first speed trials were held at Ormond Daytona, and thus Daytona is the American venue with the longest more or less continuous connection with motor sport (and in terms of sheer high speed the present banked track is not far removed in spirit from the famous 23-mile beach).

Always well aware of the value of publicity, S. F. Edge seized the opportunity offered by the completion of the Brooklands track to demonstrate the worth of a Napier, by covering 1,581 miles in 24 hours, thereby unsettling local residents, with night-long noise, and the fresh concrete of the banked track. Possibly too much has been made of Edge's track-pounding in this latter respect, for erratic settling might have been expected when a mass of concrete was put on top of the sand of Surrey. In 1913 at the track, Percy Lambert, in a Talbot, became the first driver to cover 100 miles in an hour.

Hill climbs proliferated in the early years of motoring, most of them very minor affairs. However, La Turbie—which saw fatal accidents to Bauer in 1900 and Count Zborowski in 1903—lingered on for decades, and the famous 13·4 mile Mont Ventoux climb has been in more or less continuous use since 1902, when the winning Panard took 27 min 17 sec for the climb. The Mount Washington and Giant's Despair hill climbs were inaugurated in 1904 and 1905 respectively, while the first competition on the most famous American hill climb, the 12·4 mile road up Pike's Peak in Colorado, was held in 1916, Rea Lentz winning in a Romano in 20 min 55 sec.

mph—a seeming contradiction as in 1911 a ruling that the mean of two opposite runs was to count (Héméry's 125·95 had been set in a one-way run). This lower-speed record was set at Brooklands, by I. G. Hornsted, driving a Benz with a Blitzen engine.

Other events 'against the clock' were an important feature of motor sport during its formative years, up hills and on the flat. The first sprint meeting at Achères, saw Chasseloup-Laubat's absolute record. Such events became a seaside speciality. The first Nice meet-

Giuppone's Lion-Peugeot voiturette trailing dust up the classic Mont Ventoux climb in 1909. Height of the bonnet was determined by the 100 mm × 250 mm bore-stroke ratio of the single-cylinder engine

Joys
of the Open Road
the first popular cars

It is, let us imagine, a fine summer day in 1904. As a member of the up-and-coming middle classes—a doctor, perhaps—you have ordered a car more in keeping with your station in life than the old, outmoded Benz on which you started your motoring career.

In the spring you visited Cordingley's Automobile Exhibition in the Agricultural Hall, Islington, attempting to weigh up the merits of a dozen different makes, wandering up and down the gangways with highly-polished brass headlights goggling at you from all sides, while keen-faced young salesmen in squarecut morning coats, clean celluloid collars and shiny top-hats talked technicalities with you till your head reeled.

You quite liked the look of the Prunel tonneau, but when you noticed that the English concessionaires were a gunpowder and ammunition works at Hendon, you wondered whether the make was especially liable to explosions. The Beaufort car, built in Germany for the British market, seemed a workmanlike vehicle, and there was a particularly handsome 12 hp Darracq fitted with Tonneau

The first car to be produced by the Ford Motor Company was the 1903 Model A. This restored example owned by Edgar Beatty of Walled Lake, Michigan, is driven by one of the authors . . .

Middle-class motoring 1904 style—the
9 hp Peugeot swing-seat tonneau

Grand Luxe coachwork (dark red,
lined black, picked out in white) that
almost took your heart, but in the end
you decided on a 9 hp Peugeot, for it
looked just like a Mercedes in miniature.

There was a delay in delivery, for
you wanted the coachwork finished in
your own livery, but it was worth the
wait, for Mr Friswell, the London
agent, managed to secure one of the
latest live axle models–chains are becoming rather *démodé*, except for highpowered racing cars–fitted with the
most up-to-date swing-seat body. This
is a great improvement on the old
pattern tonneau, where you had to
climb into the back seats from the
muddy road through a door in the rear
of the coachwork; now you enter from
the front, as the entire passenger seat is
hinged and swings open on a brass
track. The 6 ft 3 in wheelbase is not
long enough to allow side doors to the
rear seats; few makes have yet thought
of fitting doors to protect the legs of the
driver and front seat passenger from
the elements, and Peugeot isn't among
them.

At last, the car has been sent down
from London by train, and ignominiously dragged up to your house behind
the local carrier's horse. You have
decanted two gallons of petrol through
a gauze-lined funnel into the tank
beneath the driving seat, replenished
the square-headed radiator with rain-
water from the butt, filled the lubri-
cating tank on the dash, pressurised
it with the hand pump fitted alongside
and unscrewed the regulators on the
oil sight-glasses which show the steady
drip of oil to the engine bearings.

Now, having switched on the ignition, you open the inspection hatch in
the side of the bonnet and check that
petrol is reaching the complex Le
Rhône carburetter, which incorporates
a spring-loaded 'automatic choke' to
richen the petrol/air mixture at starting
speeds.

You go round to the front of the car
and grasp the starting handle firmly,
thumb on the same side of the grip as
your fingers to avoid injury should the
motor backfire, and pull the engine
sharply over compression.

No result . . . you try a couple more
times, then adjust the hand controls for
the throttle and ignition, set on a brass

quadrant at the centre of the steering
wheel to give a little more spark
advance and a little more throttle
opening, and try again . . . success!

Suddenly the engine is teuf-teufing
away merrily, so you rush round, jump
in the driving seat before it stops, and
pump away at the lubrication system
until the exhaust shows just a tinge of
blue oil smoke.

Now comes the big moment–moving away from rest for the first time.

You push the tall gear lever forward
until it clicks into the first speed notch
on its quadrant–it just moves fore-and-
aft, not in an H-slot like the Mercedes
or a T-slot like the Argyll–holding
down the clutch pedal as you do so.

Then you ease off the handbrake and
gently bring up your clutch foot, with
the engine just ticking over. As the
massive leather-faced cone clutch bites
home in the flywheel, the car bounds
forward with a neck-snapping jerk.
Then, very gradually, you speed up
the engine with the foot throttle (an
advanced touch this, and a definite
improvement over the hand throttle
except on bumpy roads).

As the two-cylinder engine begins
to turn over faster, a shattering vibra-

Four faces of the Edwardian motor car.
England *(right)*: Herbert Austin at the
wheel of a typical horizontal-engined
Wolseley, *circa* 1904.
Belgium *(centre)*: a Minerva tourer of
1909, the year before the Knight
sleeve-valve engine became universal
on all the products of this Antwerp
company, who had built their first car
in 1900.
Italy *(bottom left)*: curiously
proportioned laundalette coachwork
adorns this 1910 Fiat Tipo 54 5.7-litre
model. Among the features of this
luxury touring model was a fan-bladed
flywheel to aid cooling and a
water-cooled transmission brake.
America *(bottom right)*: the very first
Chevrolet car to be built was this 1912
Classic Six 30 hp tourer, designed by
racing driver Louis Chevrolet. During
the first year, 2,999 vehicles were
produced
Following pages: a splendidly
proportioned Rolls-Royce 40-50 hp
limousine, circa 1910

Cyclecar primitive: the Bédélia of 1910 represented motoring at its most basic. On racing models the front passenger changed speed by shifting the belts with a piece of wood

Cyclecar sophisticated: the Bébé Peugeot, introduced in 1912, was designed by Ettore Bugatti. It had a 6 hp four-cylinder engine and gear change by concentric prop-shafts

tion builds up under your feet, and the acetylene headlamps begin nid-nodding in unison.

So you declutch, ease up on the throttle and move the gear lever into second, glancing down to make sure it's in the notch, and not in the neutral space that lies between each speed.

Once on the direct drive in top, the Peugeot proves a willing performer, and the vibration is greatly diminished, the steering responds instantly to the slightest touch on the heavy, wood-rimmed wheel, which needs only one-and-a-half turns from lock to lock, and while you feel potholes and bumps on the hard dirt road, they don't take charge of the steering as they do with some cars.

To stop, you use the hand brake, which also frees the clutch—this is supposed to prevent skidding on the greasy wood blocks or granite setts

Body and chassis were rivetted together on the 1913 Lagonda 11.1 hp to form a rigid unit; suspension was torsion-bar assisted

which pave the road in towns—and discover that the makers' claim that 'handbrake is as effective backwards as forwards' means that it hardly works in either direction. But the footbrake, which acts on the transmission, is hyper-fierce, and definitely for emergencies only.

The car is no speedster when it comes to hills: you change down by slipping the clutch until the engine races and pulling the lever back into the lower gears until, on the steeper gradients the Peugeot is moving at walking pace, although it's powerful enough to reach the top unaided. On your old belt-drive Benz you had to jump out and run alongside on hills. . . .

You can drive all day without seeing another car, and you plot your route by the towns where petrol is available. (You keep your own supply of two-gallon cans, sent from London by rail, in a steel-lined bunker at home).

Dust is an ever-present menace: your car sucks it up from the road, and a white cloud follows you, sometimes

not settling for several minutes (the famous aeronautical engineer Sir Hiram Maxim has suggested that the ideal way of laying the dust is to spread roads with a mixture of treacle and glue . . .).

Horses (and those in charge of them) are becoming more used to motor vehicles now, and it's unlikely an irate carter will flick at you with his whip for frightening his team. But dogs still rush out from cottages as you drive by, snapping at your wheels and occasionally getting run over—but that's usually settled by a handful of small silver for the cottager. As for chickens, the stupid birds seem to have no road sense at all, and your progress past farm entrances is apt to be punctuated by a cloud of flying feathers. Some farmers are even rumoured to scatter corn in the road in the hope that their scraggy pullets, worth more dead than alive, *will* be run over. . . .

Provided, however, you remember that the law could be lurking round any corner with a cheap stopwatch, and that you're prepared to struggle with the occasional puncture on fixed rims and wheels, motoring seems a pretty carefree pastime.

Perhaps one day you'll find it worthwhile to have a full-time chauffeur-mechanic, but at present you feel the £2 a week such a servant would command in wages can be better spent. So the gardener will have to go on washing and polishing the car for a while longer. . . .

The early 1900s saw a tremendous

In 1914 the French Charron firm introduced the 845 cc Charronette four-cylinder light car, which sold for £214 on the British market

advance in the design of light cars, and 'big-cars-in-miniature' like the Peugeot could be bought relatively cheaply. True, there were still plenty of cheap vehicles on the market, mostly of varying degrees of nastiness, though some of the small singles, like the 5½ hp Baby Peugeot, the 6 hp de Dion and the little Renault, with its dashboard radiator, were very good indeed.

But small cars seem to have a way of growing into big cars, and by 1910 the lower end of the price scale was fairly poorly served, especially for the motorist of modest means who wanted sporting performance. Oddly enough, two vehicles were being evolved almost simultaneously, one in France, one in England. And both came into being as the result of road accidents. . . .

Two young Parisiens, Robert Bourbeau and Henri Devaux, both aged 18, were collaborators in an ambitious project to produce a two-stroke aero-engine. Robert, student at an engineering college, provided the know-how; Henri, son of a rich coal merchant (funny how they turn up in motoring history–Henry Ford's first backer Alexander Malcomson was one, so was the father of racing driver Felice Nazzaro) provided the financial backing and the workshop.

The two partners owned an ancient and disreputable motor cycle with a basket trailer, on which they decided to make an expedition to Dieppe. At night, to escape parental disapproval. . . .

First the trailer came adrift, depositing the sleeping Devaux in the road.

Not unnaturally, he chose to drive once the damage had been repaired, but lost control of the outfit going through a small town and demolished it against a lamp post. The two youths took what was worth saving home by train.

Bourbeau set himself the task of creating a new vehicle from the wreckage: using the four wheels, various metal fittings and the engine, he produced a long, narrow tandem-seated vehicle with the front axle pivoted in the centre, controlled by steel cables wound round the steering column: the driver sat in the rear seat, guiding the lethal device with a wheel composed of a circle of wood that had formerly braced the legs of a chair, linked to the column by bicycle spokes. Upholstery was basic in the extreme–two coal sacks, filched from the elder Devaux's yard.

It seemed hopelessly crude, yet the two experimenters were asked to make so many copies that they decided to go into full-scale production, calling the cars Bédélia. . . .

In England H. F. S. Morgan, the young son of a Worcestershire clergyman, crashed his V-twin Peugeot motor-cycle. While he was convalescing, he built a three-wheeled car which represented almost the ultimate in simplicity. The Peugeot engine was mounted at the front of a tubular backbone chassis (which also acted as transmission tunnel) with sliding pillar independent front suspension.

Two-speed chain drive engaged by dog-clutches was standard–the Bédélia had the most basic type of belt drive–and the back wheel carried the single brake band which gave minimal re-

tarding power, especially in the wet.

Such light vehicles, part car, part motor cycle, naturally became known as 'cyclecars'. A third vehicle which had some features in common with both Bédélia and Morgan was the GN, built in Hendon by Ron Godfrey and Archie Frazer-Nash from 1910.

Cyclecaring was glamourised by the popular title of 'The New Motoring,' and in its biggest boom year, 1912, over 40 makes of cyclecar were represented at the Motorcycle Show at Olympia. But it was too insubstantial to last, and soon the craze was over and the 'little big car' concept was again triumphant.

Still among the leading protagonists were Peugeot, whose 856 cc Bébé had been designed by a young Italian engineer, Ettore Bugatti, who was starting to produce cars under his own name at Molsheim, Alsace. Le Bébé had an unusual all-direct drive transmission using twin crown wheels and two pinions on the ends of concentric propeller shafts, a layout only marginally less alarming than that used on the Sizaire-Naudin of 1908, which had three direct speeds, given by treble pinions on one shaft; the gear lever moved the pinion carrier sideways and fore-and-aft, thrusting another pinion of a different diameter into mesh with the long-suffering crown wheel.

Edwardian motoring journalists were as adept as their modern colleagues when it came to praising with faint damns, and novelist Max Pemberton was no exception when he drove the

The 998 cc air-cooled V-trim Humberette cyclecar appeared in 1912; a well-built little vehicle, it sold at £120 (water cooling £15 extra)

One of the most refined light cars of the period was the little 1,100 cc AC. Most—except this prototype—had the gearbox in the rear axle

new Sizaire, which had a thumping 12 hp single-cylinder engine. 'The only point of criticism I could possibly make concerned the gear changing, which on this particular chassis was not as smooth as it might have been . . . as a general rule these gears are to be changed quietly and pleasingly. . . .'

But the Sizaire cost over £200– cyclecars could be had for less than £70, or you could even make one at home, using a little ingenuity, and maybe even sell a few replicas.

Take–and very few customers did– the 1913 Dewcar, which had two planks as the main components of the body-cum-chassis. Propelled by a 4½ hp Precision engine, the single-seater Dewcar cost £60 in 1913; a year later

the price was up £15, due, no doubt, to rising costs at Mr Dew's local saw mill!

In the end, it was the three archetypal cyclecars which lasted the longest: Bédélia survived into the 1920s, having built a particularly suicidal light ambulance during the First World War: a stretcher replaced the front seat and the wounded *poilu* was firmly strapped in with his feet over the petrol tank and engine, doubtless pleading that he'd rather be left to die in peace! The post-war models, however, built after the company's founders had severed their connection with the marque, had little in common with the original Bédélia save excessively long drive belts.

Above: this 1910 Stanley Runabout has its boiler under the bonnet and a twin-cylinder engine beneath the car, geared directly to the rear axle. It is preserved in the Henry Ford Museum at Dearborn, Michigan

Opposite: in 1913 cycle and motor cycle agent William Morris introduced this little 10 hp White & Poppe engined two-seater. Priced at £175, the car was the foundation of the Morris empire; during the 1920s its descendants became known as 'Bullnoses'

Introduced in 1914 and produced until 1924, the 9 hp Hillman car cost £200. It had a 1,357 cc four-cylinder engine

GN grew up into the Frazer-Nash in the 1920s, but the Morgan three-wheeler survived, its basic design unchanged, until 1948, when the supply of sporting V-twin engines dried up.

The rapid demise of most cyclecars left the way clear for a new generation of light cars, with tiny four-cylinder engines of 1–1½ litres. Standard, Singer, Swift, Calcott, Calthorpe, Morris, and AC were among the leading makes, setting the scene for the rapid growth of the family car market in the 1920s.

Already, however, Henry Ford was showing how mass production of motor vehicles could bring the price of a properly-built car down within the reach of the ordinary working man. The press laughed in 1904 when Henry Ford proposed to flood the market with a 15 hp four-cylinder air-cooled car as a successor to the Model A gas buggy with which he had begun production; they mocked his forecast of a daily production of a hundred cars before

Hang out more flags—this impressive barrage of bunting heralded a display of the latest models from Renault's Billancourt factory when Louis Renault visited the USA early in 1914

Top: a big boost for the Model T Ford was its victory in the trans-American New York-Seattle race of 1909 for the Guggenheim Prize. The winning car covered 4,100 miles and twelve states in 22 days. By 1914, Ford Model T production had passed the quarter-million mark annually, the result of the introduction of the moving assembly line at Highland Park *(above)* *Following pages:* Cecil Bendall's 1912 Austro-Daimler 27/80

1906 was out. But Ford knew such a
market existed.

Woodrow Wilson, then President of
Princeton University, condemned the
motor car as a spreader of socialist envy
among the lower orders, but the desire
to acquire one of these freedom-giving
vehicles proved strong.

Ford involved himself in a single-
handed and costly fight against the
stranglehold of the Association of
Licenced Automobile Manufacturers,
which sought to control the American
industry through an alleged master
patent filed in 1895 by G. B. Selden.

The court case, which cost millions,
ended up with the ALAM interests
building a car from the patent specification to prove that Selden had designed
the first motorcar in 1877, while Ford
built a car running on the Lenoir
system to prove that he hadn't.

Ford won, but he could hardly have
failed, for the ALAM's patent had only
a few months left to run. Now he could
concentrate on production of his easy-
to-drive Model T, designed in conjunction with Joseph Galamb and
Childe Harold Wills.

In 1913, possibly inspired by the
methods used for transporting carcases
in the Chicago slaughterhouses, Ford
began experiments with the moving
production line, which immediately
cut the time needed to assemble a
chassis from twelve-and-a-half to one-
and-a-half hours.

Walter Chrysler, then managing
Buick, part of Billy Durant's General
Motors empire, was simultaneously
working in the same direction, though
without such spectacular results.

Introduced at the end of 1908 at a
cost of $850, Ford's Model T sold
5,896 cars in the first year: by 1916
sales had rocketed to 577,036, and the
price fallen, because of production
economies, to $360, establishing Henry
Ford, the son of a poor farmer, as the
world's most successful businessman.

The country boy had become the
Flivver King.

Round and Round
the first autodromes

Roads were not always available for racing, for example in England because the law of the land has always proscribed it on public highways, while in America race promoters were the first to exploit the entertainment potential of the new sport. These factors led to the first and most lastingly famous autodromes, Brooklands and Indianapolis.

Brooklands was proposed early in 1906 by Hugh Locke King, and its basic layout worked out in discussion with S. F. Edge, Charles Jarrott and E. de Rodakowsky, who was to become its first clerk of the course. The motor course was built on land owned by Locke King near Weybridge, completed in six months and opened in 1907. Its principal features were two steeply-banked curves, where the track surface soon became rough as the mass of concrete settled into the sand on which it was built. These bankings were designed for speeds of up to 120 mph, which was exceeded as a lap speed in 1922.

The first Brooklands race meeting was held in July 1907, and for a year racing was conducted on a hopelessly amateurish basis. Then E. V. 'Ebby' Ebblewhite introduced more realistic programmes. The atmosphere of Brooklands, and attitudes to it, were to remain 'amateur' until it closed for ever in 1939–this largely from choice. Unhappily, however, it meant that the track never gained real international status, and that very very few events of genuine significance were ever run on it.

The 2½ mile oval at Indianapolis was

Following pages: this 1908 11.5-litre Napier is very similar in basic conception to the 1903 car (page 42); its size is emphasized by the 'baby' Peugeot. Owner Ronald Barker regularly drives it to VSCC meetings. The Locomobile *(page 66, bottom)* is another famous survivor from 'the Age of Monsters'. It was raced in the Vanderbilt Cup, 1905–08.
Below: incongruous Brooklands trio. The wind-cutting Vauxhall KN flanked by Gore-Browne's Lancia and Fedden's Straker-Squire

Above: this Piccard-Pictet was a 'Four-Inch' TT car, was raced at Brooklands in 1909, and later converted for road use.
Right: marque racing in 1909—line-up for a Sizaire handicap event; the famous transverse leaf ifs is very obvious on the nearest cars

a thoroughly commercial undertaking from its inception. The Speedway was promoted by four Indianapolis citizens, Carl G. Fisher, James A. Allison, Arthur C. Newby and Frank H. Wheeler, and was designed by P. T. Andrews; the original plan was more farsighted than that for Brooklands in that it incorporated a road circuit within the oval, and although this was not built the lack of a road race facility was to be less keenly felt than at the British autodrome. Like Brooklands the track was built quickly, and during the inaugural meeting it

Below: a 1908 12-litre GP Itala at rest in the Brooklands paddock; the track was to keep many redundant front-line cars in active racing. The famous Fiat 'Mephistopheles' was even larger, with an 18 litre engine; it was raced at Brooklands until 1922

simply broke up. Nine cars started in the first main race, over 250 miles, which saw the first Indianapolis fatal accident, when the crew of a Knox was killed as it rolled; Buick drivers Chevrolet and Burman led for most of the distance, Bob Burman winning from Clements (Stoddart-Dayton). Strang won the 100 mile feature race on the second day of the meeting, again for Buick. The 300 mile main event on the third day was cut short at 235 miles because of accidents, when Lynch (Jackson) was leading Ralph de Palma (Fiat).

By the end of 1909 the track had been resurfaced with 3,200,000 bricks. The basic Brickyard was defined, and although the bricks which gave it this nickname were to disappear, the track within its confining walls was to remain unchanged through decades of ever-increasing speeds, to the point where cars with a 200 mph potential were expected to race closely on it, although they could hardly be expected to race safely.

Programmes of short races were run in 1910 and 1911, but May 30 of that year saw the first running of the 500 Mile Sweepstakes. The superlatives started to flow, as they have done ever since, sometimes blindly disregarding realities outside Indiana: 'the greatest automobile race ever run so far in the history of the industry . . . the greatest field that ever faced a starter' proclaimed *The Automobile*. Carl Fisher had found a formula for success, and since then Indianapolis has meant just one race. That first 500 attracted 100,000 spectators.

Forty cars lined up in eight ranks for the rolling start. Leaders during the first half were a National, a Mercedes, a Knox, a Fiat and a Simplex. At half-distance, veteran driver Ray Harroun took the lead in a Marmon Wasp, and with the aid of relief driver Cyrus Patschke went on to win at 74·4 mph. The Marmon was regarded by most as 'a peculiar looking automobile'—even then the 500 establishment was suspicious of anything out of the ordinary! The Wasp had a six-cylinder production-based engine, and slimmer lines than its contemporaries, for, most pec-

Front row of the grid for the first Indianapolis 500, May 30, 1911, with the rest of the field hidden in the smoke typical of Edwardian racing. The Stoddart-Dayton pace car is on the right, alongside it in numerical order are a Case, a Simplex, an Interstate and a National. Of these, only Ralph de Palma's 597 cubic inch Simplex finished among the leaders, in sixth place. Winning car was the 477 cubic inch Marmon single-seater *(right)*; driver Ray Harroun averaged 74.59 mph, but said that he never fully extended the car. This photograph of the Marmon coming into the pits was reputedly taken by Henry Ford

uliarly, it was a single-seater. Mulford's Lozier was second, sluggish pit work perhaps costing it the race, and Bruce-Brown's Fiat was third. A multiple accident at the pits accounted for a Case, a Westcott, an Apperson and a Fiat, and the mechanic of an Amplex was killed when the car rolled. The 500 had claimed its first life. . . .

Ralph de Palma led the 1912 race from the start until with two laps to go the engine of his Mercedes failed, and Joe Dawson came through to win at 78·7 mph on a National. The following year saw the first European invasion, when Peugeot and Itala entered teams, and a couple of independents were attracted across the Atlantic. Jules Goux drove a Peugeot with a 1912 GP engine linered down within the 450 cubic inch

limit to win by 13 minutes, at 75·92 mph. He was the first winner to drive through the 500 single-handed. A Mercer was second, a Stutz third, and the two European independents, Guyot (Sunbeam) and Pilette (Mercedes-Knight) fourth and fifth respectively.

René Thomas won for Delage in 1914, when the final order read Delage, Peugeot, Delage, Peugeot, Stutz–Barney Oldfield salvaging American pride with that fifth place, and getting the loudest reception from the crowd. Ralph de Palma won in a Grand Prix Mercedes in 1915, at 89·94 mph. The 1916 race was a lacklustre event, the first 500 to be cut short. Dario Resta stroked a Peugeot to an easy win at 94·05 mph; 'probably he had in mind the death and injury of so many of his

fellow racers, due to tyres bursting.'

That comment in *Automobile Journal* did not refer so much at that time to Indianapolis as to track racing in general. Several major new board tracks of between one and two miles were by then in operation, sponsored by the entrepreneur, Jack Prince. Racing on these was fast and close, often over long distances, 300 and 350 mile events not being out of the ordinary. The board track high noon was to come in the early 1920s, but they played a substantial part in establishing track racing as the pre-eminent form of motor sport in the USA for three decades, with the Indianapolis 500 of course always at the goal. Correspondingly, and while Europe went to war, road racing in America dwindled almost to extinction.

The Odd,
the Eccentric,
the Advanced

'If wishes were horses, beggars might ride.' And if modern methods and materials had been available to the Edwardian motor manufacturers the cars they produced would have been vastly different machines, for virtually every major design feature of the modern car was proposed before the First World War.

The patent records of the day are full of ideas that might have made good if the right technology had been available. The brainwaves started a long time ago. . . .

In 1877, for instance, George and William Ashley Wilson and George Duncan of Liverpool patented 'Engines, etc., for propelling Vehicles on Roads and Rails,' powered by a single-cylinder gas engine fuelled by gas stored in tanks, and featuring simple forward-backward-neutral gearing. While the vehicle was at rest, the intrepid trio proposed that the engine 'shall be occupied in compressing air springs or like re-action agents capable of giving off stored power say for starting, mounting an incline, or when otherwise desired.'

While Louis Renault, is frequently wrongly credited with the invention of the shaft-driven live axle, few people remember that he proposed many far more remarkable inventions. At the 1905 Paris Salon Renault showed a car with a self-starter in the form of a small auxiliary engine with a pinion meshing with teeth cut in the flywheel rim; motive power was supplied by the exhaust gases, which compressed air in a small tank. In 1910 he talked of using 'varying water pressures to take the place of the standard systems of speed-changing,' while in 1914 Renault patented a hydraulic suspension system similar in principle to the modern British Ley-

land Hydrolastic arrangement.

Transmission and springing, in fact, seem to have been major preoccupations of Edwardian inventors: in 1905, for example, Richard-Brasier offered an optional underdrive on their live-axle models, giving eight speeds forward, 'whereby the gearing of the car can be easily lowered to suit the requirements of a hilly district.'

An overdrive top-'the sprinting gear'-was a feature of early Silver Ghosts, but was dropped because owners failed to understand its use, tried to run in it all the time, and complained that their cars were noisy and inflexible.

Attempts to do away with the clash-prone sliding gear were legion-in fact, the era's most popular car, the Model T Ford, was the leading example, with a two-speed pedal-operated epicyclic gear allied to a big engine with plenty of low-speed torque.

'Pedals to push, that's all,' was the motto of the Adams car, of Bedford, designed by the American, Hewitt. Their cars had one pedal for each speed (two or three, depending on the model) but the transmission was prone to rapid wear at the feet of an unskilled driver, and a sliding gear soon became an optional fitting. In 1906 Adams introduced a remarkable V-8, with a 40 hp Antoinette aero-type engine, which the company built under licence from the designer, the Frenchman Leon Levavasseur. Hewitt produced a similar car in New York: ENV, another British aero-engine manufacturer, built a 60 hp V-8 in 1908, fitted with a two-speed rear axle. Adams also built a V-16 Antoinette, but it doesn't seem to have been used in a car.

One feels that a certain Monsieur Henriod got rather carried away by the enthusiasm for the epicyclic gear,

for his 30–40 hp air-cooled car, which caused something of a sensation at the 1908 Paris Salon, was apparently designed for a motormaniac organ player. It had no apparent gearbox, for the epicyclic mechanism was concealed inside the clutch. But to select the three speeds forward and reverse, the hapless driver had to choose from no fewer than *seven* control pedals.

'It must be conceded,' one critic commented drily, 'that the simplicity of the transmission is somewhat discounted by the intricacy of control.'

That, however, was not a criticism that one could level at the earlier and most distinguished exponent of epicyclic gearing, the Lanchester. The first car built by Frederick and George Lanchester had features as advanced as a rigid tubular space frame and (unsuccessful) overdrive, plus a virtually vibrationless single-cylinder engine with two crankshafts; the subsequent flat-twin-cylinder version, which formed the basis of production models, retained the double crankshafts, and for good measure, had *six* connecting rods, which balanced the rotating forces of the engine to a degree unknown at the time. Moreover, the Lanchester was the first British car to be designed for pneumatic tyres, while balanced tiller steering was another distinctive feature of the marque. A discerning journalist of 1903 listed other virtues:

'The Lanchester cars are not only characterised by high-class workmanship and finish, but also by great originality of design; they are quite different, in fact, from any of the conventional types. The framework is exceedingly strong, and quite free from perceptible distortion under any working conditions. The Lanchester is undoubtedly the most comfortable car to ride in of

Typical of the unorthodox approach of
the Lanchester brothers is this 1912
25 hp Lanchester tourer. The engine is
mounted between the seats, driving
through a three-speed epicyclic gearbox

any that have yet been made, the system of suspension being such that any one wheel of the car may be lifted to a height of two feet without any of the other wheels leaving the ground. The front and rear wheels are carried on separate frames, which are coupled to the car frame by parallel motion, which permits to them all the motions necessary for driving over the roughest roads, but retains rigidity in desirable directions.

'Another distinguishing feature of the Lanchester car is the adoption of large wire wheels, which the makers consider both safer and stronger than any wooden wheels of equal weight.

'The car is exceedingly roomy and exceptionally comfortable: it is also claimed to be unusually easy to drive.

'Yet another feature of the cars is

At the 1912 Olympia Motor Show, the old-established coachbuilding company of A. Meier & Son, of Redhill, Surrey, introduced this 25 hp rotary-valve Itala, fitted with 'our latest folding torpedo, whereby the back part of an ordinary four-seated torpedo can be folded away converting the body into a two-seater with fish-tail back'

that they are manufactured on the interchangeable system, each part being made and passed to limit gauges. The latter are in many cases even finer than those employed in the gun trade, which has hitherto been considered the acme of high-class workmanship.

'The users of these cars, therefore, are able at any time to obtain replacement of damaged parts without fear of a misfitting article being sent.'

Henry Ford, they say, learned a lot from Lanchester.

And one final Lancunian first—the company pioneered the driver's handbook, supplied with every car nowadays; but their book even included a section on how to perform controlled skids, like the 'Swing Round Stop' and the 'Sideways Stop.' There was one stern admonition, written, one imagines, by that bearded patriarch Dr Fred Lanchester: 'Remember that whatever the state of the road it is *bad driving* to navigate the car *sideways*.'

However, the Lanchester Company never enjoyed the success it really deserved. Lack of capital and a board of directors who were incapable of ap-

preciating the Lanchester brothers' designs, dragged it down until it became just a badge-engineered part of the Daimler group.

Although Lanchester were dogged by ill-fortune, they did manage to put their advanced designs into production. Jack Hutton's 1904 brainchild was stillborn—not only did the Hutton car, shown as an incomplete chassis, at the Agricultural Hall, have oil-operated hydraulic brakes, it also featured the complex Barber infinitely variable transmission, which was said to give all speeds from zero to flat-out.

More practical was the 1913 20/30 hp Cadillac, which reduced gearchanging to a minimum with a two-speed rear axle; the ratios were changed electrically, at the touch of a button. Since 1911 Cadillac had led the world in providing an electric self starter and electric lighting, but this latest innovation had an air of sorcery about it. Starting in cold weather was simplified by an electric heater that warmed the carburetter.

In 1915 when Cadillac brought out a V-8, their rivals, Packard, upstaged them with a V-12 inspired by the Brit-

Classic multi-cylinder: the first Cadillac V-8 *(above)* appeared in 1915. It had a 5.1-litre engine, cost $2,700, and 13,000 were sold in the first year of production

Classic multi-cylinder: Packard's V-12 Twin-Six *(left)* was designed by Jesse L. Vincent, inspired by Sunbeam's pre-war V-12 aircraft and by racing car engines. It was the world's first production V-12 car, and used aluminium pistons

Architect Maberley Smith designed the odd Sunbeam-Mabley *(top left)* with diamond-formation wheels and front-wheel drive. It was in production from 1901–04. One of the best-known steam cars was the White *(top right)*. This 1902 model, the first to have wheel instead of tiller steering, bore the unfortunate name *White Elephant.* Less successful was the Gront *(above),* based on the Locomobile. This is a *circa* 1902 model ish Sunbeam aero engine. It was, at that time, the most extreme expression of the multi-cylinder petrol engine.

Of course, petrol was not the sole means of propulsion in pre-First World War days. Steam gave it a close run at one time, and the steamers built by White and Stanley in the USA, Serpollet in France, and Turner-Miesse in England were renowned for their smooth running and rapid performance. Electric cars were common for town use, but their limited range and heavy storage batteries that needed daily recharging, limited their appeal. E. W. Hart of Luton built the remarkable 50 mph four-wheel drive *Toujours Contente* in 1900, with a motor in each hub, but the electric was really too slow except for dowagers.

Paraffin-fuelled cars enjoyed a limited vogue–the Roots & Venables of the 1890s was the best-known–and the Gobron-Brillié company claimed that in emergency their opposed-piston cars could run on 'pure alcohol, benzoline, or any good spirit such as gin, brandy, whisky, etc. . . .'

Perhaps the oddest propulsive medium was liquid air, which in 1902 was 'a motive power to be reckoned with.' The Liquid Air Power and Automobile Company was said to have large plants in America and England where air was frozen to minus 312 degrees F, becoming a concentrated liquid. And to demonstrate its potential, the company produced 'a neat little motor car,' which looked very like the contemporary steam buggies. Liquid air was poured into a well insulated copper tank and pumped into 'heating coils', where it was said to expand sufficiently to turn the engine over.

'A charge of eighteen gallons will move the car forty miles at a pace of twelve miles an hour, without any of the noise, dirt, smell or vapour inseparable from the employment of steam or petroleum,' claimed the company, but it is difficult to see how the vehicle could ever have moved *any* distance under its own power. Despite eulogistic articles in the popular press, it seems likely that the 'Liquid Air' venture was just another scheme to persuade the credulous to part with their money.

Then there was the 1902 Dunkley

No 3 Self-Charging Gas Motor Car– 'Takes its own supply from any ordinary gas pipe or street lamp post for 100 miles' run–Patent Twin Engines running together or uncoupled at will by driver, combined with Patent Double-Acting Gas Compressor.' It's stated on good authority that this little gem enjoyed a production life of several years . . . the company later went in for motorised prams!

Some of the more eccentric confections of the age boasted wheels in the oddest places. Peter-Paul Schilovsky, who managed the Tsar's motor stable, designed a two-wheeled car steadied by gyroscopes, and Wolseley built it for him in 1912 (James Scripps Booth built a monstrous V-8 two-wheeler of even more frightening aspect in America around the same time).

M. O. Reeves of Columbus, Indiana,

on the other hand, believed in the safety of numbers. His 1911 Octoauto had eight wheels on four axles and steered with six of them. It was supposed to give easier riding over bad roads, but it just promised twice as much tyre trouble. It was succeeded by a six-wheeler, called, improbably, the Sexoauto!

Six wheels also featured on the Broomell Pullman of 1903, the 1903–4 Janvier, a clumsy-looking tonneau that steered with the front two axles, and the 1905 Gros, on which the centre axle drove and the outer two steered . . . Mr Maberley Smith, a moderately successful architect, devised a strange little car like a motorised sofa, with four wheels set diamond fashion. It was claimed to eliminate skidding, and Sunbeam marketed it as the Sunbeam-Mabley from 1901–4.

The Sporting Car

The sporting car has always been part of the motoring scene, for although early enthusiast motorists were often as concerned as manufacturers to emphasize the practical uses of the horseless carriage, they equally regarded them as playthings. The cars which contested early races were simply cars, and the racing cars which came only a little later were not far removed from their touring counterparts. Touring bodies were fitted to 'racing car' chassis as a matter of course, while on the other hand the touring 60 hp Mercedes hastily prepared for the 1903 Gordon Bennett race in Ireland after the works 90 hp racing cars had been destroyed in a fire was shown by Camille Jenatzy's victory to be a very effective racing car–a sports car in fact, if not in name, for this generic term was not to be applied for many years (it had been implied earlier, in 1902, when the Gentleman's Sports Motor Co advertised turned versions of Benz cars).

The high-performance touring cars and touring conversions of racing cars in the early 1900s carried ponderous bodywork which emphasized their touring purpose. The realities of competitive motoring quickly led to lighter, lower cars, which in their make-up and the use to which they were put, were the European forerunners of the sports car. More obvious predecessors, however, were the American two-seater roadsters, a breed which flourished from about 1906 until the First World War.

These were spartan in the extreme, usually with little behind the toe board but a pair of bucket seats, a fuel tank, a spare tyre and perhaps a small locker or tool box. In appearance many were closely similar to contemporary racing cars, with wings and lights. Renault capitalized on precisely this, with the racing car replicas built for the American market in 1907; these closely resembled the 13-litre car which Szisz drove to win the 1906 French GP, but incorporated many stock components and had $7\frac{1}{4}$ litre engines.

Outstanding early American roadsters were steam cars built by the Stanleys; a Gentleman's Speedy Roadster with the largest of three alternative engines (a 30 hp unit), was capable of speed bursts of over 75 mph. But the best-known of all American roadsters came a few years later, the Raceabout version of the Mercer 35, which was built from 1911 until 1914, and the Stutz Bearcat, which was introduced in 1914 and continued in production into the 1920s. Many other manufacturers listed roadsters–Apperson, Chadwick (who offered a supercharged six for two

years from 1908), Ford with the Model K, Marmon, Maxwell, National, Peerless, Overland and Thomas, and deserving to be bracketed with the Mercer and Stutz, Lozier and Simplex.

The craze for roadsters even reached down to the humble Model T Ford, for which bodies with at least speedy names such as Cyclone and Greyhound were marketed, the latter 'specially designed to be lighter and stronger than other racing bodies . . . will relieve your Ford of a great deal of weight and increase the power and speed of your engine . . . the car will take up speed smoothly and quickly without the usual jerking motion, and will fairly sail through the air because of its peculiar non-friction shape.'

The best of the roadsters were true dual-purpose cars, which were used on roads and were raced in circuit and track events, from the early 24-hour races to the Indianapolis 500. In these they mixed it with stripped 'specials' based on stock models, and with pure European racing cars. Lozier claimed that the car driven into second place in the first 500 by Ralph Mulford was 'identical with the model put out by the factory,' while a Marmon roadster (more conventional in appearance than the single-seater which won) was running third when the last of its coolant

Sports forerunners.
Left: Jenatzy in full cry with the 60 hp Mercedes he drove to win the 1903 Gordon Bennett (and thus incidentally gain the first major victory for the marque), and Ferdinand Porsche driving the 1910 Prince Henry Austro Daimler, which had sports lines that would have been acceptable through the 1920s
Right: the roadster line. An Apperson Jackrabbit of 1907, and a 1908 Chadwick Six. Both marques were prominent in American racing, and a supercharged works Chadwick was successful in sprint events

drained away on the last lap (it was classified fifth behind a racing Fiat and a racing Mercedes). In 1912 Hugh Hughes placed a standard 4·9 litre Mercer 35C third, even though this car had the smallest engine in the race and Hughes had to push it for half a mile when he ran out of fuel. A pre-Bearcat Stutz roadster finished 1½ minutes behind the Mercer, indicating that contemporary Mercer and Stutz roadsters were closely matched (the more usual comparison between 35 and Bearcat inevitably favours the later design).

The proper setting for this generation of roadsters, however, was in road events, in races such as the Vanderbilt and Elgin series, and in hill climbs, where they were perhaps the first competition sports cars.

In Europe the sports car evolved along different lines, largely from cars which ran in the trials which were the forerunners of rallies. Early events such as the Thousand Miles Trial in 1900 were intended to demonstrate to a still largely doubting public that the horseless carriage was a practical proposition. Within a very few years this case was obviously proved, and a competitive element began to creep into trials. Trend-setting events were the German Herkomer Trials in 1906 and 1907, and in the subsequent Prince Henry Trials. To the consternation of some diehard entrants who anticipated gentile and leisurely affairs, these trials were, however, very definitely competitive, and successful Herkomer cars wore very light aluminium bodies, some with rakish wings which served to underline departures from the Roi des Belges style which the old school felt appropriate to touring cars.

This move away from bulky touring bodies was more pronounced in some of the Prince Henry contendors, and the 1910 event saw the appearance of two significant sporting cars. Austro-

Daimlers took the first three places, the winning car being driven by the company's design director, Dr. Ferdinand Porsche. This had a long-stroke 5·7 litre engine with shaft-driven overhead camshafts, which produced 86 bhp at 1,900 rpm, sufficient to give the car a top speed of 87 mph, doubtless aided by the small frontal area of its notably compact four-seater body. The only reactionary aspect of the car was its chain final drive, although this was an improvement on the Mixte transmission of Porsche's previous competition car, built for the 1907 Kaiserpreis (in the Mixte transmission, the engine was used to generate current for electric motors in the wheel hubs; its value was proved in military vehicles).

The three cars of the Vauxhall team also performed well in the 1910 Prince Henry Trials; their 3 litre side valve engine was developed by Laurence Pomeroy from a two-year old design, and in 1910 produced 52 bhp at the high engine speed of 2,500 rpm. The Prince Henry had a handsome body with a distinctive vee radiator, and to all intents and purposes was the forerunner of the first British production sports car. In 1911 its engine capacity was increased to 4 litres, and from this Prince Henry came the Vauxhall 30/98, in 1913. The first example of this model was built at the request of John Higginson, whose modest requirement was for a car to break the Shelsley Walsh hill climb record. Vauxhall obligingly stretched the engine to 4½ litres (and 98 bhp), mounted it in a lightweight chassis—and produced a sporting classic. A few were built before the First World War, and the model remained in production until 1927, for its last five years with a 4¼ litre pushrod ohv engine designed by C. E. King.

Throughout this period many other sporting tourers appeared, some genuinely high-performance cars, others

marriages of sporty bodies with very standard mechanical parts, while at the extreme end of the scale were stripped 'specials' and racing cars (erstwhile grand prix cars ran in Prince Henry events). These were seen together in some races such as the Targa Florio, which was first run in 1906 over Sicilian roads which for the most part were little more than tracks. The first Targa was won by Cagno, driving a very stark 7·4 litre Itala to average 29·07 mph over 227 miles. In the following year the great Felice Nazzaro won the one and only Kaiserpreis in a similarly basic 8 litre Fiat. By their nature, these events were the first European sports car races, for the first Tourist Trophy, run in 1905, was strictly a touring car event.

Vincenzo Florio's Targa was a testing event even by Edwardian racing standards, from its first running over three laps of the 92·48 mile 'Great Madonie' circuit in 1906, 50 days before the first Grand Prix was run. For the most part roads were no more than tracks, and this was reflected in Allessandro Cagno's very low winning speed (he fought his Itala round the Madonie mountains for 9½ hours, to win by over half an hour). The 1907–11 races were of varying lengths; in 1909 the event was over only one lap, as the island was recovering from the 1908 Messina earthquake—but Florio's determination and Sicilian pride in the event ensured that it took place.

The 1912–14 Targas were point to point round the island Tours of Sicily. Two fell to SCATs, produced by the Ceiranos (works test driver Cyril Snipe winning in 1912 and Ernesto Ceirano in 1914), while Felice Nazzaro drove one of his own Nazzaros to win in 1913. These races attracted a wide variety of sporting machinery, many of the entries stark devices for all the world resembling American runabouts—minimally equipped ALFA, Isotta Fraschini, Lan-

cia, Ceiranos as well as SCATs, Elka, SPA, Nazzaro, de Dion and others. De Dions are usually associated with the voiturette category, but almost improbably one Borra ran one of the stodgy V-8s in the 1912–14 races, placing it fourth in 1913. In Sicily, then, one of the classic sports car races, in retrospect and reality if not in contemporary definition, was well and truly established before the First World War.

The only older surviving race, the RAC's Tourist Trophy, has sometimes been a sports car race in its chequered history, but from its first running in the Isle of Man in 1905 until 1908 was very firmly a touring car event, with regulations covering fuel consumption, load and bodywork; in 1906 'touring suitability' had to be demonstrated in pre-race trials; in 1907 entries in a concurrent Heavy Touring Car race had to carry enormous screens to simulate limousine frontal area! These early Isle of Man TTs were closer in spirit to contemporary trials than to races (although contrarily they were unquestionably

races). Winners were Napier with an Arrol Johnstone in 1905, the Hon C. S. Rolls with a Rolls-Royce, E. Courtis (Rover) and W. Watson (Hutton) in the 1908 'four inch' race. The TT then lapsed until 1914, when the cars were much more sporting; it was won by Lee Guinness in a Sunbeam at 56·44 mph, from a pair of Minervas.

Meanwhile, development of voiturette sporting cars was stimulated by the Coupe de *l'Auto* races. In 1908 a

notable Isotta-Fraschini had appeared, with an advanced 1,327 cc overhead camshaft four-cylinder engine, which revved to 2,500 rpm. It had a scaled-down two-seater body, similar to those of the larger American roadsters and much better proportioned than some contemporary small European sporting cars, such as the de Dion-based specials.

A year later the first Bugatti appeared, and in some respects this was so similar to the Isotta that latter-day Mol-

In late Edwardian years, Vauxhall and Mercer built highly-respected sporting cars, the 30/98 and 35, which showed divergent European and American lines of development. The 30/98 *(above)*, photographed in 1916, has adequate bodywork, while the 1912 35T in the Cunningham Museum *(left)* starkly proclaims that it is 'sporty'. The 4.8-litre T-head Mercer engine developed 55 bhp, and the 4.5-litre Vauxhall unit rather more; cars had a maximum speed of around 75 mph *Below:* the Renault Grand Prix Replica of 1907 was outwardly, just that— compare with the 'real thing' on page 84—but with a 7.2-litre 35 hp engine. It was more than a boy racer machine, however, and achieved some racing success in America. The Fiat 28/40 *(opposite)* was a contemporary of the Renault. Vincenzo Lancia placed this one second in the 1907 Targa Florio, behind team-mate Nazzaro

sheim propagandists have gone to lengths to show that Ettore Bugatti must have designed the Isotta. More probably it inspired his T13. This was a delightful little car in its own right; like the Isotta, it had a four-cylinder shaft-driven ohc engine of 1,327 cc, which developed 22 bhp at 3,000 rpm and gave the T13 a maximum speed of

60 mph. Several hundred were sold.

The 1910 Coupe de *l'Auto* was won by a 2·6 litre Hispano-Suiza, designed by Marc Birkigt. Its T-head engine had the long stroke (65 × 200 mm) still required by the regulations, but in the following year this was replaced by a more rational 80 × 110 mm 3·6 litre unit in a production derivative, the 15T.

This soon became known as the Alfonso XIII, for Spain's motoring monarch used one. A short wheelbase version was offered with very sporting two-seater bodywork—one of the first spiders.

The Coupe rules had been revised for 1911 to restrict engines in the only sensible way, by capacity, and some of the cars built to this 3 litre limit had notable sporting derivatives. The Sunbeam 12/16 which was catalogued in 1911 was based on the Coupe racer, and was succeeded by a model closely following the cars which placed 1–2–3 in the 1912 race. These cars were broadly similar to contemporary Vauxhalls which sprang from a different background (although Vauxhall also entered top-flight racing at this time), and if it comes to that to models from Talbot, SPA, Isotta-Fraschini.

That striving for low-cost racing which has punctuated the motor sport decades became reality in pre-First World War days in the cyclecar class, where a limit of 1,100 cc was normal. Cyclecars had rudimentary chassis and running gear, and were usually powered by single- or twin-cylinder motor cycle engines–indeed, nobody seemed quite sure where to categorize these devices, and races for them were frequently run as part of motor cycle meetings.

The archetypical cyclecar was the French Bédélia, which both members of a crew played a very active part in driving. The driver, at the back, was responsible for steering, accelerating and stopping, his colleague at the front for starting the vee-twin engine, on some models for gear changing, and on all presumably for worrying more about the gravity fuel tank mounted directly atop the engine and the antics of the front wheels in their centre-pivot axle! Nevertheless, these spindly machines were capable of surprisingly high race speeds; in 1913 the 163-mile

A long pointed tail was almost *de rigeur* in the immediate antecedents of the sports car, such as this 1914 15/20 Talbot and 1915 Calthorpe 10 hp two-seater, although it was oddly at variance with the frontal area of the usual blunt noses

Cyclecar Grand Prix at Amiens was won by a Bédélia at 41·46 mph.

The outstanding contemporary of the Bédélia was the British GN.

At the other end of the scale, Rolls-Royce had a final sporting fling in the 1913 Austrian Alpine Trial, stung into entering a team when a privately-owned Silver Ghost failed to start on a hill in the 1912 event. The Derby firm entered three 40/50 Continentals, and after they had won the event the model was dubbed Alpine Eagle. A Continental won again in 1914, and privately

Top: first of a famous line, an ALFA 24 hp spyder of 1911
Above: the Hon C. S. Rolls racing a Rolls-Royce Light Twenty in the 1906 Tourist Trophy–he won at 39.3 mph

owned cars also took first and third places in the 1913 Spanish Grand Prix, a tough touring car event in the Guadarrama Mountains.

These were of course high-performance touring cars rather than sporting cars–but that after all is where the sports car story had started, a decade earlier. . . .

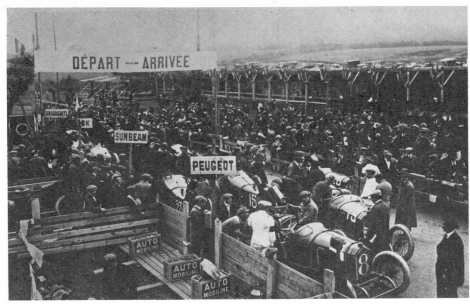

Microcosm of a late Edwardian motor race, the 1913 Coupe de *l'Auto*.
Left: Preparations for the start, with the Peugeots and Sunbeams nearest the camera.
Below, left to right and top to bottom: Jean Chassagne's Sunbeam moving away from the pits, and Repusseau's Buick about to start. The Buicks were prepared by the company's British agent, E. Keith-Davis; Repusseau retired with engine trouble, his team mate Drouillet crashed into a ditch, after colliding with a postman who wandered onto the circuit!
Two shots which show the atrocious state of the roads used. The first shows an unusual car, the Argentinian Anasagasti with a Picker engine. It was driven by d'Avary. *Right:* Lee Guinness' Sunbeam. The Vauxhall driven by A. J. Hancock at speed in a country section of the 32-mile circuit, and Goux' Peugeot passing under a temporary footbridge at St Martin

81

From Gordon Bennett to Grand Prix

The first circuit race was the minor Course du Catalogue over two 45-mile laps near Melun in 1900, which for the record was won by Panhard driver Girardot. Two years later the Belgian Automobile Club organized the true forerunner of today's road races, the first Circuit des Ardennes. This had a lap distance of 53 miles, approached in recent years only by the Targa Florio. But it was an out-and-out race, with none of the impediments of controls or neutralized sections usual in city-to-city races. Charles Jarrott won, on the sixth and last lap when his duel with Gabriel was resolved as a chain broke on the Frenchman's Mors.

In 1903 the Gordon Bennett Trophy race became a circuit event, and because of the 1902 British victory it became the first major international sporting event to be run in Britain. It would probably have been a circuit race wherever held in 1903, for the Paris-Madrid had ended the open-road era. On British soil it could never have been in the old tradition, and as it was a special Act of Parliament had to be passed before it could be run at all, on remote Irish roads centred on Ballyshannon. British, French, German and American teams competed, and the result was a clear-cut victory for the modified touring 60 hp Mercedes driven by Camille Jenatzy, from the three cars of the French team.

The following year saw international racing introduced into America, in the Vanderbilt Trophy event on Gordon Bennett lines. The 10-lap, 284-mile, race on Long Island was won by Franco-American George Heath driving a Panhard, by 2½ minutes from the only other runner to complete the full distance, Albert Clément's Clément-Bayard. Lyttle's Pope-Toledo was

third, Schmidt's Packard 'Grey Wolf' fourth.

That Packard was a track car, for already the seeds of the American circuit versus track schism were germinating. The Americans were racing on short ovals before the Europeans started racing on circuits, in this recognizing that the spectator was an important person—his rating in Europe was to be lowly for a few years yet.

The first star driver—and constructor—in these oval races was Alexander Winton (whose cars were never successful in road racing); he was later supplanted as a driver by the flamboyant Barney Oldfield, who raced Ford

and Winton cars, and by Ford works driver Frank Kulick, who in 1904 set the first sub-minute lap of a one-mile dirt track. Early track programmes consisted of races from five to fifty miles, but in 1905 the world's first 24-hour race was run on one of these ovals, at Columbus Ohio, when the winning Pope-Toledo covered 829 miles.

On European roads, Jenatzy's victory meant that the Gordon Bennett was run in Germany in 1904, where the German court from Kaiser to princelings gathered at the Taunus circuit to suffer the spectacle of watching Léon Théry retrieving the trophy for France, with a Richard-Brasier. In Italy, Vin-

Gordon Bennett scenes. *Left:* American cars were rare in early European races, and those that did appear were dismally unsuccessful. This four-cylinder Winton completed five laps in the 1903 race in Ireland
Below: winner of the last Gordon Bennett race, run in 1905 on the demanding Auvergne circuit, Léon Théry. His Brasier trails the cloud of dust common in any early race run on dry roads.
Right: spectators and cars shaded from the Spanish sun, as an Hispano driver waits to start in the 1910 Catalan Cup

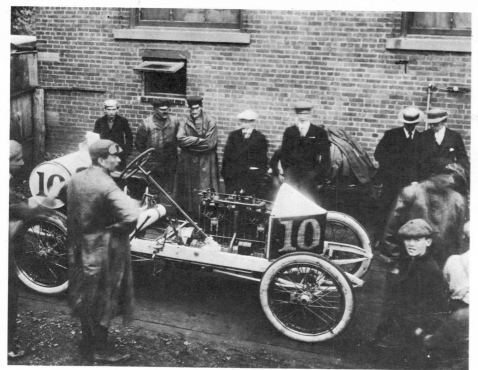

cenzo Lancia scored the first significant victory for Fiat, in the Coppa Florio.

In 1905 the French hosted the Gordon Bennett. Grudgingly. They felt that as the leading automobile nation they should have the largest entry, proposing 15 French cars, 6 British and 6 German cars, 3 each from Austria, Belgium, Italy, Switzerland and the USA. However, the race was run to the old rules, over a challenging 85-mile circuit in the Auvergne mountains, and French honour was satisfied as Théry, 'The Chronometer', led the Fiats driven by Felice Nazzaro and Alessandro Cagno at the end.

The French had their way, and in 1906 inaugurated the French Grand Prix, which was open to teams from any number of manufacturers. Further benefit came from French high-handidness, in that as a result of the fracas motor sport's first governing body, the Alliance Internationale des Automobile Clubs Reconnus (AIACR) was established, albeit to continue as a strongly French-influenced body for many years.

The European top-flight racing car remained a fairly stereotyped device, with the largest possible four-cylinder engine in a car weighing no more than 1,007 kg. Chain drive was yielding to shaft drive; multi-plate clutches had replaced the cone type; gearboxes were being mounted so as to be insulated from flexible chassis. Mors had experimented with friction shock absorbers, and in a lower class Bollée had essayed independent front suspension. Engines were slowly becoming more efficient, a notable example being the 1905 16 litre Fiat unit, which had push-rod operated inclined valves and developed 120 bhp at 1,100 rpm.

In the light car classes the merits of all-round balance were appreciated, and there was real progress, for example, in the independent front suspension of the Sizaire-Naudin which was built for the Coupe de l'*Auto* (a voiturette race, introduced in 1906 with regulations which restricted engine

bore, but not capacity–this gave rise to some outlandish long-stroke engines). Europe had seen a few really original cars–Clément Ader had built eight-cylinder racing engines in 1903, when the Gobron-Brillié had also appeared, with tubular frame, opposed-piston engine, and even a fuel-injection essay–but for a while technical innovations were American. Alexander Winton built an 'eight' in 1903; Pope-Toledo and Thomas produced racing 'sixes'; in 1905 Franklin and Premier entries for the Vanderbilt Cup had eight-cylinder air-cooled engines; Walter Christie persevered with his front-wheel drive monsters (and even tried a fearsome four-wheel drive, twin-engined, version!); in 1906 a Frayer-Miller had an underslung frame, so that its crew sat low, with only their heads projecting above the scuttle.

The term 'grand prix' was not new in 1906–it simply means great prize, and had first been applied to a motor race at Pau in 1901. But the idea of a national grand prix was new in 1906, when a cornerstone of modern road racing was laid. In introducing it, the French certainly did not envisage a series of national grands prix of equal status, but with the arrogance typical of the French-dominated first decade of motor sport, simply one grand prix–that of the AC de France, of course.

The first French Grand Prix was run on two hot June days in 1906, six laps of a 64·12 mile circuit near Le Mans having to be covered on each day. The heat aggravated crews' problems, with road surfaces which broke up, tyres that failed and save on a few cars had to be replaced on the wheel beside the road (some cars had wheels with detachable rims) and above all, unwieldy cars which had to be manhandled every mile of the 769. Eleven cars finished of the 32 which started, headed from the third lap by Ferenc Szisz on a flame-red 13 litre Renault. He averaged 62·88 mph, to finish over half an hour ahead of Felice Nazzaro on a 16,286 cc Fiat.

These placings were reversed in 1907, when the race was run over 477 miles at Dieppe, and Nazzaro won comfortably from Szisz. The 1908 result was a crushing blow to French pride. Almost half of the 48 cars which started in the Grand Prix at Dieppe were French; 9 were German, 6 British, 6 Italian and 3 Belgian, and there was a lone American Thomas. Christian Lautenschlager, driving his first race, won for Mercedes at 69·05 mph, and Benz took second and third places.

It was hardly coincidental that the majority of French manufacturers, together with a few from other countries, agreed to abstain from grand prix racing (while continuing to contest voiturette events, where French superiority still seemed assured).

The 1907 race, incidentally, saw the largest engine ever used in a GP car, the 19,891 cc V-4 in Walter Christie's front-wheel drive car, which was ob-

served with disapproval by the French establishment. It completed four erratic laps before retiring (but Christie did drive it to win a 250-mile race at Daytona Beach). For the 1908 teams, the first 'pits' were provided; these in fact were trenches with counters at ground level, but the term has stuck although the later French 'boite' or Italian 'box' is much more appropriate.

Meanwhile, for a brief period, road racing flowered in America. In 1908 the American Grand Prize was inaugurated with a splendid race at Savannah. In contrast to earlier American races, this was a well-organized event, on a circuit in part prepared by convicts. Ralph de Palma (Fiat) led, then Hanriot (Benz), Wagner (Fiat), Hémery (Benz), Wagner again, then into the last lap Nazzaro. He lost two places when a tyre punctured, leaving Wagner to beat Hémery by 56 seconds. This race saw the first appearance of a supercharged GP car, a Chadwick which retired after four laps, and the last for a GP Renault, which retired after six laps.

The Grand Prize was next run in 1910, when it was a straight battle between Fiat and Benz, the brilliant newcomer David Bruce Brown winning for Fiat by a mere two seconds from Hémery's Benz. Bob Burman placed a Marquette Buick third, Ray Harroun a Marmon sixth and last. Bruce Brown won for Fiat again in 1911, from Hearn in a Benz. That was the year the Indianapolis 500 was first run (and won by Harroun in a Marmon), and although the Grand Prize and Vanderbilt Cup races were run until 1916, they were increasingly overshadowed by the track event.

In Europe, an attempt was made to revive grand prix racing in 1911, in a Le Mans event dubbed the Grand Prix des Vieux Tacots ('Old Crocks'), which was contested by 14 cars ranging from a 1906 GP Lorraine-Dietrich to a 1·3 litre T13 Bugatti. Hémery won in a Fiat which was no more than a tuned touring model, while the Bugatti was second, albeit two laps behind in a 12-lap race!

Throughout these lean years of front-line racing, the voiturette class had thrived, especially the Coupe de l'Auto. The early regulations had encouraged outlandish power units, by restricting the bore of engines but not their stroke or capacity. Sizaire-Naudin and Peugeot were the outstanding marques in the first three Coupes, 1906–8, and in 1908 both used single-cylinder 100×250 mm engines which were so high that drivers had to look round the scuttles of their cars rather than over them!

From 1909 sanity increasingly prevailed, and by 1911 a 3 litre capacity limit was the principal restriction. Thus, until the series ended in 1913, the Coupe regulations inspired some classic designs. Marc Birkigt's 2·6 litre Hispano-Suiza, which Paul Zuccarelli drove to win the 1910 event, became the Alfonso XIII. Bablot won for Louis Delage in 1911, and in the 1912 race Sunbeam achieved a 1–2–3 with their side valve cars (the last engines of this type to power the winner of a major road race). Moreover, the Coupe was run concurrently with the Grand Prix, and these three cars of the four-car Sunbeam team were third, fourth and fifth overall–Rigal in the Sunbeam placed third averaged 65·29 mph over the 956 miles, compared with George Boillot's winning speed in a 7·6 litre Peugeot of 68·45 mph.

That Peugeot was the first 'modern' grand prix car, with a fast-revving twin-ohc four-valve engine. Its principal rival was a Fiat on very traditional lines, with a 14·1 litre engine, artillery wheels, and chain final-drive. One car of each team finished the race, Wagner taking second place some 13 minutes behind the Peugeot.

This to all intents and purposes ended the age of monsters in grand prix racing, although three Mercedes redolent of the type were entered by André Pilette in a secondary race for GP cars at Le Mans in 1913, where they were outrun by a pair of 6·2 litre Delages. The Mercedes used four- and six-cylinder versions of the 75/80 aircraft engine, in a development exercise, and

Top: preparations for the 1907 French GP at Dieppe, with a pair of Renaults and a Germain in the foreground—racing numbers in this event gave a clue to the make of the car
Right: tyre changes were the purgatory of early racing. Here Hémery's mechanic struggles with a wheel on their winning Fiat in the 1911 Grand Prix de France at Le Mans

Above: the 1912 GP Peugeot was an advanced car which set new standards, although it did not look strikingly novel, in part because its long-stroke engine and tall overhead camshaft valvegear enforced a high build. Jules Goux drove this car to victory in the GP de France in 1912, and in 1913 won the Indianapolis 500 with a similar car.

Right: Ralph de Palma's 14-litre Fiat, passing the pits during the 1912 French GP at Dieppe, was the last effective car in the line of road-racing giants, with its wooden-spoked wheels, chain final drive, and overall emphasis on brute power

were the last GP cars to have chain drive.

The Peugeot design, by the Swiss Ernest Henry in collaboration with two drivers, Georges Boillot and Paul Zuccarelli, was to have a profound influence on road-going as well as racing cars, which can be traced to 1950, when Henry died forgotten and penniless.

Boillot took the Grand Prix for Peugeot again in 1913, and all France expected him to win in 1914. For the first time the Grand Prix regulations imposed a limit on engine capacity, which has been fundamental to virtually every subsequent successful set of racing rules. This was $4\frac{1}{2}$ litres, and was coupled with a maximum car weight of 1,100 kg (2,425 lb). Whereas only 20 cars started in the 1913 race, 37 ran in 1914, representing France, Germany, Britain, Italy, Belgium and Switzerland. All the engines except the sleeve-valve units in the Swiss Piccard-Pictets had overhead camshafts, and five types had twin-overhead camshafts (the Delage engine even had mechanically-operated valves, which were thus positively operated as they did not rely on springs). The best power units were in the order of 120 bhp, produced at up to 3,000 rpm (although the Vauxhall engine was designed to run at up to 4,000 rpm). Another great advance was in the use of four-wheel brakes, by Delage, Fiat, Peugeot and Piccard-Pictet.

A spectacular and challenging new circuit near Lyon was chosen for the race. Paul Daimler's new Mercedes was a straightforward design, but the cars were painstakingly tested, the team studied the circuit carefully, and their five drivers drove their own cars to it from Stuttgart. In contrast, their principal opponents, the Peugeot and Delage teams, returned from Indianapolis only just before the race, apparently over-confident and with only two short practice periods in which to become familiar with the circuit and cars (these practice sessions were reluctantly permitted by the local authority, at the grisly hour of 3.30 am; crack-of-dawn activity was part of the Edwardian racing scene–the earliest GPs started at 6 am, and the 1913 race was scheduled to start at 5 am!). The new Peugeots were virtually untested– had they been, some faults might have been eliminated. In this respect, perhaps above all, Peugeot missed the talented Paul Zuccarelli, who had been killed while testing in 1913.

The hills around the circuit were crowded with an estimated 300,000 spectators as the cars were started, at intervals as in the past, but for the first time in pairs. To the consternation of the French, the 'unknown' Mercedes driver Max Sailer took the lead, and lap by lap extended it over the 'greatest driver of the day,' Boillot. He fought his ill-handling Peugeot round the cruel circuit, thus compounding his problem of tyre wear.

At the end of six laps Boillot led, and Sailer's Mercedes lay silent by the road. But stolid Christian Lautenschlager was menacingly close in second place, and with two laps to go he moved into the lead. Boillot could not counter-attack, for his brakes and engine were failing. When a valve dropped on the last lap, Boillot stopped. According to legend, he wept as he was helped from his car; according to an ACF official who was on the spot, he hopped out to answer the pressing calls of nature, then went into a nearby café where he discussed the race.

Christian Lautenschlager headed a Mercedes 1–2–3, at 65·66 mph, Goux and Rigal placed their Peugeots a distant fourth and seventh, Resta's Sunbeam was sixth, the other four finishers were outrun.

This race was a climax to a grand prix era in which car design had progressed enormously, from the muscle-bound monsters to cars in which efficiency was a prime consideration. The part played by motor racing in 'improving the breed' has often been questionable, but there is no doubting its value as a forcing ground in the years before the First World War.

Clear pre-race favourite for the 1914 French GP was Georges Boillot, who had won the 1912 and 1913 GPs for Peugeot. The reverse side of his signal board *(left)* reflects this confidence, but in fact the Peugeots were outclassed by the Mercedes. Winner was Christian Lautenschlager *(above)* in a straight-forward but superbly prepared Mercedes

Below: many erstwhile GP cars from Europe were raced in the USA. At Santa Monica early in 1914, J. P. Marquis' 1913 GP Sunbeam rests ignominiously on somebody's fence; a 1908 GP Mercedes thunders past

Cars Fit for Heroes

the post-war boom

'Don't use a motor car for pleasure,' shrieked a huge placard erected in London's Trafalgar Square during the First World War. And with petrol rationed and new car production curtailed (except for military purposes) there was little enough incentive for car owners to go motoring.

But once the war was over the story was quite different. Countless thousands of men whose only pre-war ex-

perience of motoring had been the occasional ride on an open-top bus had been given their first chance at actually driving a motor vehicle in this first petrol war, liked the experience, and decided to have a car of their own as soon as peace came.

So there was a tremendous new market for virtually anything with wheels and an engine, and one initial result was that the cyclecar, which in its nastier manifestations had seemed dead and buried, rose from its shallow grave. Some of the post-war examples were cheaper and arguably even nastier than their predecessors.

There was, for instance, the Gibbons,

built in suburban Essex from, it appears, old tea chests mounted on motorcycle wheels, and powered by a single-cylinder air-cooled engine bolted to the offside, out in the open air. Its contemporary, the Tamplin, was built largely of fibreboard, braced, surprisingly, by a sliding-pillar independent suspension. Power for this cramped machine was provided by a thumping JAP Vee-twin. And while a passenger could sit in a tiny recepticle in tandem with the driver, there was no room for his feet, which had to take their chance amid the whirring drive belts.

Other cyclecars, like the Castle-Three, the TB and the LSD, striving for

For many thousands of First World War soldiers, working in a repair depot like this one was their first chance to handle a motor car. A whole generation of motorists learned to drive on Crossley, Sunbeam and Ford staff vehicles . . .

Right: the year is 1919, the place the Burford Bridge Hotel in Surrey, and Mr and Mrs William Morris are attending the JCC rally in their wooden-bodied Morris Cowley. *Below:* The Earl of Cavan directs the route of a Hertfordshire Hunt point-to-point from his Edwardian Vulcan early in 1920

the respectability of a 'real car,' achieved little more than an aldermanic increase in weight which took them over the 8 cwt taxation limit for three-wheeled vehicles. The extraordinary Ashton-Evans went the other way. A four-wheeler, it had the rear pair set so close together that they counted as one to the taxation authorities.

Cyclecars, however, were just one minor manifestation of the motor boom of the post-Armistice period.

In Europe, the cessation of arms contracts left many firms, especially in the aircraft and engineering fields, high and dry, with factories expanded to meet the demands of war, with stockpiles of raw materials, with large staffs of skilled workmen . . . and no work.

To stay in business they looked around for other products which would utilise these resources profitably; and many of them chose the motor industry as an outlet.

Take the Grahame-White Company, which had large works at the London Aerodrome, Hendon; their post-war activities included the manufacture of cyclecars (including a £75 Buckboard entirely devoid of springing), coachbuilt bodies for Rolls-Royce chassis stripped of the armour plating they had worn in the war and . . . bedroom furniture!

Grandiose production schemes were proposed: the British Motor Manufacturers' Mass Production Syndicate proposed to take over the moribund Whitehead Aircraft Company, capitalise the venture for £5 million to build a 16 hp car to sell for £235, at the rate of 150,000 vehicles a year. Even in those car-hungry days, the scheme was too over-reaching: and it is doubtful whether even one Whitehead-Thanet saw the light of day.

A little more successful was the Angus-Sanderson, built in County Durham. Again, massive production figures were projected, based on the American concept of assembly of bought-in components, but few cars were built during the make's spasmodic existence. Perhaps four survive today.

Incidentally, the marque's handsomely-cast power units were provided by Tylor, who also made lavatory cisterns. . . .

A similar engine was used on some of the cars built by Varley-Woods, a partnership between Ernest Vernon-Varley, former soup-canner, mouth organ manufacturer and government surplus dealer, and John Woods, an East African river trader. When the company failed, Woods returned to Africa. And was killed by a lion. . . .

But perhaps the most ambitious pro-

ject of all was the British Motor Trading Corporation, which was an attempt to link several companies to form a self-sufficient whole, in much the same way that William Crapo Durant had organised General Motors in America.

Most prominent of the group was Bean Cars, which proposed to build 50,000 cars in 1919–20; then there were the Swift, Vulcan and ABC motor companies, plus steel and aluminium suppliers, component makers and radiator makers. The venture was capitalised at £6 million; but sales were

hardly up to expectations—Bean probably sold less than ten per cent of their target—and the companies were soon all going their own separate ways again.

In fact, all the vast post-war expansion plans of the British motor industry were premature; the anticipated boom collapsed almost as soon as it had got under way. Companies lacked the capital to expand, cheap skilled labour was a thing of the past, the cost of raw materials rose rapidly.

So did the prices of new cars, often in horrifying leaps reaching several times pre-war levels and the contrast was all the more noticeable when models which had come through the war substantially unchanged were compared with their 1914 counterparts. The 12 hp Rover is an example: the 1914 five-seater tourer cost £350; the 1919 equivalent was priced at £750, which

despite design improvements was a quite disproportionate increase, especially when the 1919 British-assembled Model T Ford cost just £275. It was hardly surprising that the Ford had 40 per cent of the English market that year.

The successful singlemindedness of the Ford organisation had not gone unnoticed in France where, amid the almost universal burgeoning of the cyclecar industry, the former manager of Mors, André Citroën, announced that his new company would produce just one model, a 10 hp *torpédo*, in great quantity at a remarkably low price.

Unlike some post-war French ventures into mass marketing, such as the abortive ASS (l'automobile pour tous) which was only produced in penny—or centime?—numbers, the new Citroën proved an immediate success. By 1922 100 Citroëns a day were leaving the

company's works on the Quai de Javel, Paris. And the marque's success was consolidated by the introduction, in 1922, of the Type C 5 cv 'Trefle,' built in the former Clément-Bayard factory.

De Dion, already past their prime, were no longer a force to be reckoned with: the *'superiorité formidable'* of the pre-war models had long vanished. Now the company's products, still built to the highest standards, were old-fashioned and its output negligible.

Renault, on the other hand, had expanded from the garden shed where the company had been founded in 1898, to factories covering 87 acres, equipped with steel, brass, aluminium and iron foundries, forges and press shops and an assembly area covering 360,000 square feet. Like Ford, Louis Renault mistrusted financiers, and ploughed profit back into the expansion of his business. However, apart from a new 10 hp four that replaced the old twin-cylinder 'Marne Taxi' chassis, his post-war offerings were just updated versions of the 1914 range, a line-up of such complexity that all-out mass production was impossible. It wasn't until 1923, when the little 8·3 hp model appeared to challenge Citröen's 5 cv 'Cloverleaf' that Renault really moved into the mass market. Renault even upstaged Citröen, the astute publicist who at one stage hired the Eiffel Tower to advertise his cars, by sending an apparently driverless 8·3 hp on a several days' tour of the streets of Paris.

Peugeot, too, faced the post-war boom with a widely diversified range. In 1921, however, they introduced a new model, the Quadrilette, which really went all-out for the economy market. With the smallest four-cylinder engine then produced, a toy-like 667 cc unit, the Quadrilette was a quasi-cyclecar with, at first, tandem seating, based on a cheap pressed-steel punt chassis with a rear track of only 30 inches. Later versions were rather more orthodox in layout, and the little Quad was produced until 1929, and sold through a network of agents that covered all Europe, from London to Petrograd in Bolshevik Russia.

Apart from these huge companies, there were dozens of tiny firms all fighting for a share of the market. So many, in fact, that in 1922 the French Motor Show overspilled the art nouveau portals of the Grand Palais to such an extent that cyclecars were housed in an annexe across the Seine in Les Invalides. The 1920–21 London Motor Shows had been similarly oversubscribed, and had to use the White City as well as Olympia to house the ex-hibitors, a shuttle service of charabancs linking the two sites.

There were 125 French manufacturers at that 1922 Paris Show and 86 British manufacturers at the 1921 London exhibition (plus several foreign makes built specially for the English market); these figures included only those makers rich enough to afford the price of an exhibition stand. . . .

Other European countries offered less opportunity for expansion. Germany, financially crippled by the war, counted herself lucky to have retained any form of motor industry, and, as in so many periods of runaway inflation, there seemed to be more call for the higher-priced vehicles as, presumably, the lower-income groups who would normally have bought economy cars, ran out of money before their richer compatriots. It was not until the mid-1920s that things settled down sufficiently for mass-production to become a viable proposition.

Italy, on the other hand, had always been a poor country, and most of the products of its pre-war motor industry had been limited production quality machines aimed at the rich minority. Despite the rapid expansion of the industry during the war, the old distribution of wealth still remained much the same in the 1920s, and the anticipated mass market was slow to materialise (moreover, during a trade slump in 1921 it was officially dictated that 90 per cent of output should be exported). Italy's biggest maker, Fiat, introduced the country's first mass-produced model, Tipo 501, in 1919; in view of the political situation, and the fact that

Spacious days: the Model T Ford *(top)* filling up at an early petrol pump in Stockholm, Sweden, in the early 1920s has no parking problems, while the AA scout helping the Sunbeam owner in distress is so confident that no traffic will disturb him that he has left his BSA and tools across the road

The Hudson Motor Company of Detroit introduced the Essex as a low-priced range in 1918. This 1919 roadster was typical of their early production, but the 1922 saloon made Essex a best-seller

the car was relatively expensive in its compulsory export markets, sales of 46,000 in the years 1919–26 were quite remarkable.

Across the Atlantic, the end of the war had been greeted with qualified euphoria. The country was rich, manufacturers had expanded their facilities to meet military contracts, home taxation was low and in export markets, even allowing for high rates of import duty – in England the McKenna Duties added $33\frac{1}{3}$ per cent to the price of a complete car – American vehicles could more than hold their own when it came to price and ease of obtaining delivery.

Within five days of the Armistice, production was getting under way

again: soon, announced *Automobile Topics*, all the major companies were 'increasing production as rapidly as possible, and expect more business than they can possibly deliver this year.'

Willys-Overland planned an output of 180,000 cars in 1919; Dodge and Studebaker were forecasting sales of 150,000. Billy Durant committed the companies in his General Motors grouping to an expansion programme costing almost $40 million. Ford, whose Model T had been upgraded to include an electric lighting and starting outfit, was aiming at a daily production of 4,000 cars – over 1·2 million a year, twice as many cars as then existed in the whole of Europe!

Even though an epidemic of strikes slowed down the industry's production, American makers managed to reach a new record output of 1,876,336, with Ford taking 750,000 (40 per cent)

of the total, Dodge, established only in 1914 with the money that Henry Ford had paid to buy out the shares that the Dodge brothers held in his company, reached 124,000, Willys-Overland turned out 94,800, while Studebaker fell badly short of their target, producing only 29,356.

Already there was a backlog of 2,500,000 unfulfilled orders, and an output of 3,450,000 vehicles was forecast for 1920.

In March 1920, the industry produced a record 220,000 cars – roughly equalling the entire car population of Great Britain – and seemed set to go on to even greater achievements.

But the factors that had made the boom possible were all ephemeral: and this was just the high water before the ebb. When the tide of success started to go out, it went with such suddenness that companies all over the world, from the largest to the smallest, were left stranded. Before the end of the year many of the biggest American factories had been forced to suspend production: by the spring of 1921 the motor manufacturers of Europe were also caught up in the slump, probably the worst that the industry has ever experienced.

It would, it seemed, take a miracle to save the situation. . . .

The 1920 Stanley Model 735 steam car looked like a petrol car, but moved with absolute silence. Price tag was $2,600; cruising speed 45 mph

Fiascos and Flivvers

The sudden collapse of the post-war boom hit the American industry hardest.

Henry Ford, who had just gained sole control of his massive company by buying out all the other stockholders for nearly $106 million, had tried to boost flagging sales by cutting prices in September 1920 by as much as $155 on a $550 car, much to the annoyance of

Main Street, USA, in the early 1920s. Cars as far as the eye can see, and virtually every one of them a Model T Ford. Henry Ford had certainly fulfilled his ambition of producing 'The Universal Car'

other mass-producers. For a time it looked as though this drastic move, which entailed selling the cars at a loss and making up the profit on spares, would succeed, but the market collapsed and on Christmas Eve 1920 the huge new Ford plant on the River Rouge shut down 'indefinitely;' for weeks the empty building just echoed to the sound of roller skates as the company's former chief executives, now reduced to the status of watchmen, sped round on their tours of inspection. Others packed spares for shipment, while half a dozen of the most senior, including Henry Ford's son Edsel, laid

concrete in a machine shop–'the million dollar floor' they called it, from the total regular salaries of those concerned. Even the contents of the staff canteen were sold off in an effort to rationalise finances.

Other companies were even harder hit, for Billy Durant's General Motors combine showed signs of collapse, brought on by the depressed market and the cut in Ford prices. Frantically, Durant tried to buy up huge blocks of shares in the company, but he was way out of his financial depth, and a syndicate formed by the DuPont and J. P. Morgan banking interest bailed the

company out. Durant went, replaced by Alfred P. Sloan, who began to lay the foundations of the modern General Motors organisation, and the company emerged from the crisis stronger than before. Less than a month after his expulsion from the group Billy Durant bobbed back into the arena with a new $7 million company, Durant Motors, backed by money subscribed by friends.

Ford was luckier. Although he had to pay off the remainder of a $60 million loan, plus between $18–30 million in taxes–a total of $50 million or more–in April 1921, he saved the day by shipping cars from stock to his dealers for immediate settlement.

The dealers grumbled . . . but paid up. The clouds over the industry were lifting. On January 3, 1921, Packard resumed production, followed by Reo, Studebaker and Willys; by the beginning of February the first 15,000 men were back on the Model T line and by April the company was aiming at an annual production of a million cars.

Henry paid his debts on time with several million dollars in hand.

Across the Atlantic, the sagging market proved a major setback to those companies that were trying to emulate Ford's mass-production philosophy.

Bean, who could produce twenty cars a day, were one of the first to feel the pinch; in October 1920 they claimed that they had reached the 'economical point of manufacture,' and slashed the price of their four-seater model by £105. The effect was minimal.

But in February 1921, William Morris, an ex-cycle agent from Oxford who was attempting to break into the mass market with a car based firmly on American design principles, cut the prices of all his models by up to £100 in an effort to clear his factory of unsold stock . . . and it worked. By 1926 Morris cars were Britain's best-selling range, with 41 per cent of the market, the same figure that Ford had held in 1920 before the crippling horsepower tax imposed in that year lessened the 22 hp Ford's considerable price advantage over the 11·9 hp Morris.

Ford had adopted the moving production line technique in their Manchester factory soon after its introduction in the company's American factory in 1913, but Morris didn't follow this logical step until the 1930s. Until then, chassis were pushed through the factory by hand to the various assembly stages, but even so, Morris managed to produce 54,000 cars in 1925.

One strange side effect of the 1920 slump was that it eventually gave Morris his keenest competitor.

Frank Smith, who ran the Wolverhampton based Clyno Engineering Company, motorcycle manufacturers, planned to go into production after the war with a 10 hp ohv-engined sports car on similar lines to the Bugatti. When the market failed, the project was abandoned and the company liquidated. Re-formed in 1922, it began production of a 10·8 hp side valve model with a Coventry-Climax engine, designed from the start to match the Morris, price for price. Soon 300 cars a week were being produced in a cramped factory in the back streets of Wolverhampton.

In France, André Citroën failed to bring off a proposed $10 million alliance with Ford–'shall be absolutely master of the French market' he telegraphed the unimpressed Henry, who turned him down flat–and decided to compete with the Americans on their home ground. He spent three weeks in the United States in the spring of 1923, and proposed to set up a factory in New York State producing 80,000 cars a year, priced at between $800–$1,250.

'American car manufacturers do not know how to advertise,' bombasted Le Petit Juif, 'When I enter the field, this part of the business will be handled differently.'

It was, however, all talk. Citroën did set up a British assembly plant at Slough during the 1920s, but the American venture remained an idle dream. Perhaps he had recalled the ill-starred attempt by Fiat to set up an American factory at Poughkeepsie in 1910, which like most attempts by European manufacturers to beat the

Rival British popular cars in the 1920s were Morris and Clyno; a bull-nosed Morris-Cowley 'Chummy' is about to be passed by a 'Royal' Clyno

94

Silent film comedians like Laurel and Hardy *(top left)* found the Model T's unique characteristics made it an ideal laughter-making machine; second-hand Ts could be bought for $5 or $10, to be smashed or turned into a tram sandwich, as in this scene from *Hog Wild*. Last of the Ts was built in 1927 *(top right)*; its replacement, the Model A *(above)* had similar styling, but mechanically was 19 years younger

American industry on their home ground, ended in a strategic withdrawal.

To be sure, the American market was vast–over 10 million cars were registered in 1920–but there were sufficient home manufacturers to fight over the two-fifths left after Ford had taken his share to make it virtually impossible for any outsider of any sire to become established.

It was a market, too, in which the car had become far more of an accepted part of everyday life than it had in Europe, and in which serviceability counted for more than detail finish. The popular American car was 'designedly a vehicle with only just those essentials

necessary for the purpose of taking one safely from place to place, everything being carried out with an eye to the saving of money, always provided that each unit will do its work satisfactorily.'

Alongside this philosophy, the Americans introduced that of annual model change, which automatically depressed the market for second-hand cars and promoted the sales of new vehicles. By 1925 there were 20 million vehicles on the roads of the United States: four years later the total was $26\frac{1}{2}$ million, one vehicle for every five Americans.

Even in such a sellers' market, the going was not always easy. Two of the biggest companies, Maxwell and Willys, found themselves in difficulties in the early 1920s and their banks called in the gifted engineer Walter Chrysler to save them. The Willys group was liquidated, John North Willys managed to regain control of the company, but the popularity of his Overland model was on the wane.

The reorganised Maxwell company

proved an excellent basis on which for Chrysler to develop the first truly up-to-date American popular car, aided by a brilliant trio of young engineers, Carl Breer, Fred Zeder and Owen Skelton. The new Chrysler Six, which appeared in 1923, caused a sensation, for its high-compression engine, inspired by the work of Harry Ricardo in England, gave it a genuine 75 mph performance.

Before long the Maxwell name had been dropped. Sales of Chrysler cars reached 43,000 the year after the marque's debut, and by 1928 Chrysler was strong enough to buy the Dodge motor company, a move which placed them firmly third behind General Motors and Ford, who had lost his pre-eminent position when he closed his factories down for six months in 1927 during the traumatic changeover from the Model T, of which between 15 and 16 million had been built world-wide, to the more conventional Model A.

Even so, Henry was confident enough in the future of his company to turn down the astronomical offer of

Chevrolet agents in Montana had to resort to horsepower when snow held up delivery of their new car stock *(top)*. In 1924 Walter Percy Chrysler produced the first car to bear his name, under the auspices of Maxwell-Chalmers. Designed by Skilton, Zeder and Breer, the Chrysler 70 *(centre)* had outstanding performance. First year sales of 43,000 were an industry record. The Buick 50 of 1928 *(above)* had overhead valves, a feature typical of all Buicks from 1903 to date

£200,000,000 made in a bid by New York stockbroker W. Prentiss early in 1927.

Fourth, but fading fast, was Durant Motors, propped up solely by their popular Star range. Then came Hudson, Nash, Packard, Studebaker and Willys-Overland. Behind these came a bewildering host of relatively small manufacturers, for the most part assemblers of proprietary parts.

It all added up to an industry that by the end of the 1920s was building 85 per cent of the world's cars; that exported a tenth of this output as well as operating overseas subsidiaries (GM had bought Vauxhall and Opel in Europe, Ford had assembly plants there), which produced a record 5·3 million cars in 1929, compared with just over 200,000 built in Britain.

Small wonder that by the late 1920s the American car had become a standardised–dull even–part of everyday life.

As recently as 1926 Ned Jordan had introduced the marketing technique of selling the sizzle, not the steak, with his flowery 'somewhere West of Laramie' advertisement, which extolled the virtues of riding into the sunset at the wheel of a Jordan Playboy, 'the cross of the wild and the tame.' In reality, the Playboy was a nondescript assembled model of no especial merit. Its advertising made it memorable.

The typical American car of the late 1920s was a closed sedan, a type which outnumbered open tourers by nine to one, exactly reversing the trend of a

Visionaries of the 1920s: O. D. North and R. Lucas designed this streamlined, unit construction car *(left)* in 1923. It had a rear-mounted five-cylinder radial engine and independent suspension all round. It was inspired by the Rumpler 'Teardrop' of 1921 *(below)*; this had a six-cylinder radial power plant. The Julian *(above)* from Syracuse, New York had a 60 hp aircraft-type radial and a central driving position

decade earlier. It had an internal-combustion engine, for steam and electric propulsion, which had lasted longer in the USA than anywhere else, had become virtually extinct. Now that the Model T was no more, the typical American car had four-wheel brakes, mechanically-operated on cheap models, hydraulic on costlier vehicles.

To emphasise the car's utilitarian role, such 'convenience' features as synchromesh gearboxes, radios, heaters and easy-clean cellulose and chromium plate became increasingly common.

Even though the large engines of American cars designed for a home land where fuel was cheap attracted higher road-tax in Europe, as well as import duties, these vehicles posed a stiff challenge to the home products. In 1930 an eight-cylinder Marmon Roosevelt could be bought in England for £395; a new Hillman, the lowest-priced British-built eight, cost £445....

To emphasise the difference between the British and American markets, the nearest approach to the Model T produced by an English maker was the diminutive Austin Seven introduced in 1922, which attracted much the same sort of affectionate banter as the 'Tin Lizzie', but which had an engine of only 747 cc compared with the T's 2,844 cc power unit—a decided advantage in Britain, where cars were taxed on horsepower after 1920—plus correspondingly smaller overall dimensions.

Like the T, the Austin Seven repre-

sented the triumph of good selling points over inherent design defects, and its life-span was almost as long as that of the Ford, although it underwent more drastic design changes in that period.

Equally, low-priced cars in America tended to look and behave very similarly, while their British counterparts preserved a good deal of individuality.

Indeed, it was still possible for British manufacturers to survive on an annual output of one or two cars built to bespoke order for local customers. G. H. Waite of Leicester made a living in this way for some 30 years with his Clyde cars and motorcycles; another of these independent makes of which no more than a few dozen were made over a long period was the Jewel.

In their way, such tiny manufacturers were possibly more secure than many larger makers who were faced with the virtually impossible situation

of being too small to produce in sufficient numbers to be competitive with such makes as Morris, yet lacking the capital to expand to the necessary degree. As a result, many of the most famous names in the British industry—Bean, Swift, Star, Hampton, Vulcan, HE—vanished in the late 1920s and early 1930s. Even Clyno, whose meteoric rise had eclipsed many older makes, collapsed in 1929, the victim of an overambitious expansion programme, coupled with the ill-advised introduction of the '£100' Century model—'Only fit to carry manure in,' commented one of the design staff.

In Europe, manufacturers tended to follow—at a respectable distance—the American lead. The products of Italy's leading maker, Fiat, became more and more American in appearance as the 1920s progressed, and sales rose by leaps and bounds.

Above: the 856 cc Citroen 5CV—
punningly known as the Citroen pressé
from the characteristic yellow colour of
its three-seater cloverleaf body.
left: under the direction of S. F. Edge,
AC built a range of 1.5-litre fours and
2-litre sixes. The six-cylinder engine,
announced in 1919, had a single
overhead camshaft engine with
sufficient development potential to
remain in production until 1963, by
which time output had risen from
35 bhp to 103 bhp.
Opposite, top: the Lancia Dilambda of
1929 had a 4-litre engine in a massive
chassis with, of course, Lancia's famous
sliding-pillar ifs.
Opposite, below: one of the more
refined assembled cars of the later
1920s was the 1.5-litre Lea-Francis, with
a Meadows power unit

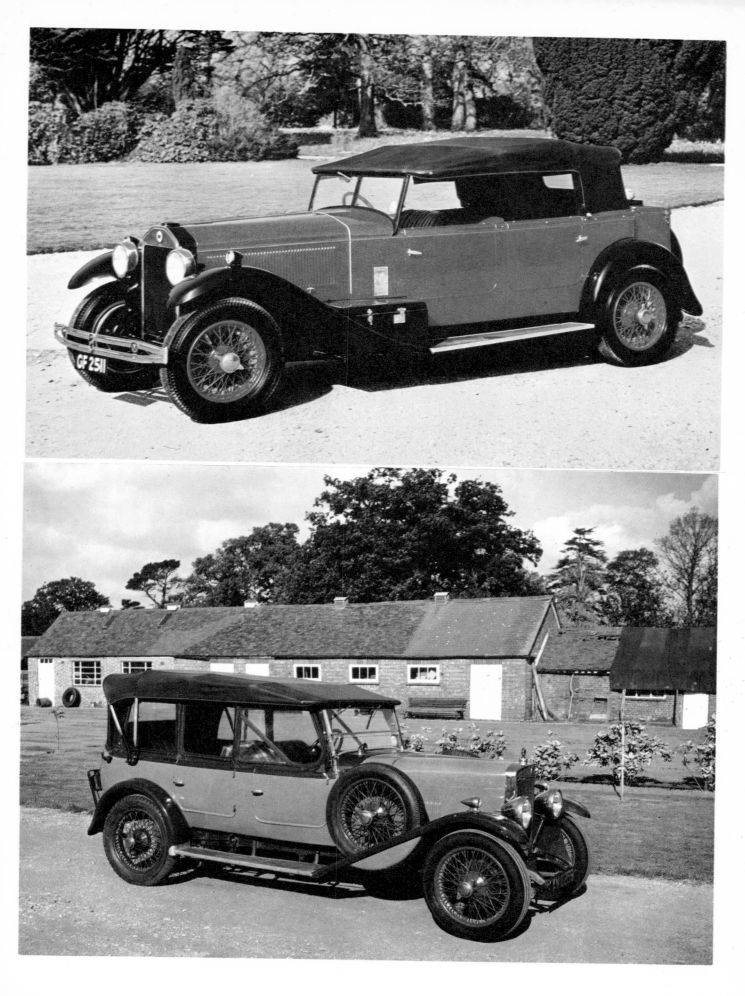

Sir Herbert Austin at the wheel of the prototype Austin Seven, 1922. Initially greeted with derision, the Seven became one of the immortals of motoring history, although its basic design had many endearing shortcomings

American influence was apparent, too, in many of the models produced in post-war Germany, though it was galloping inflation rather than fashion that shaped such crude economy vehicles as the 200 cc three-wheeled Goliath Pioneer of 1926 or the ugly Hanomag Kommisbrot ('Utility Loaf') of the mid-1920s.

The popular Opel Laubfrosch of 1924 was a straight licence-built version of the Citroën 5 cv. Its success made Opel important enough for General Motors to acquire the company in 1928 to gain a Continental foothold comparable to the Ford European assembly plants.

By the end of the 1920s the typical German car was a square-rigged saloon of definitely transatlantic appearance, and by 1929 there were over 500,000 cars on the roads of Germany, though many of the smaller makers had vanished in the preceding years.

The American influence even reached as far as Sweden, where the Volvo, introduced in 1927 by a combine of engineering companies, looked as though it had originated in Detroit rather than downtown Gothenburg.

There was no doubt about it: as more and more people could afford to motor, and as the industry expanded to meet the demand, so motoring was becoming perceptibly duller and the old individualities of makes from different countries were being eradicated.

Except, perhaps, in France, where the Motor Show was 'controlled by designers proud of their craft in which the production expert had relatively little say.' In fact, on display were 'types of chassis which . . . were as wildly unconventional as they were probably unsaleable.' It was an approach which would, paradoxically, ruin André Citroën, yet result in his company becoming stronger than ever and give the lie to the glib generalisation that unconventionality was unsaleable.

As the 1930s opened, in the wake of world economic depression, it was becoming apparent that the motor industry needed more than styling gimmicks—of which there were far too many on the new cars—to ensure its profitable survival.

The Singer Ten of the mid-1920s was a refined version of a basic concept dating back to 1911; this 1926 example *(left)* has the overhead valve engine and unit gearbox introduced in 1923.

Crossley's first ohv car was the 1927 18/50, which was also the company's first six-cylinder model. This early production model is being tested over the Bwlch-y-Groes pass in Wales

The Morris Cowley driving compartment of *circa* 1926 *(top left)* looks spartan, but in fact has better instrumentation—speedometer, clock, ammeter, fuel gauge—than many modern small cars. A sporting light car of the 1920s was the Rhode *(top right)*. Immediately below is its French counterpart, the 10/20 hp Salmson of 1927, here with Weymann fabric saloon bodywork. Anything but sporting was the weird two-stroke Trojan *(centre)*; in 1926 this solid-tyred tourer was driven overland from Singapore by three intrepid Chinese. By the late 1920s small saloons like this 1927 Swift 10 *(right)* were ousting open tourers

Milan Cathedral

The "NOMAD"

Fabric Saloon

BUILT to meet the requirements of those who prefer a closed car for all the year round use, this beautiful Fabric Saloon is the exact counterpart of the "MIGRANT" model, but has a fixed roof. Surprisingly roomy, extremely comfortable, luxuriously equipped and of superior appearance, so different from the mass-produced varieties. Moreover, like all Swifts, the "NOMAD" is a car of remarkable performance, economical to run and to maintain, and one that provides the service of a big car at but a fraction of the running and maintenance costs.

Combinations of choice colourings to suit all tastes are available in a wide range. The price is £260 and Wire Wheels cost only £7 7 0 extra.

Nature improved by art . . . The Lea-Francis 12/40 of 1927 *(top left)* was hardly likely to rocket up a mountain pass in the exhilarating manner suggested, nor would the owner of a Trojan Achilles fabric saloon *(top centre)* be likely to live in an ivy-girt castle! Swift's Nomad *(above)* represented a last-ditch stand by this manufacturer against mass-produced cars from Austin and Morris, but Swift faded away in 1931. The 1925 Bianchi Tipo 20 *(opposite bottom)* was a well-made, if expensive, tourer, while the MG 18/80 *(left)* was aimed at those with more sporting pretensions

103

A Golden Age of Racing

Racing got into its stride hesitantly after the First World War, and in 1919 and again in 1920 only two major events were run, the Targa Florio on the twisting roads of the Madonie circuit in Sicily, and the '500' at the Indianapolis track. These were in almost every respect to opposite ends of the racing spectrum, yet racing was still one sport –Ballot ran one of his Indianapolis cars in the 1920 Targa. The overlap between European road racing and US track racing was to dwindle through the first few years of the 1920s then virtually disappear for a decade. Both principal forms of motor sport were to pass through golden ages to twilight periods during the 1920s.

On the grand prix circuits this was a period of new names, expansion, and

changes. The Automobile Club de France ran their Grand Prix again in 1921, for the last time as an exclusive super-race; later in the same year the Italian Grand Prix was inaugurated; later in the decade came the Belgian, German, British, Spanish and Monaco Grands Prix, and although for a while the French GP remained pre-eminent, it was no longer The Grand Prix.

The 1921 race was run at Le Mans, over a circuit later to become famous as the venue of the 24-hour race. The Grand Prix and Indianapolis regulations, 3 litres or 183 cubic inches, for once coincided, and at the American track the straight-eight engine had been proved. So all but two of the GP starters had eight-cylinder engines. The race was between the Ballots and the American Duesenberg team which was a last-minute entry. The Duesenberg was the first grand prix car to have hydraulic brakes, and although this gave the team an obvious advantage, the ex-

ample was not wholly followed by European constructors for several years (Bugatti and Rolland-Pilain used them on the front wheels of their cars in 1922).

The condition of the circuit was abominable, which made the race as great a physical challenge as any pre-war GPs. In the second half, Jimmy Murphy built up a secure lead in one of the handsome blue and white cars, averaging 78·10 mph over the 321 miles to finish 15 minutes ahead of Ralph de Palma's Ballot; 41 years were to pass before another American won a French GP; the victory for an all-American car remains unique in grand prix history.

The Italians ran their first GP at Brescia later in the year; the very fact that another grand prix was organized hardly pleased the French, and there was the additional aggravation that starting money was paid–hitherto entrants had been expected to pay for the privilege of starting. Only six cars ran in the race on Brescia heath, three Bal-

American surprise. Jimmy Murphy in the 1921 French Grand Prix, on his way to victory in the handsome blue and white Duesenberg. This was the first straight eight car to win a GP

Worthy but lucky winners of the 1922
French GP, Felice Nazzaro and his Fiat
804
Below: French oddities—Foresti's Ballot
leading de Vizcaya's Bugatti in the 1922
GP, the last for Ballot, the first for
Bugatti

lots and three of the twin-ohc straight-eight Fiat 802s, which had not been completed in time for the French race because of industrial troubles (a familiar affliction of Italian teams in more recent years!). Pietro Bordino led the race for Fiat until an oil pipe broke, when Jules Goux led Chassagne in a Ballot 1–2, at 89·44 mph.

In 1922, grand prix racing entered a brilliant four-year phase under a new 2 litre formula, which stimulated technical development to an unusual degree and brought to the fore a new generation of drivers. The first 2-litre grand prix was the French race, which in its ever-nomadic progress around the circuits of France was run near Strasbourg.

It was contested by six teams. From France Ballot entered their last GP with cars basically designed in 1921; Rolland-Pilain entered theoretically advanced cars; Ettore Bugatti entered GP racing with the forerunner of a line of famous eight-cylinder cars, the Type 30. Bugatti had been enjoying considerable success in voiturette racing with the T13 and T22, although as was to become almost usual with Bugattis this success was in part illusory, and was not sustained once Talbot-Darracq and Fiat entered the class.

Britain contributed two teams of cars, both types with four-cylinder engines. The 1·5 litre Aston Martins were outclassed on paper, and in the race; more was expected of the Sunbeams.

From Italy came a team of handsome Fiat 804s, to dominate the event from practice to finish. The Fiat design team, ignored the eight-cylinder trend and produced a six-cylinder unit, which for its first race outing produced 95 bhp at 4,500 rpm.

From the first massed start in grand prix history, the three Fiats ran away from the field. However, there was a weakness in the 804, which showed with tragic consequences in the closing laps. The rear axle casings were faulty, and two failed; Biagio Nazzaro, nephew of the great Felice, was killed as his car crashed, Bordino escaped as his lost a wheel. Felice Nazzaro completed the 498 miles in six and a quarter hours, to

win at 79·33 mph–and then it was found that his rear axle was near to failure. Two other cars, Bugattis, completed the distance, second man de Vizcaya finishing 58 minutes behind Nazzaro!

With the engine of the 804 developed to produce 112 bhp, the Fiat team completely dominated the Italian GP, run at the new Monza autodrome.

Fiat came up with another surprise in 1923, the first supercharged grand prix car. Lee Sherman Chadwick's forced induction essays in 1908 had not been directly followed up, and the supercharger was not proved until the First World War, when it was successfully used on aircraft engines. Mercedes used Roots-type superchargers on four of their six cars in the 1922 Mille Miglia, and on the three which ran in the 1923 Indianapolis 500. A low-pressure blower was used on the Fiat 805 in 1923, on a straight-eight which produced 130 bhp

at 5,500 rpm. This was some 15 bhp more than the Sunbeam engine, which until the Fiats arrived at the Tours circuit for the race was regarded as the most potent contender. Those Sunbeams were the famous 'Fiats in green paint,' for their resemblance to the 804 could hardly be denied.

The Fiats led the race convincingly, until one by one they stopped as their unshielded Wittig superchargers inhaled road grit. Sunbeams took up the running, and H. O. D. Segrave drove his through to the first British victory in a grand prix, followed by team mate Albert Divo.

The only Bugatti to finish was another Type 30 oddity, this time with a wheel-enveloping body–hence its 'tank' nickname–and dubious road-holding habits. A novelty of greater significance was the first V-12 grand prix car, a Delage which was barely

The Bugatti Type 35 is one of racing's all-time classics, beautifully proportioned, appearing almost too dainty for the rough roads of the 1920s, the product of precise craftsmanship rather than advanced technical thinking. Used in the T35 and its derivatives from 1924 until 1931, the rigid chassis and competent suspension made for good road holding, which helped to offset the modest power output of the 2-litre straight eight in its unsupercharged form. A supercharger was introduced in the T39 variant built for the 1926–27 Grand Prix formula, and retained in the 2.3-litre T35B and 2-litre T35C

Right: the Alfa Romeo P2 was the dominant car of the 2-litre Grands Prix in 1924–25. It was a perfectly orthodox car, unlike the Bugatti with chassis and running gear just adequate for the power of its supercharged straight eight. Less tangibly, it came to typify the blood-red Italian racing cars of the period

Top: unorthodoxy from Germany and France. The rear-engined Benz *tropfennwagen* was designed by Edmund Rumpler, and was perhaps too unconventional to be successful without a development programme that was beyond the resources of its builders. Gabriel Voisin's 1923 GP essay was built around many production components; advanced aerodynamics and semi-monocoque construction could not compensate for the handicap of its 75 bhp sleeve-valve engine
Left: start of the 1923 French GP at Tours. Guinness' Sunbeam leads a Rolland-Pilain, a Voisin and a Bugatti, a Fiat and another Sunbeam

completed in time for the race, and retired in the early stages.

The Italian GP saw the debut of an exceptionally unorthodox car, bearing the ancient name Benz. This was a decade ahead of its contemporaries in conception, with an aerodynamically smooth 'tear-drop' body covering a *rear*-mounted twin-ohc engine and gearbox *behind* the cockpit; its suspension was independent all round, by swing axles at the rear, with inboard brakes. It was not a notable success in racing (two of the three cars at Monza placed fourth and fifth), and was not properly developed when Benz amalgamated with Mercedes. But it was prophetic, and in the next decade one of the team drivers at Monza, Walb, became racing director of Auto Union, a team with a race-winning rear-engined car.

Fiat took the first two places in that Italian GP, ahead of Jimmy Murphy's straight-eight Miller, a track car adapted for Monza simply by the addition of front-wheel brakes.

The high noon of the grands prix of the 1920s came at Lyon in 1924. Sunbeam returned to defend their 1923 victory, with supercharged versions of their 1923 cars; Fiat returned with improved versions of their 1923 Italian GP 805s, for what was to be the company's last entry in a major race; Delage were there with improved V-12s; Bugatti was there with half a dozen T35s; there was a privately-owned Miller. There were Alfa Romeos.

Alfa Romeo, to become one of the great marques of grand prix racing, had abandoned their P1 after a fatal test crash in 1923 and followed a well-worn path in enticing a member of the Fiat design staff, Vittorio Jano, to undertake its successor, the P2. Nicola Romeo's emissary to Jano was Enzo Ferrari, who was henceforth to play a central role in Alfa's racing affairs, and almost 30 years later a major part in bringing their grand prix efforts to an end. Jano's P2, which inevitably had strong echoes of recent Fiats, had a Roots-supercharged straight-eight, which initially developed 135 bhp at 5,500 rpm. Antonio Ascari had driven it to a trial victory in a race at Cremona before a team was entered for their first important event, at Lyon.

Segrave led the Grand Prix for Sunbeam, Bordino led it for Fiat, Guinness for Sunbeam, Ascari for Alfa, Campari for Alfa. The Fiats all retired, the Sunbeams slowed with magneto trouble, Ascari's engine failed. Burly Giuseppe Campari won the 503 mile race at 70·97 mph, finishing just over a minute ahead of Divo's Delage. Another Delage was third, Wagner's Alfa fourth, Segrave's Sunbeam fifth.

The last runners were Bugattis, hopelessly outclassed. Yet of all the cars at Lyon in 1924, the Type 35 is most often recalled and has probably been the subject of more adulation than any other grand prix car. It was certainly a most attractive little machine, with a well-proportioned body tapering back from the horseshoe radiator which virtually became a Molsheim trade mark, and unique broad-spoked light alloy wheels. But at Lyon it was underpowered with an unsupercharged straight-eight producing only 105 bhp. Somehow, the impression is established in motor racing lore that the T35 was an immediate race-winner—Bugatti addicts have done a job of which any latter-day motor industry press propagandist would be proud—but in fact whenever other top-line teams were in a race, the original T35 was not a competitive car. . . .

The 1924 French Grand Prix was perhaps the greatest race of the decade, with a superb entry. Among those present were Zborowski's Miller and Segrave's Sunbeam *(above)* and the brand-new V-12 Delage (driven by Thomas and Benoist, *above right).* Before the race, Ettore Bugatti proudly unveiled his new T35 *(right)*

The superiority of the Alfa Romeo P2 was summed up at the start of the 1925 Belgian GP *(below)* when two of the P2s were leaving the field behind within a few metres of the start

Apart from one isolated effort in 1927, and through their recent support of Ferrari, Fiat severed their long link with grand prix racing, one reason being Agnelli's understandable displeasure at seeing designer after designer lured away to produce Fiat-inspired cars to beat Fiats! Coincidentally, Mercedes fleetingly returned to the grand prix scene, with a 160 bhp straight-eight designed by Porsche, which gained a reputation for accidents resulting from dubious road-holding, rather than for race successes.

In the second major race of the year, the Italian GP, the Alfa Romeo team scored a 1–2–3–4, headed by Ascari at 98·76 mph, to round off a triumphant debut year for the *quadrifoglio* (the four-leafed clover device worn by all Alfa team cars).

This was also the last grand prix where riding mechanics were required by international regulations, although for a few years cars were to remain outwardly two-seaters. The lot of the riding mechanic had been a hard one since the dawn of racing, but their job had become increasingly redundant as machines became more sophisticated and races were confined within short-lap circuits. Two-man crews were to be seen in some sports car events for many years, but a largely unsung breed of heroes disappeared from the grands prix. . . .

In its last year, the 2-litre formula

faded away. The only threat to the Alfa P2s came from the Delage V-12s, now supercharged to produce 190 bhp. The Alfa team won the first Belgian GP on the classic Spa circuit very much as they pleased, in a very leisurely fashion. The French GP moved to its first artificial venue, the Montlhéry road cum track autodrome, where Antonio Ascari was fatally injured when he crashed, whereupon the Alfas were withdrawn, and Delages finished first and second ahead of a Sunbeam. The Italian GP saw P2s finish 1–2–4.

The increasing speeds of cars worried motor sport's governing body, which consequently reduced the engine capacity limit to $1\frac{1}{2}$ litres for 1926–27, a size previously considered appropriate for voiturettes. Spasmodically through racing history attempts to cut speeds by this obvious regulation have been shown to be misguided. Had Fiat seriously campaigned their 806 in 1927 it would almost certainly have been proved fallacious once again. This remarkable car had a Roots-supercharged, twin crankshafts (geared together), three ohc V-12 which produced 175 bhp at its one race appearance, 185 bhp at 8,500 rpm in bench tests, thus easily matching the power of the Alfa P2 engine. However, the 806 ran only in the secondary Milan GP, winning easily; the Fiat management reaffirmed their 'no racing' policy, and the 806 was never seen again.

So the $1\frac{1}{2}$ litre standard was set by Albert Lory's straight-eight Delage—a superb engine in a mediocre chassis. The power unit had four valves per cylinder, twin-overhead camshafts, twin Roots-type superchargers, and a crankshaft which ran in ten roller bearings (the use of over 60 roller or ball bearings was a feature of the engine). It was designed

Top: the V-12 Delage in its 1925 form, driven by Wagner in the French GP at the new Montlhéry autodrome
Left: last Fiat GP car was the remarkable 806, which was raced only once, to win the minor Milan GP at Monza. Pietro Bordino waits in the car on the grid, the old maestro Felice Nazarro beams approvingly beside the cockpit
Right: a Bentley looming over a delicate Bugatti in a modern race for historic cars at Oulton Park—a pairing not wholly ludicrous, for sports and racing cars ran together in many events in the late 1920s, and Etancelin drove a Bugatti to narrowly beat Birkin's $4\frac{1}{2}$ litre 'Blower' Bentley in the 1930 French GP

Left: in the Grands Prix of 1927, the 1½ litre supercharged Delage was unbeatable; in the French GP, Robert Benoist headed a team 1–2–3

Below: Grand Prix racing at Brooklands in 1927, on a contrived 'road' circuit. Divo, third in another Delage 1–2–3, negotiating a sandbank chicane. This was the last race for the Delage works team

to rev to 9,000 rpm–a remarkable speed for its time. Unhappily, similar attention was not given to the chassis, and the car had one extraordinary fault–the exhaust overheated cockpit and driver beyond endurance. For 1927 the exhaust was placed on the left, as far as possible from the driver. In that season the engine gave 170 bhp; in voiturette racing in the mid-1930s 195 bhp was to be extracted from it.

Bugatti at last took to the supercharger, in the straight-eight T39, a derivative of the T35. And at last he gained grand prix victories. The once-mighty French race was a farce, at the featureless Miramas track, where three Bugattis were the only starters. Veteran Jules Goux won, second man Costantini was lapped 15 times! For the European Grand Prix, at San Sebastian in Spain that year, the Bugattis had opposition, the then self-defeating Delages, one of which was nevertheless second between two Bugattis.

In 1926 the RAC ran their first Grand Prix, on a circuit contrived with sand banks at Brooklands–'while cars will naturally race at their highest speeds on the open sections of the Track, the "road" portion with its narrow turns and gradient will provide a real test' the programme patiently explained to a British public unaccustomed to road racing. The regulations rose above mere jargon, for example in preferring 'replenishment stations' to pits. . . . In the race, the Delage drivers, two to a car, persevered and took turns to cool their feet, to be rewarded with first and third places, Sénéchal and Wagner winning at 71·61 mph.

Delage retired for the winter, and the only challenge to Bugatti in the Italian GP came from the first cars of a new

The Monaco Grand Prix, most glamorous of all motor races, was first run in 1929. That first race was won by expatriate Englishman William Grover—'Williams'—in a Bugatti T35B *(right)* at 49.83 mph. Part of the reason the race was so firmly established in that depressing period is obvious in this shot of a quartet of Bugattis in the 1930 race *(above)*

marque, the Maserati Type 26, derived from Alfieri Maserati's Diatto design. Both Maseratis retired in the race.

Delage won every major race in 1927, when Bugatti even withdrew his French GP entries rather than risk almost certain loss of face. In that event, the last active driver who raced in the first Grand Prix, Louis Wagner, raced for the last time. He drove a Talbot, and this was also the last appearance of a works STD car. In the Italian Grand Prix, OM ran a team in a GP for the only time, and were rewarded with second place, behind a Delage and ahead

of an Indianapolis Cooper Special Miller.

The last race of the 1·5 litre formula was run at Brooklands, where two drivers whose careers spanned 50 years of GP racing might have met. Three Fiats were entered (they did not appear, of course) and their nominated drivers included Comm. Felice Nazzaro; the nominated driver of the third Bugatti was one M. Giron (the programme should have read Chiron). Nazzaro had raced in the 1906 GP, Chiron raced a GP car in 1956. . . .

Delage scored a 1–2–3 (Chiron was

fourth), the last effective formula of the 1920s ran out, and the British GP disappeared from the sporting calendar for more than 20 years.

In the rest of the 1920s few races were run to the promulgated formulae, most were *formule libre* or sports car events. Only Bugatti ran works cars, spasmodically at that, and the field was left to independent drivers and *equipes*. Their cars included the left-overs of the mid-1920s, Alfas, Delages, Talbots, and some new machines, produced by Bugatti, above all, and the Maserati brothers. Bugatti, as has often been pointed out,

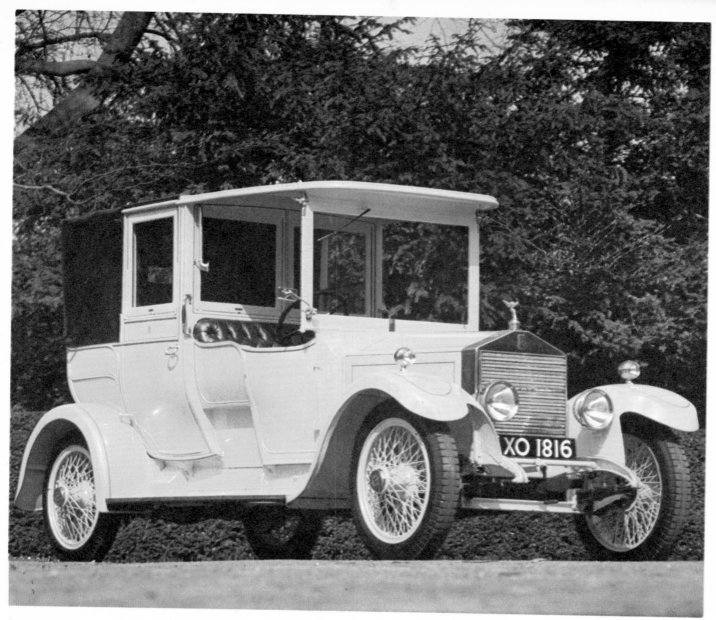

Opposite, top: this elegant Rolls-Royce Phantom I sedanca dates from 1912, and is still in regular use during the summer months

Opposite, below: the 1930 Rolls-Royce Phantom II Continental had elegant closed sporting coachwork, and a top speed of 90 mph. This car was originally owned by Sir Henry Royce, and is reputedly the only Rolls-Royce prototype ever to fall into private ownership. *Above:* when Lord Lonsdale traded in his Edwardian Fiat for a new Rolls-Royce 20 in the mid-1920s, he had the upright coachwork of the old car transferred to the new chassis, to produce this curiously archaic vehicle

built racing cars for sale—and that was his really great contribution to racing, through its leanest years. The cars changed little, this in itself helping to preserve continuity, if not Bugatti's chances of success when racing started to pick up again.

The 1926–27 catalogue of Ettore Bugatti Automobiles of Clapham makes fascinating reading in the 1970s, not least in that it quoted RAC horse-power figures. Top of the range was the 17·8 hp (!) 2 litre Grand Prix Type 35—listed at £1,100. A supercharged 11·9 hp (!) 1½ litre Type 37 Grand Prix Model could be obtained for £550, complete with grease gun and toolkit....

The period was marred by tragedy, and brightened by one outstanding innovation. An accident in the 1928 European GP at Monza was the first to involve grand prix spectators; 22 died

when Talbot driver Emilio Materassi crashed into the crowd. In 1929 the first 'round the houses' race was run at Monaco, a happy conception by Lionel Noghès and Louis Chiron to run a race entirely within the confining and built-up boundaries of the Principality. The first race was entirely successful, with a field of 16 cars which was outstanding at the depressed end of the 1920s. Expatriate English driver Williams won in a T35B Bugatti at 49·83 mph, from Bouriano in another Bugatti and Rudolf Caracciola in a 7·1 litre SSK Mercedes, a cumbersome machine for the sinuous circuit—yet Caracciola led the race at half-distance!

From that point, racing in Monaco flourished. The same could not be said of the grands prix generally for another year or two, although in fact the worst days had passed.

High Noon on the Tracks

Track racing appeared to have a promising future in Europe in the 1920s, as new autodromes were built and Brooklands seemed to flourish. It very positively did have a future in the USA, where apart from odd incidental road events, it was the only form of racing to be practised. The European tracks in fact produced little–if anything–of real significance; American racing inspired some outstanding machines.

Brooklands was re-opened in 1920, and it did flourish so long as it was the only racing venue on the British main-

Below: this bump in the Brooklands banking was a favourite spot for photographs of cars with wheels clear of the track. This particular jump ended in tragedy, as a few yards further on Clive Dunfee crashed, and was killed
Bottom: an extraordinary assortment of cars setting out on an MCC high-speed trial

Top left: Gwenda Stewart's Derby Miller in 1931; she was most successful with it at Montlhéry, but did set a ladies' record of the Surrey track at 139.95 mph. *Top right:* George Eyston's MG during the 1934 British Empire Trophy. *Above left:* the single-seater Bentley on the rough banking, wearing the obligatory Brooklands silencer. *Above right:* Harvey's fwd Alvis came to grief in the 1926 200 Miles' Race

land—a rather negative virtue! Its limitations, however, were all too apparent, and in the mid-1920s the first attempts to simulate road racing conditions were made, with sandbank corners. In 1930 the 'Mountain Circuit' was devised, and in 1937 the Campbell Circuit; this was a Good Try, but by that time there were honest mainland circuits in use (at the Crystal Palace and Donington Park). By 1939 Brooklands had outlived its usefulness, and during the Second World War was so cut about as to be unusable for racing, even if much of it had not been occupied by an aircraft factory; arguably, it was as well that it lived on only in nostalgic reminiscence, for its continued existence could well have distracted effort from the new boom in mainstream road racing.

Many of the Brooklands programmes were made up of very short races,

and handicaps were popular as a means of matching ill-assorted cars—a cynic might suggest that historic car racing was invented at Brooklands long before it actually was (in 1930). The Motor Course inspired numerous curious specials, of which the best-known to the general public were Count Louis Zborowski's Chitty-Chitty-Bang-Bangs (I-III, the first of which had a 27-litre Maybach aero engine); it was never important enough to give rise to a pure racing strain, as did Indianapolis.

Efforts were made to run races of real status, for example the JCC 200-mile races of the 1920s, the Essex MC six-hour events, the 1926–27 Grands Prix, and the Double-Twelve. 'It was the success of the classic race in France . . . that made many patriotic Englishmen regret the total absence of anything approaching the race in their own land.' Objections from local residents were as much the bane of Brooklands as of some latter-day British circuits, so this attempt to emulate the Le Mans 24-hour Race had to be run in two distinct daylight parts ('All motorists know that a lightly-tuned sports engine is not always the most amenable piece of mechanism first thing in the morning. The start should, therefore, be most

intriguing and should not be missed' urged the programme). That 1929 Double-Twelve was won by Ramponi in an Alfa Romeo at 76 mph; it was run twice more, then discarded in favour of a simpler 1,000 mile event, which was run only once (and won by two girls, Elsie Wisdom and Joan Richmond, in a Riley Nine at 84.41 mph).

The Outer Circuit record stood to John Cobb in the Napier-Railton at 143.44 mph when the Track closed in 1939.

A banked track built at Sitges in Spain in 1922 was soon abandoned (somebody miscalculated, and the bankings were absurdly steep), and a 2.8 mile high speed track was opened at Monza to complement the new road circuit in the royal park near Milan; this was little used, and was demolished in 1939. The most promising of all European tracks seemed to be at Montlhéry in France.

This Paris Autodrome was built in 1924, incorporating a 1.58 mile banked track which could be linked to road circuits. Like Brooklands, it was used for many record attempts as well as races, and unlike Brooklands it continued in use after the Second World War. The French GP was run at Montlhéry in 1925, 1931 and from 1933 until 1937.

The home of track racing since the First World War has been America, with the international interest inevitably focussed on the International Sweepstakes, run at Indianapolis every Memorial Day–the 500. With the last of the Elgin series in 1920, road racing virtually died until 1933 when the first of what were to be spasmodic revivals (until the late 1940s) took place, for stock-based specials. These ARCA events, together with Daytona races on a beach cum road circuit, were the distant forerunners of NASCAR stock car racing. But the emphasis between the wars was almost totally on the ovals.

The board tracks did not last long, most being closed by the mid-1920s, but there were uncounted dirt ovals, banked and unbanked, throughout the country. These were the base of the racing pyramid; at the top was Indianapolis (although some folk-legend drivers did not even aspire to the 500, but were content to make a living on the dirt tracks). On the fast tracks–the boards and the Brickyard–sophisticated racing cars such as the Duesenbergs and Millers dominated; through the 1920s the predominant cars on the dirt, were the Fronty Fords. Chevrolet's Frontenac company built 'proper' racing cars, and did a very substantial business in ohv conversions of Ford engines–in

the mid-1920s, the eight-valve Frontenac version produced 65 bhp, the twin-ohc 16-valve version some 80 bhp. Some Fronty-Fords even ran in the 500, Corum placing one fifth in 1923 (Alfred Moss, father of Stirling, took 16th place with one in 1924).

The first race of any consequence to be run anywhere after the 1918 Armistice was the 1919 500, where some notable new machinery appeared–the Packard V-12, and the Duesenberg and Ballot straight-eights. The former led the race in its early stages, but otherwise made little impression (although it is said to have sparked Enzo Ferrari's obsession with the V-12 format); the 'eights' were the first successful racing engines in this format, and both designs in part, derived from Bugatti's wartime aero engines. The single-ohc Duesenberg unit produced 92 bhp, and was installed in a handsome body; the twin-ohc 140 bhp Ballot engine was in a square-cut car, reminiscent of pre-war Peugeots–hardly surprising, as the designer of those cars, Ernest Henry, had been commissioned to start work on them on Christmas Eve, 1918. There would be nothing remarkable in a 101 days drawing board to track car nowadays, but in 1919 this was an astonishing achievement.

The fact that 1914 Peugeots took first and third places in the race, bracketing a 1915 Stutz, detracts little

from the story–the significant thing is that the 'eight' arrived as a strong force in racing.

The 3 litre (183 cubic inch) races in the following three years were won by a Frontenac four, a Frontenac eight, and a Miller-engined Duesenberg. Then came the 2 litre (122 cubic inch) and 1½ litre years, and the rivalry between Duesenberg and Miller.

Perhaps the single most significant car was the Duesenberg which Corum and Boyer drove to victory in 1924, for its straight-eight had a centrifugal supercharger. As BRM were to demonstrate a quarter of a century later, this type of forced induction restricts the effective rev range within narrow limits, which is acceptable on an oval track, but imposes a great handicap on a road circuit where many gear changes are required through varying corners. 'The 1924 Indianapolis 500 mile race will stand out as a high point in American racing history' commented Motor Age; it does, but it was also the point at which track and road racing really went their separate ways.

Duesenbergs won in 1925 and 1927. Thereafter, Harry Miller's exquisite V-8s powered the winning cars, year after year, even through Speedway owner Eddie Rickenbacker's ill-considered formulae intended to attract major manufacturers. Like other essays on these lines through racing history,

Opposite: two outstanding Indianapolis cars. *Top:* one of Harry Miller's classic 91 cubic inch cars, this one the rarer front-wheel drive type. The 1.5-litre twin-ohc straight eight was centrifugally supercharged, initially producing 154 bhp at 7,000 rpm; later examples gave more than 280 bhp. In fwd or 'conventional' form these Millers won a vast number of track events
Right: the Maserati 8CTF was designed as a Grand Prix car, but achieved fame when Wilbur Shaw drove this 'Boyle Special' to victory in the '500' in 1939 and 1940. Its 3-litre twin-ohc straight eight had two Roots-type superchargers, and produced 355 bhp at 6,500 rpm

Left: efforts to establish road circuits at Brooklands were only partly successful. These two cars in the 1938 JCC International Trophy–Bira's blue 2.9-litre Maserati passing an MG–are on the Campbell Circuit. The colour stripes on the tails of cars indicated which of three 'handicap channels' drivers had to take at the Fork (these were artificial bends intended to 'equalize' lap speeds of cars in different classes)

they failed. But Ford (Edsel) was at-tracted to the Speedway, by a package offered by entrepreneur Preston Tucker, and Ford (corporately) couldn't completely duck out of the commitment. On paper, the idea of Harry Miller-designed cars powered by basically stock Ford V-8s was promis-ing. The cars looked good, but were unconventional front-wheel drive machines, were built in a hurry, and were hardly tested before the tedious business of qualifying start-ed. Four made the start, all retired. Ford (Henry) saw to it that his company had no more to do with racing (thirty years later it was, how-ever, to be heavily involved with the winning car, once again produced by the leading designer of the day, around a basically stock Ford V-8). The 1935 chassis kept re-appearing in assorted guises for many years, with Offen-hauser, Novi and even Mercury engines (the latter being Andy Grana-telli's Grancor Special, with which he began his long love-hate relationship

Left: first lap of the 1919 '500', with Thomas' Ballot on the inside, Wilcox' winning Peugeot in the centre

Below: the field moving off at the start of the 25th '500', in 1937. Riding mechanics in the cars appear completely anachronistic, a decade after they were last seen in GP cars

with the Indianapolis Speedway).

The 1937 race was won by Wilbur Shaw in a Gilmore Special, which was very special in that it introduced the Offenhauser engine to the winner's circle. This four-cylinder engine is the most remarkable in track-racing history. Based on a marine unit designed by Miller back in 1926, it was still pushing cars into the winner's circle in the 1970s, far removed from the original in some respects, but still basically the same strong, beefy lump of metal.

Wilbur Shaw drove the next novel Indy winner, too, in 1939. This was the first European car to win the race since 1919, a Maserati 8CTF. He drove it to win again in 1940, and was leading in it when he crashed in 1941. Surprisingly, its straight-eight did not start another Indianapolis dynasty (where a cardinal rule so often is 'what's right, copy'), although its lines did spark off an improvement in the overall appearance of track cars.

As major racing had restarted at Indianapolis after one world war, so the story wound up there, as another European conflict became world-wide. . . .

Above: the Gulf-Millers were advanced cars which ran at Indianapolis 1938–41, but never finished the race. The 3-litre six-cylinder engine was rear-mounted and drove through all four wheels.
Left: there was no questioning the quality of the 2-litre Duesenbergs, however. Peter de Paolo (in cockpit) and Norman Batten drove this one to win the '500' at over 100 mph, in 1925

Sporting becomes Sports

The sports really came into being as such after the First World War, and during the 1920s sports car racing blossomed with the inauguration of such classic events as the Le Mans 24-hour Race and the Mille Miglia. A post-war European priority was to produce cars of any sort for an eager market, but alongside the high-performance cars carried over from 1914 at the 1919 London Motor Show there were a few new sporting cars.

Probably the most frequently-recalled sports cars of the 1920s are the Bentleys, and the most notable new marque to exhibit at Olympia was therefore Bentley, although the company showed only a chassis and an incomplete engine. This was the first 3 litre (incidentally, a novel form of capacity nomenclature in Britain in those days), intended as a fast touring car. It had a 2,996 cc four-cylinder 16-valve ohc engine, mounted in a conventional chassis, with brakes to the rear wheels only. It did not actually become available until 1921, when the never more than modest Bently production got under way (the company's annual production exceeded 400 cars only in occasional years). Variants followed, and by 1924, Bentleys were well and truly established in racing, with a first Le Mans victory to the credit of a 3 litre.

This image was hardly to the advantage of the six-cylinder 6½ litre model introduced in 1926, for this car was aimed at the limousine market, and did not come into its own until the

W. O. Bentley's substantial cars are regarded with a reverence which attaches to few other marques. This stems in large part from the almost legendary great green cars at Le Mans, 'the Bentley boys', and the sheer solidness of the machines.
Above: the first 'main-line' appearance for a Bentley team was in the Isle of Man in 1922, when three 3-litre cars were run in the TT, placing 2-4-6. Obviously, it was felt that only the driver merited protection from road debris thrown up by the front wheels.
Above right: the 6.6-litre Speed Six which Barnato and Birkin drove to win the 1929 Le Mans 24-hour Race.
Right: last Le Mans victory for Bentley came in 1930. Kidstone takes the winning Speed Six, which he shared with Barnato, past the flag. The Clement-Watney sister car which placed second follows; the 1.5-litre Bugatti on the left was driven by Mmes Siko and Mareuse

Sporting contrasts. The Amilcar GCSS Surbaisse *(left)* was a pretty little machine, and much more—in terms of performance it was one of the outstanding small sports cars of the vintage decade.
Top: near the end of a famous Vauxhall sporting line, a 1925 30/98. The General Motors take-over was imminent, and coupled with the rather dated basic conception of the car this damned it. Later models of sporting appearance were in fact very mundane machines. *Above:* there was nothing mundane about this mighty Mercedes, the SSK, which had a 250 bhp supercharged engine and speed of over 120 mph

Speed Six sports version appeared in 1928. By then the $4\frac{1}{2}$, to all intents and purposes an enlarged 3 litre to answer the challenge from Sunbeam and other rivals, was established. The $4\frac{1}{2}$ and the Speed Six achieved magnificent competition records–which offset the abysmal showing of the supercharged $4\frac{1}{2}$, the 'Blower Bentley', produced in small numbers at the behest of Sir Henry Birkin and contrarily the Bentley which most caught the public imagination.

A few heavily-bodied saloons apart, Bentleys are nowadays recalled as one of the archetypical sports cars of the 1920s, yet as late as 1928 Bentley Motors felt it necessary to introduce their $4\frac{1}{2}$ catalogue: '. . . the Company wishes it to be understood that the car is definitely in the class generally designated as "sports" models. . . .' The $4\frac{1}{2}$ was 'offered to those discriminating motorists to whom the joy of motoring lies in fascinating acceleration and high speed.' Which still holds good as a sports car definition–if 'above-average handling' could be added . . .

Bentley's principal British equivalents in the 'heavy-metal' class were Vauxhall and Sunbeam. The Luton company reintroduced the 30/98 after the war as the E type, and in 1922 endowed it with the ohv OE, which lasted until after the General Motors takeover. Vauxhall's twin-ohc engine was not used in production cars, but Sunbeam did build a few 3 litre Super Sports with race-inspired power units on these lines. They were reluctant to retain their tune, and were mounted in inadequate chassis.

The other really outstanding large sports cars of the period came from Germany, from Mercedes (later Mercedes-Benz). Mercedes won the 1921 Coppa Florio with a supercharged 28/95, and by 1925 were producing supercharged sports cars for sale. These six-cylinder cars were designed by Porsche, and were the forerunners of the famous SS models, the SS, SSK (short chassis) and SSKL (lightened short chassis). In normal form the 7 litre engine produced 170 bhp, rising through 225 bhp with a 'normal' supercharger, to a claimed 300 bhp with the large supercharger fitted to some SSKL models, which made these not insubstantial cars formidable performers. Rudolf Caracciola scored many race victories in big white Mercedes, above all perhaps in a brilliant drive in the 1931 Mille Miglia.

The Bentleys and Mercedes had their near-equivalents in Europe throughout the inter-war years, large cars which fell somewhere between sporting touring and sports cars. Among French manufacturers, Ariès, Bignan, Chenard-Walcker, Lorraine-Dietrich, Hotchkiss and Peugeot all built large tourers with strong sports characteristics–a 3 litre Chenard-Walcker won the first Le Mans 24-hour Race, $3\frac{1}{2}$ litre la Lorraines won it in 1925 and 1926, and took the Spa 24 hours, a Bignan won the first Spa 24 hours in 1924, a Peugeot the 1926 race, a 3-litre Ariès led the 1927 Le Mans race until the 22nd hour.

Belgium produced the 5.3 litre Excelsior, heavy but with the stamina to win duration events. An often overlooked car, the Austro-Daimler ADM 11, was a formidable sports car in the later 1920s, especially in the hands of that master of hill climbing, Hans Stuck

(its successor in 1931, the ADR6, was named the Bergmeister). Even Spain produced large cars with sporting pretensions, such as the 3 litre Elizalde Type 20. In the first post-war Alfa Romeos, 4 and $4\frac{1}{2}$ litre cars, there was no hint of the great cars that were to come; these were on a par with European contemporaries, and certainly much better machines than the flashy but ineffectual Nazzaros which on paper were their Italian equivalents.

American interest in sporting cars dwindled between the wars, and almost totally vanished by the late 1930s. Mercer continued into the 1920s, the Raceabout becoming more staid, and less distinguished sporting models were marketed by Dupont, Essex, Kissel, Jordan and other companies, but in many cases speedster appearance outweighed performance potential.

During the second half of the decade, F. E. Moscovics revived the Stutz company and introduced some excellent sporting models with single-ohc straight-eight engines. The 4.9 litre Black Hawk was proved capable of holding its own with similar European cars when Bloch and Brisson placed one second to a Bentley at Le Mans in 1928. In 1932 the twin-ohc DV32 was introduced, and the name Bearcat revived; the Super Bearcat had a guaranteed 100 mph capability. Hard economics were against this type of car, however, and the Stutz company faded away.

Meanwhile, E. L. Cord had been behind several cars of real potential; notably in the late 1920s the Auburns which rivalled Stutz as Mercer once had, and the Duesenberg Model J. The Auburn-Duesenberg-Cord consortium built some fine cars in the 1930s. A V-12 Auburn was introduced in 1931, and the 851 and 852 speedsters later in the decade, while a handful of the superb Duesenberg SJs were built. Sporting if not sports, the Cord 810 and 812 came in the middle of the decade, and have as firm a place in the novels of the period (and later) as in automotive history. These were outwardly distinctive front-wheel drive cars, with 4.7 litre V-8 engines–the largest power units to drive private

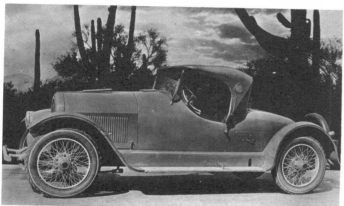

cars through their front wheels until the Oldsmobile Toronado came along late in the 1960s.

America in the 1930s was stony ground for purveyors of fine cars, and the quality of the Auburns, Duesenbergs and Cords was not appreciated until years after the firm had collapsed, in 1937. . . .

At the other end of the scale from Bentleys and Mercedes, small sports cars proliferated in Europe, although in many cases rakish bodies were coupled with pedestrian performance. In this class, the French excelled, with cars such as the BNC, EHP, SARA, front-wheel drive Tractas and others,

but above all with the twin-ohc Salmsons, the supercharged 1,100 cc San Sebastian at the top of the range, and the twin-ohc straight-six 1,100 cc Amilcars which became dominant in their class.

Out of Herbert Austin's humble little 1922 Seven on the other side of the Channel ultimately came the blown Ulster, while out of Morris Garages and Cecil Kimber came MG. The 847 cc ohc M-type Midget which appeared in 1930 essentialised the small English sports car; its performance in standard production form may not have been startling, but the Midgets and larger six-cylinder derivatives were rapidly

Sporting Americana. *Top left:* the 4.1-litre Chrysler roadster which Stoffel and Benoist drove into sixth place at Le Mans in 1929. *Top right:* Brisson's 4.9-litre Stutz trailing the Clement/Benjafield 4.4-litre Bentley at Le Mans in 1928; the Stutz finished second, highest placing for a US car until a Ford Mk 2 won in 1966.
Above left: the Kissel Speedster was a two-seater wholly in the tradition of pre-war roadsters.
Above right: completely out of the ordinary—the 400 bhp V-16 four-wheel drive Chancellor-Miller, which came at the end of the roadster era

Very British. W. Cooper with his Morris Sports, a Cowley chassis with an aluminium body *(left)*, and a decade later Norman Black on his way to victory in the TT with a supercharged MG C-type Midget *(right)*

developed under the stimulus of racing. In 1936 the ohc engine gave way to a pushrod ohv unit in the TA, first of the classic T series.

The 'in-between' capacity class was perhaps the most interesting of all. In England, AC produced Anzani-engined 1½ litre fours until 1925, then introduced an advanced light-alloy ohc six (Bruce and Brunell won the 1926 Monte Carlo Rally with one of these). Alvis introduced their familiar 12/50 in 1924, essayed front-wheel drive cars from 1925 and put one into production in 1928, before partly turning their back on their splendid sporting record, with more mundane cars in the 1930s.

The singular—some might have the temerity to say idiosyncratic—chain-drive Frazer-Nash grew out of the GN (one of the best of a dubious bunch of early-1920s cyclecars), and the line culminated in the TT Replica before the company turned to importing the significant BMW 328 in the later 1930s.

Bugatti offered sports derivatives of the T35 range, T35A, T37 and T37A (indeed, in that happy age the addition of wings, lights and a spare wheel was sufficient to transform many racing cars—even the Alfa P2s were so equipped for their last races). From the T37 came the T40, and Jean Bugatti's first design followed, the T43 which was a

Above: the Talbot 105 was a sterling Georges Roesch design, introduced in 1931, and extensively and successfully raced and rallied. Outwardly following stolidly British lines, it was light and had a very efficient 3-litre six-cylinder engine

Opposite, top: Jaguar forerunners were Swallow-bodied cars, such as this Austin Swallow two-seater, announced by William Lyons' company in 1927. Small Fiat, Morris, Standard, Swift and Wolseley models were also used as the basis of sporty Swallows. All were dumpy little cars, in contrast to the sleek 2½-litre SS Jaguar 100 *(opposite, below)* announced in 1935—the year SS Cars Ltd introduced the name Jaguar

The beautifully streamlined Bugatti Type 57C at Le Mans in 1939, when it was driven to a clear victory by Wimille and Veyron. Ettore Bugatti's son Jean was killed while testing this car later in 1939

good car by any standards (the 4·9 litre T50 on the other hand gained a lethal reputation). In the 1930s, Bugatti's cars tended to be larger; the T55 and T59 were elegant in standard form, but were also clothed in some of the more hideous bodies to come out of French coachbuilders during the period. Late in the 1930s Bugatti was for once ahead of the times, with the out-and-out sports-racing T57S and T57C which won at Le Mans in 1937 and 1939.

The outstanding sports cars built between the wars, in the middle weight or any other category, came from Milan. From 1925 Alfa Romeo pro-duced a succession of lithe elegant six- and eight-cylinder cars which set new standards, not least in demonstrating that all-round balance and efficiency was worth much more than sheer power. In 1929 the winning 6·6 litre Bentley at Le Mans covered 1,821 miles; in the following year the win-ning 2·3 litre Alfa Romeo covered 1,875 miles. . . .

The first new post-war sporting Alfas were Giuseppe Merosi's RL, RM and RLSS, competent six- and four-cylinder cars which enjoyed some rac-ing successes and were listed for several years. Vittorio Jano took over from Merosi, and once he had finished with the grand prix P2, turned his attention to sports cars. The Alfa Romeo manage-ment were spurred on by OM racing successes, especially in the first Mille Miglia, and by the Italian government's beneficient attitude towards success in competitions and exports.

Jano's first sports car was the 1925 6C, with 1½ litre single-ohc engine, which was quickly followed by twin-ohc 1,750 cc models, including the supercharged Supersport which Cam-pari drove to win the 1928 Mille Miglia.

Thereafter, with only one break, the Mille Miglia fell to Alfas until 1938. With the introduction of the 8C in 1931,

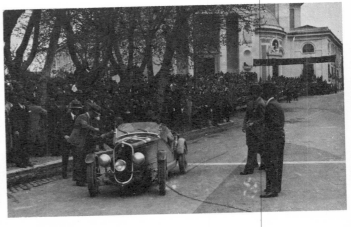

Above left: a pair of six-cylinder Alfa Romeos in the 1934 Mille Miglia, Ruesch forcing inside Bataglia (and perilously close to a couple of roadside stones). This scene typifies the race in the 1930s, when save for that German victory in 1931 it was dominated by Alfas.
Left: Guidotti and Boratto with a beautiful 2.3-litre six-cylinder Alfa Romeo coupé raced in the 1937 Mille Miglia—in all save contemporary designation a GT car.
Above: Fiat's delightful little 508S Balilla, which was based on bread-and-butter saloon components, was the Italian equivalent of the numerous small British sports cars. It had a 995 cc engine. This Balilla Sports MM was raced by Gilera and Manoni in the 1934 Mille Miglia

Alfa Romeo domination of sports car racing became absolute. The 8C, which in normal form had a 2·3 litre engine and a variety of bodies, became immensely respected throughout Europe, a reputation reinforced by their relative rarity (fewer than 200 were built).

A simpler six-cylinder 2·3 litre was marketed more widely from 1934, its derivatives continuing for several years. However, further full-blooded 8Cs were developed directly from the P3 grand prix car (in fact the 1935 Mille Miglia was won by Pintacuda in a road-equipped P3); the Alfa Corse 8C 2,900 coupe which led for most of the distance at Le Mans in 1938 was one of the first front-line GT cars in the modern idiom.

When the earlier 8C was at the height of its career in 1933, Fiat chose to list a sports car again. Their delightful little 1 litre 508S Ballila was virtually the only small Italian sports car with international appeal to appear between the two world wars; a few carried attractive 'Mille Miglia' coupe bodies—mini GT cars!

Imitation is a gross form of automotive flattery, and in the Dolomite 2·0 litre straight-eight of 1934, Triumph carried it to the point where Alfa Romeo could have objected, and Triumph abandoned this model when only six examples had been built!

Below left: astonishing debut. First major race for the most famous of all racing MGs, the K3 Magnette, was in the 1933 Mille Miglia, when George Eyston won the 1,100 cc class.
Below right: it is easy to forget that Riley was a sporting marque in the 1930s. A pair of French drivers placed this 1.5-litre car second overall at Le Mans in 1934. Gwenda Stewart's Derby and a 4.9-litre Bugatti follow

The Dolomite was an isolated example in a widely diversified range of British sports cars which appeared in the 1930s, most of them built in penny packets, to be sure, and some of them sporty rather than sports, but at no time before or since has such a wide variety of sporting machinery been built in a country in a decade. From Aero Minx and Wolseley Hornet, they ranged up through Rileys, Aston Martins, HRGs and the first Morgan four-wheelers, to the extremely efficient Roesch Talbot 105s and Lagondas which were almost throwbacks to the late-1920s mammoths in terms of bulkiness (but a Fox and Nichols 4½ litre Lagonda Rapide narrowly won at Le Mans in 1935) and to a new breed of hybrids, British chassis exploiting the abundant lazy power of big American power units, Railtons, Broughs, Allards and Atalantas, for example.

The Dolomite's equivalent in fierceness was the MG Magnette K3, which had a supercharged 1,100 cc six producing 120 bhp. The K3s gained some notable successes in the hands of leading drivers, as a major race debut taking first and second in class in the 1933 Mille Miglia, while later in the year Tazio Nuvolari put in an epic drive to win the TT in a K3.

As street eye-catchers, William Lyons' SS cars had few equals. The first Swallow cars had been rebodied Austins, Fiats, Swifts and Wolseleys, but the 1931 SS1 built around Standard mechanical components was a striking close-coupled coupe with a long low bonnet. The SS90 sports two-seater followed, then in 1935 came the SS Jaguar 100, and the marque began to gain a competition record on the

strength of rally and race successes.

William Lyons' cars were always much cheaper than their appearance suggested; similar lines–low bonnet and long flowing wings–were also a feature of one of the most expensive (pound for pound) sports cars of the period, Adrian Squire's 'ideal' Squire. This was powered by a supercharged Anzani 1½ litre engine, which gave it a top speed of over 100 mph. The chassis cost almost £1,000 in 1934, when one could buy a complete Bertelli-designed Aston Martin for £610. A year later the 100 mph 1½ litre Ulster Aston was marketed, and in the following year a BMW 328 could be purchased for under £700. This was one of the most forward-looking sports cars of the 1930s, with an efficient but uncomplicated 2 litre six-cylinder engine in a light chassis, clothed in a smooth body –a package which added up, to all intents and purposes, to a 100 mph car. With sleek coupe bodies, 328s placed 5–7–9 in the last pre-war Le Mans 24 hours, and in open form won the 1940 Mille Miglia.

Racing in the later years of the 1930s saw a resurgence of French sports cars, large and small. Delage and Delahaye came together, and produced some workmanlike and effective cars, as did Talbot. By happy coincidence these could be stripped and run as unsupercharged GP cars under the 1938–39 formula (as the grand prix prospect had been a bleak one of German domination in the preceding years, the ACF had even run their premier event for sports cars). At the other end of the scale, Amedée Gordini did amazing things with little Simca-Cinqs and 1 litre Simcas.

Left, top: sports cars have come and gone; Morgan 4/4s seemed everlasting. This is the 1938 1,267 cc Standard-engined prototype
Left, below: last Bugatti produced—the term is relative—was the T57. This is one of 43 T57S, with a slightly squat Corsica body and out-of-period wheels

The Sports Car Classics

To many the proof of a real sports car is in competition, at least it was in races in the days before highly-specialized quasi-racing cars ruled the sports car classics. The beginnings of modern sports car racing in the 1920s are inextricably mixed up with touring car events. The 1921 Corsican Grand Prix is often quoted as a starting point. In 1922 came Europe's first 24-hour race, the Bol d'Or, and in 1923 the first Le Mans 24-hour Race. The first race was not even to be an end in itself, but the first round in a three-year contest (or 72-hour race!) for the Rudge Whitworth Cup, which officially became secondary to the *Coupe Annuelle à la Distance* only from 1928.

The race caught on, not least with the British, who were to be very strongly represented from the mid-1920s at least until the 1960s. Until 1939 it was an event for catalogued models (sometimes perhaps not too strictly), and initially all cars over 1,100

cc had to be four seaters and all had to carry ballast equivalent to passengers. Fairly soon, however, streamlined and specialized types appeared in the smaller classes, and by 1937 the only accommodation requirement was 'two comfortable seats facing forward,' a fortunate change for Bugatti whose T57S sports-racer won the event!

In 1923 Lagache and Léonard won in a 3 litre Chenard et Walcker at 57·20 mph; in 1939 Wimille and Veyron won in a 3·3 litre Bugatti at 86·85 mph. In the meantime the circuit had twice been shortened and simplified, to the 8·36 mile form retained until 1968, and the roads making it up transformed from a series of loose-surfaced lanes to a broad billiard-table track.

Today, the Mille Miglia begins to sound improbable, and indeed it was a remarkable event to be conceived even in the 1920s—a thousand miles over a great figure of eight of public roads from Brescia down to Rome and back again, on good highways and over rough Appenine passes, through villages and towns with normal traffic halted. Aymo Maggi and Renzo Castagneto thought it up, the Italian government blessed it. . . .

The first Mille Miglia, in 1927, attracted 77 starters, and rather surpris-

Driven by the maestro. *This 2.3-litre 8C Alfa Romeo was raced in the 1931 Mille Miglia by the great Tazio Nuvolari (*below: *the car being moved to the start through an enthusiastic crowd). He finished ninth, but won the race for Alfa Romeo in 1930 and 1933, finished second in 1934 and 1947*

ingly the Brescia-built 2 litre OMs scored a 1–2–3, Minoia and Morandi winning at 47·99 mph. Thereafter, it was contested by increasing hordes of cars, from humble little Fiats to the latest full-blooded sports models. Alfa Romeo almost made a habit of winning, save for that triumph gained for Mercedes by Caracciola in 1931. In 1938, the last pre-war year the race was run over the traditional course (an accident

involving spectators meant that it was not held in 1939), Biondetti and Stefani averaged 84·13 mph in a 2,900 Alfa.

The Targa Florio came into its own between the wars, too, over the 67·11 mile 'Medium Madonie' circuit until 1930, then over the 44·74 mile 'Short Madonie' until 1936. Broadly thought of as a sports car race, the Targa has always been an event unto itself, until quite recently defying close catergorisation; in the 1920s a just-redundant GP car, with a spare wheel strapped on and a top-line driver in the cockpit was a very effective Targa car. Bugatti had a great run of successes from 1925 until 1929, then it was Alfa's turn. Varzi took the 1930 race in an adapted P2, then Alfa sports cars won until the race was emasculated in 1936.

The 'senior' surviving motor race, in terms of the date of its first running, is Britain's Tourist Trophy. Between the

Top, left: from 1924 until 1927 Le Mans cars had to race part of the distance with soft tops erected. In this rustic shot d'Erlanger in a 3-litre Bentley leads a Th Schneider in the 1927 race. *Left:* ten years later a streamlined 1.5-litre Adler is surrounded by an assortment of cycle-winged small cars—Ford, Simca-Cinq, two Austins and an MG. *Below:* Borzacchini's Alfa Romeo in the Sicilian mountains during the 1933 Targa Florio

wars, this had a characteristically chequered history, moving from the Isle of Man to Ulster and then to Donington, being run only spasmodically, sometimes achieving greatness.

The 1928–36 TTs were run on the 13·6 mile Ards circuit in Northern Ireland, and saw some great drives against the RAC's handicap system as well as between drivers. Kaye Don took the first of these races in a Lea Francis, by 13 seconds from a front-wheel drive Alvis–an appropriate result, as these were closely bracketed by contemporary sports car buffs. Caracciola took the 1929 race in a big Mercedes, and 1930 saw an Alfa Romeo 1–2–3 scored by that formidable triumvirate, Nuvolari, Campari and Varzi. The pre-war highlight came in 1933, when Nuvolari drove an astonishing virtuoso race to narrowly win in an MG K3–to achieve this against runner-up Hamilton's more favourably handicapped MG J4, Nuvolari more or less had to break the lap record seven times!

TT scenes. *Top:* heavy metal in the 1936 race, Hall's Bentley and Lewis' Lagonda. *Right:* oops! McFeanan's Bugatti a little out of hand in Newtownards. *Below:* Newtownards again, in 1933. Hamilton's MG Midget and *(right)* Nuvolari's K3, being forced on to beat the handicap

Following pages: the BMW 328 was one of the great sports cars of the 1930s, and influenced development in post-war years. It had a 2-litre six-cylinder engine in a light chassis, clothed with an elegant and efficient body. The accompanying Bücker Jungmeister is a contemporary and wholly complimentary, for it was an outstanding aerobatic machine—a sports aircraft

Voitures de Grande Luxe

'White, magnificent as a royal barge, yet earthbound, poised on powerful wheels. . . .'

That was the French author Pierre Frondaie's picture of the car which he glorified as a symbol of the aristocratic life in his novel 'L'homme a l'Hispano'. And no vehicle sums up the luxury vintage car better than the 37·2 hp Hispano-Suiza of 1919 marketed under the uncompromising slogan 'The dearest *but* the best,' and described with more attention to superlatives than grammar by its makers as 'The most exclusive, luxurious, speediest and silent automobile the world has ever produced.'

Designer of all the Hispano models was the brilliant Swiss engineer Marc Birkigt, who, having been called to Barcelona to redesign the local water supply system, stayed to become an electrical engineer, then, like his contemporary, Frederick Royce, bought a twin-cylinder Decauville.

By this time he was working for a not-too-successful motor manufacturing company called Castro, and the Decauville was doubtless the inspiration for the 1902 10 hp live-axle Castro. Inevitably, a four-cylinder model followed, but this failed to save the company, which was crippled by strikes.

However, a group of local businessmen obviously felt that the cars were too good to vanish from the market, so they reorganised the company, put Birkigt in charge, and renamed it, elegantly if ungrammatically, Hispano-Suiza in his honour.

From 1905 the marque featured unit-construction of engine and gearbox. 'The most difficult layout to copy' claimed the company, hoping everyone had forgotten about Decauville. . . .

Before long, the Hispano-Suiza was considered worthy to share the garage of that most discerning of royal motorists, Alfonso XIII of Spain, with his 50 hp Panhard. When a new sporting model was developed from their 1909 Coupe de *l'Auto* winner, it was called the Type Alfonso XIII, in his honour.

By 1911 the Hispano had achieved such international prestige that a factory was opened at 27 Rue Cave, Levallois-Perrel, Paris, plus showrooms in the Avenue Malakoff. Soon titled scorchers like La Baronne de Laroche were tearing around the Bois de Boulogne in their Alfonsos. Now the Paris factory, based at Bois-Colombes from 1914, set the pace.

During the First World War, the French factory devoted itself to producing V-8 aero engines of advanced design, built under licence in England as the Wolseley Viper. The V-8, claimed Hispano, had powered around 60 per cent of the allied aircraft on all fronts.

It was this engine that provided the experience which led to the company's post-war power unit, a single-overhead camshaft 6,597 cc six. This made unprecedented use of light alloy, with light screwed-in steel cylinder liners and a 99 lb seven-bearing crankshaft machined from a solid billet of steel weighing 770 lb. This advanced engine, which developed 135 bhp, was mounted in a massive chassis, fitted with four-wheel brakes. Though a Mercedes had been experimentally fitted with brakes on the front axle in 1906, and Argyll, Arrol-Johnstone and Isotta-Fraschini had catalogued such a fitment before the war, the Hispano system was far in advance of anything previously attempted, for it featured servo-assistance, to give light, powerful operation.

Above the austere radiator of the Hispano soared a silver stork mascot, emblem of the French air ace Georges Guynemer, whose Spad biplane had been Hispano-powered. The squadron of French aces–N3, *l'Escadrille Cigogne*–to which Guynemer belonged had become such a feature of contemporary French folklore that three other quality car manufacturers, Bucciali, Fonck and Bignan, adopted the flying stork as a symbol, and the road in which the Parisian Hispano factory was based was renamed Rue de Capitaine Guynemer.

The Hispano had only three, widely-spaced forward speeds, a feature that didn't matter too much on the 37·2 hp H6 model, designed to travel virtually anywhere in top gear, but which became a major drawback on the 'economy' version of this car, the Barcelona-built T49 of only 3,750 cc. Since the smaller engine had to cope with the same heavy chassis and bodywork as the more powerful version, frequent use had to be made of the gearbox, which, in a well-preserved T49 proved fearfully noisy, emitting a piercing shriek like a circular saw cutting through hardwood.

An announcement in 1923 that the French factory was soon to market two small cars, a 2-litre 12–14 hp four and a 3-litre 18 hp six, came to nothing, perhaps fortunately, for the T49 showed that economy models were not really Birkigt's forte. Small cars of this type were built by the Barcelona factory, however, under a 'bread-and-butter' contract for the Spanish government.

The H6 series, current until 1931 was unquestionably one of the great designs of the 1920s. Its successor, the even more splendid 9·5 litre Type 68 V-12, introduced at the height of the Depression at a chassis price of £2,750, was

Although Hispano-Suiza did produce some mundane cars, the company is usually recalled for its *voitures de grandes luxe*, such as the 1928 32CV coupe de ville *(left)*. 1935 35CV on the right has an elegant *torpédo* body

followed by a true *folie des grandeurs*, the 11,300 cc Series II Type 68, which was powered by an engine originally developed for high speed railcars.

Alongside the Hispano-Suiza, the Rolls-Royce Silver Ghost looked distinctly old-fashioned. Its durability and reliability had been amply proven in the war, when the standard touring car chassis had proved substantial enough to carry armoured car bodywork, but the Rolls was still basically a 1906 design, which had benefitted little from the company's wartime venture into aero engine design. Its four speed gearbox had an unnecessarily complex 'locking-gate' to prevent the lever from springing out of gear, which took the edge off the car's very real merits as a touring vehicle. Unlike most other luxury cars of the early 1920s, it did not have front-wheel brakes, due to Royce's firm insistence on not making any innovation without exhaustive testing. When four-wheel brakes appeared in 1924, the design was based on the Hispano-Suiza layout. In 1925 the Phantom I replaced the Silver Ghost, though the chassis remained much the same; the Phantom II of 1929 was a much more thorough redesign.

Rivalling Rolls-Royce for quality was the Lanchester 40, introduced in 1919, and based on George Lanchester's sporting Forty design of 1914, the first of this idiosyncratic marque to have a 'conventional' bonnet. The new 40 retained the epicyclic gearbox of its forebears, and its single-overhead camshaft six-cylinder engine owed much to contemporary aero engine practice. Its welded aluminium coachwork and torsionally stiff chassis were noteworthy, but it did not have front-wheel brakes until 1924, an unusual omission in view of the fact that the 'little Lanchester', the 21 hp model introduced in 1923 to combat the new 20 hp Rolls-Royce, had them from the start. The answer, it seemed, was that the '40' was designed to be driven by chauffeurs, who had no need for aids like four-wheel brakes to get them out of trouble, while the 21 hp was for owner-drivers, who lacked the experience of professionals, and might drive too fast for safety. . . .

However, when the 40 did acquire front-wheel brakes, they were very good indeed, with servo-assistance from an hydraulic ram. Its chassis price in 1924 was £1,800, only £100 less than the Rolls-Royce Silver Ghost.

Though commercial pressures forced Lanchester to conform to a more conventional layout in the 1920s, one manufacturer, at least, seemed to be successful enough pursuing a completely individual – eccentric, even – course, building cars of distinct individuality; his name was Gabriel Voisin, already established as an aircraft manufacturer, and one of the first Frenchmen to fly in a heavier-than-air machine.

Voisin's autocratic attitude to his customers is epitomised in the story of the irate customer who stormed into the company's workshops in the Avenue Gambetta, Issy-les-Molineaux, Paris, complaining that his new 17 cv 'wouldn't pull.' A little man in blue overalls, who seemed to be some kind of foreman, offered to test the car, and took it for a run round the locality, to try the acceleration and braking. After a while, he handed the car over to the dissatisfied owner, and asked him to drive. Three minutes later, the man in the blue overalls snapped: 'Drive back to the factory.'

He marched straight to the cashiers: 'Give this gentleman his money back,' he ordered. 'He cannot drive, and is unworthy to own a Voisin!'

The 'workman' was, of course, Gabriel Voisin himself. . . .

In their day Voisin's cars, with their lightweight, aerodynamic bodywork and high-performance sleeve-valve power units–one of the company's latter designs had a straight-twelve engine which projected into the driving compartment to give the necessary balance for exceptional handling characteristics at very high speed, allied to a short drive line–seemed daringly unorthodox.

But they sold well enough–total production between 1919–1936 was over 27,000–despite ambivalent Press comments like: 'The body lines are distinctively French, having a sobriety which might not appeal to English tastes,' which masked such ingenious innovations as the electrically-operated Solcar sunshine roof of 1929.

Certainly the Voisin did far better than another luxury car built by aviation pioneers, the Farman of 1920–31, which was one of the few cars worthy to be mentioned in the same breath as the Hispano-Suiza–and which was superior in one respect, with a four-speed gearbox with well-chosen, *silent* ratios.

Italy's premier offering in this period was the straight-eight Isotta–Fraschini from Milan, which was introduced in 6 litre form in 1918, and uprated to 7·3 litres in 1925. Designed with the profitable American market in mind by Guistino Cattaneo, the Isotta was the first straight-eight to go into serious production, and, good car though it was, it suffered in comparison with the Hispano.

Commented one connoisseur with considerable experience of the Isotta: 'It handled like a truck!'

You couldn't say the same of Belgium's best-known luxury car, the Minerva, which had its origins back in 1899 when an engineer named Sylvain de Jong built a light power unit for bicycles. By 1910 Minerva had progressed through the usual voiturettes to a range of luxury cars, all powered by Knight sleeve-valve engines.

Their 1920s offerings were all big and aristocratic. Typically, the 1921 instruction book advised owners (or, rather, their chauffeurs) to top-up the rear axle with 'a wine-glass of oil' every 2,000 miles.

Despite a wheelbase of 12 feet 6 inches, Minerva's 32/34 hp six of 1927 was a highly manoeuvrable machine with a surprising turn of acceleration.

Only the inevitable blue haze of oil smoke in the exhaust revealed that it had sleeve valves. The long cantilever springs characteristic of the make gave the car a curious gait like a galloping horse over rough going.

More like a galloping elephant was France's biggest car de luxe of the 1920s, the gargantuan Renault 45, introduced in 1921. Nearly half its overall length of over 16 feet was devoted to keeping its six-cylinder 9·1 litre engine dry, and even then, opening the bonnet revealed that the rear cylinders vanished beneath the typically Renault dashboard radiator. Despite its archaic layout, the 45 was a car of great elegance; its replacement, the 7·1 litre Reinastella of 1929 was a poor substitute.

One great make which vanished from the luxury car scene in the 1920s was Napier, whose *eminence grise*, S. F. Edge, had parted with them after a dispute in 1912 on condition that he kept out of the motor industry for seven years. In return, he received a 'golden handshake' of £160,000, which he used to set up a very successful pig-farming operation on the Sussex Downs. The post-war Napier 40/50 had a rather dated chassis layout, which was a pity, for its overhead camshaft engine was a fine design. Contemporary owners, however, were obviously not so conscious of the chassis shortcomings as modern commentators. One proud customer praised 'the 40/50 hp Six Cylinder Napier in which we have now

done 5,000 miles of the most enjoyable travelling we have ever had in any car; my wife and I think that as this has turned out such a grand success, we should have another 40/50 hp Six Cylinder Napier with landaulette body, and I have much pleasure in placing the order with you for same.

'May I add that we (together with many of our friends) consider your new type engine simply the last word in locomotion.'

It was also the last word as far as Napier's car-producing activities were concerned, for the company's diversification into aero engines had become so important that the motor side of the business was dropped in 1924. Napier did make an attempt to acquire the moribund Bentley Motor Company in 1931, but this was thwarted by Rolls-Royce who apparently feared the potential competition, and bought Bentley themselves.

Oddly enough, at the same time Rolls-Royce were winding up another expansive venture, their American factory at Springfield, Massachussets, which was operational from 1920 until 1931. This attempt to save on shipping costs and import duties failed because the wealthy Americans who wanted a Rolls-Royce were fully prepared to pay extra for the 'genuine' British-built Rolls-Royce, which carried an extra cachet of exclusivity.

In fact, America was an excellent market for luxury cars. While European manufacturers were accustomed to a modest output of high-priced cars for an exclusive clientele, American makers were able to provide top quality vehicles in huge numbers.

Cadillac's V-8 sold 13,000 in 1915, its first year of production, at prices ranging from $2,700 to $3,350, yet even at that volume of production the transmission was so silent that Rolls-Royce bought a V-8 to find out why it was quieter than their product!

There was, of course, still room for limited production behemoths like the 8·5 litre Locomobile 48, ('The Exclusive Car for Exclusive People'), introduced in 1911 and still listed in 1929, or America's biggest car, the 9·3 litre McFarlan, built in penny numbers in

The austere lines of this 1932 Voisin C14 *(left)* are probably less striking nowadays than when the car was new. But Gabriel Voisin (who died, aged 93, in 1973) built for lightness and practicality rather than the dictates of fashion. He also succeeded in turning the sleeve-valve engine into a high performance unit: this 2.3-litre six could reach 75 mph. Giant of the 1920s was Ettore Bugatti's 12.7-litre *La Royale (top);* this is the prototype with a Packard body. Six of these T41 cars were built; only three were actually sold. More practical was the 1931 Delage D8 *(above)*

Connersville, Indiana, and boasting a triple ignition system incorporating 18 spark plugs for its six-cylinder engine. Most ornate of the McFarlans was the Knickerbocker Cabriolet, described by one owner as 'the largest possible motor car in the worst possible taste . . . looks like nothing so much as a Moorish castle on wheels.' It cost $9,000.

Another $9,000 car of the period was the V-8 6-litre Cunningham, arguably one of America's greatest cars. Listed from 1916 to 1933, it was bought by such celebrities as William Randolph Hearst, Harold Lloyd and Mary Pickford. The ultimate in high price, if not elegance, was the V-12 Heine-Velox of 1921, built in San Francisco, fitted with hydraulic front brakes, and so ugly that even a price of $17,000 couldn't save the company from early failure.

For the customer who wanted the refinement and smoothness of a V-12, there was the Packard Twin-Six, introduced in 1915 at prices ranging from $3,150 to $4,600. Who would buy the unknown Heine-Velox when they could buy Packard's 'Boss of the Road' for a third of the price?

By European standards, production of Packards was phenomenal. In the nine-year production life of the Twin-Six, over 35,000 examples of this prestige model were built, while output of Packard's lower priced model, the Single Six, priced around $2,700, grew to 40,358 in 18 months in 1925–26. Even the Company's new top model, the Eight, 'equipped with every luxury and embellishment the markets of the world afford' sold 12,766 in its first 20 months of production, at prices ranging from $3,650 to $4,950.

Compare this with Hispano-Suiza's *total* output in 40 years from two factories of around 8,600, or Bugatti's most prestigious vehicle, the 12·7 litre Royale, of which only six were built, priced at half-a-million francs!

Perhaps the best-known of the 'volume classics' was the Lincoln. The Lincoln Motor Company had been formed in 1917 by Henry Leland, who had headed Cadillac since its inception, to build Liberty V-12 aero engines. After the war, they turned to car production, their first V-8 appearing in 1920. Although the Lincoln was fully up to Henry Leland's exacting mechanical requirements, its styling was awkward.

The Parry-Thomas-designed Leyland Eight *(left)* was magnificently engineered, but ugly disc wheels with prominent hubs marred its appearance. Between 1920–1931, Rolls-Royce were built at Springfield, Massachussets; this Brewster Phantom I speedster *(below)* is typical . . .

The company's finances, overstretched by the building of elaborate production facilities and sales figures that failed to come up to expectation, suffered a fatal blow when an incompetent income tax official filed a claim against Lincoln for arrears of taxes amounting to $4,500,000. This figure was eventually found to be nine times the correct amount, but by that time it was too late. The company had gone into receivership and had been bought by Henry Ford for $8 million.

Within months Leland and his son Wilfred had left the company, unable to compromise with the Ford way of doing things.

Under the Ford regime Lincoln production rose to 40 cars a day, cars that were as far removed from the utilitarian Model T as could be imagined. They were, claimed the company, 'created

Cadillac's proud slogan was 'The Standard of The World', and magnificent multi-cylinder cars like the V-16 of 1930–38 and the V-12 of 1931–38 upheld this. Top picture shows a 1931 V-12 6-litre town car, while the 1930 7.4-litre V-16 *(above)* carries vee-fronted landaulette coachwork

and assembled to standards never before attempted in the making of manufactured product . . . admits nor accepts no compromise with standards other

Top left: the first Lincoln cars appeared in 1921, with 81 bhp 5.8-litre V-8 power units which had full-pressure lubrication. The company was acquired by Henry Ford in 1922, after less than two years' independence.
Top right: perhaps the most striking American cars of the mid-1930s were the 'coffin-nosed' Cords, designed by Gordon Beuhrig. This is the supercharged 812 version. Imposing car behind it is a 1934 Cadillac series 20 V-8 sedan. *Below left:* this 1929 Packard 645 Victoria had a 6,350 cc straight-eight engine developing 106 bhp. *Below right:* the 1931–32 Model KB Lincoln had a 7.2-litre V-12 power unit

than the highest.' Edsel, Henry Ford's son, took a great interest in Lincoln, and many of the styling and mechanical lessons learned from the Lincoln operation proved invaluable when it came to developing the new Model A.

Two things were most impressive about the Lincoln: its magnificent top gear performance and its ultra-light steering.

Spare a thought though, for Childe Harold Wills, the gifted engineer who had formed part of the elite team that designed the Model T Ford (and, indeed all the Fords since 1903). Wills, the 'mechanical genius of Highland Park,' was so vital a part of the Ford organisation that he commanded a share of Ford's own dividends, and when he left the company in 1919 to set up on his own, Wills took a final payment of $1,592,128 with him.

The car he built from 1921–26, the Wills Sainte Claire, was a beautifully engineered vehicle which pioneered the use of molybdenum steel and initially featured a 4 litre V-8 engine with overhead camshafts. In 1924 came a long-stroke six-cylinder ohc engine, replaced towards the end of production by the retrograde step of pushrod ohv. Production reached 1,500 in 1923, but the company never really recovered from the 1921 slump.

Another maker of luxury cars with advanced ideas of metallurgy was Pierce-Arrow, whose mid-1920s models made extensive use of light alloy: prototypes were built with 85 per cent alloy construction and power-steering. Apart from its superlative quality the Pierce-Arrow was remarkable for its fender headlights: 'the owner is never embarrassed by having his car mistaken for any other make,' claimed the company, and their products were used by American Presidents from Woodrow Wilson to Franklin D. Roosevelt.

Another great name of the 1920s was Duesenberg, whose model A of 1920–28 incorporated many lessons learned from wartime production of Bugatti aero engines. The Model J of 1928, built under the aegis of Erret Lobban Cord, ensured the company's place in motoring history. The most powerful car of its day, the Model J was current until 1937; the supercharged, 130 mph, SJ version first appeared in 1932.

Over 470 Duesenbergs Js and SJs were sold, at prices ranging from

$11,000 to $25,000, yet Fred Duesenberg contended that his car was priced in exactly the same way as a Ford, on a dollar-for-dollar, cost-plus, value-for-money basis–it was just more expensive because it had cost more to make. The sheer ostentation of the coachwork by Bohmann & Schwartz, Rollston, Murphy and other leading coach-builders set the Duesenberg apart from more prosaically styled luxury cars as the supreme emblem of a gilded era.

The Model J was a car for the Gatsbys of America; it was, considered Crown Prince Nicholas of Rumania, who owned–and raced–several examples of the marque, 'the world's finest automobile, from every point of view.'

Top: the 1926 Wills St Claire was a far cry from the Model T Ford—but both were designed by Childe Harold Wills. *Above:* this Pierce-Arrow of the mid 1920s lacks the 'fender headlamps' found on most examples of this marque.

Opposite, top: Prince Nicholas of Rumania racing a much-modified Duesenberg Model J at Le Mans in 1935. *Opposite, centre:* the rare Thomson & Taylor modified low-chassis Daimler Double-Six—a sleeve-valve V-12!—with bodywork by Corsica. *Right:* George Brough, famous for his motor cycles, built a range of sports cars in the mid-1930s, using Hudson six- and eight-cylinder engines. *Opposite, bottom:* the 3.6-litre Ford V-8-powered 1936 Jensen, and Bugatti's last production car, the T57 of 1934–39

Ten Years of Progress

1927–a crazy year; the year of Lindbergh, talking pictures, the De Havilland Moth. Of the Louis Armstrong Hot Seven, of Clara Bow, the 'It' Girl, of the last Model T Ford and the first transatlantic telephone conversation....

In your B & P Urban Motor House (price £16 15s, designed specially to comply with the bye-laws of Urban District Councils) stands a new Clyno Royal tourer, a typical mass-produced model of the day, with conservative styling, and a Mulliner coachbuilt body

A spacious coach-built Mulliner body was standard equipment on the Clyno Royal models. This is the 1927 10.8 hp version, with a Coventry-Climax engine

whose excellence of finish belies the car's modest price of £199 10s.

Indeed, this is probably the lowest-priced car in which anyone with a pretension to a position in society could make their calls without feeling *infra dig*: it has real leather upholstery, nickel-plated brightwork and a mahogany dashboard, while the four-wheel brakes and balloon tyres are features by no means universal at this end of the market.

While the Clyno is little different in external appearance compared with similar vehicles of ten or a dozen years earlier, its basic equipment is far more comprehensive.

It has, for example, electric lighting and starting, with a dynamo built in as part of the engine design–though there's still a fixed starting handle and a raucous bulb horn for emergencies. The engine, squarer cut, still with side valves, and less elaborately finished than the power unit of an Edwardian light car, is more powerful, developing around 23 brake horsepower from 1,368 cc–enough to propel the car, with its heavy four seater body, at 45–50 mph, and to enable it to tow one of the trailer caravans that are just beginning to become part of the leisure scene.

The windscreen opens for clear visibility in fog and frost, but an efficient

Italian middle-class motoring of the mid-1930s is represented by this 2.5-litre Fiat 522S pillarless sports saloon, one of few surviving examples

electric screen wiper is fitted; only a few years earlier hand-operated squeegees were a rare luxury, when all too often there was no means at all of cleaning rain off the glass.

In many ways, however, the concept of this car is behind the times—perhaps that is what gives the vehicle its air of middle class respectability. The gearbox, for example, is separate from the engine, mounted on a torque tube which keeps the back axle in place, the entire unit moving up and down as the car rides over rough surfaces, causing the gear lever to rock backwards and forward in a disconcerting manner.

It is a layout that has many advantages—the entire transmission can be removed for inspection within the space of thirty minutes or so—but it does not conform with the current fashion for unit construction. The clutch is the old-fangled (and sometimes fierce) cone type, heavy in operation and needing under-

standing for clean gear changing—synchromesh, an American invention, has yet to appear. The lighter, simpler plate clutch is now almost universal on older makes.

Other signs of conservatism are the right-hand gear change and central throttle pedal features, rapidly vanishing from the specification of most right-hand-drive cars, and the dashboard of solid mahogany rather than pressed steel. Although the car is called a 'tourer', it has only a tiny underseat locker and a rear folding grid for luggage—but a six footer can sit in the rear seat with his legs fully stretched in real comfort.

The steering is light and positive—the design, they say, was based on that of a grand prix Peugeot owned by one of the Clyno company's directors—with just one-and-a-half turns from lock to lock. On the road, the car is commendably lively—it will, for instance, out-perform a Bullnose Morris of officially greater power—yet has sufficient flexibility, thanks to a massive flywheel, to move away from rest in top gear without stalling.

It will, at the still-current British speed limit of 20 mph (which everyone, save the occasional police trappers, ignores) consume a gallon of 60 octane motor spirit, price 1s 7d, served from a hand-wound pump at one of the growing numbers of roadside service stations, every 35–40 miles.

The roads, too, are changing. A post-war programme of reconstruction and development has made them far more suited to the needs of motor traffic, and already bypasses are being built to relieve congested town centres. But speculative builders are nullifying this trend to some extent by lining these new roads with estates of identical semi-detached houses, recreating many of the urban problems the bypasses were intended to solve. There's already an outcry against this 'ribbon development,' but legislation to prevent it will not be forthcoming for several years.

And there are so many cars now on the roads that in city centres one way traffic schemes are beginning to make an appearance, while in Wolverhampton the go-ahead chief constable is ex-

The motorist of 1927 took open-air motoring as a matter of course, even in winter *(above left)*; public buses offered even less protection from the elements than this Clyno tourer in London. Ten years later, most popular cars were saloons like this Talbot Ten *(top right)*; the interior is noticeably cramped compared with the Clyno, and rear-hinged doors are a source of danger

perimenting with automatic traffic lights to regulate the vehicles at a busy intersection.

Let's move ten years into the future, to the Coronation year of 1937. The new occupant of the garage is a Talbot Ten, a car in the same price and social bracket as your old Clyno. Though its side valve engine capacity is slightly less than that of the earlier car, it is nearly twice as powerful, thanks to improvements in engine technology. But by the same token, it is less flexible–the gearbox has four speeds instead of the Clyno's three–less economical and has more exacting fuel requirements.

They advertise the Talbot as 'track-bred,' but that's rather a dubious claim, for Rootes, the owners of the marque name, are trading on the racing achievements of the old Georges Roesch designed cars, built by the original Clement-Talbot Company. The 'Ten' is little more than a disguised Hillman Minx with a high-compression cylinder head and coachbuilt bodywork by Thrupp & Maberly, another Rootes subsidiary.

It is much lower slung than the car of a decade earlier, with a transmission tunnel between the seats, and footwells dropped inside the chassis frame. The floor on the older model was entirely above the chassis, giving a high seating position, with the driver's eye-level over five feet above the road.

The 1937 car, with its fashionable Airline Saloon body, puts the driver's viewpoint almost 18 inches lower, and

he's seated low in relation to the high bonnet, with a narrow windscreen; forward vision is correspondingly restricted, and as the driver cannot see the nearside wing, width judgment is difficult. All-round vision is restricted by the styling of the body, with its ample blind spots. A tiny luggage boot is provided in the sloping tail. One advantage of the Talbot's sporting pretensions is its stubby remote-control gear lever, which gives moderately precise control; all too many 1937 cars have willowy central gear levers like anaemic pokers, which make selecting a speed unnecessarily difficult.

All in all, the car of 1937 is faster, fussier and flashier, than its 1927 counterpart; and the adoption of such extras as radio, sunshine roof, semaphore direction indicators and hydraulic brakes cannot hide the fact that somewhere along the way much of the charm has gone out of motoring.

The roads are becoming more crowded, yet new motor road construction has slowed almost to a halt–between 1933 and 1935 only 194 miles was added to the trunk road system. Of nearly £75,000,000 collected each year in motor tax, only a third of this goes on building new highways.

Ten years earlier motorists were promised vastly improved dual car-

riageways, with trees separating the tracks, with flyover bridges and 'all the latest conveniences,' but precious little has happened since.

In 1934 a 'Five Year Plan' for the roads was announced, but the results so far have been negligible, unlike the activity in Germany and Italy, where the authoritarian governments have created huge new motorways, 600 miles in two years, in Germany alone.

Restrictions on the British motorist are on the increase–the 20 mph speed limit was lifted in 1930, only to be replaced four years later by a 30 mph limit in built-up areas, while Mr Hore-Belisha, the Minister of Transport, has inaugurated a new form of pedestrian crossing marked by flashing beacons.

The old haphazard rules for obtaining a driving licence have been swept away–now all new drivers have to pass a test, and third party insurance is compulsory.

Motoring is, in short, becoming far more organised, far more of a commonplace part of everyday life, as it has been in America for some time.

The 1937 Englishman's home, even if it's a speculative semi on the local bypass, is still his castle; his car, says one contemporary journalist, is 'the magic carpet that completes the tout ensemble.'

Winter Roads to Monte Carlo

The earliest rallies, as events we would recognize today, were trials, and the term 'rally', possibly less appropriate in English, was first used in France. 'Trial' continued in erratic usage, until well after the Second World War: in the title of a demanding round-Australia event, in British affairs with strong traditional and recreational flavours, and in that curiously British breed of trials cars, devices basically intended to ascend as far as possible tortuous short routes up steep rural banks in the only form of motor sport in which time plays no part.

Although its reputation is dubious among the modern rallying hardcore, the Monte Carlo Rally *is* rallying to most of the world, just as Le Mans is sports car racing and Indianapolis is track racing. At times, though, it has unquestionably been the outstanding rally. Monte Carlo rallies were run in 1911 and 1912, gentle affairs in no way comparable with the Alpine Trials of the period. They were won by G. H.

Rougier, who drove a Turcat-Méry from Paris, and J. Beutler, who drove a Berliet from Berlin.

The event was revived in 1924, when the winner was J. Ledure, in a 2 litre Bignan. He was the only starter from Glasgow, which somehow sounds implausible. But the basic plot was that competitors could choose their own start point, provided there was a recognized local motor club which would collaborate with the AC de Monaco in despatching them. In terms of scoring points, the further from Monaco the better, and 1925 winner Repusseau (Renault) even started from outside Europe (from Tunis). British interest was scanty, and in 1926 when the Hon Victor Bruce won the event in an AC he was the only British runner to start from Britain.

Just to get to Monaco was the aim, albeit an ambitious aim when a long car journey was still something of an adventure, and a long journey in the depths of winter from some of the

furthest flung corners of Europe was a very chancy undertaking.

Soon, however, some form of tests were needed after these concentration runs, and from 1925 in fact the regulations started to stipulate more than 'get here'. In 1930 there were 57 possible start points, ranging from Genoa (at a mere 190 km) to Talinn (3,474 km) and Athens (3,756 km). Maximum and minimum average speeds were 40 and 35 kmp (specifically, an average of more than 43 kmh meant instant disqualification), and the object was to arrive in Monaco between 10 am and 4 pm. Nothing would seem simpler than starting from Genoa? Each competitor was assigned 45 basic points; to these 0·015 points were added for every kilometre over 1,000, or 0·015 subtracted for every kilometre under 1,000. Hence the choice of starting from Athens (although nobody got through the wintry Balkans from Greece until 1931) or the Gulf of Finland was not urged by some sort of masochistic heroism in open

Goal for every leading rally competitor during his career—Monte Carlo. Crowds throng round the finishers in a mid-1930s 'Monte', with some open cars hinting at very spartan drives. *Below:* stamping around in the snow can have brought little relief from the cold inside this Singer Junior in 1927! *Following pages:* Isotta-Fraschini Tipo 8A of 1924–31 was a top vintage luxury car

cars through winters which invariably seemed to be snowy!

Further points were gained by the speed average (that ideal 40 kmh earning 200 points), and for passengers carried (hence four-man crews). And then there was a regularity test from la Turbie over two laps of the 50-mile Col de Braus circuit, where 'any delay caused by the closing of the Railway stile at Sospel will be neutralized;' the required average was 32 kmh, or 20 mph—tell that to latter-day Flying Finns!

In the mid-1930s the notorious driving tests, wiggle-woggles round pylons, decided the rally, and led to some odd specials. Zamfirescu and Cristea drove a Ford V-8 with trick brakes to win in 1936, from Berlescu's Ford V-8, which was a stripped chassis with a canvas body; then Donald Healey drove an Invicta, using very small 'spare' wheels for the tests—he lost to Vasselle, who changed the back axle ratio of his Hotchkiss en route, to give it a maximum speed of 37 kmh but outstanding performance in the vital 'flexibility test'.

This sort of thing spoiled what was in itself a most demanding winter event. Its nearest summer equivalent, for a few years from 1929, was the Alpine Trial (later Rally), where the timed climbs throughout the route where much more akin to modern special stages. In 1933 only three drivers completed the route without penalty, thus qualifying for Coupes des Alpes (there was no outright winner, and the real target was to complete three events without penalty and thus gain a gold Coupe). The 1931 Alpine, incidentally, saw the best British performance since Rolls' last works appearance in the event's distant predecessor, the Austrian Alpine Trial, when the three team Talbots completed the course without losing a mark.

The RAC Rally of Great Britain was also inaugurated in the 1930s, as a gentle concentration run to a common route, usually to a seaside resort. It was decided by driving tests, and as in the Monte Carlo Rally the associated concours d'elegance was almost unnecessarily important. Certainly there was no hint of the fierce international event the RAC was to become in the 1960s.

Indeed, rallying through the period is best not judged by today's standards, but by heroic individual performances. Like Jacques Bignan getting the first car through to Monaco from Athens, his big Fiat consuming seven sets of tyre chains en route. Or Mrs Vaughan, a surgeon, who started from Umea in northern Sweden in a small Triumph in 1932, stopped at a multiple accident in southern France and reputedly set four broken legs by the roadside—and she didn't lose her lead in the Coupe des Dames. Or Donald Healey, who won in an Invicta in 1931—from Sweden, where it savaged a telegraph pole, to Monaco it was a crab-tracked Invicta (this inveterate Monte trier later had one of the Alfa-inspired Triumph Dolomites torn to pieces around him by a Danish train when he was on his way to the Principality). In the 1930s, the 'Monte' was the Great Winter Adventure.

Cartoons from Monte Carlo Rally regulations suggest that from preparation to finish pre-war events were rather carefree! *Above centre:* the Col de Lecques was a familiar part of the Monte Carlo route for decades; a Delahaye *(left)* and a Ford climbing it in 1938. *Above right:* a Lancia in the snow-powdered Gorge de Verdon in 1938. *Far left:* a Peugeot in one of the wiggle-woggle tests used to decide many pre-war rallies. *Right:* SS1 tourer and coupe, travel-stained at the end of the 1933 Alpine Trial. *Below left:* testing trial—Aldington and Berry drove their Frazer Nash through the 1933 Alpine without losing any marks. *Below right:* scenic tour—an SS Jaguar 100 in the 1939 Scottish Rally

Planned Obsolesence and Peoples' Cars

The Wall Street Crash of 1929 had an immediate and dramatic effect on the American motor industry. That year production had reached an all-time record of 5,337,087, a million cars more than in 1928. The sudden collapse in buying power saw sales figures plummet faster than a lift in the newly-built Empire State Building: in 1932 output bottomed at 1,331,860.

Though new car production had dropped by 75 per cent, the number of vehicles in use remained remarkably constant, falling only 10 per cent, from 26,500,000 to 23,877,000 over the same period. It was obvious that, even though many Americans could no longer afford a new car, the old one had become too valuable a part of everyday life to be jettisoned at the onset of an economic crisis. It would just have to be kept going until things got better again. . . .

At first, the motor industry hoped that the depression was just a temporary setback and for Ford, at least, buoyed up by the continuing demand for the new Model A, the signs looked hopeful.

In the first five months of 1929, Ford made 30·5 per cent of all America's cars; in June the figure rose to 40 per cent of the market as other companies began to feel the force of the gathering storm.

On October 29, 'Black Tuesday,' the Stock Market collapsed in a frenzy of selling; within a year six million unemployed were asking plaintively 'Brother can you spare a dime?'

Ford sales fell from $1,145 million in 1929 to $874 million in 1930; General Motors sales from $1,500 to $1,000 over the same period. Ford had managed to outsell General Motors by some 300,000 vehicles–not bad for a one-model firm.

Chrysler managed to come through 1930 with a modest profit; Studebaker, Nash and Hudson were just surviving; Durant, Stearns, Moon, Kissel, Gardner and many other smaller independents just faded from the scene.

It was even tougher in 1931; Ford, pushing ahead with a world-wide expansion plan, saw sales cut by a half, a situation only marginally improved by the introduction of the new Model B– 'a corking good four'–and the brilliant V–8 in 1932.

Others were moving in to the attack. Willys-Overland were actually undercutting Ford prices with their Whippet model, a policy that probably aggravated financial problems that led to a second liquidation; Chevrolet, though slightly more expensive, were running Ford sales close; Chrysler, thanks to their lower-priced Plymouth range, were consolidated in their position as one of the big three of the Motor industry.

The improved Plymouth of 1931 offered a low, double-drop frame, freewheel and a flexibly mounted 'floating power' engine. A jubilant Walter Chrysler presented the third New Plymouth off the line to Henry Ford; within weeks the Plymouth was outselling both Ford and Chevrolet in some areas.

But none of these new cars was an economy model as Europe understood the term; despite their low price, all were relatively large vehicles, a type only possible in a country where fuel was cheap.

In fact, the differing social conditions in America and Europe led Ford to design their first 'all-European' model, the 8 hp Model Y (sold in Germany as the 'Köln') of 1932, conceived in Dearborn and modified at the new Thames-side Dagenham factory to suit the British market.

In Britain, where the depression began to bite in 1930, the big manufacturers were obsessed with an old preoccupation, the development of a £100 car.

Morris managed it in 1931 with a no-frills version of their 8 hp two-seater, and advertised that to become

In 1932, Hudson replaced the Essex with a new model, the 2.6 litre Terraplane; the Terraplane chassis was used in England as the basis of the Railton sports car. This is one of the first Terraplanes, still with Essex hubcaps: the driver is aviatrix Amelia Earhart

During the 1930s Ford organised their own motor show at the Albert Hall; the £100 8 hp Popular saloon was launched at the 1935 exhibition *(left)*. Morris' £100 Minor of 1931 *(above)* was an austere two-seater

'the two-car family ideal,' you only had to spend £214 on a side valve Minor saloon and a two-seater; Ford beat this in 1935 with the first £100 saloon car, the 8 hp Popular.

But even in the depression, little economy cars seemed too austere for the customers, who demanded extra refinements that cost just a little more–and eventually the economy models were issued in de luxe form; the cheap versions were dropped, and the cycle was complete, with the situation back where it started.

The £100 car was a chimera, but the quest for it occupied several makers who should have known better, for many years. Only the Ford Popular enjoyed any concrete success and even that didn't remain at £100 for long.

Nevertheless, by the mid-1930s the £100–£150 8 hp–10 hp class was dominating the market; apart from the Ford and Morris Eights, the Austin Seven, Singer Bantam and Standard Nine were competitors in this field.

These were positive giants compared with the smallest practical car on the European market, the Fiat 500, the price of which was inflated to £120 by import costs and modifications to conform with English taste.

The Fiat had a toylike four-cylinder engine of 570 cc and could carry two passengers at 50 mph, with a fuel consumption of 45–50 mpg; it was one of the sensations of the 1936 Paris Show (Simca built this model under licence for the French market).

The Fiat was the smallest example of the craze for streamlining which had swept Europe in the early 1930s, once the easing of the Depression made it possible for manufacturers to develop new models.

One of the first popular cars to be built in Japan was the Austin Seven-inspired Datsun of 1932 *(right)*. One of the smallest cars of the inter-war years was the 570 cc four-cylinder Fiat Topolino *(below)*, which cost £120 in 1937, and offered 50 mph *and* 50 mpg. Citroen's *traction avant* of 1934 nearly ruined the company, yet had a production life of 23 years

For, although purists regard the year 1930 as a watershed in car design ('pre-1931 GOOD, post-1930 BAD') in fact the true vintage car was already vanishing by 1928, to be replaced by an intermediate breed of car which stood between the uncompromising uprightness of the 1920s and the more meretricious charms of the 1930s.

It was in 1934 that André Citroën introduced his Traction Avant, which completely broke away from existing canons of design. Body and chassis were combined in one unit, and the 12 hp engine drove the front wheels. Torsion bar springing gave the car exceptional stability on bends–they called the Citröen 'the car you can't overturn.' It

American original: the Chrysler Airflow *(above)* foreshadowed future styling trends; this Airflow Eight of 1935 has a V-bonnet, added to soften the car's appearance. Japanese copy: Toyota model AA of 1935 *(top)* followed Airflow styling. The 1938 Corsair *(right)* had a Lycoming V-8 engine in a Cord chassis; its front seat was wide enough for four people

could reach 70 mph and cruise at 60 mph.

It was 'a car of daringly unconventional design,' and it broke André Citröen. Control of his company passed into the hands of the Michelin Tyre Company, but the Traction Avant continued in production until 1957 when its design features still seemed modern.

Other makers found that adopting independent front suspension enabled them to move the engine forward in the chassis to give extra leg room on a short wheelbase, and the system grew rapidly in popularity. In 1931 only 1·57 per cent of the cars on the British market had independent front suspension; by the end of 1936 the percentage had risen to 36·4.

Independent suspension formed a major part of the specification of the car which epitomised the streamlining craze, the Chrysler Airflow, designed by Carl Breer, who discovered by wind-tunnel testing that the conventional motor car was more aerodynamically efficient going backwards. So he set out to design a 'back-to-front' car.

The result, making Chrysler's tenth anniversary in 1934, was the revolutionary Airflow, a streamlined sedan with all the seats within the wheelbase, and chassis and body frame built as one unit. It was a pure Art Deco fantasy based on scientific tests and its influence on other manufacturers was widespread. But it was a commercial flop.

Even so, within months, Singer, normally one of Britain's more conventionally-minded mass-producers, were offering the 1·4 litre Airstream Eleven, which combined independent front suspension, a hydraulic clutch, free-wheel, and a Chrysler-style 'low air resistance shape' for a mere £300.

The Singer Airstream lasted only a few months in production, despite the claims that it was 'The Car of Tomorrow—Today,' and it was not long before commercial pressures forced Chrysler to modify their design in the interests of increased sales.

In 1935 the Airflow design was hurriedly modified to include a dummy bonnet with more conventional lines—'Added beauty without sacrifice of aerodynamic efficiency,' claimed Chrysler—and the Airflow range lasted until 1937.

By that time streamlining had become an accepted fact of motoring life—even some Rolls-Royce had acquired streamlined tails—but perhaps the movement's most bizarre flowering was seen at the October 1936 Paris Salon, held at a time of major political and industrial unrest in France.

Renault had adopted the new styling with enthusiasm, with the bonnet top merging into a rounded-off radiator shell, while the new Peugeots had the radiator curved to follow the contour of the front wings, with the front headlamps mounted beneath the grille. The front wings merged into the radiator shell and bonnet sides, with ample side valances, the rear wings enveloped the wheels to below hub level, and no running boards were fitted.

Centerpiece of the Peugeot stand at the Salon was 'the car of 1940,' a 402 saloon designed by the aerodynamicist Andrean; it had a rounded windscreen and a stabilising tail-fin, a feature shared in less exaggerated form by the Skoda coupé from Czechoslovakia.

The latter car, featuring a tubular backbone chassis and all-round independent springing, had its headlamps let into the wings under tiny slatted replicas of the radiator shell; so, too, had the extraordinary Panhard Dynamic, which had a sleeve-valve six-cylinder power unit and independent torsion-bar suspension all round. Body and chassis were built as a unit, all four wheels were concealed under metal spats and the driver's seat was in the centre of the windscreen, which had curved end panels for extra side vision. The windscreen was so shallow that triple wiper blades were necessary.

One of the foreign exhibits at that Paris Salon was the 'coffin-nosed' Cord from Auburn, Indiana, originally introduced in 1935, which had a bonnet with no visible radiator, just horizontal louvres wrapped around, plus retractable headlamps in the wings. Like the other model to carry Erret Lobban Cord's surname, the L-29 of the Depression years, the 'coffin-nose' had front-wheel drive: its advanced styling, by Gordon Beuhrig, was widely copied in watered-down form, but never in such a bizarre manner as by the Parisian *carossier* Henri Binder that October of 1936.

Monsieur Binder had taken a Rolls-Royce Phantom II and converted it into a passable replica of the Cord with a peaked 'coffin-nose' bonnet, with a raked front which completely concealed the traditional radiator, the only concession to convention being a tiny

By the mid-1930s, most popular cars followed the streamline fashions. The Riley Kestrel of 1933–38 *(top)* was one of the first fastbacks. Less well-balanced was the Flying Standard range of 1936 (Flying Twenty, *right*), with the engine pushed forward over the axle to give a curiously distorted profile. BMW were noted for their elegant sports two-seaters, but the designer of this 1937 saloon *(lower right)* obviously ran out of ideas when he reached the windscreen. The French Hotchkiss Ten *(bottom right)* is altogether crisper

Silver Lady where the radiator cap should have been. The car was only on show for two days before being withdrawn, apparently at the earnest request of the Rolls-Royce representative.

A couple of weeks later another unorthodox vehicle with wrap-around grille made its debut. This was the Fitzmaurice Special, based on the Ford V–8, and offering 'beauty of line combined with a semi-streamline form and exceptional body width'–but this time carrying the blessing of the chassis manufacturers, who exhibited it at their Albert Hall show.

The streamlining craze even reached Scandinavia: the Volvo PV 36 of 1936 was scarcely distinguishable from the remodelled Chrysler Airflow, while the same company's experimental Venus-Bilo of a couple of years later went *totus porcus* with full-width aerodynamic bodywork of singularly repellent aspect.

The radical changes in car styling during the early and middle 1930s seem

The 1930 Type 770 was the first
Mercedes to be dubbed 'Grosser', and
was indeed an imposing car. It weighed
53 cwt in normal form—armour-plated
versions for state occasions were of
course even more tank-like in
construction and weight—and was
propelled by a 7,655 cc straight-eight
engine, which in supercharged form
developed 200 bhp, giving the 770 a
maximum speed of 100 mph

Maybachs of the 1930s were equally
large, but their more elegant lines
concealed their bulk. This pair are both
V-12s, a 1938 cabriolet *(far left)* and a
1936 Zeppelin, a name recalling
Wilhelm Maybach's one-time association
with airship pioneer Count Zeppelin

Two British classics of the 1930s. The Siddeley Special *(left)* had a light-alloy 5-litre engine which gave this 1935 limited-production vehicle a 90 mph top speed. The 1936 Lagonda V-12 *(right)* was perhaps W. O. Bentley's finest design. Top gear range was from 7 to 104 mph, and the sporting version took third and fourth places at Le Mans in 1939.

to have been devised to make motorists dissatisfied with their old vehicles and buy new, despite the world depression. It was noticeable that as America climbed out of the depression in 1936, a year second only to the record of 1929 for new car sales, styling changes for 1937 were kept to a minimum.

'It is not,' pontificated one pundit, 'the habit of the industry to make daring innovations in the midst of a good buying cycle.'

Even so, whereas in 1935 manufacturers had been talking about marketing 'economy' models stripped of all unnecessary fittings and designed for low fuel consumption, in 1936 they were tempting the customers with bigger and better packages. Longer wheelbases, extra headroom gained by lowering the floor, bigger engines and wider, more spacious bodies were offered. All-steel coachwork, hydraulic brakes and independent front suspension were

almost universal, as were warm air heating and defrosting.

Overdrive–automatically coming into action at 35 mph on the Studebaker President–was becoming available on lower-priced cars, and there was optimistic talk of fully-automatic gearboxes in production cars by late 1937. And, as a sign of the times, between 30 and 35 per cent of new cars were being fitted with car radios.

In short, motoring for the man in the street was now more luxurious than it had formerly been for the wealthy. But there were drawbacks. The old idea that a car, properly maintained, should last for ever had become as obsolete as acetylene lamps.

Final-drive ratios had become progressively lower in an attempt to recapture the flexibility of the old cars with their low-compression, heavy-flywheel engines–the 1932 Talbot 65 had a 6·75:1 back axle gearing–and this,

coupled with the fact that engines now revved at twice the speed of the popular power units of the 1920s, meant that cylinder bore life was generally short: 'some engines will run 50,000 miles or

The changing shape of the American popular car: apart from its raked-back radiator and valanced wings, the 1934 Oldsmobile Eight *(below left)* has fundamentally the same profile as a late 1920s sedan. It is obvious, though, that the stylist has taken over from the engineer. The 1938 Mercury *(bottom left)* is a much more sophisticated packaging job, though its corpulent lines give it a more dated appearance to modern eyes than the earlier car. Mercury cars were introduced by Ford's Lincoln division in 1938 as an up-market version of the successful Ford V-8. They were directly competitive with the Buick *(below)*, which had coil springing all round. *Opposite page:* Ford's contemporary British lineup included this Eight *(top)*, with a basic shape which would epitomise the cheapest Ford cars until 1960, and the 22 hp Model 60 V-8

Mercedes-Benz moved into the economy class with the 'Heckmotor' (rear-engined) range of the mid-1930s, though this 1934 150 sporting two-seater *(right)* seems to be an object lesson in the mis-application of space. However, Daimler-Benz experience with rear-engined cars stood them in good stead when it came to building pre-production prototypes of the Volkswagen in 1937 *(below)*. In 1938, Adolf Hitler (with Ferdinand Porsche) laid the foundation stone of Volkswagen's Wolfsburg factory *(lower right)*

more without showing signs of wear, others may develop it in 10,000 miles,' commented *The Autocar*.

Yet many 1920s engines were capable of running ten times as far before a rebore was necessary–and generally at a lower fuel consumption.

The stubby right-hand gearchange of the early days had been replaced by a wavering bent-poker central change, distinctly lacking in precision. All-steel saloon bodies were prone to 'drum' and magnify the chassis noises. The concentration of weight above and ahead of the front axle, combined with low-geared spongy steering, meant dismal handling characteristics. But as so many of the motorists of the 1930s were first-time car buyers, naturally enough they were unaware of these shortcomings.

Earlier motorists may have bought their cars for the accessibility of their greasing points or the ease with which brakes or valve clearances could be adjusted, but it was styling which sold cars of the 1930s. The all-enveloping wings made it almost impossible to adjust the brakes without removing the wheels; the low-slung chassis were too near the ground for a conventional jack to be of any use in raising the car and the wheelnuts were all too often hidden under a chromed nave-plate.

'Modern cars,' complained one dissatisfied owner in 1936, 'would be 100 per cent more "get-at-able" if their designers were made to work in a garage or workshop for at least two years. On one popular American car the front wheel and half a mudguard have to be removed to get at the tappets.'

But he was wasting his breath, and the sales figures proved it.

Between 1930 and 1935 the volume of traffic on Britain's roads increased by 47 per cent; private car registrations rose over the decade between 1929–39, from 1,042,300 to 2,134,000–but America's annual output exceeded the latter total by 100 per cent.

These were sales figures achieved in free societies, where consumers had a free choice as to what they could buy. But Adolf Hitler, leader of the new Nazi government in Germany, believed that public demand could be channelled to political ends. He offered a modest subsidy to Dr Ferdinand Porsche to develop a cheap 'People's Car' which would attract the German car-buying public, and keep their money inside the Fatherland, strengthening Germany's currency.

The more people who bought, the cheaper the car–it was a Teutonic ad-

aptation of the Model T Ford success story, but with the grim twist that the 'Kraft durch Freud' (Strength through Joy) car could easily be adapted for military use.

The new Volkswagen, it was claimed, owed much of its inspiration to a design by Hans Ledwinka, the brilliant engineer at the Tatra car works in Czechoslovakia, and was intended to be produced at the rate of a million a year, to sell at £80. The war intervened, and only 100,000 or so Volkswagens were produced during the period of hostilities. The heyday of the VW was yet to come.

There was something prophetic in the birth of the Volkswagen: it was a car built to create a market, not to meet an existing need, and was a modern expression of a concept that had become unfashionable with the passing of the Model T. It was a design which would span an era of major change in automobile design, during which standards were to become more and more debased, until production engineers learned to control the new methods they had created.

The motor car of 1939 came off badly in comparison with its predecessors, but things were to get a great deal worse before they improved.

The Speed Kings

The nature of the Land Speed Record changed rapidly after the First World War: the machines became increasingly specialized; speeds soon became too high for roads or even relatively spacious banked tracks to be suitable venues for attempts—only vast naturally flat areas, seaside beaches or later salt flats, could provide the required unimpeded distances; with only two exceptions between the wars, the Land Speed Record became the property of a handful of British drivers. Segrave, Thomas, Campbell, Eyston and Cobb were the heroes of the Golden Age of record-breaking, in cars which became household names—*Babs,* the '1,000 hp' Sunbeam, *Bluebird, Thunderbolt,* the Railton Special.

The most famous names in 'tween-wars record breaking were Campbell and *Bluebird.* Here Sir Malcom breaks the record for the sixth time (Daytona, 1933)

First Hornsted's 1914 record had to be beaten, and so for that matter did Héméry's 125·95 mph set in 1909 (see Chapter 7). Ralph de Palma improved upon it in 1919, and in 1920 Tommy Milton exceeded 150 mph (156·03 mph) in a twin-engined Duesenberg. Both however were one-way runs, and the record did not fall until 1922, when for the last time it was broken by a multi-purpose car and on a track. The car was the 18·3 litre 350 hp Sunbeam, in which K. L. Guinness achieved a mean of 133·75 mph at Brooklands. Malcolm Campbell later used this car, as *Bluebird,* to break the record three times, in 1925 raising it to 150·87 mph.

In the previous year, the record had twice been raised in an encounter which was reminiscent of an earlier age of motor sport, when on a narrow tree-lined road near Arpajon in France René Thomas and Ernest Eldridge met at a sprint meeting. Thomas took the world record at 143·31 mph in a relatively sophisticated 10·6 litre Delage, then Eldridge bettered his speed in a crude Fiat special—this had a 21·7 litre aircraft engine and chain final-drive appropriate to a pre-1912 grand prix car. Eldridge's time was disallowed on the technicality that the car had no reverse gear; with this rectified he recorded 146·01 mph, and the last outright record set on a public road.

The sophistication of the next Sunbeam to take the record was almost ludicrous in contrast. This had an engine of only 4 litres, made up of two straight-six 2 litre GP units mated in a V-12. Henry Segrave drove it on Southport Sands to inch the record up to 152·33 mph. Later in 1926, however, on consecutive days on Pendine Sands, Welshman J. G. Parry Thomas nudged it well on towards 200 mph, with

Above: H. O. D. Segrave on Daytona Beach with the '1,000 hp' Sunbeam in 1927, when he became the first man to lift the record above 200 mph
Right: Frank Lockhart with the ultra-efficient Stutz Black Hawk Special —with a mere 3 litres, this car exceeded 200 mph, before Lockhart crashed

speeds of 169·30 mph and 171·09 mph. His car was the equal of the Eldridge Fiat in crudity; under its streamlining, the Higham Special *Babs* had a 26·9 litre Liberty V-12, which drove through an old Benz gearbox and chains. Making another attempt at Pendine, in 1927, Thomas was killed as *Babs* went out of control and rolled over.

Thomas was attempting to regain the record from Campbell, who had averaged 174·88 mph in a new 22·3 litre *Bluebird*. This was to undergo several reconstructions, the first in response to a dramatic new machine, the '1,000 hp' Sunbeam. The two 22·5 litre V-12s in this car probably mustered less than 900 bhp, but there was an impressive ring to a four-figure power output; the whole car certainly looked impressive, with its smooth bodywork extending over the wheels. Segrave took it to Daytona, and exceeded 200 mph (203·79 mph).

This was beaten by Campbell within a year, and then by Ray Keech in the monstrous White-Triplex, which had three 27 litre 12-cylinder Liberty engines, one ahead of the driver, two side-by-side behind him! Keech set a brave 207·55 mph in this 81-litre device, while Frank Lockhart with the petit 3 litre Stutz Black Hawk Special threatened humiliation (Lockhart exceeded 200 mph on his first run, and was travelling faster on the return when the Stutz

crashed, and Lockhart was fatally injured).

Before turning to speed on water, Henry Segrave shattered the record again, with the dramatically handsome Irving-Napier *Golden Arrow* (231·44 mph), then for the first half of the 1930s the record was Campbell's. By the end of 1935 he had pushed it over 300 mph (301·13 mph), at a significant new venue, the Bonneville salt flats in Utah. Here every subsequent outright record was to be set.

In the three years before the outbreak of the Second World War, two Englishmen with two outstanding cars attacked the LSR at Bonneville. George Eyston's *Thunderbolt* was impressive rather than handsome. It weighed 7 tons, was powered by two Rolls-Royce 36·5 litre V-12s with a combined output of some 4,700 bhp, had six wheels (of which the front four steered), and a form of disc brake, mounted inboard on the second pair of front wheels and the transmission at the rear. With *Thunderbolt* in its

original form, with a vast radiator intake in the nose and a large tail fin, Eyston took the record in 1937 (312·00 mph) and 1938 (345·50 mph). Later in 1938 he lost it to John Cobb, who raised it to 350·20 mph in the beautiful Railton Special, but regained it on the following day with a speed of 357·50 mph; between his two 1938 records, Eyston modified *Thunderbolt* to improve its aerodynamics, fairing the nose and relying on tank cooling, and removing the tail fin.

The last word belonged to John Cobb in the Railton, however. In August 1939 he set the record beyond immediate challenge at 369·74 mph. On the salt flats, Reid Railton's car was not to be matched in sophistication for another 20 years (although it might have been if Porsche's Mercedes-Benz T80 had not been stillborn). The two 26·9 Napier engines of Cobb's car drove through all four wheels, and their combined 2,500 bhp had to propel only 3 tons. The driver sat in a closed cockpit

in the extreme nose, and the smooth body lines were only slightly marred by the humps which accomodated the wheels. The design speed was 400 mph, which was to be so nearly achieved in 1947. . . .

Throughout the 1920s and 1930s all forms of record breaking flourished, as never before or since, although by no means all of the achievements were officially-recognized records, rather exploits which caught public imagination and were meat and drink to advertising copy-writers.

Duration and distance record-breaking was popular. Thus Studebaker advertisements in 1929 could shout 'Round the World in Sixteen Days!,' a reasonable interpretation of 30,000 miles at 68·36 mph (less reasonably, disregarding niceties like classes, they claimed in the Brooklands Double 12 programme 'every officially recognized world's record between 10,000 and 30,000 miles . . . not won by specially constructed racing cars but by eight-cylinder cars taken at random from normal production').

An extreme case was the marathon drive by Marchal and colleagues in the Citröen *Petite Rosalie*, which circulated Montlhéry apparently interminably in 1933 (actually for 133 days, covering 180,000 miles at 58·07 mph). Ab Jenkins really put the Bonneville salt flats on the record map with his long-distance records with Auburn, Duesenberg and Mormon Meteor specials from 1932. These culminated in 1940, when Jenkins covered 3,868 miles in 24 hours.

This type of record-breaking was also George Eyston's real forte, for although he is best remembered for his Land Speed Record efforts, at times he

Above: George Eyston first took the LSR with the dramatic *Thunderbolt* at Bonneville in 1937. The car had to be push-started by a mundane vehicle. *Right:* Eyston in one of the many machines he drove to break class records, in this case MG EX120, the first 750 cc car to exceed 100 mph. *Below:* the 40 hp Lanchester during an attempt on the 12-hour record at Brooklands in 1924, driven by Parry Thomas, Lionel Rapson and George Duller

Top: twin rear wheels were favoured on hill-climb cars for many years, here by Raymond Mays, in a typical attitude as he flings his ERA up the Shelsley Walsh climb, and by Hermann Lang, in a GP Mercedes at Vienna in 1939.
Above: foretaste of things that were to come—Opel's rocket-propelled RAK 2

held many distance or duration records, from one hour to 48 hours, in a variety of cars. Eyston was one of the drivers associated with special MGs which set some astonishing capacity class records. For example, EX120 was the first 750 cc car to exceed 100 mph (at Montlhéry in 1931); EX127, the Magic Midget, exceeded 120 mph three years later, and in 1936 raised the 750 cc flying mile record to 140·6 mph. EX135, which was to become associated above all with Goldie Gardner, had a Railton-designed body as svelte as that on the Cobb LSR car; on the Dresden autobahn in 1939 Gardner drove it to cover the flying-start kilometre at 203·54 mph with an

1,100 cc engine, which was undoubtedly one of the outstanding pre-war record performances (and closely approximates to Segrave's world record with the 45-litre Sunbeam only 12 years earlier!).

The folly of using roads, even roads as advanced as autobahnen, for record attempts had been tragically demonstrated early in 1938, when the brilliant racing driver Berndt Rosemeyer attacked Caracciola's 268 mph Class B records, which had been set in a Mercedes. His ultra-streamlined Auto Union went out of control on the Frankfurt-Darmstadt autobhan during the attempt, and Rosemeyer died as it crashed into a wood.

A decade earlier a German sprint novelty had appeared, and disappeared without seeming at all significant. However, the Opel rocket-powered RAK cars of 1927–28 foreshadowed developments then many years away—in

not using internal-combustion engines, in not using any form of drive through their wheels, and in using stub wings to induce downforce.

The carefree era of hill climbing in Britain ended when a spectator was injured at Kop Hill in Buckinghamshire in 1925. Until then, some police forces had turned benevolently blind eyes to at least this type of competition on public roads, and amateur meetings had flourished; after the Kop accident, hill climbing was restricted to a few short hills on private ground, such as Shelsley Walsh, where the challenge of shaving fractions of a second from times continues at amiable gatherings. A new impetus was given to this branch of the sport when the European Mountain Championship was introduced in 1930, and attracted some of the top road race drivers and teams—Hans Stuck took the first championship, Hermann Lang the 1939 series.

Power without Glory
racing as a propaganda weapon

By 1931 grand prix racing was recovering from its doldrums. In the previous year the Maserati brothers had produced a new eight-cylinder car, and had raced the V4 16-cylinder car, the first of several 'twin-engined' machines which were to appear in the early 1930s (the V4 had two 'eights' mounted side by side on a common crankcase). The 8C was very successful, albeit there was no modern machinery to oppose it.

This was remedied in 1931, when a complex set of GP regulations was abandoned in favour of two simple requirements—two-seater bodies and 10-hour minimum race durations for *grandes épreuves* (full national European GPs, as distinct from lesser local grands prix, such as the Rome or Tunis GPs). As far as the complexity of regulations are concerned, those must have been halcyon days for anybody connected with the sport: the 1931 International Sporting Code of the AIACR was a 76 page book, the equivalent section of the 1971 FIA Year Book occupied 256 more closely packed pages.

The prospect of stability encouraged Alfa Romeo and Bugatti to build new cars. Vittorio Jano took the successful six-cylinder sports Alfa as his basis, designing a 2·3 litre eight, which had its cylinders in two blocks of four, with a central gear train to drive twin overhead camshafts, Roots supercharger and ancillaries; initially this unit gave 165 bhp, which sounds modest enough compared with the engines of the mid-1920s, but proved adequate for a season.

Ettore Bugatti introduced the T51, which closely resembled the T35 'family' in layout, but had a twin-ohc hemispherical cylinder head 2·3 litre engine (Bugatti had clung overlong to his three-valve single-ohc design; in 1929 he had acquired two 'Packard Cable Special' Millers from Leon Duray, who was financially embarassed after the Monza GP and traded the cars for three T43s and the Atlantic fare; twin-ohc Bugatti engines followed, the first in the T46 touring car).

The Alfa and the Bugatti took the major honours in 1931, and in 1932 there was a further stimulant to constructors when the anachronistic requirement for two-seater bodies was dropped, and race duration cut to five hours. One result was the first monoposto grand prix car, and the finest GP car in the vintage tradition, the Alfa Romeo Tipo B, or 'P3'. Jano enlarged his eight to 2·65 litres, to give a still-modest 180 bhp in 1932; it drove through two propeller shafts, splayed at 30 degrees behind the gearbox, to twin final bevel drives. Nuvolari drove the P3 to a debut victory, in the Italian GP, and thereafter it dominated the season, with 1–2–3 placings in the French and German GPs, and defeats only in the Czech and Marseilles GPs.

Leading drivers during this period—which was to prove to be an interlude between GP stagnation and revolution—were men from the 1920s: the great Tazio Nuvolari, whose fiery brilliance epitomised the Latin racer; Giuseppe Campari, who was to die in an accident which should never have been allowed to happen, in what was to have been his last race (the 1933 Monza GP, when Campari, Czaikowski and Borzacchini all crashed fatally because oil was not properly cleared at one corner); Louis Chiron, the dashing Monégasque who upheld the honour of France; Rudolf Caracciola, who performed miracles

Monaco, 1933, and an assortment of Bugattis and Alfa Romeos typical of the period. There was one big difference about this race, however—Varzi, in a works Bugatti T51, is starting from the pole position he earned by setting fastest lap in practice

1934 saw advanced German technology change the face of Grand Prix racing. But it did not reach down to the many minor provincial events once a vital part of the racing scene. On a typical French road circuit, at Dieppe, Louis Chiron on an Alfa P3 leads Lord Howe in a T51 Bugatti *(left)* and that happy warrior Phi-Phi Etancelin forges on in an 8CM Maserati

with cumbersome Mercedes sports cars before turning to Alfas for a brief period; Achille Varzi, in temperament so unlike Nuvolari, but so often his bitter racing rival. For Britain only George Eyston and Sir Henry Birkin featured among the leaders in GP results, and Birkin contracted fatal scep-

ticeamia from a minor exhaust burn during the 1933 Tripoli GP meeting.

That season saw glory returning to the GP circuits, and the final flowering of a line of cars which could be traced back to 1912. Alfa Romeo withdrew, entrusting their reputation to the new Scuderia Ferrari, and jeopardizing it by witholding the P3s until mid-season! The Maserati brothers revamped their straight-eight, with a 3 litre engine and −12 years after Duesenberg had demonstrated their efficacy at Le Mans—hydraulic brakes 'all round'. Bugatti had the T51, by the grace of Alfa suddenly competitive again, although there were obvious misgivings at Mol-

sheim, for as in 1927, the Bugatti team was scratched from the all-important French GP.

Late in the year, the Bugatti T59 appeared, in a way fittingly, for it was the last of a line of GP cars in the old style. It had a supercharged straight-eight, a superbly-proportioned 'two-seater' body, and aesthetically-attractive wire wheels. It had rigid suspension, front and rear (ironically, in view of Bugatti's much-quoted jibe about Bentley making the fastest lorries in Europe, a leading British independent driver later

Monoposto. The Alfa Romeo Tipo B—popularly P3—which was one of the greatest GP cars in the old tradition

Out of period, yet almost true to period. J. Venables Llewellyn's 1935 ERA at Pardon, during a VSCC Prescott hill-climb in 1972

commented that this Bugatti handled like a lorry!). The T59 was exceedingly handsome; it is also a hard truth that as a GP car it was useless.

Bugatti took the Monaco GP in 1933, after one of racing's classic duels; Varzi –who had taken pole position on the first grand prix grid to be determined by practice times–and Nuvolari fought 'tooth and nail' throughout the 100 laps, Varzi conclusively winning when the engine of Nuvolari's Alfa failed on the last lap. By mid-season, Bugatti and Maserati successes had persuaded Alfa Romeo to release the P3s to Ferrari, and these cars resumed their winning ways.

Through the year a new set of regulations had been known. Stipulating a *maximum* weight of 750 kg and a minimum body cross-section at the cockpit, these seemed to promise to prolong the active life of existing cars, which would require only minor modifications. But in Germany, two constructors, state

aided and abetted, started from scratch and within the same rules came up with startling new designs.

Dr Ferdinand Porsche designed a radically new car for a consortium of minor manufacturers, linked under the name Auto Union. His P-Wagen had a 4·35 litre V-16 engine mounted between cockpit and rear axle in a rigid tubular frame, and independent suspension to all four wheels. For Daimler Benz, Nibel and Wagner designed the W25. Although outwardly less unconventional than the P-Wagen, this Mercedes brought together for the first time in a front-engined car independent suspension all round, hydraulic brakes, and a gearbox differential attached to the frame, and therefore sprung weight. The straight-eight M25 engine of the W25 followed orthodox Mercedes practice, and in its initial 3·36 litre form, produced over 350 bhp.

Both cars had a considerable power advantage over Italian and French cars, and both had new handling qualities. The Mercedes was 'soft', when jarring rigidity had been considered funda-

mental to racing cars in the past, but was otherwise straightforward; the handling of the Auto Union posed problems for drivers, who had to adapt to new techniques (in fact, of established drivers only Hans Stuck was able to make the transition easily).

These German teams were not all-conquering in their first season, most notably when they first raced outside Germany, in the 1934 French GP. One by one the Mercedes and Auto Unions fell out, and only three Alfa Romeos

Bugatti built this adventurous, albeit cumbersome, four-wheel drive T53 in 1931. It proved difficult to drive, ran in practice for one GP, and was mainly used in hill climbs

The old and new orders met in full strength for the 1934 French GP at Montlhéry. Chiron made a brilliant start—perhaps a jumped start—in his Alfa Romeo, and led an Alfa 1–2–3 at the end of the race. No other cars were classified as finishers, for as the race went on, the dead car park filled up. *Below:* among the mechanical casualties were Dreyfus' Bugatti T59, Fagioli's Mercedes, Momberger's Auto Union, and Nuvolari's Bugatti

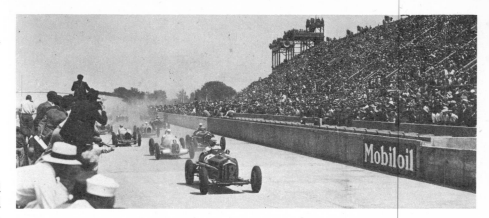

completed the full race distance, headed by Louis Chiron. As the teams gained experience, however, they went from strength to strength, and stop-gap measures by other constructors were fruitless—hastily enlarged engines, still in chassis which were now obsolete, were no answer to modern technology applied to racing. Auto Union won the 1934 German, Swiss and Czech GPs, while Mercedes took the Italian and Spanish races, as well as secondary events.

The Germans changed their cars in detail for 1935, both Mercedes and Auto Union enlarging their engines (to 3·99 litres and 430 bhp and 4·95 litres and 375 bhp respectively). Bugatti drifted haplessly towards grand prix oblivion; Maserati enlarged their 'six' and worked on a sound V-8-engined car (which had their development resources been anything like adequate, might have become a worthy contender); Alfa Romeo worked too slowly on a V-12; Scuderia Ferrari revamped the P3, grafting on independent front suspension and enlarging the engine to as much as 3·8 litres, and put together two of the infamous *bimotore*. This car used P3 components, and two P3 engines (one ahead of the driver, one behind him) which had a combined power output of around 540 bhp; the car handled badly, and had a phenomenal appetite for tyres; Chiron managed to place one second in the Avus race, Nuvolari and Chiron the pair fourth and fifth at Tripoli.

The season belonged to Mercedes, whose cars were beaten only four times, to Auto Union who were distant runners-up with victories in the Italian GP and two lesser events, and to Tazio Nuvolari. In an amazing virtuoso drive at the Nürburgring he led the might of Germany in the German Grand Prix at the end of 10 laps; an inept fuel stop cost him five places, but he overcame even this handicap to thrash his out-

classed P3 back up the order to start the last lap in second place. The leader was Manfred von Brauchitsch, very much a German of those nationalistic times, hungry for the honour of winning the *Grosser Preis*; justice was perhaps done when one of his rear tyres blew, and the astonishing Nuvolari passed him to win.

Engines were larger still in 1936, demonstrating once and for all the folly of regulations which do not restrict capacity. Mercedes' 4·74 litre M25E developed 494 bhp, and in the C-type Auto Union, the V-16 was enlarged to 6 litres, to produce 520 bhp. But Mercedes mounted their unit in a new short chassis, which proved very difficult to handle; Caracciola won the opening races of the year, at Monaco and Tunis, but thereafter the team was consistently defeated—indeed, their entries for three late-season races were withdrawn.

The German, Swiss and Italian GPs fell to a brilliant newcomer from the world of motor cycle racing, Berndt Rosemeyer. He had no pre-conceived ideas about a car's handling qualities, and took to the Auto Union immediately. Mercedes shortcomings let Alfa Romeo into the top placings, for the

new V-12 performed well—excellently by P3 standards, although those were no longer the norm. The German teams did not cross the Atlantic, for the first American race for Grand Prix cars since the First World War, albeit on the 'Mickey Mouse' Roosevelt Raceway on Long Island. Nuvolari won the 300-mile G. Vanderbilt Cup in a V-12 Alfa at 65·99 mph.

The next year was different, and in terms of sheer power the all-time pinnacle of grand prix racing. Mercedes came back with the W125—a new chassis, de Dion rear axle, and a 5,660 cc straight-eight, where, for the first time on a Mercedes the mixture, rather than air to the carburetter, was compressed by the supercharger. In its maximum state of tune, this engine produced 646 bhp at 5,800 rpm, 114 bhp per litre. The 6 litre Auto Union engine (incidentally, the largest seen in GP racing since 1913) gave 520 bhp, the Alfa Romeo V-12 little over 400 bhp.

To drive their formidable cars, Mercedes looked hard for a team of German drivers, but team manager Neubauer was forced eventually to give priority to ability. Caracciola was ever a Mercedes stalwart; Hermann Lang had

Motor racing for prestige—the legendary German cars of 1937. Donington *(top)* saw the last race of the formula: three Mercedes lead at the start; Rosemeyer *(top right)* won the Donington race, which was to be his last; a Mercedes leaping over the crest of the hill up from Melbourne corner. *Above:* in this classic German GP pit stop shot of Lang's Mercedes, a mechanic is lifting a new wheel onto a rear hub before the discarded one has come to rest. *Right:* Caracciola and Brauchtisch leading at Monaco

With very few exceptions, the major single-seater races between 1934 and the outbreak of the Second World War fell to the German Auto Union and Mercedes teams. *Left:* H. P. ('Saucy' to the English!) Muller on the way to his only Grand Prix victory, driving a V-12 Auto Union in the 1939 French GP at Rheims

Left below: Manfred von Brauchitsch throwing his Mercedes W154 into a corner on Berne's beautiful but demanding Bremgarten circuit during the 1938 Swiss Grand Prix

Below right: voiturettes, in all but designation the Formula 2 cars of the mid 1930s. Richard Seaman enjoyed a run of success in 1936 with the one-time GP Delage, revamped by Giulio Ramponi. The Isle of Man crowd looks extraordinarily unprotected by modern standards.

The trio of ERAs *(bottom)* are leading the field away at the start of the 1935 Dieppe GP des Voiturettes. Seaman is driving the 1,500 cc R1B (no 10), next to him are Mays in the 1,500 cc R4B and Fairfield in the 1,100 cc R4A

risen from the ranks, and as a one-time mechanic was never wholly acceptable to some of his driver colleagues (but within two years was to mature into the best Mercedes driver); Brauchitsch was less talented, but made up a leading trio of Germans. The *auslanders* were Neubauer's second string: Italian Geoffredo Zehender, Swiss Christian Kautz, and Richard Seaman, who was to prove the best of the three, and was to gain immortality in now-fading British racing lore when he won the 1938 German GP.

Mercedes (seven victories) and Auto Union (five victories) completely dominated the 1937 season; Auto Union's respectable tally was largely owed to Rosemeyer; in those 12 principal races, only a single third place fell to a non-German car, Rex Mays' eight-cylinder Alfa in the Vanderbilt Cup.

The 1937 season, and the 750 kg formula, ended in England, where top-line single-seaters had not been seen for years. Oddly, perhaps, this was not in a British GP, but in a race at Donington Park which roughly equated with the Coppa Acerbo, or a latter-day event like the Race of Champions at Brands Hatch. The 'locals'—teams and spectators—were shattered by the performance of the German cars. Here, Berndt Rosemeyer won his last race, for during the winter, glory-seeking by Auto Union led to his death in an insignificant class record attempt on the Frankfurt-Darmstadt autobahn.

One result of German GP might in the mid-1930s, was an upsurge of interest in second-level racing, which in today's terminology would be called Formula 2. Here, as in most other fields, Bugatti was fading, but Maserati were strong with the 4CTR and from 1936 the 6CM, and Britain was a force in single-seater racing.

The ERA sprang from the famous 'White Riley' raced by Raymond Mays. It followed orthodox early-1930s monoposto lines, with a straightforward pushrod ohv 'six', of three alternative capacities, 1,100 cc, 1,500 cc and 2 litres, with Roots-type superchargers; in 1,500 cc form this engine produced 150 bhp at 6,500 rpm. Nothing startling about it—save that it was a competitive British single-seater.

Between 1934 and 1936, 17 A- and B-type ERAs were built. In the hands

173

Throughout his career, Raymond Sommer would race anything, anywhere. He placed this outclassed Alfa Romeo 8C 308 fifth in the 1939 French GP

of drivers like Seaman, Mays and Bira, they became familiar on the circuits of Europe (and as well as winning races, they took hill climbs and class records), and indeed they remain familiar in British historic car races today. Later ERAs, which had Zoller-supercharged engines, were less competitive, as development lagged behind when Continental constructors took 1½ litre racing more seriously.

A pace-setter in voiturette racing in 1936 was a car almost ten years old—one of Lory's Delages built to the 1926–27 1½ litre grand prix formula. After passing through the hands of Louis Chiron (who placed it seventh at Indianapolis in 1929) and Lord Howe, it was bought by Dick Seaman, and virtually rebuilt by Giulio Ramponi. He extracted 195 bhp from the engine, some 25 bhp more than the Delage team in 1927! Seaman really confirmed his stature with this car, consistently beating 'modern' machinery, before joining the Mercedes grand prix team.

By the late 1930s, 1½ litre racing was becoming much more professional, and standards rose rapidly as companies like Alfa Romeo entered the class. By one of those odd racing coincidences, the most sophisticated circuit cars of the 1920s and 1930s, the 1½ litre Fiat 806 and the 1½ litre Mercedes W165, were both raced only once. A pair of W165s were designed and built in less than six months, when the Italians announced their decision to run the rich Tripoli

GP for 1½ litre cars. Outwardly, the W165 resembled the contemporary W163 GP Mercedes, and in fact had identical chassis, running gear and transmission. Like the W163 it departed from Mercedes precedents in having a vee engine, a compact V-8 which produced 260 bhp when the cars raced at Tripoli. Here, to the consternation of the Italians, Lang won at 122·91 mph from team mate Caracciola.

The German team might not have enjoyed such an easy victory if the Alfa Romeos 158s had not over heated, for Farina drove a 158 with a revised cooling system to win the 1940 Tripoli race at 128·22 mph.

The 158 which was to become famous as a grand prix car from 1946 until 1951, first appeared as the 'Alfetta' in 1938. Colombo designed around one bank of cylinders from the Alfa V-16 GP engine, and the twin-ohc Roots-supercharged straight-eight produced 195 bhp at 6,500 rpm when the car was first raced, to win the 1938 Coppa Ciano. In 1939 the elegant 158s were beaten only once, at Tripoli.

Maserati's answer to the 158–although never its equal–was the 1939 4CL, which was also to become a grand prix car, and as the 4CLT, a leading private owner's car in the late 1940s. This also used a 'half engine', although in this case the 3 litre 8CTF 'eight' was derived from the four-cylinder unit.

Meanwhile, in 1938 a rational engine capacity grand prix formula had come into force, and proved its value as a stimulant to design progress. This admitted unsupercharged engines of up to 4½ litres, supercharged units of 3 litres, and the supercharged German cars built

to it proved to be no slower round circuits than their 5·6 and 6 litre predecessors.

Mercedes had the W154 and in 1939 its sleeker W163 derivative, with a 2·96 litre V-12. This most 'un-Mercedes' format was adopted in a search for more power per litre; greater piston area than would have been possible with a straight-eight, was coupled with higher rpm in this twin-supercharged engine, to achieve 483 bhp at 7,800 rpm in 1939 (163 bhp per litre). Auto Union also used a V-12 in their D-type, and in 1939 this produced 485 bhp at 7,000 rpm; very much to the point, the cockpit of this car was further back in the wheelbase, so that drivers' 'seat of the pants' reactions were no longer so irrelevant as they had been in earlier Auto Unions.

The Maserati brothers' resources were pitiful compared with those available to the German teams, otherwise their 8CTF might well have been a challenger for top honours; as it was, Trossi led the Mercedes for a while in the 1938 Coppa Ciano, and Paul Pietsch briefly led the German GP with an 8CTF. With this model, the supercharged multi-cylinder engine was firmly re-established as a force at Indianapolis, when Wilbur Shaw won the 500 with the 'Boyle Special' 8CTF in 1939 and 1940.

Despite their increasing pre-occupation with 1½ litre racing, for the GPs, Alfa Romeo essayed an 'eight', a V-12 and a V-16. None produced adequate power (the best in this respect, the V-16, gave some 350 bhp), but somehow Farina overcame this handicap to place a V-16 second in the 1938 Coppa Acerbo and the Italian GP. These cars, incidentally, were run by Alfa Corse, for Enzo Ferrari had severed his long association with Alfa Romeo.

French constructors opted for the unsupercharged alternative, Talbot and Delahaye running adaptations of their big sports cars. They were enormously encouraged when Dreyfus in a Delahaye beat the Mercedes in the first race of 1938, a minor affair at Pau. But, in fact, the ratio of 3:4·5 favoured the supercharged cars, and equality was not to be achieved until a decade later, when

Below: Mercedes sophistication. The German team raced the sleek W163 in the 1939 GPs, when their most successful driver was one-time mechanic Hermann Lang, here on his way to victory at Pau. The very efficient W165 *(right)* voiturette was raced only once, in the Tripoli GP, and once again Lang won
Bottom left: Hans Stuck drove this Auto Union into sixth place in the 1939 French GP; Rene le Begue follows in the Talbot he placed third.
Bottom right: distasteful nationalism— Richard Seaman looks mildly abashed after winning the 1938 German GP for Mercedes, but doubtless *Korpsfuhrer* Huhnlein is making the most of the occasion in his oration

supercharged engines were restricted to 1·5 litres, and 4·5 litre normally aspirated engines, were still permitted.

Mercedes reigned until the Autumn of 1938, taking coveted 1–2–3s in the French and Swiss GPs. Towards the end of the year, however, Nuvolari gave Auto Union fortunes a much-needed fillip, when he took the Italian GP by a clear lap, and the Donington GP after a fiery drive.

The Mercedes team was the most successful in 1939, too, when Lang emerged as their leading driver. Rudi Caracciola scored his sixth German GP victory, which was fitting, as it was to be his last major race victory. Dick Seaman died in the burning wreck of a W163 at the sometimes beautiful, too often grim, Spa circuit in Belgium. Yet another motorcyclist turned Auto Union driver, H. P. ('Saucy') Muller, won the French GP. Tazio Nuvolari scored the last victory of the season, in the Yugoslav Grand Prix, on September 3, 1939.

The era which ended in Belgrade is usually recalled as a glorious one of power and speed. Technically it was

indeed rich, but only in its last two seasons was all-round efficiency the aim; the earlier striving for sheer brute power was less laudible. Mercedes showed just what could be achieved in performance and race results, if vast resources were applied to motor racing; Auto Union pointed the way ahead, although in retrospect they might in six seasons have advanced to the stage where when racing resumed the accepted place for a grand prix car's engine to be was behind the cockpit?

On the other side of the coin, GP fields were often very thin, and races frequently processional; when the French GP was run for single-seaters again in 1938, nine cars started, three completed only one lap, four finished— which made for a very tedious three hours at Rheims.

Racing was debased as never before, or since, as an instrument of state propaganda—on that score alone, the pre-1934 battles between archaic Alfas, Bugattis and Maseratis were surely to be preferred to the startling technical progress and occasional spectacle gained at such a heavy moral price?

Something Old, Something New

The ink was hardly dry on the surrender documents that ended the Second World War when Britain's motor manufacturers began reorganising their plants to produce cars once again. It was a task of considerable magnitude, for most of them had totally converted their factories to produce aero engines, aircraft frames, tanks, armoured fighting vehicles, munitions, guns and ammunition; output of utility vehicles and staff cars was just a small part of this activity. Not only did the manufacturers have to retool for new models, or in most cases the old ones, they also had to find the appropriate raw materials, a difficult problem at a time of universal shortages.

Nevertheless, in the first month of production, July 1945, Britain's motor industry turned out 258 cars and 5,113 commercials; by January 1946 the figures had risen to 10,620 cars and 9,153 commercials. Within six months output had almost doubled: in June 1946, 20,139 cars and 12,934 commercials were produced, rising to a combined total of 34,477 by September, contributing to an annual production from October 1945 to September 1946 of 151,322 cars. Already the industry was bettering pre-war production levels, yet the demand for cars was almost insatiable.

Waiting time for delivery of most cars was a matter of many months, partly caused by an edict of Clement Attlee's Socialist Government that half the industry's output of private cars should be exported. Motorists counted themselves lucky if they could take delivery of any new car, regardless of make, nationality or engine size. In November 1946, London dealers were quoting a possible (no promises, mind you) delivery time of two years, and were turning away deposits from prospective buyers because they already had more orders than they could cope with.

Another factor was the shortage of steel sheet, caused partly by reduced imports from the United States, partly by the British Government's decision to give priority for steel supplies to other industries, especially housing.

The motor industry was planning for a target of 600,000 cars in 1947, but the shortages caused them to rethink their plans. Vauxhall, for instance, cut back from a target of 80,000 vehicles to a more realistic 55,000. One consequence of this restriction was that prices and costs could not be accurately controlled, nor could economical production levels be reached.

New car prices – 80 to 90 per cent higher than pre-war levels – were only one of the problems facing the British motorist in 1946: the Government added 30 per cent purchase tax to the cost of his new car, then taxed it at £1 per horsepower. And to make matters worse, petrol was strictly rationed by the Petroleum Board, formed at the start of the war. The unbranded 'Pool' petrol cost 1s 11d a gallon (10 pence in today's terms); it was rated at 70 octane, and the ordinary family motorist got just about enough for 270 miles' motoring every month.

Even when he managed to take his car for a run, he could not buy new tyres for it unless he was one of the fortunate few who held an 'Essential' petrol ration book. Not that there was a shortage of rubber – the tyre makers hadn't had time to change over from the huge moulds needed to produce military truck and aircraft tyres to the smaller car tyre moulds.

Just to add to the muddle, many of the 1,790,000 pre-war cars still in use were in a fairly derelict condition, and manufacturers just couldn't afford to make enough spare parts to keep them all running.

'The rate at which old cars will be dropping out altogether, and existing cars reaching the condition when their owners will want to replace them,' claimed *The Times*, 'would probably outstrip the total production of new cars today.' Even if half that output had not already been earmarked for export. . . .

The first British car to appear after the war that was not just a reworked 1939 model was the 16 hp Armstrong Siddeley, made by a firm whose products had hitherto been noted for a combination of high engineering standards and ponderously ugly coachwork. But the new car was regarded as among Britain's most handsome post-war cars; it was available with three types of coachwork, with names – Hurricane, Lancaster, Typhoon – that recalled Armstrong-Siddeley's contribution to the wartime aircraft industry. Available with either a four speed synchromesh gearbox or the marque's traditional preselector transmission, the 16 hp Armstrong Siddeley had torsion-bar independent suspension at the front, and could exceed 70 mph.

A complete about-face was also apparent in the post-war programme of the Jowett Motor Company, whose early models with the famous flat-twin 'little engine with a big pull' once had a

Austin's first post-war model was the 16 of 1945 *(top)*, which used a 2.2-litre ohv engine in a body designed in 1940. The Morris Eight *(below)* was a pre-war model which remained in production. It was replaced by 1949 by the famous Morris Minor

Jowett's Javelin *(above)* was one of the most advanced popular models of 1947, while the Invicta Black Prince *(above right)* boasted a specification too complex for commercial success. Vauxhall's 12 hp saloon of 1941 *(right)* looked conventional enough, but featured unit body/chassis construction, as did the Issigonis-designed Morris Six introduced in 1948. The Vauxhall remained in production in the post-war period

clothcap image entirely appropriate to their Yorkshire hometown of Idle, near Bradford, where racing pigeon lofts dot the hillsides above the mills. But the 1946 Jowett Javelin was a remarkably sophisticated design aimed at the mass market. Its welded-girder body/chassis frame had separate panels, while the suspension was by torsion bars all round, independent at the front. Its flat-four engine gave a lively performance, its low profile and low centre of gravity, coupled with soft suspension that hardened up on corners, gave excellent roadholding. The Javelin may not have enjoyed the sales its manufacturers envisaged, but it certainly achieved a lasting reputation.

New, too, was the 3·8 litre Jensen, whose luxury specification even included an electric immersion heater in the cylinder block for easier starting in cold weather and the Bentley-designed $2\frac{1}{2}$ litre Lagonda, with twin-overhead camshafts and Cotal electrically-controlled transmission. The most remarkable post-war vehicle of all was almost certainly the Invicta Black Prince, which pioneered automatic transmission, its Brockhouse Turbo-Transmitter being controlled by a 'forward, reverse, neutral' switch on the dashboard – there was no clutch pedal. 'Driving the Invicta therefore requires the very minimum of effort and skill.'

The 3-litre engine of the Black Prince had twin-overhead camshafts, three main carburetters, two starting carburetters, 24 volt silent dynamotor starting

plus 12 volt lighting, and an electric heater in the radiator helped those 24 volts to turn the engine over in cold weather. Originality didn't stop there: the welded box-section frame, braced by a massive cruciform girder, was independently sprung all round on hydraulically-damped torsion bars, inboard hydraulic brakes were fitted on the back axle, permanent hydraulic jacking was featured, and the light alloy coachwork had seats on a rubber-mounted panel to isolate the passengers from any body or chassis vibrations.

Its makers might have guessed that the Black Prince was altogether too advanced for commercial success; only a handful were built.

Conventionality, it seemed, was the most profitable course. Ford announced in October 1946 that their Dagenham factory had produced a million vehicles since its inception in 1931, while the Morris-dominated Nuffield Group was capable of building a million pounds' worth of cars a month – £500,000-worth for export, of course!

In America, however, restrictions were even more severe. After VE Day, the industry was granted permission to produce a total of 200,000 private vehicles during the remaining months of 1945 – provided that it could find materials to build them with. Although the numerical restriction was lifted after the Japanese capitulated, an outburst of wildcat strikes combined with the shortage of raw materials to push production costs sky-high. But the Office of Price Administration, which the

Truman administration had instituted to try and check post-war inflation, decreed that new-car prices should be based on 1942 costs.

On the face of it, this was a logical demand, for the 1945 models were little changed from their immediate predecessors: but the big mass-producers were unable to turn out sufficient cars to bring down the unit costs to anything like this level.

'It costs us $1,041 to make a car' complained Henry Ford II, who had taken over and revitalised the Ford Motor Company from his ailing grandfather, 'but we are restricted to selling it at a maximum of $780.'

'Mr Ford is selfishly conspiring to undermine the American people's bulwark against economic disaster,' countered Chester Bowles, head of the OPA, whose terms of reference apparently blinded him to the fact that the members of the motor industry were American citizens as worthy of attention as any car-buying consumer.

The main result of the OPA's restrictions was that virtually any piece of rolling junk could be sold at an inflated price on the car-hungry market.

Fortunately, the price controls were lifted in 1947, and the increased output of new cars soon restored the financial balance of the industry, though inflation had lifted the cost of the new car to twice pre-war levels. In 1949, the average new American car cost around $1,800, had an eight-cylinder engine and, almost certainly, heater and radio. Automatic transmission, still a rare luxury item in Europe, was a commonly demanded option in the USA.

Even at the higher prices, the customers bought – to such good effect that in 1949 the industry turned out 5 million cars, at last exceeding the record output level of 1929. In 1950 more than 8 million cars and trucks were built and even the outbreak of the Korean war failed to have more than a marginal effect on civilian production.

The rise in output was matched by a major road building programme to cope with the 25-million-plus cars that were now registered in the United States; this figure was to double by the mid-1950s, and almost treble by the late 1960s, despite a minor recession after the peak year of 1955, when nearly 8 million cars were built.

The rise in output had frozen out the smaller independent companies, who had been able to compete successfully while restrictions had held back the big three – General Motors, Ford, Chrysler – but who could not compete with the economics of mass-production on the grand scale.

Even old-established companies like Studebaker-Packard faded away gradually, and the bold attempt by Henry J. Kaiser to establish a new automotive empire foundered on the Kaiser-Frazer Corporation's inability to establish a solid marketing network for its Kaiser, Frazer and Henry J models, which had managed to grab 5 per cent of the 1948 sales charts, only to vanish completely by the early 1950s.

Nor did Preston Tucker, with his radical rear-engined Torpedo, or Powel Crosley with his sub-compact Hotshot, manage to break into the industry, despite the enthusiastic acclaim for the design of their cars. It seemed as though, when it came to buying a new car, the American motorist would always go for the safe, conventional choice, with a known service and spares record. But the minor export successes of European models on the American market showed that there were weak spots in the sales armour of the big three which determined sales tactics could penetrate.

Perhaps the most striking post-war revival of all was that of the German Volkswagen. Apart from the stigma of its pre-war Nazi backing, the much-vaunted 'People's Car' was to be built in a factory that had been flattened by Allied bombing and, apparently, had no export hopes. British experts had looked over the works to see whether it had any commercial future, and condemned the Volkswagen out of hand:

'This car does not fulfil the technical requirements which must be expected from a motor car. Its performance and qualities have no attraction for the average buyer. It is too ugly and too noisy. Such a type of car can, if at all, only be popular for two to three years at the most.'

So the army of occupation smiled gently when a handful of former VW employees asked permission to restart production among the ruins; starting with salvage work, they built 1,785 cars in the remaining months of 1945, raised production to an astounding 10,020 in 1946 and, despite growing

Dollar grin days: the 1951 Buick *(below left)* typifies the exaggerated styling of the immediate post-war American car, while the designer of the 1949 Nash *(below right)* seems to have been determined to keep the wheels out of sight. The Kaiser and the Frazer *(bottom)* represented the last major attempt to launch a new American car group; one reason for its failure was the lack of an adequate dealership network

Bombing had reduced the Volkswagen factory to near ruins during the war, and when the Allied commission inspected the factory after the Armistice, they were distinctly unimpressed by the product. Even the amphibious *Schwimwagen (left)* failed to live up to their 'technical requirements'. Yet the Volkswagen went on to become the most popular car in motoring history, with a body shape little changed (1964 version, *top*), apart from more window area, from the 1937 prototypes shown on page 162. Ambitious cosmetic coachwork can be fitted to the VW chassis platform: one of the most sophisticated conversions is the Brazilian-built Puma GTE *(above)* from Sao Paulo. More widely familiar were the many open fun cars or beach buggies based on the Beetle, normally using its chassis and mechanical parts with skimpy plastics bodywork. These originated in California, the first being the Meyer's Manx

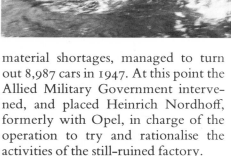

material shortages, managed to turn out 8,987 cars in 1947. At this point the Allied Military Government intervened, and placed Heinrich Nordhoff, formerly with Opel, in charge of the operation to try and rationalise the activities of the still-ruined factory.

'The future,' said Nordhoff portentously, 'begins when all ties with the past have been severed.' He insisted on sole command of the factory, without interference from anyone, even the occupying Powers!

To be sure, Nordhoff had problems: 'I knew neither the factory nor the product, I had to start absolutely from scratch,' he recalled a decade later. 'With 7,000 workmen we built under great stress 6,000 cars in one year – provided it didn't rain too heavily, as the

roof and all the windows of the factory had been destroyed!'

Even in war-shattered Germany, there was a vast demand for transportation, and Nordhoff, without any tangible financial backing, did his utmost to fulfil that need.

He asked his dealers for cash in advance – and got it, brought to the works in pockets, parcels and suitcases bulging with new notes. He had even bartered cars in exchange for production necessities, and by the beginning of the 1950s had managed to open export markets in Switzerland, Holland and Belgium. The much-needed foreign currency provided a solid basis for the rebuilding of the works and the expansion of production. In 1950 the daily output was 515 cars; by 1954 this

figure had been doubled, and the next year the millionth Volkswagen left the factory. By the end of 1957, the second million had been reached, and the rate of expansion continued to rise – 5 million had been produced by 1962. A decade later VW exceeded the Model T Ford's all-time record of 15 million plus, even though the company had diversified into more sophisticated designs to capture a greater market spread.

Even now, there seems to be no end in sight for the jelly-mould shape of the VW 'Beetle,' which seems to flaunt its 1930s contours as a symbol of permanence in a changing world. The 'no-change' policy transformed the ruins of a Hitlerian dream into one of Europe's biggest car factories within 15 years.

Hard Times for the Specialists

The post-war materials shortages and sales restrictions may have been a nuisance to the large-scale producers; to many smaller manufacturers they proved fatal.

Isotta Fraschini, for example, planned a comeback after the war with a new luxury model for the American market, the Monterosa. Announced in 1947, it had a rear-mounted 3·4 litre V-8 with a single-overhead camshaft, driving through a five-speed gearbox; independent suspension was fitted at the front, while the rear end was 'semi-independent,' mounted on rubber cushions and hydraulic shock absorbers. But probably no more than 20 Monterosas were built, none seems to have been sold, and by 1949 Isotta had ceased production.

Other classic marques were finding survival impossible, especially in France where the taxation structure had been heavily weighted against luxury cars. Delahaye had taken over Delage in the mid-1930s, and the group's post-war plans included continued production of the 1935-designed Type 135 six-cylinder 3½ litre model – 'a superlative machine built with great care and precision based on the fruits of long experience' – fitted with the Cotal electromagnetic gearbox. This was controlled by a miniature steering column-mounted lever working in a gate 'with four speeds, either forward or reverse or neutral.' At least one owner proved that his Delahaye was as fast in reverse as it was in forward gear before he lost control. . . .

At first it looked as though the combined efforts of Delahaye and Delage would succeed in spite of the restrictions; in 1946 a total of 417 cars was produced, and by 1950, when a reasonable export business had somehow been built up, 483 cars were turned out. But the collapse, when it came, was rapid: only 77 Delahaye/Delage cars were built in 1951, and by 1952 the Delage was no more.

The old Type 135 Delahaye appeared for the last time in 1952, alongside the firm's last fling, the 235, a reworking of the 1935 model with the engine – which was basically the firm's bread-and-butter truck power unit – up-rated from 130 to 152 bhp, but the new model was too costly for the post-war buyer. The black two-door saloon bodied by Antem of Paris shown at the 1952 London Show was good for around 120 mph; but so was the XK 120 Jaguar, which cost less than £1,800 against the Delahaye's £4,750.

In 1954 Delahaye had been taken over by Hotchkiss: car production was found to be less profitable than truck manufacture, and though the Delahaye name faded away in 1956, Hotchkiss are still active builders of *camions*.

Slightly better fortune was enjoyed by Britain's luxury car makers, who in the main built cars as a spin-off sideline from more profitable ventures, like aircraft engineering.

Lagonda and Aston Martin had shown how necessary a second string was to the car manufacturers' bow. Lagonda, having taken on W. O. Bentley as chief designer in 1935, planned to use

Isotta Fraschini's last new car was the rear-engined 8C Monterosa of 1947 *(below)*.
Gregoire followed up the post-war 600 cc front-wheel drive saloon with this 2-litre flat-four. It was later built by Hotchkiss

his name on a post-war 2½ litre model aimed at a wider market than the V-12 of the late 1930s; the 'Lagonda-Bentley' was designed with all-round independent suspension, a Cotal gearbox and twin-overhead camshafts. But Rolls-Royce, owners of Bentley Motors (1931) Ltd, instigated costly legal action to restrain Lagonda from using 'Bentley' in the name of the new model, the Labour government refused to allow more steel than could be used to build 100 cars and the company ran out of money. Two new Bentley designs, a five-cylinder radial-engined 1,360 cc model and a torsion-bar suspended air-cooled flat six, were shelved, and the company passed into the hands of the David Brown organisation in 1947, as did the ailing Aston Martin concern. At first Aston Martin used their own design 2 litre four-cylinder engine with

Last of the *grands routiers*: the two Delage D6 dropheads *(below)* appeared at the 1946 Paris Show—the one with the lightning flash along the side was bodied by Antem—but only a few were produced before the company was absorbed by Hotchkiss, whose 3½-litre Model 686 of 1949 *(bottom left)* was descended from the 1928 AM80. The last new Bugatti model *(bottom right)* was the Jaguar-like T101

pushrod valve gear, but by 1950 both marques were fitted with the Bentley six, a power unit that proved capable of much development over the next two decades. Within the security of the David Brown group, which specialised in gear manufacture, the two companies flourished, although their designs became more rationalised in the interests of more efficient production, and it was no great surprise when the Lagonda name was dropped in 1963.

Harder hit than the car makers, who, even for limited production luxury machines, could use up-to-date techniques developed by such allied industries as aircraft manufacture, were the quality coachbuilders. The coming of the all-steel, integral body/chassis unit hit them hard, especially the host of body-builders who had existed before the war by series-producing special coachwork for mass market cars. In any case, the coach-building industry had been contracting since the end of the vintage era: at the 1928 London Motor Show, there had been 62 exhibitors in the carriagework section; ten years later the total had fallen to 27, and at the 1953 show, there were just 15 coachbuilders. Of these, six were divisions of the major manufacturers, including three companies that were showing un-

modified production bodies, the rest covering the entire range from convertible or estate versions of mass-produced saloons to Rolls-Royce and Bentley limousines costing well over £6,000.

The British coach-building industry had learned much from wartime experience, with techniques such as forming curved wood framing from laminated strips rather than sawing from the solid, or fabricating metal parts from welded-up components rather than blacksmithing them from the raw iron; but the market for coach-built cars was contracting rapidly – even Rolls-Royce announced a 'standard steel' saloon, which eliminated yet another traditional sector of the coachbuilder's clientele.

Eventually, apart from the very few special-bodied Rolls-Royce Phantoms built for royalty, the activities of the luxury coachbuilders who had once offered a bespoke body for every purchaser of a luxury chassis were restricted to minor trim alterations.

One of the most famous Rolls-Royce coachbuilders, in fact, had become just a facade by the late 1960s, with conversion work carried out, not in their luxurious premises, but by a sub-contractor based under a London railway arch.

The first post-war Rolls-Royce model was the 4.4-litre Silver Wraith *(above)*, here seen with 1952 Mulliner coachwork. Mulliner was also responsible for the fastback Bentley Continental of 1952 *(right)*. Rover's 75 saloon of 1949 *(below)* was a complete breakaway from this firm's previous models; for some time a third headlamp was a characteristic feature of this car The 2.6-litre Lagonda of 1948 was W. O. Bentley's last car design *(below right)*

In America, changes had been even more sweeping. Packard, once the supreme arbiter where elegant coachwork was concerned, had been persuaded by President Franklin D. Roosevelt to sell nearly all their body dies to the Russians during the war; from October 1945 to September 1947 they produced just one model, the 21st series Clipper, from the 1942 dies that remained. Then they unveiled their new model, the 22nd series, based on a pre-war 'dream car'. Its bulbous styling earned it unkind nicknames like 'inverted bathtub' and 'pregnant elephant', but it sold in numbers great enough to justify its $15 million development cost. In 1949 Packard marked its golden jubilee with the 23rd

Series, with the new Ultramatic transmission. Sales of 104,593 were a near-record for the company, but they were selling to a new kind of customer, who was spending surplus post-war income on a once-in-a-lifetime purchase, and would not come back for a new model in the future. Packard's traditional customers had deserted in droves, for the more opulent charms of the Cadillac and Lincoln Continental, and the net result was a dramatic drop in Packard sales.

In an effort to save the company, the board brought in a new president, Jim Nance, whose whiz-kid sales techniques had dramatically boosted sales of Hotpoint domestic appliances. But what was good for washing machines

proved to be quite ineffectual for cars. All the company's records and spares for their classic models were ruthlessly scrapped, and a hasty new model development plan undertaken. Inevitably, the company overstretched its finances, the new model proved to have too many teething troubles, and a 1954 merger with Studebaker turned out to be a disaster. By 1958 the new management had killed Packard; Studebaker followed six years later.

The role of the coachbuilder in America was reduced even further than that of his European counterpart; the famous coachbuilders became just design studios, whose names were perpetuated in badges stuck on the sides of mildly modified production limous-

Lincoln's 1952 Capri pillarless coupé *(above)* had a 5½-litre V-8 power unit—and dummy air scoops on the rear wheel arch!
Right: The same company's Mercury 4.2-litre sedan of 1949 *(right)* had all-new styling plus coil-spring independent front suspension.
Below: the decline in standards of a once-proud name is evident in the horrid Packard Patrician 400 of 1952, an object-lesson in misapplied decoration. Even the old Packard pelican mascot seems to have been restyled into a chrome-plated vulture!

ines. One American coachbuilder for example, learned sufficient of his trade in Paris to call himself a *carossier*; his output consisted mainly of vulgarly bodied Cadillacs for oil-rich sheiks whose sole desire was for vulgar ornamentation to indicate how many thousands of dollars they had spent on their vast, chrome-bedecked vehicles.

More fortunate, perhaps, was the fate of the Lincoln Continental, originally conceived as a 'dream car' for Edsel Ford, using so many standard parts from the 1939 Lincoln Zephyr range as possible, but with panels cut-and-shut to give the car lower lines. The spare wheel was mounted externally on the car's tail, a position that had been unfashionable since the late 1920s. In October 1939 the Lincoln Continental went into limited production, and was declared by an avant-garde architect as 'the most beautiful car ever designed.' The company, more modestly, claimed the low, sleek Continental as 'a friend of the wind and not an obstruction.' Just 5,322 of the original model were produced in the 1939–42

and 1946–8 periods, and three years after the model had been dropped, the New York Museum of Modern Art selected it as one of eight cars outstanding in their excellence as works of art.

In 1955 came the Continental Mark II, but it was overpriced, and lacked the panache of its forebear; so did the Mark III and Mark IV Continentals of 1959–60. For 1961, however, Ford announced a new Lincoln Continental in the classic tradition, with severe, unadorned lines that stood out among its over-chromed contemporaries. Half the model's production time was taken up with checking and testing including

a 12-mile road appraisal for each car. Less than 100 of the new model were produced daily, a tiny output by Ford standards. Though by European standards the 1961 Continental looked a shade ponderous, the American Press was enthusiastic, praising its combination of classic beauty with modern functionalism.

Though such eulogies tended to exaggerate the car's virtues, they did show that even in the mass-production-oriented atmosphere of the late 1950s and early 1960s it was still possible for a thoroughbred marque name to be revived with dignity.

Austerity and Flamboyance

Pre-war methods and models may have been sufficient to carry most manufacturers through the immediate post-war period, but it was obvious that this state of affairs had to change. One technical advance that had made its first tentative appearance before the war was the pressed-steel monocoque body/chassis structure, which offered increased torsional rigidity and could give increased interior space; but it did mean that production methods had to be rethought, for the necessary jigs and dies were expensive, and their cost could only be absorbed over a considerable production run.

One of the first all-new post-war designs was the 1948 Morris Minor, designed by Alec Issigonis, which had torsion-bar independent front suspension and a rigid rear axle on leaf springs housed in a unit-constructed body/chassis which aped, as nearly as post-war austerity would permit, post-war American styling. The fact that the car had to use the pre-war 918 cc Series E side-valve power unit, rather than the more powerful 'flat four' driving the front wheels that had originally been planned for the Minor, was hardly noticed among the post-war climate of shortages. Most of the early production went for export, but among those who managed to secure delivery of one of the few 1949 Minors released on the

May 1950—post-war petrol rationing ends in Britain, and London motorists queue to fill their tanks with coupon-free fuel

Standard's Vanguard *(top left)* was one of the first post-war unit-constructed models. Its styling was obviously influenced by American trends, as was the 1949 Morris Minor *(top right)* designed by Alec Issigonis. This car could have become the British equivalent of the Volkswagen—it was produced for well over 20 years—had BMC production been more rationalised. *Above left:* Triumph's 1800 of 1946 harked back to pre-war styling; the 1951 Hillman Minx *(above right)* updated a theme dating from 1932. The Minx name was finally dropped in 1970.

British market was the racing driver B Bira – Prince Birabongse of Siam.

Another post-war unit-constructed design came from the Standard Motor Company of Coventry, which had merged with Triumph in 1945. They planned a one-model programme based on a six-seated family saloon, the Vanguard, with a 2·1 litre ohv wet-liner four-cylinder engine; the car had the bulbous, overblown look common to so many of the early unit-constructed cars. Although Triumph adopted the 2·1 litre Vanguard engine for their post-war model, originally intended to be equipped with a 1·8 litre Standard unit, this Renown epitomised traditional British styling, with 'razor-edged' coachwork in the idiom of the late 1930s. In 1949 a smaller version of this car was announced, the 1¼ litre Triumph Mayflower, which had a maxi-

mum speed of 63 mph and remained in production for only four years, (although the Renown lasted until 1955).

In fact, at the beginning of the 1950s, the most highly regarded British cars blended 'traditional' and 'aerodynamic' styling in a not-always-happy combination. Forward engine mounting and generously skirted wings were ill-suited to traditional radiator shells, though the post-war Rileys managed to preserve much of the elegance of earlier models.

Austin, on the other hand, had thrown out most of its pre-war sense of middle-class conservatism after the death of Lord Austin in 1943, and the company's post-war family models, the 1·2 litre Devon and Dorset were styled for the export markets, especially the US where over 85,000 Austins were sold in 1948. Unashamedly aimed at America was the A90 Atlantic, which in 1949 broke 63 American stock-car records at Indianapolis, averaging 70-plus mph over 11,875 miles in appalling weather conditions. Priced at £888, the Atlantic boasted such refinements as an electrically-operated hood, but sales were not up to expectations and the model's production run was shorter than anticipated.

On the Continent, manufacturers were less dominated by the mechanical convention that bound English and

American manufacturers to the front-mounted water-cooled engine, rear-wheel drive layout. Citroen, for example, had been working in secret throughout the German occupation to develop a super economy car with front-wheel drive – 'four wheels under an umbrella,' was how Citroen's general manager, Pierre Boulanger, described the project. Based on a 1939 prototype, the 1948 2 cv Citroen had a geared-up 375 cc flat-twin engine developing a road burning 8 bhp, giving a 34 mph top speed. Bodywork, painted a utilitarian grey, had the gawky air of an illicit liason between a Nissen hut and a deckchair.

But the concept was ideally suited to the French market, and even a production rate of 1,000 a day wasn't enough to meet demand: by the 1970s well over 2·5 million 2CVs – now with a choice of 435 cc or 602 cc engines – had been sold, yet demand was still rising. One thing puzzled the French – foreigners never took enthusiastically to the model.

Renault, too, had come up with a new economy model for the new Europe; again developed secretly during the Occupation, the 760 cc 4 cv had a rear-mounted four-cylinder ohv engine developing 19 bhp, with a 60 mph top speed. Over a million were built before the model was dropped in 1961,

With all the elegance of a four-wheeled Nissen hut, this is the sole surviving prototype of the 2cv Citroen

and the 4 cv was built under licence by Hino of Japan.

One of the most ambitious post-war economy car projects, however, was French by birth, British and Australian by adoption. In 1945 the front-wheel drive pioneer J. A. Gregoire announced a new design, a 600 cc front-wheel drive saloon with a frame and dash made from Alpax aluminium alloy; this assembly weighed only 100 lb. Its flat-twin engine developed 15 bhp, and suspension was independent all round.

The car was never put into production as a Gregoire, but several companies bought manufacturing rights. Panhard used this model as a basis for their Dyna, which featured torsion bar

Variations on a theme by J. A. Grégoire —the 1946 Kendall *(left)* was an unsuccessful 'People's Car', while the Dyna Panhard *(right)* was the foundation for Panhard's last production models

valve springs and light-alloy coach-work, but which had a solid beam axle in place of the Gregoire's independent rear suspension.

This design was also fixed on by the British Member of Parliament Denis Kendall as a suitable basis for manufacture at Grantham, Lincs, in a £200 'People's Car' project, but only a few were built before the factory closed in November 1946.

The story then shifted to Australia, where J. A. Hartnett, who had helped launch General Motors' Holden in 1948, felt that there was an untapped market for a small car, and eventually secured the Gregoire rights. But he did not get all the state backing he anticipated, and the bodywork supplier failed to deliver the panels on time, so that eventually only 120 hand-built Hartnett-Gregoires were built, in 1950–51.

Fiat, who dominated the Italian industry, were concentrating on economy, too. The faithful 500 was available in 1949 in three models, a saloon, a

convertible and a 'Belvedere' station wagon. There were also an 1,100 cc and a 1,500 cc model: one variant of the '1100', the 1100S sports saloon, carried neat swept-tail coachwork by Pinin Farina; it had a greater compression ratio than the standard model, which gave it a maximum speed of 87 mph, at which speed it consumed petrol at the rate of 22 miles per gallon.

In America, however, economy seemed to be the last thing that manufacturers were thinking of: instead, it was the period of the 'Dollar Grin', when stylists endowed cars with a profusion of chromium plating, especially about the radiator grille and light assemblies.

Lincoln, for example, gave the Continental more bulbous wings plus a redesigned chrome-bedecked, front end – and completely destroyed the model's classic appearance. Edsel Ford, the Lincoln Continental's progenitor, had died, and without his guidance the corporate stylists had run wild.

But the late 1940s didn't just bring an

over-exuberance of styling to the American car; there were also significant technical advances, like the adoption of automatic transmissions on most ranges. Automatics had long been a dream of motor manufacturers, but the necessary manufacturing ability was missing until the late 1940s (though the fluid flywheel had long been a feature of Daimler cars).

Buick, indeed, announced that their 1949 models had virtually eliminated gear-changing, manual or automatic: the Dynaflow torque-converter was said to be 'devoid of clutch and all gears save reverse and an emergency "low".'

When in 1950 Buick became the fourth manufacturer ever to produce over half-a-million cars in one year, 429,903 of the total of 552,827 were fitted with Dynaflow.

Sealed-beam headlights, too, were becoming almost universal as were heaters and car radios.

But these innovations apart, the typical American car of the period was quite unadventurous mechanically. It seemed as though mass-production had reached the point where only detail refinements to a basically conventional package were possible.

In 1951 Simca launched the Aronde *(top)* which was a complete breakaway from the old Fiat-based Simca Huit. Its Italian Fiat equivalent was completely redesigned as the 1100/103 in 1953 *(below)*. The Mercedes 170 *(right)* of 1947 was an updated version of a model introduced in 1931.

Commissars' cars. The Zis of 1945
(right) was a Packard which was 'given'
to the Russians. Its successor, the 1956
Zil *(below)*, was a more up-to-date
Communo-Packard, built complete with
all the chrome ornamentation felt
essential in the capitalist West.
Bottom: the 1968 Zil 114 was more
restrained

Proposals for cars driven by reaction engines are as old as motoring history—indeed, models driven by simple steam engines ('acolipyles') were built in the 17th Century. But it was not until 1950 that the first successful 'jet' car appeared, built by Rover as a logical development of their Second World War work with gas turbines.

This car, the JET 1 *(top left)* won Rover the Dewar Trophy in 1951. In the following year it reached 151.965 mph over a flying kilometre.

BMC's gas turbine car *(top centre)* was based on an Austin Princess, and appeared cumbersome with its nose extension. The last Rover gas turbine passenger car *(top right)* on the other hand was a polished design, with front-wheel drive and disc brakes all round. Its sleek unit-construction body served as the basis for the Rover 2000 piston-engined car.

In 1963 Rover carried the gas turbine theme into competition, with an entry in the Le Mans 24-hour Race *(above left)*. This car used a BRM Formula 1 chassis. As a formula equating its engine with a conventional power unit could not be agreed, it ran with the other cars, but not in direct competition against them (driven by Graham Hill and Richie Ginther, it covered the eighth greatest distance in 1963, at an average speed high enough to have won the 1955 24-hour race outright).

In 1965 a more polished version of this car ran in open competition with piston-engined cars *(above centre)*. Later it was driven on public roads in England, and road-tested by *The Motor*. The journal recorded a maximum speed of 127.3 mph (although on the long straight at Le Mans it had reached 142 mph); at 100 mph it achieved 21 miles per gallon of kerosene. This Rover was a much more practical design than the ludicrous General Motors Firebird *(above right)* which was hawked round the motor shows in 1956. This was a far cry from the first gas turbine car actually to run on American roads, the 1955 Chrysler *(far left, top)* which was outwardly identical to the contemporary Plymouth, save for its wide exhaust duct. Dodge's Turbo Dart *(far left, lower* with its engine compartment, *left)* was released in limited numbers to private motorists in 1962 for experimental everyday use.

So far, however, the gas turbine has proved impractical for motor cars, although a few gas turbine trucks have been marketed

Last Classic Racing Era

Racing picked up quickly in Europe after the Second World War – indeed, the French contrived to run a meeting in a Paris park only three months after fighting ended. Something like a season of races was run in 1946, when the settings and many of the performers appeared to have been carried over almost without interruption from 1939. There were no German cars, of course, and there were no new cars. But there were front-line cars, the Alfa Romeo 158s which had been carefully hidden during the war. They were raced four times in 1946, failed at their first outing but in the Grand Prix des Nations at Geneva began a fabulous run of success. Through 1947, the Alfas set the standard for the new Formula I which came into effect in 1948.

This equated 1·5 litre supercharged engines with 4·5 litre unsupercharged units – a much more realistic equation than in 1938–39, and one which in time was to lead to parity between the two types of power unit. Immediately, the Alfas were little changed – 275 bhp was adequate in 1947, 310 bhp in 1948, especially as the driving squad of Alfa Corse was so formidable (Varzi, Trossi, Wimille, with Sanesi a first reserve).

The supercharged opposition largely consisted of four-cylinder Maseratis, while the French ran unsupercharged cars, notably the Lago-Talbots. Though seldom able to challenge in terms of sheer speed, these benefitted from their much better fuel consumption, which meant that they could run through a 500 km grand prix with only one fuel stop, whereas the blown cars had to stop two or three times.

As so often through racing history there were white elephants. France had the CTA-Arsenal, with a V-8 designed by Lory of Delage fame installed in a chassis of antiquated conception. Raymond Sommer, associated with more than one lost cause, made the only race start in a CTA-Arsenal; a half shaft broke as he let in the clutch at the start of the 1947 French GP. There was the E-type ERA, which failed to make any impression. There was the very ambitious Cisitalia 360. Commissioned by Piero Dusio, the Porsche Buro designed a space-framed, rear-engined car, with two- or four-wheel drive which could be selected by the driver. The target peak power of its two-stage supercharged flat-12 engine was 550 bhp at 12,000 rpm. Finance ran out before the car was developed to raceworthiness; had it reached the tracks, the subsequent history of racing might have been very different.

Some of the old circuits came back into use. Berne's Bremgarten, for example, tricky at the best of times, desperately dangerous in bad weather (the 1948 Swiss GP meeting claimed the lives of Varzi and Kautz). The wide-open Rheims circuit was used again for the French GP in 1948; at the other end of the speed scale, the Monaco GP was run again in 1948, for the first time since 1937. Monza was re-opened in 1948 (although the Italian GP was run in Turin's Valentino Park that year), and so was Spa.

Lacking any pre-war mainland circuits, the British discovered airfields; among the acres of concrete were perimeter tracks, and some of them made adequate race circuits. Some lasted only a short time, none became at all permanent so long as the pretence that they might be needed in a national emergency was kept up. Of all of them, Silverstone was to become the most famous. Here in 1948, the RAC ran a Grand Prix, using runways as well as perimeter track to form a curious circuit – at the point where the runways intersected, drivers raced towards each other, before turning away sharply! That RAC Grand Prix was won by Luigi Villoresi in a Maserati 4CLT/48 at 72·28 mph.

The Alfas did not run at Silverstone, but wherever they did in 1948 the result was almost inevitably a 1–2–3. In hindsight, the French GP was the most notable of the year, for at Rheims the great Tazio Nuvolari raced a GP car for the last time (sharing with Villoresi the

Right: unsophisticated start—but a talent that was to dominate European racing was nurtured in the Argentine *mecanica national* races such as this. *Below:* brave start—the Coupe de la Libération field in the Bois de Boulogne in 1945. Louveau (Maserati, right) won this 1.5-litre race at 61 mph. It was preceded by the first post-war race, won by Amédée Gordini

Maserati placed seventh), and a little-known Argentinian, J. M. Fangio, raced in a major GP for the first time (he retired). The names Ascari and Alfa Romeo were coupled again, too, for Alberto Ascari drove the third-placed 158 in his only race for the team which his father had led in the 1920s. Jean-Pierre Wimille won – his last success in France, for he was to be killed while practising for the 1949 Buenos Aires GP in a Simca-Gordini.

Ferrari was flexing his muscles down in Maranello. The first GP Ferrari was underpowered, had a fragile transmission and suspect handling qualities. It had a single-stage supercharged single-ohc V-12 designed by Gioacchino Colombo, which produced 225 bhp in 1948. In the following year the Ferraris were more competitive – but then so were Maseratis, Talbots, et al, for Alfa withdrew for a season. But even while a new twin-ohc Ferrari was showing its potential, Aurelio Lampredi moved to Modena, to design the large-capacity unsupercharged engine which was eventually to end the reign of the Alfa Romeo 158.

Meanwhile, the first BRM was unveiled late in 1949. The roots of BRM were in the old ERA company, and in

Above: French dependables—Talbots driven by Levegh and Cabantous among the straw bales of Silverstone. *Below:* Italian masterpiece—the Alfa Romeo 158

the determination of Raymond Mays and Peter Berthon to build an all-British GP winner. Design work began in 1946, and the very complex car took shape slowly. The engine was a four-ohc V-16, with a Rolls-Royce designed two-stage centrifugal supercharger. The tubular frame was conventional, but the suspension (independent front, de Dion rear) incorporated oleo-pneumatic struts. The engine was powerful

Above: plan view of an ERA at Silverstone, courtesy Geoffrey Ansell in the 1948 British GP. *Right:* return of the *maestro* — Nuvolari in a Maserati, about to be lapped by Trossi in an Alfa in the Grand Prix des Nations at Geneva, in 1946

(475 bhp at 11,500 rpm), but effective power was available only in a very restricted rev range, which made life difficult for drivers. Sommer was nominated to drive the car in its first race; a drive shaft failed on the start line.

Before Formula 1 was abandoned for the grands prix at the end of 1951, BRMs only once scored world championship points, in the 1951 British GP. Thereafter, the cars were relegated to secondary *formule libre* races, and eventually a degree of reliability was achieved in the Mk 2 version. The car continued to fascinate the racing world, and BRM were able to persuade top-line drivers to race it. But whatever claims its apologists might make for it,

the V-16 BRM was a failure.

Had the BRM worked as intended, it would have added spice to the battle which developed through 1950 and 1951, as Ferrari challenged Alfa Romeo. The 158s returned to the circuits with engines boosted to give 350 bhp, and the famous 'three Fs' team – Farina, Fagioli and Fangio. Ferrari's unsupercharged V-12 first appeared in 3·3 litre form, but by the end of the season had been enlarged to a full 4·5 litres. With this 375F1 Ascari was able to hold the 158s, and in the Italian GP even led them briefly.

Despite the writing on the wall, Alfa Romeo resolved to run the cars again in 1951, revising them and redesignating some 159. The engine was persuaded to deliver up to 425 bhp, at the expense of over-stressing the 13-year-old design, and fuel consumption increased to 1·6 mpg – this called for extra tankage, and with a full fuel load handling conse-

quently deteriorated (to combat this, the swing axles were replaced with de Dion rear suspension). The newer Ferrari engine gave 380 bhp. Alfa lined up Farina and Fangio; Ferrari had Ascari and the fiery Argentinian newcomer Froilan Gonzalez, plus Villoresi and Taruffi.

The Alfas just came out on top in the early races. The turning point came at Silverstone. Fangio led until his fuel stop, when Gonzalez went ahead. He flung the Ferrari round, cutting corners with all four wheels off the track when he felt there was a centimetre to be gained. Gonzalez won at 96·11 mph from Fangio. The Alfa Romeo run of victories unbroken since 1946 ended. Ferrari vanquished the marque he had served so long.

Ascari won clearly at the Nürburgring, where the German GP gained real status for the first time since 1939, and in the Italian GP. In the last GP of the year, in Spain, the Ferraris threw tyre treads, and Fangio won in a 159 (and took his first world championship). Alfa Romeo could not afford to build new cars, and withdrew from GP racing. And the age of the supercharger in grand prix racing ended.

The formula collapsed prematurely, for race organizers were not confident of the attractions of processions of Ferraris followed by erratic BRMs and aged Talbots. So in 1952–53 the world championship races were run for 2 litre

Redundant airfields were a welcome legacy of the Second World War, although they could be the most inhospitable places in England on a summer day. This is Boreham in 1952; the Essex circuit had a very short life in the early 1950s, later a very much longer one as a Ford test track, and the base of the Ford competitions department

Above: great British hope, the BRM V-16 in its first season, driven by Parnell at Goodwood, and *(right)* the car it was to challenge, an Alfa 158 being flung round Silverstone by Fangio. *Below:* the successful 4.5-litre Ferrari (*left:* Ascari followed by Moss in an HWM at San Remo in 1951). *right:* Hawthorn in the 'Thin Wall Special' at Goodwood in 1953

unsupercharged Formula 2 cars.

This proved to be a period of technical sterility, but full of racing interest. Ferrari was on top almost throughout, with the Type 500 (basically a Lampredi four-cylinder engine in a chassis derived from the supercharged V-12 cars). These cars failed the team only once (in the 1953 Syracuse GP) and they were beaten fairly and squarely only twice, by a Gordini at Rheims in 1952 and a Maserati at Monza in 1953. Driving the T500, Ascari gained two successive world championships.

That Rheims race was one of eight in the GPs de France series, of which the Rouen race ranked as the French GP. Seven of these fell to Ferrari, but at Rheims Jean Behra triumphed in a Gordini. This was a rare moment for French racing enthusiasts, although it was not a championship race – a first championship victory for a French car was 16 years off, and that was to be scored by a British team, using British engines in French chassis.

With $1\frac{1}{2}$ litre, 2 litre and later $2\frac{1}{2}$ litre cars, Amédée Gordini struggled to work miracles with shoestring resources. His cars were necessarily simple (he even continued to use live rear axles) and his 2 litre engines produced 155 bhp at the best (although 180 bhp was sometimes claimed for them). He managed to keep 'the blue' represented in racing until 1957.

Maserati, owned since 1947 by Orsi, worked to make the A6CGM and in 1953 the A6SSG competitive, while the

Maserati brothers produced a neat little Osca six-cylinder F2 car, but like Gordini lacked the resources to develop it fully.

This 2-litre Formula 2 saw several British cars in the field – an unprecedented GP state of affairs. None of them won a GP, true, but this inexpensive formula meant that teams and drivers gained a lot of experience. There were the HWMs, which had an engine based on the Alta unit; in 1952 Stirling Moss, Peter Collins and Lance Macklin strove to make up for its lack of power as they chased round after the Italian cars. There were the first front-engined cars built by Cooper, the T20 and 1954 T23, which were normally fitted with a Bristol pushrod ohc six which had its origins in the BMW 328. These Coopers are nowadays raced as bravely in historic car events as they were in their heyday, in 1952 most notably by young Mike Hawthorn (his Cooper drives

earned him a place in the 1953 Ferrari team, for whom he beat Fangio out of the last corner at Rheims to win the French GP, the first English driver to win a race of such status since 1938).

Connaught built the very sound Type A, which had excellent handling qualities but was sadly underpowered with a pushrod ohv engine based on a Lea-Francis unit (in 1953 the works car pioneered the racing use of Hillborn fuel injection). There was the last of the ERAs, the G–type, and a few other one-offs, while from Germany came the AFM and the Veritas.

In the world championship series, Ferrari was as dominant as Alfa Romeo had been a few years earlier. Then in the last 2 litre championship race, when one of those incredibly close Monza battles was being fought out by three drivers. In the last corner, Ascari led, slid wildly as he changed line to avoid a Connaught which was being lapped, and was rammed by Marimon (also lapped). Farina took his Ferrari onto the grass to avoid the melée, and Fangio slipped through to win for Maserati, at 110·69 mph. Thus the 2 litre championships ended on a high note.

The new 2½ litre formula promised much, and in its seven-year span racing was to see an upheaval which could never have been imagined in 1954. As that year opened, the big talking point was the Return of Mercedes – an event which by coincidence seemed to happen at 20-year intervals: 1914, 1934, 1954.

Ferrari and Maserati were prepared to do battle, of course, while Gordini and sundry British teams were prepared to mop up any places that might fall to them as major contenders fell out. There was an unknown quantity: Lancia were preparing to enter the field, and nobody would underrate a car from the drawing board of that old master Vittorio Jano.

Mercedes were confident that their W196 was a very superior car. They reverted to a straight-eight configuration in the engine – the last eight-in-line in GP racing. Most notably, it had fuel injection and desmodromic valve gear, a mechanical method of positive operation which had been experimentally used on a GP engine as far back as 1922, by Rolland-Pilain. This unit, which ultimately produced some 290 bhp, was laid almost flat in a space frame. Brakes were mounted inboard at the front as well as the rear; the ifs was conventional, but at the back a swing axle arrangement was used, the designers attempting to overcome its inherent drawback with the exceptionally low roll centre.

Mercedes contracted Juan Manuel Fangio to drive the W196s, together with two second-rate Germans. And Fangio was the factor which made the car superior in 1954. Much of the technical novelty was superfluous, the

Above: too late—the Mk II version of the V-16 BRM, here driven in real anger by Juan Manuel Fangio
Opposite: 2-litre Grands Prix. Mike Hawthorn made his name in 1952 with a Cooper *(top left,* at Spa), and became a star when he joined Ferrari in 1953 and beat the great Fangio in the French GP *(top, right).* Climax to the 2-litre championships came at Monza in the 1953 Italian GP. Here, Chiron (Osca) and Bira (Maserati) on the left make way for the leaders, Fangio (Maserati), Farina and Ascari (Ferraris) and Marimon (Maserati). This Ferrari T500, the supreme car of 1952–53, was raced to several championship victories by Ascari and is now in the Donington Collection

whole car lacked the 'touch' which made the little W165 of 1938 such an outstanding machine. But Fangio won four of the major GPs in which he started in a W196 in 1954, and was the leading W196 driver in two others, the British (fourth) and the Spanish (third). Otherwise, the team collected a second, a third, two fourths and a fifth – without Fangio, the return on a substantial investment would have been poor.

The racing world was duly impressed when the W196s, wearing full streamlining, ran away with the French GP, less than impressed when the cars looked clumsy at Silverstone and Gonzalez and Hawthorn scored a Ferrari 1–2 in the British GP. Fangio won the German GP. the last Swiss GP, the Italian GP, placed third behind Hawthorn's Ferrari and Musso's Maserati in

Return of Mercedes. The great German company came back to GP racing at Rheims in 1954, when they unveiled their W196 *stromlinienwagen* straight eight. The world of racing was appropriately over-awed, especially when the cars driven by Fangio (18, *above*) and Karl Kling (20) ran away with the race (Fangio won at 115.67 mph). A fortnight later at Silverstone *(left)* the tables were turned when Gonzalez led the British GP from start to finish in a Ferrari, winning at 89.69 mph. Oil drums marking corners handicapped the Mercedes drivers

Spain, in the last race on the Pedrables circuit.

In 1955 Mercedes signed another top driver to back Fangio, Stirling Moss, who had led the Mercedes convincingly in his private Maserati at Monza in 1954. The team lost only one race, when both cars failed at Monaco; Moss dutifully followed Fangio in two of the few races run in 1955, and headed him to win the British GP.

The season was cut short in the aftermath of the Le Mans disaster (see chapter 33), when some countries such as Switzerland placed an absolute ban on further racing on their soil. It was also disappointing in that the Lancia D50 was withdrawn from racing before the potential it had shown at the end of 1954 was fully developed. Drivers had problems with the car – its basic hand-

ling characteristics would have been quite acceptable to a driver in the 1970s, but its well-reasoned weight distribution made it unduly 'nervous' for drivers accustomed to a decreasing fuel load in the tails of their cars (the D50 had its fuel tanks in outrigged sponsons between the wheels). Jano used a very light tubular frame, and a compact V-8 to which the front suspension was directly mounted, so that it played a load-bearing role.

In 1955 Ascari won the secondary Naples and Turin races in D50s, and was poised to take the lead at Monaco when he crashed into the harbour. A few days later he was killed 'getting his hand in' with a sports Ferrari in a Monza test session. Coincidentally, the Lancia company was in a parlous financial state. So their racing department was

closed, and the D50s handed over to Ferrari, who also collected a useful Fiat subsidy, to enable him to uphold the prestige of the Italian motor industry on the circuits of Europe.

It might better have gone to Maserati, who had a most effective car in their 250F. This was a simple car, developed from the 1953 F2 Maserati, ideal for private owners and highly competitive in the works team – it was soon lapping circuits faster than the costly Mercedes W196 ever had. It was also to have a longer active life than any other $2\frac{1}{2}$ litre GP car, and was perhaps the last truly classic front-engined GP car.

Things were stirring in England, although the most prophetic development was hardly noticed – as Mercedes scored a 1–2–3–4 in the 1955 British GP at Aintree, one Jack Brabham re-

Top: the 1955 GP on the Monza combined circuit. Fangio in a streamlined Mercedes is leading his team mates Taruffi and Kling in open-wheel W196s off the old road circuit; Hawthorn (Ferrari) and Moss (Mercedes) are completing a lap on the banked track
Right: Fangio leads Moss in the early stages of the 1955 British GP at Aintree, which Moss won at 86.47 mph
Below: Lancia D50s lined up to be handed over to Ferrari—modern GP teams would be happy to have so many cars!

tired from the race in a rear-engined Cooper-Bristol, an adapted sports car. BRM and Vanwall seemed to carry Britain's real hopes.

The front-engined BRM Type 25 was as simple as the V-16 had been complex, with a straightforward four-cylinder engine. It was hardly less troublesome, but after many drivers had tried it (and several had lucky escapes as Type 25s crashed), BRM at last won a championship race, when Jo Bonnier won the 1959 Dutch GP.

C. A. Vandervell was an industrialist of the old school, who had given up his association with the earlier BRM in disgust, and ran the 'Thinwall Special' 4·5 litre Ferrari in opposition to the V-16s. Through 1954–55 a Vanwall GP car was developed, finally emerging in full 2·5 litre form. It had an unusual

Last years of front-engined glory.
Left: Fangio in a Mercedes W196, and
Mike Hawthorn (Ferrari) in the 1954
Spanish Grand Prix. Against the run of
the season, Hawthorn won the race, at
97.93 mph, while Fangio nursed his
ailing Mercedes through to third place.
In 1957 Juan Manuel Fangio gained his
fifth world championship, when he was
46 years old. In his last full season, he
drove for Maserati (*below,* rounding the
Gasworks hairpin at Monaco on his way
to victory in a 250F). That year saw the
first British victory for a British car in a
world championship event, when a
Vanwall was driven to win the British
Grand Prix at Aintree. Moss *(right)* led
until his car started giving trouble;
his team mate, Tony Brooks, not fully fit
after an accident at Le Mans, was called
in to hand over his Vanwall to Moss,
who drove it through from ninth place
to the lead, and an historic victory

Top: in October 1955 Tony Brooks won a surprise victory in the Syracuse GP with a Connaught. The Ferrari and Maserati opposition was not at full strength, but Brooks was driving his first race in a GP car, and one had to look back to the 1924 Spanish GP for the previous 'all-British' victory in a Continental GP.
Grand Prix cars on a public road hemmed by stone walls appear strange to modern eyes, and this type of regional secondary F1 race has long passed into history
Above: Silverstone, however, has remained a constant part of the GP scene. In the 1956 International Trophy, Fangio in a Lancia-Ferrari leads Hawthorn in a BRM and Moss (3) and Schell in Vanwalls. Moss won at 100.47 mph — averaging a higher speed over the 180 miles than the previous lap record. Fangio, Hawthorn and Schell all retired

Front-engined twilight. *Top, left:* the neat but ineffectual '16' with which Team Lotus started contesting Continental GPs in 1958, here driven by Hill in the French GP. *Top, right:* Chuck Daigh driving one of Lance Reventlow's beautifully built, but hopelessly outclassed Scarabs in practice for the 1960 Monaco GP. *Above, left:* Mike Hawthorn takes refreshment as he motors a Ferrari away from the Aintree pits after a wheel change in 1957. *Above, right:* Fairman testing the Ferguson P99, which was raced to prove its four-wheel drive system. This car was driven by Moss to win the 1961 Oulton Park Gold Cup

four-cylinder engine, which owed much to Norton motor cycle practice, while the chassis was reminiscent of Ferraris. In 1956 the space frame and rear suspension were reworked by Colin Chapman, then an *enfant terrible* of racing, and the car was reclothed in a striking low-drag body designed by Frank Costin. Stirling Moss, then the Maserati number one driver, raced this Vanwall to victory in the 1956 Silverstone International Trophy, and as leader of the Vanwall team was to do great things with it in 1957. That 1956 Silverstone victory somehow came to overshadow the fact that the previous autumn a British car driven by a British driver had beaten Continental works cars in a grand prix. And that hadn't happened for more than 30 years. The

event was the Syracuse GP in Sicily, the driver an amateur, C. A. S. Brooks, and the car a Type B Connaught.

Unhappily, that had to be Connaught's greatest moment. The team was always short of money, like Gordini's having to race whenever possible for start and prize money, while to preserve engines drivers had to restrict rpm in racing, and thus could not fully exploit the car's excellent road-holding. In 1956 reliability saw Flockhart and Fairman finish third and fifth in the Italian GP. But through 1957 the effort ran down, and eventually collapsed under an auctioneer's hammer. Ironically, Connaught had started work on an advanced rear-engined car at that time. . . .

Meanwhile, in 1956 Ferrari had the services of Fangio. The partnership was unhappy, but it gained the world championship. In 1957 Maserati had Fangio, a happier arrangement for what was to be the last full season for both constructor and driver. It brought championships to both, for in 1957 the Formula 1 Constructors' Championship was inaugurated.

In 1957 Britain at last became a real force in GP racing, as Vanwall promise became fact. Moss and Brooks drove for the team, and shared the car which was first in the British GP – the first

all-British win in a championship race. Moss also won the Pescara GP (elevated to championship status for one year), and the Italian GP at 120·77 mph.

By this time, constructors with 'conventional' front-engined cars were working towards a dead end, for at Monaco in 1957 Brabham had raced the first Cooper-Climax GP car. Maserati gave up racing at the end of that year, near-bankrupt after some costly sports car accidents. Ferrari abandoned the Lancia-based cars for 1958, after failing to win a single GP with them in 1957, and introduced the compact Dino 246, which two years later was to be the last front-engined car to win a championship race. Lotus joined the GP ranks, Vanwall and BRM continued. They were handicapped more than most constructors, for their four-cylinder engines took least kindly to the 'commercially available' fuel which became obligatory in racing.

Moss won four GPs in 1958, one in a Cooper (see chapter 37), three in Vanwalls. Hawthorn won one race for Ferrari, but took five second places, a third and a fifth, and so amassed enough points to win the drivers' championship (Brooks' two victories for Vanwall ensured that the British team took the constructors' championship however). Mike Hawthorn, upset at

Above: the last really effective front-engined GP car was the Ferrari Dino 246, here driven by Collins in the 1958 British GP
Below: start of the 1960 French GP.

Three of the leading cars are Ferraris, but even on the fast Rheims circuit these were matched by less powerful Coopers—Brabham, second here, won the race

mid-season by the death of his friend and team mate Peter Collins in the German GP, retired, and late in the year died in a senseless road accident in a Jaguar.

Tony Vandervell gave up GP racing, too – perhaps at an appropriate moment, for the generation of GP cars which his handsome Vanwalls represented was about to be swept into oblivion. Too late, Aston Martin entered GP racing with a classically-proportioned car, which made an excellent debut in the Silverstone International Trophy, but thereafter was sadly outclassed. A year later Lance Reventlow's Scarab made even less impression.

In 1960 only the Italian GP fell to a front-engined car – and that was a race the British teams decided to boycott, because it was felt that the combined Monza road and banked track on which it was run was dangerous. So the honour of closing a chapter with a front-engined victory fell to American Phil Hill, who averaged 132.07 mph over the 311 miles.

Ferrari and BRM were by this time the only true GP constructors in the old tradition. Changing times, and especially the availability of Coventry Climax engines, meant that the 'kit car' era had arrived. And so had the time when the only place to mount engines was in the backs of chassis.

World of Rallies

For a few years rallying retained its pre-war atmosphere, but commercial pressures inevitably led to increasing professionalism, and to works participation on a sometimes lavish scale. The nature of rallies began to change, too, as in many parts of Europe they were crowded off public roads. It became less of an achievement to motor from one end of Europe to the other, so special stage tests became more and more important – and this in time meant that the RAC Rally could be transformed into one of the leading and more competitive events on the calendar, hitherto a most unlikely possibility in a country where hostility to competitive motoring on public roads is deep-rooted!

At its lowest level, rallying can be a simple navigational exercise, a fun and games treasure hunt. Much above that level, any competitor who hopes to succeed has to adopt a professional approach, even if his resources limit professional equipment. A major international event will see leading teams deploy vast resources, send 'recce' crews back and forth over the route, develop modifications which may never be seen on production models, test and test. Crews are equipped with lavish technical aids to 'navigation', with ice notes and pace notes, have intercoms built into crash helmets so that they can communicate in the appalling racket inside a closed car at

Mild-weather Monte. A Renault 4CV and a Jaguar pause before the Col des Lecques timed section in 1954, while a Jowett Javelin passes by

high speed on rough roads, and perhaps have radios for communicating with their team managers. Cars have become very specialized, truck loads of tyres are available to cater for any climatic fluctuations, service crews carry out major repairs in impossible times in impossible roadside conditions, publicity men hover anxiously, to exploit the best or explain away the worst.

Rallying has become an over-elaboration of a once-simple sport, ironically at a time when general conditions in many countries are increasingly hostile to it.

But it has also developed into a surprisingly popular spectator sport – surprising, that is, if your idea of unpleasantness is standing in the bonechilling dampness of a Welsh forest in the small hours of a winter night. Identification with the competitors and their cars is part of the reason, and then for some enthusiasts racing has no spectacle to compare with a rally car 'flat' behind a battery of headlights on a Welsh track, or bouncing off snow banks on a Provençal col, or trailing the red dust of East Africa.

The greatest change to come over

rallying in the 1960s – or thereabouts – was not mechanical, for here progress was fairly logical, and front-wheel drive, rear-engined, and 'conventional' cars all held sway (the outstanding cars of recent years have included the little fwd Saabs, the Mini-Coopers which for a spell were all-conquering, the Austin Healey 3000, Porsche 911s, Ford Escorts, Lancia Fulvias from Italy, Alpines from France). The change was the influx of Scandinavian drivers, at times almost overwhelming. Through the decade the winners of the RAC Rally were Carlsson, Trana, Aaltonen, Soderstrom, Lampinen, Kallstrom – a stranglehold which was not broken until 1972 when Roger Clark won in an Escort. The Finns and Swedes exploited their natural assets, such as an ability to 'read' conditions, and sense what lay ahead, sheer ability with cars on tough going, and bravery to a point which others might jokingly or ruefully define as 'bone headedness'.

Accidentally, rallying threw up a new branch of motor sport, rallycross. In 1967 the RAC Rally was cancelled because of an outbreak of foot and mouth disease. So to satisfy the hungry TV cameras, a mock special stage was

arranged at Brands Hatch for leading rally competitors. Out of this has grown a sort of circuit event, usually run on mixed tarmac and earth courses, which is rallycross. By 1973 there was a European Rallycross Championship, which had precious little to do with rallying. . . .

Mainstream rallying got under way again in 1946, when the Alpine Rally was run, and won by Huguet in a Hotchkiss. This event entered its greatest period in the 1950s, when Ian Appleyard (Jaguar) and Stirling Moss (Sunbeam Talbot) both won coveted *Coupes des Alpes en Or* for three consecutive penalty-free runs. During the next decade it went into a decline, eventually being restricted to the French Alps and retitled Coupe des Alpes. Its fate was symptomatic, for the extravagent use of public roads through tourist regions could no longer be justified.

The same reason foredoomed one of the fiercest events ever run in Europe, the Marathon de la Route. This successor to the pre-war Liège-Rome-Liège (a title which stuck at least until the event deserted Italy for the Balkans in the late 1950s) set a pattern for really

Opposite: Alpine scenes. *Far left:* Ian Appleyard's Jaguar during the 1952 event, when he won his last *Coupe*. *Left:* cloud veils the distant view, but the loose surface and daunting drop must have been very obvious to the crew of this Porsche 356 in 1953. *Lower left:* freak weather in June played havoc with the 1954 Alpine – Slatter's AC Ace in the aftermath of a blizzard on the Umbrail Pass. *Left:* the Morley brothers built up a splendid record in international rallies, and so did the Austin Healey 3000. The Morleys' 'big Healey' in characteristic Alpine conditions, in 1965.

Right, top: the Tulip in the days before rallying became wholly professional. Venner's Frazer Nash and Kuiper's Jaguar at a frontier in 1954. *Right:* a quartet of Standard Eights in a test at Zandvoort in 1956 – the year the handicap favoured puny cars in the aftermath of the Le Mans disaster

tough rallies, totally demanding of cars and crews. The avowed intent of the organizers was to achieve the ideal of just one finisher, and to that end a high average speed was required over as much of the 3,000 plus mile route as possible (nearest to the 'ideal' was achieved in 1961, when 8 of 85 starters survived). In the Marathon's heyday the route ran from Spa, across neutralized Austria, to the more frightening of the Dolomite passes, such as the Vivione and the Gavia, to the then-destructive rocky and dusty Yugoslav roads, ultimately to Sofia. Then back again, virtually non-stop. On passes like the Stelvio there were no hill climb half-measures – the timed stages were ascent and descent. At times this rally was as near to a road race as a rally could be. Inevitably, it could not survive, and in 1965 was confined to 84 hours of lapping the Nürburgring circuit.

It naturally produced an annual crop of epic stories. For example, of 1952 winner Johnny Claes driving the last 1,700 miles single-handed while his co-driver had medical attention at every control. And breaking into the list of male winners – Gendebien, Mair-esse, Storez and others – came a pair of girls, Pat Moss and Anne Wisdom, winners in an Austin-Healey 3000 in 1960, the first ladies to win an event of such stature outright.

Most countries have their major rally, or have had one. Sweden's Midnight Sun and Finland's 1000 Lakes survive as archetypical Scandinavian forest events, which have given the game some of its leading drivers and expressive terms such as 'yump', Italy's San Remo (one-time Sestrieres), Portugal's TAP, the poor-relation Polish Rally, the Moroccan, the Austrian, and in 1972 a newcomer to the Championship for Makes, the Press-on-Regardless organized by the SCCA and won by Henderson and Pogue in an AMC Jeep Wagoneer.

The Dutch Tulip Rally was far from being a flat meander round the bulb fields – like most, it had to head for mountains to sort out an order, and the Dutch made especial use of the Vosges. It was reckoned to be a good rally for amateurs, and some of the results which its handicap system produced seemed improbable – in 1956 a private Austin A30 was first, followed by four Standard Eights!

Greece has had a rally of status since the mid-1950s, in the Acropolis (inaugurated as a national event in 1952 and won by one Pezmazoglova in a Chevrolet). Stretches were traditionally run on unsurfaced roads, and this coupled with the high averages required meant that the Acropolis was almost a successor to the Marathon. It was in this dusty, demanding event in 1972, that Fiat's overt return to motor sport was finally rewarded with a victory, when a 124 Spyder crewed by Lindberg and Eisendle won by a mere 29 seconds.

In parts of the world where roads are less congested, rallies have had different characters. The Round-Australia Trial was an event matched only by South American *turismo carretera* races, a 9,000 mile test to near-destruction on dirt surfaces a long way from 'civilization'.

One or two trans-continental marathons have been essayed, but most leading works teams ignored them. The 1970 World Cup Rally, London to Mexico, was perhaps successful (it certainly was for Ford, who made much capital out of the victory by Mikkola and Palm in an Escort).

The East African Safari is the only major annual rally to have the 'adventure' qualities of the 'tween-wars Montes, where simply to finish is still an achievement. It was inaugurated as the local Coronation Safari in 1953, and for many years was run in Kenya, Tanzania and Uganda. The name changed in 1960, and through a decade its reputation as a challenge to Europeans grew to a legend. Many tried, Erik Carlsson finished second, Pat Moss and Anne Hall were third, but there seemed to be no substitute for local expertise in East African heat and dust, mud and floods. This held especially true in wet years, and when Z. Nowicki and P. Cliff won for Peugeot in 1963 and 1968, there were only seven other finishers (of 84 and 91 starters respectively). In 1968 these were two Peugeots, two Fords, two Datsuns and a Triumph – the three pairs representing marques which took most of the Safaris in the 1960s, when the importance of the event in prestige and shop window terms became fully recognized. Hence Ford's heavyweight approach, which paid its fullest dividend in 1972 when Hannu Mikkola and Gunnar Palm won in an Escort RS1600 – a victory which put paid to the well-publicized myth that the Safari would never be won by European drivers.

Political changes in East Africa meant that the Safari route varied from time to time, and in 1974 it was run wholly in Kenya. Only 16 cars finished in that very wet event, headed by Joginder Singh's Mitsubishi Colt Lancer.

Top: an Austin 1800 crewed by Tony Fall, Mike Wood and Brian Culcheth in Australia during the London–Sydney marathon.
Centre: Ford preferred to use two-man crews in inter-continental events – in the 1970 World Cup Rally, the crew of the winning Escort relax on one of the 'easier' stretches in South America. Major teams ignored the 1974 world cup event.
Left: leisurely days – a trilby-hatted driver with a Jaguar Mk VII in RAC Rally seafront driving tests

The RAC Rally is an exception to a recent European trend: it has increased in severity, competitiveness and status, and amongst the rally hardcore it is one of the most popular events. In 1960 special stages replaced the old wiggle-woggle type tests, and in 1961 organizer Jack Kemsley took it onto special stages in forests. Soon names like Coed-y-Brenin and Clocaenog became part of the vocabulary of international rallying (and latterly it has come as something of a mild shock to hear foreign team managers making a better job of pronouncing these than British crew members!). Save when there is heavy snow, as in 1971, the open-road sections of the RAC count for nothing, and the result is decided on special stages, most on rough forest tracks. As the rally is held late in the year conditions on these may be muddy, crisply dry, or snowy. Britain's Forestry Commission presumably makes a profit out of the rally, charging for every mile per car which starts, and nearly everybody enjoys the five days.

'Enjoyment' is a word seldom applied nowadays to the Monte Carlo Rally. But it still attracts world-wide attention, and is therefore the rally which few teams can afford to miss. Haphazard organization, obstructive French police, and high costs have all detracted from the event, and it still cannot quite live down past iniquities.

There was a time when experts reckoned to be able to forecast which car the organizers intended to win, as soon as the regulations were published. And they were too often correct!

This era reached rock bottom in 1966, when three Mini Coopers and a Lotus Cortina finished in the lead. This was not what had been intended: Citroen were supposed to win, and the best-placed DS21 was fifth. So a day was spent minutely scrutineering the British cars until – voila! – a trivial means of disqualifying them was found. Never mind that the British team managers had scrupulously cleared that very point with the FIA (the international governing body) before the start – the Citroen driven by Toivonen and Mikander was declared the winner. More publicity accrued to the disqualified Mini Coopers, and ever since the AC de Monaco has run an honest rally!

After the Second World War there were no bonus points to be earned by motoring to Monaco from far-flung corners of Europe, and save for the very unfortunate the rally was decided on a long common route, and special stages to sort out some sort of running order on arrival at Monaco. The best are then despatched on a long decisive test in the Alps Maritimes, where in January the weather can play some odd tricks.

Hotchkiss won the event in 1949–50, to bring their score of victories to an unbeaten six. Sydney Allard started from Glasgow in 1952, to win a very icy rally in his own Allard J2 saloon. Monegasque Louis Chiron won in a Lancia in 1954. In 1961 the ancient name Panhard headed the finishing list, 1–2–3 as the regulations suited their odd little 24CT coupe to its last hiccuping exhaust note. Burly Erik Carlsson gained consecutive victories for Saab in 1962–63; Mini Coopers should have won four successive rallies in 1964–67, but at least Aaltonen's win in 1967 was poetic justice after the 1966 fiasco! Then Porsche scored a hat trick, Alpine won for France in 1971 and were hot favourites to do so in 1972. Conditions in the final tests meant that they did not, but that Munari and Manucci in a Lancia scored the first all-Italian victory in the rally's long history.

Problems over the use of public roads increasingly beset this type of rally, and the future of some events must always be in jeopardy. By rallying itself is immensely popular, and obviously has a continuing future in events run in less populated areas outside Europe, especially in Africa, or in events where the competition is on private ground. So Britain's RAC Rally, so long a Cinderella, has set an ideal pattern for future rallies.

Unprecedented Expansion
rise of the Japanese industry

In 1902, just under half a century from the opening of Japan to the Western world by Commodore Perry, the Land of the Rising Sun built its first car, the work of Shintaro Yoshida and Komanosuke Uchiyama. It had, apparently, an American power unit. Five years later another design by Uchiyama appeared; called the Takuri, it was the first Japanese car to reach production status, as around a dozen examples were made.

Meanwhile, Torao Yamaha had constructed a steam car in 1904; it was not a success, and the engineer removed the power unit and fitted it in a fishing boat which survived until 1944.

In 1906 Mitsubishi are reported to have built a number of steam cars; but such ventures were merely token attempts to emulate Western progress, and when the competitors in the New York–Paris race passed through Japan in 1907, none of the people on their route had ever seen a car before. After the First World War, Mitsubishi built a handful of cars, apparently based closely on the contemporary Fiat Zero, at their Kobe shipyard. This experimental venture lasted only until 1921.

In the early 1920s the Jitsuyo Jidosha Serzo Company manufactured Gorham and Lila light cars, but the great earthquake of 1923 put paid to many Japanese car makers. Indeed, the local motor industry was on a tiny scale and composed of ephemeral companies which only produced a few cars before going out of business.

Some of the short-lived names of the between-wars period were Kyosan, Kuragne, Ohta, Raito, Tsukaba, Wakaba, and, one of the most successful, Hakuyosha. This company was set up in 1917 by Junya Toyokawa, who had studied automobile engineering in the United States. Several models were built, including the air-cooled Ohtomo, and an export trade was built up in the Far East.

Typical of the tiny cars fostered by the Japanese taxation system was the 1962 Mazda Carol, which had a 360 cc transverse four-cylinder engine

Fuji Heavy Industries was formed after the Second World War, manufacturing many things from scooters to aircraft. Their Subara 360 *(top left)* was introduced in 1958, with a rear-mounted twin-cylinder engine and torsion-bar independent suspension. Mazda's R360 coupe *(top right,* with the Carol) had a 356 cc power unit. Toyota's Crown range *(above)* was originally launched in 1955, and the first Toyopet Crown *(left)* looked similar to contemporary Vauxhalls. By 1962 the Crown line had more indiviuality (RS40, *centre),* while the 1969 Crown RS50 *(right)* was smarter yet

But Toyokawa's venture was swamped by the more sophisticated imports; and when Ford opened an assembly plant in Japan, most of the indigenous manufacturers just faded away.

The outstanding motor company of the interwar years was DAT, which had its origins in an experimental vehicle built by the Kwaishinsha Motor Works of Tokyo in 1912; the DAT (the name was made up of the initials of the owners of the company) appeared a couple of years later, but was production overshadowed by the firm's output of trucks. In 1926 the factory moved to Osaka, and in 1931 the Datson ('Son of DAT') appeared; its name was changed to Datsun a year later in honour of the rising sun symbol of Japan.

During the 1930s Datsun built an upgraded version of the Austin Seven; in 1933 the company moved to Yoko-hama and in 1934 they merged with the new Nissan company, which, with liberal help from the American firm of Graham-Paige, built a large car based on the Graham Six.

Next in the field were Toyota, already well established as textile manufacturers, who began experiments in 1935 with a six-cylinder car that looked like a cross between a Ford and a Chrysler Airflow. From then on, they produced a range of American-inspired sixes. But the catalyst which really spurred the development of the Japanese motor industry was the country's rapid technological expansion during the Second World War.

Toyota made their comeback in 1947 with a 27 hp backbone chassis economy car, styled on similar lines to the Volkswagen. Only 215 of this model were produced between 1947 and 1952, but output rocketed dramatically in 1953, when 16,500 cars were built; from that time the company's expansion was continuous, and by the late 1960s annual production was nudging the million mark. During this period, Toyota had moved into first place in the Japanese industry, overtaking Nissan-Datsun by a narrow margin.

The Nissan name had been dropped from the firm's cars after the war, and the group had concentrated on turning out Datsuns, plus licence-built Austin A40s and A50s. When the Austin line was phased out in 1950, the Nissan title was reintroduced for the new Cedric range which had been designed to succeed it.

In 1966 the company expanded further, taking over Prince Motors of Tokyo, which had had its origins in the post-war Tama electric car. In 1952 the Prince name was introduced for the firm's first petrol model, named in honour of Crown Prince Akihito; by 1957 Prince had become confident enough to attempt Japan's first exports to the European market.

Toyota, too, had been involved in a takeover in the 1960s, absorbing the faltering Daihatsu concern, which, having begun production with a three-wheeler in the 1930s, had concentrated its energies on the sub-mini market encouraged by Japan's restrictive motor tax laws, building mostly 360 cc models, plus a handful of 1,000 cc cars. And in 1966, Toyota took over Hino, originally truck manufacturers, who had started car manufacture in 1952 with a licence-built version of the 4 cv Renault. After nine years they introduced their own design, the Contessa, but sales were only 4,692 at the time of the merger.

Takeovers were the order of the day in the late 1960s, for Mitsubishi, an industrial giant with interests in ships, aircraft, agricultural machinery, petrol refining, nuclear equipment, railway

Honda had been making motorcycles for many years before they turned to four-wheelers in 1962. This is their N600 four-seater introduced in that year *(above)*. Hino of Tokyo built Renaults under licence from 1953 until 1961. When they launched their own line in 1962 (coachbuilt model at the Turin Show, *left*) their cars still bore obvious traces of Renault ancestry

factorily than their European counterparts. In 1973 Mazda were the world's biggest producer of rotaries, turning out 20,000 a month.

It was a remarkable level of sophistication for an industry that had only begun to establish itself firmly after the Second World War.

In 1950, the combined Japanese industry produced just 1,594 cars, 3,502 buses and 26,501 commercial vehicles; by 1961 over 250,000 cars were being turned out every year and by 1967 output had increased by 37.6 per cent to become the third largest motor industry in the world, with a total output of 3,146,486 vehicles – 1,375,755 cars, 27,363 buses and 1,743,368 commercials.

But even then most of the industry's efforts were devoted to meeting home demand, for only one Japanese in ten owned a car at that period, compared with one in two in the USA, one in five in West Germany, one in six in Britain, one in eight in Italy. . . .

Only 11 per cent of Japanese production was exported in 1967, mostly to America; but already a bridgehead had been established in Europe, 12,000 miles away, following the example of their motor cycle manufacturers.

Because the Japanese were late starters in the European market, setting up a sales and service network was an expensive and difficult business. But they had already managed to make a decided impact on the American market (aided by an import policy that hampered sales of foreign makes in Japan) and they repeated the feat in Europe, to such good effect that by the end of 1973 the Datsun Sunny family saloon had reached the exalted ranks of Britain's top twenty cars in the sales charts. Perhaps a contributory factor was Datsun's keen participation in Western motor sport, including a well publicised win of the tough East African Safari Rally with a 240Z sports model in 1973. Whatever the reason, of the 74,175 Japanese cars sold in Britain in the first nine months of 1973, almost 49,000 were Datsuns.

Whether, however, the Japanese can continue to maintain this level of market penetration over such tremendous distances in a world increasingly jealous of its energy supplies is a question that will only begin to be answered in the next few years.

rolling stock and construction equipment as well as motor vehicles, who sold 105,950 cars in 1967, joined forces that year with Isuzu. That company had built Hillman Minxes under licence for some years, and their power units still showed Rootes influence.

Mitsubishi's output for 1968 ranged from the 21 bhp 360 cc Minica, through the Colt, available with 1,000 cc, 1,200 cc and 1,500 cc power units, to the 2 litre six-cylinder Debonair, a not-too-successful attempt to break into the large car monopoly ruled by Toyota and Nissan.

The growing interest in larger cars was the natural outcome of increasing affluence, despite the financial advantages given by the authorities to the under 360 cc class.

Honda, rulers of the motor cycle market, moved into cars in 1962 with a 600 cc sports model, later uprated to 800 cc. In 1966 Honda produced a 360 cc saloon to challenge the successful Fuji Subaru model. In 1968 they too moved into the larger car market with an air-cooled 1,300 cc model with a 110 mph top speed; within six years they had become a major force in the industry.

Even more surprising was the rise of Toyo Kogyo, a company that had originally been, of all unlikely things, a cork manufacturer. They produce cars under the Mazda marque name. Their growth rate soon put them in third place behind Toyota and Nissan; by 1968 they had begun production of Wankel-rotary-engined cars, for which they held the Japanese licence, and which seemed to perform more satis-

In 1964, Mazda introduced this 1000 cc saloon *(top row, left)*, with a front-mounted water-cooled engine developing 40 bhp. Nissan's 1962 Cedric *(top right)* boasted 'low-price luxury'. The Cedric was built in the Datsun factory, and the photographs below it show two Datsun products of the late 1960s, the 1967 Bluebird *(left)* and the 1000 GTL Sunny of 1969—in 1973 the Sunny became the first Japanese car to be listed among Britain's top-selling 20 cars.
In 1973 Mazda were offering a choice between conventionality (Mazda 1000 models, *above*), and rotary-engined unorthodoxy (RX4, *right*)

Dream Cars and Disappearing Marques

If anything characterised the motoring scene in the early 1950s, it was the gadget – sometimes decorative, sometimes bogusly technical and only occasionally of the slightest practicality.

It was an era of 'roof racks' and 'heavily chromed' headlamp cowls, of screw-on 'portholes' for the bonnet sides and scallop-shaped exhaust pipe deflectors, of tartan car seat covers and widow's peaks for the windscreen. You could buy suction-fitting windscreen defrosters that tried to clear a patch of glass perhaps a foot wide and four inches deep; you could bolt a symbolic bird moulded in repellent amber plastic to your bonnet to sweep insects clear of the screen; you could fit a water injection 'bomb' to your fuel system and 'save petrol.' Then there were the stylised wheel discs, the spotlights and the flashing indicators that replaced the old semaphore signals that always used to stick in damp weather, but usually responded to a sharp thump on the appropriate door pillar.

Daimler attempted to play on the cult of the gimmick in their 1956 One-o-Four Ladies' Model which was virtually the same externally as the normal One-o-Four, but cost £300 more. Radio was standard, as were power-operated windows; on the passenger's side a burr walnut drawer beneath the glove box contained a torch, notepad and gold pencil, sunglasses and a cigarette packet sleeve; beneath this again was a sectional touring map mounted in slides. Forward of the passenger door was a special pocket containing a folding umbrella; sheepskin rugs were provided for the floor and a travelling rug for the seat. In the rear armrest was a fitted vanity case containing dry rouge, foundation cream, lipstick, cleansing lotion, a powder compact, comb and cleansing tissues. In the boot were four lightweight suitcases, a picnic hamper, an icebox and a shooting stick.

All this conspicuous consumption was the tangible sign of the end of austerity, and in America the 1950s saw the development of exaggerated styling, which emphasised the power and prestige of the car at the expense of its utility or its real performance.

Engines became larger and more powerful, while body styling became more and more bizarre. To a display of chrome that would have done credit to a juke box were added garish two-tone paint schemes. And throughout the 1950s tailfins, which had originally been just a rudimentary feature on the 1950s Cadillac, became commonplace on virtually every model on the American market, housing huge stop, turn and brake lights. Eventually the tailfins became so large that they became something of a hazard when reversing a car 18 to 20 feet long overall.

It was also the era of the dream cars, advanced design concepts which were built to test public reaction to styling and engineering innovations before they were translated into production terms.

For instance, in 1954, Cadillac showed the El Camino two-door hardtop, featuring 'Aircraft Styling, emphasised by super-sonic tailfins on the rear fenders . . . long-range pencil beam, aircraft landing-type lights that are auto-

The rising cult of the tail fin: from the rudimentary bumps on the 1950 Cadillac *(below)* fins grew to ridiculous proportions, epitomised by the 1957 Chrysler Windsor *(left)* with its FliteSweep styling

matically shut off completely by the autronic eye when in traffic . . . "aircraft type" hydromatic gear shift selector lever.'

Sometimes the specification of these dream vehicles bordered on the bizarre: witness the 1953 Lincoln X-100, Car of Tomorrow, which did the round of the motor shows in 1954.

'Its most revolutionary feature,' claimed its manufacturer, 'is undoubtedly the sliding transparent non-glare plastic roof over the driver's compartment. This canopy is actuated in three ways. It can be rolled forward or backwards by an instrument panel switch. If closed, it can be rolled back by pressure on the door latch button. (The electrical system of this button is adjusted so that the canopy does not automatically open when the door is opened, but only if extra pressure is applied to the button). If the roof is open when the car is parked and unat-

The changing shape of the American car during the 1950s. Models in the 1953 Studebaker range were exceptionally low and elegant *(top left)*, but in 1954 the company merged with Packard, whose styling was as clumsy as its model names (Clipper de luxe Club Sedan, *top right*), and a result was mutual disaster. 'Juke-box' styling reached its zenith with cars like the 1958 Oldsmobile Dynamic 88 Holiday Coupe *(above)*.
Pontiac's Firebird II *(below)* at the Paris Motor Show was a dream car design exercise

In 1957 Ford's Lincoln-Mercury Division launched the Edsel *(top)*, after careful market research in the upper middle-class price bracket. This failed to anticipate a slump in big-car sales, and only 35,000 Edsels were sold. Chevrolet's unorthodox rear-engined air-cooled Corvair *(above and left)* was damned by critics as 'unsafe at any speed'. This car started Nader's safety crusade rolling

tended, the canopy and windows will close in event of rain when a moisture-sensitive electrical device on the top of the car starts the roof motors. The special high-compression overhead valve engine delivers 300 bhp. The outstanding feature of the engine is an induction system which is entirely new, including 12 Venturi Carburettor System. When in city traffic the engine operates on 2 venturi, when on the highway it operates on 4 venturi, but for all-out operation it automatically converts to a full racing manifold with a carburettor venturi for each cylinder. Power transmission is through a newly

developed automatic transmission with electrical operated gear selector. The car is equipped with 4 windshield wipers and a rear window wiper, power steering, power brakes including an electrically power-assisted emergency handbrake. Front-wheel brakes are cooled with automatic thermostatically-controlled blowers when their temperature goes above 150°F. Two front power seats each provide 6-way adjustment, up-down, forward-backward, tilt front and back. Front seats are heated with built-in electric heating elements. Built-in electrically-operated jacks for each wheel. Bonnet

and luggage compartment lids are electrically opened and closed. This car is equipped with a 12-volt electrical system powering 24 electrical motors; 44 electronic tubes; 50 light bulbs; 92 control switches; 29 solenoids; 53 relays; 23 circuit breakers and 10 fuses. Approximately 8 miles of electrical wiring is used. In addition it contains dictaphone, ship-to-shore type telephone, electric shaver and a signal-seeking radio with separate controls for front and rear seat passengers.'

There was so much gadgetry in the Lincoln X-100 that an eighth of the car's total weight was accounted for by the complicated electrical equipment.

Some of the car's styling features, like its huge circular tail lamps, appeared on Fords of the late 1950s, but the double-bubble cockpit of the 1955 Ford Futura was quite impracticable. However, that model's heavily hooded lamps and scowling grille were echoed on the 1957 Lincoln Premiere.

But dreams could become nightmares, as Ford found when they attempted to launch a new model to fill a gap in the middle range market. Following considerable research, including hiring the poetess Marianne Moore to think up names that were never used, the company introduced the Edsel range in 1958. It couldn't have been launched at a worse time: the market was in recession, its fussy styling followed a trend that had already been outmoded, and customers were turning away from big cars for more manoeuvrable vehicles.

The Edsel lasted just two years in production: it was an error that is reported to have cost the company $250 million. Its passing marked the end of the era of the tailfin and the ever-increasing size of the average American car and heralded the rise of the compact.

Partly this was precipitated by the gowing success of the imported European cars – tiny by American standards – partly it was the natural result of the home product having become too big and clumsy to operate and too expensive to buy and run.

Not that the compact was an entirely new concept: the smaller independent manufacturers had been building compact-sized cars for years, but it was a new approach for the 'big three' – General Motors, Ford and Chrysler, whose compacts all made their debut in 1959.

Most unorthodox was the Chevrolet Corvair, with a rear-mounted flat-six 2·3 litre air-cooled engine, all-round independent suspension and unit body/chassis construction; the Chrysler Plymouth Valiant and Ford Falcon were more conventional, the smooth 'European' lines of the Ford contrasting strongly with the company's larger products, such as the Thunderbird, which acquired extra chrome ('bright metal spears on the side panel projectiles') in 1959.

Rambler, the only American manufacturer to concentrate on compacts, saw sales rising steadily throughout the 1950s, reaching virtually 500,000 a year by the end of the decade: Nash, Rambler's *alter ego*, were pioneers of the sub-compact with their experimental NX1 of 1950, powered by the

British Austin A40 engine. In 1954 Austin began to build. this model, named Metropolitan, for Nash to sell in North America. A 40 mpg petrol consumption was something new to the American market; but the Metropolitan could be had with all the comforts of the larger cars, like 'Weather Eye' air conditioning.

Smaller cars still were popular in Europe, and the petrol shortages and rationing which resulted from the Suez crisis of 1956 boosted the sales of these sub-economy vehicles, especially the curious little bubble cars, a fashion started by the Italian Iso company in 1953 with their 236 cc Isetta three-wheeler, which was produced under licence in France and by BMW of Germany, who built it until 1964, nine years after its progenitors had stopped making it. A feature of this little three-wheeler was the full-width front door, with the steering column and wheel swinging open with it for easy access. Late one rainy night two friends of the author arrived in their aged Isetta at an expensive country hotel for a meal. The uniformed commissionaire saluted smartly, grasped the door handle and pulled – to find himself holding the entire door and steering assembly in his hand, courtesy of two rusted-through hinges!

Messerschmitt and Heinkel, who had supplied the Luftwaffe with aircraft in the war, now invaded Britain with bubblecars. The three-wheeled tandem-seated Messerschmitt 'Kabinenroller' was produced from 1953 until 1962, mostly with a 200 cc Sachs engine: but a 'highpowered' version, the four-wheeled 500 cc Tiger was made from 1958–60.

With their noisy air-cooled engines and cramped accommodation, the bubblecars were a fairly crude solution to the problems of economy. Austin-Morris engineer Alec Issigonis thought that a more polished approach would

Nash Airflyte in miniature—the Austin-built Metropolitan (above) of 1954–61 was a curious mixture of European engineering and American styling, the end-product being an Art Deco mess on wheels. Right: the Isetta was the original bubble car, best known in its BMW version, built through to 1963. Messerschmitt's Kabinenroller (far right) seated two in tandem. The four-wheel 'high-performance' Tiger version had a 500 cc engine in place of the normal 200 cc unit

secure his company a large share of the market. Hurried development of his concept of a tiny box-on-wheels – introduced as the Mini in 1959 – with a transverse engine, front-wheel drive and all-round independent suspension by rubber-in-torsion meant that the existing BMC A Series power unit had to be adapted to fit – and anyone who has attempted to work on the engine of an early Mini will have realised that the installation was not exactly tailor-made!

There were problems, too, with water leakage and with the vulnerable distributor, which shorted-out in rain. But the virtues of the model far outweighed its vices, and the Mini became the most prolific British model, with sales well in excess of two million. It also proved surprisingly successful in racing and rallying.

As the Mini came in, a production legend was on its way out. Ford's Popular, which lasted until 1959, had 1938 styling and the 1,172 cc side valve engine originally designed for the 1935 CX 10 hp, but soldiered on through the 1950s as Britain's cheapest full four-seater saloon, with a basic price before tax of only £295 in 1958 (British purchase tax added another £149). Its replacement, the overhead valve Anglia, was far more up-to-date featuring the reverse-rake window that had first been seen on some American Lincoln models.

But while the cheaper models

Alec Issigonis' Mini was conceived as an economy box on wheels in the late 1950s. The prototype *(top left)* looked odd with its Austin A35 radiator grille, but the first production model *(top centre)* had the cheeky appearance which endeared the Mini to over 3 million owners. Fastest recent Mini is the 1275 GT *(top right)* but the earlier Cooper versions performed better than the designer could have imagined, and for years dominated their classes in saloon racing *(above, at Brands Hatch).*

Opposite: Ford's 1954 Anglia 100E *(top)* was up to the minute in styling, but its side-valve engine had its origins in 1935. The Zephyr Six broke with Ford tradition, in having an ohv engine and independent front suspension. The 1959 Austin A40 *(far right)* had clean-cut Farina styling, but the A105 Westminster of 1956 was anything but clean-cut

thrived, many of the smaller British companies faded away during the 1950s.

Armstrong-Siddeley, for example, introduced two new 2·3 litre models for 1957, the six-cylinder 236, which pioneered the Manumatic transmission, which provided 'two pedal control and simple but not automatic gearchanges,' and the faster, four-cylinder 234. Neither was a great success, and they were soon dropped. Armstrong's last car, the 4 litre Star Sapphire, had little better fortune, though it was a superior car, for in 1960, as a result of the marque's parent company, Hawker Siddeley, having merged with the Bristol Aeroplane Company, car production ceased.

One of Britain's oldest marques, Lanchester, had been taken over by Daimler long before, in 1931, but had managed to preserve some individuality over years of badge engineering in which Lanchesters became lower-priced Daimlers. The company's last venture was the Sprite of 1955–56, which never reached serious production status. It had unit construction of body and chassis, torsion-bar independent front suspension, and a Hobbs fully automatic transmission.

But it was no more than an impressive swansong, and in 1956 Lanchester celebrated their golden jubilee by dying.

Other casualties of the 1950s included Lea-Francis (which unsuccessfully tried a comeback in 1960), Invicta, acquired by Frazer Nash (which itself gave up production in favour of its Porsche agency in 1960), Healey, HRG and Jowett.

In France, the motor industry, already reduced to a handful of monolithic enterprises, contracted still further when Citroen, whose shark-like, hydro-pneumatically suspended DS19 was the sensation of 1955 (and is still not outmoded), acquired an interest in Panhard & Levassor. The marque which had introduced the classic concept of the motor car became a wholly owned Citroen subsidiary in 1965 and

vanished completely two years later.

During the decade Simca acquired Unic trucks, the Ford-France factory, Saurer's French operation and Talbot; in 1958 Chrysler acquired a minority interest in the company as a first step in setting up a European operation, making the purchase absolute five years later.

Such transactions were not really a phenomenon that was likely to bother the motor industry in the totalitarian states behind the Iron Curtain, but in fact their operations enjoyed something of an expansion at this period, even attempting to break into foreign markets.

The Czech Skoda company, for instance, which had started off with high hopes in 1923 building Hispano-Suizas under licence and gradually became more and more utilitarian, by the 1950s producing a rather ugly range of saloons of obviously pre-war antecedants. But in 1954 they established a British sales agency, presumably in an attempt to acquire some Western currency, even though the car was hardly an attractive sales prospect, being priced some £200 above comparable British models.

Nevertheless, an agent was appointed, with an office more than somewhat off the beaten track at Blindley Heath in rural Surrey; whether enough Skodas were sold at this time to justify even this modest agency is a moot point.

Russia's motor industry, for so long geared to Model A Ford derivatives, produced mainly modified Packard models for high officials in the 1950s.

But towards the end of the decade prototypes of a new popular model began to appear. Initially the new car was called the Communard, and had a VW-type flat-four engine: but by the time it was shown in 1960, a 750 cc V4 was fitted, with a curious balancing arrangement consisting of a counter-rotating shaft running at full engine speed inside a hollow camshaft turning at half that rate. The new model was called the Zaphorozhets, after the town in which the factory was located.

Poland introduced the Syrena in 1955, East Germany the Trabant; both were utilitarian two-strokes which were hardly comparable with Western models. Later, some East European countries turned to licence-built versions of Western designs, Fiats being particularly favoured.

Red China's offerings at the same period had no need of comparison with anything, for the only customers for that vast country's tiny industry were the Maoist bigwigs, who could choose between the older 5·6 litre Red Flag limousine or the newer, Chrysler Plymouth-inspired Peace, built in Tientsin, and like its predecessor, a V-8.

The whole world, it seemed, was taking to the car: even in the most repressed societies, this new personal freedom was becoming more popular.

The Australian Holden Special Sedan *(top)* of 1959 was similar in conception and styling to contemporary Vauxhalls—hardly surprising, as both companies were part of the mighty General Motors organization.
The Mercedes 220S of 1956 typifies the styling of the company's post-war models. The 220S was advertised in Spain as 'el elegante Sedán con el impetuoso motor de 6 cilindros'—a rather extravagant claim

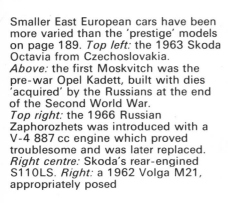

Smaller East European cars have been more varied than the 'prestige' models on page 189. *Top left:* the 1963 Skoda Octavia from Czechoslovakia.
Above: the first Moskvitch was the pre-war Opel Kadett, built with dies 'acquired' by the Russians at the end of the Second World War.
Top right: the 1966 Russian Zaphorozhets was introduced with a V-4 887 cc engine which proved troublesome and was later replaced.
Right centre: Skoda's rear-engined S110LS. *Right:* a 1962 Volga M21, appropriately posed

Luxurious High Performance

In the vintage years, you knew where you were with quality cars. They were large and upright – 'a sports car is any vehicle you cannot walk through with your hat on!' – and bore aristocratic names like Rolls-Royce, Hispano-Suiza or Delaunay-Belleville.

But in the changing world of post-war motoring exotic makes originated in the most unlikely circumstances, and were quite likely to carry the name of an engineer of far from aristocratic birth.

Take Ferrari, one of the most sought-after modern marques; its founder, Enzo Ferrari was born in 1898, son of the owner of a little wood-and-metal-working business in Modena, Italy. He entered the motor industry on being demobbed in 1919; within a year he had joined Alfa Romeo as a driver and tester, eventually leading the company's racing division.

In 1929 he founded his own racing team, Scuderia Ferrari, its emblem the black prancing horse on a yellow shield that had been carried on the plane of an Italian air ace during the First World War. In 1940, Ferrari built two eight-cylinder 1½ litre prototypes, based on Fiat components. The first post-war model – the first actual Ferrari – was the 1½ litre Tipo 125, powered by a type of engine that was to become the hallmark of the marque, the V-12. Although most of the company's early products were racing and sports cars, touring models were produced, with bodies built by leading Italian coachbuilders.

In 1951 came the first of a range of large-engined models aimed at the United States market, the 4.1 litre America; by 1955 this had grown into the 4.9 litre Superamerica, with a V-12 which developed 340 bhp in touring form, and was good for 165 mph. In 1959 disc brakes were added to the specification; as the Superfast, costing a cool £11,519, the model remained in production until 1966. These super-luxury models, magnificent though they were, commanded only a limited market, and Ferrari production of them has deliberately been limited. Demand for the elegant 365 GTB 2 plus 2 was never satisfied, and the latest in the line, the Berlinetta Boxer was designed for an annual production of fewer than 100 cars.

What has kept the company going were large cash injections from Fiat and the Dino engine, a V-6 2-litre named after Ferrari's son, who died in 1956. The mid-engined Dino coupe is as near as Ferrari has ever got to mass-production, and its price tag of over £6,000 reflects this fact. In 1973 a V-8 Dino 308 2 plus 2 was launched.

Another of Italy's top marques, Lamborghini, has a curious origin. Ferruccio Lamborghini, an amateur mechanic, built a tractor in 1948 using war-surplus Ford, Morris and General Motors parts. Surprisingly the venture prospered, and by the mid-1960s twenty tractors were being produced daily, as well as a new product, oil burners. In 1963 Ferruccio Lamborghini decided to go in for car production – as a hobby! Story has it that he made his decision after being rebuffed by Ferrari, and this sparked the ambition to beat Ferrari at his own game (although Lamborghini has resolutely refused to enter racing).

Like Ferrari, his car had a V-12 engine; its success was immediate, and, by 1966 production of the 350 GT was running at four a week. In 1965 the rear-engined 4-litre Miura appeared, bringing 180 mph performance to the Lamborghini range, then the elegant Espada. Latest in the Lamborghini supercar line up is the Countach, with similar speed potential to the Ferrari Berlinetta, and intended for much the same discerning clientele; the smaller Urraco has a transversely-mounted 2.5 litre V-8, and nominally at least is a

Left: smallest Ferrari is the pretty little Dino, which has a V-6 engine mounted transversely behind the cockpit.

Opposite: the Ferrari V-12 tradition is handsomely represented in the 365 GTB 4 Daytona *(top)*. The open *spyder* version of this model is much rarer. Behind it in this photograph is another classic, a 1966 275 GTB 4 (in Ferrari nomenclature, '275' refers to the capacity of each cylinder in this gran turismo berlinetta, while the '4' is an afterthought denoting that this model has a four-camshaft engine)

The four photographs at the top of this page show the earliest Lamborghini, the d'Allara-designed 3.5-litre V-12 GT coupe, contrasted with three 1974 models, an Urraco (top right), a Jarama S and an Espada 400 GT Mk III. Immediately below these are two de Tomaso models, the Deauville (left) and the Pantera GTS; under Ford ownership of the company, the Pantera has been developed into a practical luxury high-performance car.

Two more top Italian models are the 1973 Maserati Khamsin (above left) and the 1969 Iso Fidia (above right).

The Lancia Stratos (left) is emblazoned with the name of the Lancia works rally team sponsor. The Stratos was rallied in selected events from 1973

four-seater, aimed at capturing some of the Dino market.

One of the oldest names in the Italian high-performance field is Maserati, founded in 1926 by the Maserati brothers of Bologna. But the *fratelli* had moved on long before the company entered the *gran turismo* field. Road versions of the 2-litre A6G in the mid-1950s were hardly practical everyday devices, but a decade later Maserati entered the exotica field with cars like the 1964 4·2 litre Quattroporte, which had the option of automatic transmission. Later came the 4·7 litre 175 mph Ghibli, and then the mid-engined Bora, which lacked the fine lines of some contemporary cars in the same category, but offered real luggage space in compensation.

Maserati finances, it seems, were always fairly finely balanced, and it was not until a substantial holding in the company was taken over by Citroen (which is itself controlled by Michelin) in 1968 that its future seemed certain, although the union has not been entirely harmonious.

One of the main fruits has been the Citroen SM, one of the last of the French *grand routiers*, its 2·7 litre V-6 Maserati engine neatly slotting into the complex French car tax system, which savagely penalises the larger engined vehicles. With fuel injection and front-wheel drive, the SM has a road performance in the region of 140 mph. The same power unit is used in the Maserati Merak.

Fourth of the Italian luxury car makers is De Tomaso, lately acquired by Ford, and incorporating the Ghia and Vignale coach-building companies. De Tomaso's Pantera succeeded the beautiful but much criticized Mangusta. It has a 351 Ford V-8 engine, and was sold through American Ford dealers, which made it a wholly realistic project.

American power propelled France's most famous luxury car of the 1950s and 1960s, the Facel Vega, which used a Chrysler V-8 of 4·5 litres swept volume; it was designed for the motorist who could afford to sneer at the French taxation system.

Facel had originally provided bodywork for Panhard, Simca and Ford-France, which accounted for the model's squarecut good looks. Eventually the power unit was uprated to 6·3 litres,

giving a top speed of 135 mph, coupled with good handling by the standards of the day, though the death of the French author Albert Camus in his Facel, gave rise to popular doubts on this score.

However, the smaller Facellia, introduced in 1960, proved somewhat of a curate's egg, and contributed towards the company's eventual bankruptcy.

Top: latter-day French *grand routier*, the Citroen SM, results from an alliance between Citroen and Maserati.
Centre: Raymond Loewy's attempt to improve on the Jaguar XK140 in 1955.
Above: Pegaso was Spain's only recent manufacturer of 'luxury' cars, from 1951 until 1957. This pair of 2.8-litre Z-102s have Touring bodies.
Following pages: the Alfa Romeo Montreal *(top left)*, and the Monica *(bottom left)*, designed in England but built in France. *Right:* the Maserati Bora

British limited-production variety.
Top row, left to right: the 3-litre Alvis of 1955–67 was the last private car built by this company; Gordon-Keeble built fewer than 100 of these elegant 5.4-litre GT coupés, but the model became a legend; the Aston Martin DBS V8 was a well-mannered thoroughbred.
Centre: Bristol's 401 of 1949 betrays its BMW ancestry—its smooth contours gave it a 100 mph-plus maximum speed with only 85 bhp; the 410 introduced in 1966 had a modified Chrysler 5.2-litre V-8, and a maximum speed of 132 mph.
Above: the Jensen 541K of 1957 and the four-wheel drive FF

Its twin-ohc 1·6 litre engine burned oil copiously and pistons frequently, and in a death-throes spasm the company turned to Volvo engines in the Facel III.

Hopefully, a better fate awaits the new Monica, sponsored by railway-rolling stock maker Jean Tastevin, de-signed by Englishman Chris Lawrence and initially powered by a 3·5 litre Martin V-8, designed in England. Be-fore the car got into production, a 5·6-litre Chrysler V-8 was sensibly substi-tuted.

Certainly the Monica deserves a better fate than the Gordon-Keeble, which built up a tremendous reputa-tion during its chequered production career. Powered by a 4·6 litre V-8 Chevrolet engine housed in an elegant Bertone-styled body, the Gordon-Keeble proved to be under-priced, and the company failed after less than 100 cars had been built; subsequent attempts to make the project viable proved only temporarily successful.

The Ford of Britain GT 40, a road-going version of their classic sports car, was an uncharacteristic venture. The GT 40 became something of a legend in its own time and several of the cars built for racing have been converted for road use.

In 1971 Aston Martin survived the latest financial crisis in their long history and passed into new owner-ship; their 1973 V-8, priced at £9,600, has a top speed of 160 mph.

Jensen, who introduced the revol-utionary FF 6·3 litre four-wheel drive coupe in 1966, have also had—and overcome—their problems; their main product since the FF was quietly discontinued, the Interceptor, is very much in the company's tradition of quality coach-building. Well-ap-pointed, too, is the Bristol 411, another limited-production model to use Chry-sler power.

There will, it seems, always be a market for specialised super luxury cars. How long they can continue to be sold on performance as well as sybaritic luxury is another matter entirely.

TCs to GTBs
the wide wide world of the sports car

The conception of a sports car has changed greatly since the Second World War, to the point where there is no longer a sports car type that can be closely defined. Some developments had been foreshadowed by 1939: coupes which would now be regarded as GT cars had been raced by companies such as Alfa Romeo; sports-racing cars had been raced by companies such as Bugatti; smoothly efficient bodies had been produced by coachbuilders, and more important by companies such as BMW.

A key early post-war sports car was an MG Midget, the TC. This had the qualities which some critics still seem to think essential in a true sports car: it was noisy, it had a very hard ride, weather-proofing was inadequate; in other words, it was uncomfortable. It was not shatteringly fast – its 55 bhp engine propelled it to a near 80 mph maximum – but the manner of its going was a revelation to Americans. It was old hat to Britons who had known the like through the 1930s, but this sporty little device was utterly different to the wallowing automobiles that were all most Americans knew. They bought TCs by the thousand (6,000 to be precise), and the great American reawakening largely stemmed from this unremarkable yet remarkable little car.

This 'traditional' sports car theme was to be carried through decade after decade, while overall ideas of a sports car became increasingly diversified – the role of the once-definable type was filled by cars ranging from high-performance saloons and 'sports compacts' to businessman's expresses, from bug-gies to svelte GT machines, from trials cars to thinly-disguised GP cars, from kit conversions for humdrum chassis to the most powerful road-racing cars ever built.

Through this, MGs continued to be built, sometimes as badge-engineering by-products of BMC and BLMC models. In the sports line, the TC was followed by the TD and the TF. This was succeeded in 1955 by the MGA, which slowly evolved through into the 1970s, in 1973 gaining a 3·5 litre V-8 in its coupe MGB GT version. Meanwhile, the Midget theme and name had been picked up again in a version of the Austin Healey Sprite (which it outlived, as BLMC dropped their Healey association).

Few manufacturers outside England bothered with this type of car, until Datsun essayed the mediocre Fairlady

An MGB GT racing through the streets of Campofelice in the 1967 Targa Florio. The carabinieri show little interest

For decades Jaguar and MG have been leading manufacturers of sports cars. From the first XK120, Jaguars have always had smooth bodies and superb engines, even if the suspension of the XKs may have been a little rudimentary. Jaguar gained their second Le Mans victory in 1953, when Hamilton and Rolt won, and Moss *(right)* and Walker drove the car placed second. The E-type *(above)* is perhaps a grand touring car rather than a sports car, but with tremendous performance—which can hardly be exploited in many speed-restricted countries in the 1970s!

The post-war MG story is summed up by the pair of cars opposite, a TC and a V-8 engined MGB GT

Top left: Donald Healey's Healey in the 1948 Mille Miglia. *Top right:* his name was coupled to Austin in the 'frog-eye' Sprite in 1958. *Centre left:* the 'rival' small Triumph, the Spitfire, was developed through to the GT6; *Centre right:* Healey's name re-appeared on a new 'traditional' sports car, the Jensen-Healey. *Above:* Triumph's TR series evolved from the car shown at Earls Court in 1952 through to the masculine TR6

and then introduced the immensely successful 240Z. But British manufacturers found that it stubbornly remained a worthwhile category. Donald Healey built a few sports cars in his own name, and Nash-Healeys, then his 1952 Healey Hundred was adopted for mass production as the Austin Healey 100S; the later six-cylinder version became a familiar rally car, and so in the face of probability (bearing in mind limiting factors like clearances) did the '3000'.

This was a beefy masculine car, with body closely similar to the 100-6, and a 2·9 litre pushrod ohv 'six' which propelled it at 117 mph (123 mph in the 1961 Mk 2 version). BLMC were largely content to see the 3000 continuing to sell in a market where more modern 'soft' alternatives were available, at least until US safety regulations were introduced in 1968. It was then felt that the cost of modifying it to meet these was beyond commercial realism, and as without the major US outlet the market for the 3000 was too

small it was discontinued (what might have been was shown by the success of the Datsun 240Z – 'the last of the big Healeys' according to some enthusiasts when the 240Z began to appear in rallies!).

Soon the Austin-Healey link was discontinued, too, and Donald Healey developed a modern sports car in the old idiom to be produced by Jensen, using a Lotus engine. This turned out to be as undistinguished as the anachronistic 3000 had been distinguished.

Major competition for the BMC cars came from Triumph, which of course was to become an associated company under the BLMC umbrella. Triumph's Roadster, with its curious revival of the dickey or mother-in-law seat, hardly rated as a sports car, but in 1950 they showed a very definite sports car with a streamlined body (unlike some other firms, Triumph ignored the exemplary styling of the stillborn 1940 BMW Mille Miglia in their bulbous and complex TRX). The production TR2 which appeared in 1953 was a much chunkier car; major components derived from other Triumphs (the chassis frame from a pre-war Standard), and the engine was basically a Vanguard unit, in 90 bhp form which gave the TR2 a 108 mph maximum. From that point the TR series has evolved, through the TR3, the first mass-production car with disc brakes (over 80,000 were built), the TR4, TR4A with a major chassis redesign to accept the independent rear

suspension from the 2000 saloon, TR5 with 2·5 litre six-cylinder engine (and its PI fuel injection option), and the 1969 Ghia-bodied TR6.

In 1962 the Herald-based Triumph Spitfire equivalent of the Sprite/Midget was introduced, with the Herald's swing axle arrangement at the rear giving anxiety-inducing cornering if the little car was driven hard. It was successful in the market place, and went through the customary evolutionary process, most notably with the GT6 2 litre fastback which came in 1966.

Through the 1950s there were many small-production sports cars in the same vein. Frazer-Nash built cars with names like Le Mans Replica, Mille Miglia, Targa Florio and Sebring, which reflected race successes (a Frazer Nash was the only British car ever to win the Targa, driven by Cortese in 1951). HRG restarted modest production of their pre-war cars in 1946, and introduced the Aerodynamic; a completely new 1½ litre car appeared in 1955, as modern as its forerunners had been 'vintage' in conception, but only prototypes were run before HRG ceased production. AC introduced the first post-war British sports car with independent suspension, the Ace, in 1953. Based on John Tojeiro's cars, this had the 2-litre six-cylinder engine which had first seen the light of day in the 1920s, which propelled it to 103 mph; the Ace was to go much faster in the fulness of time.

Connaught built a few sports cars. Bristol developed the BMW 328 engine, and their most sporting model, the 450, was based on the chassis of the ERA G-type (the team 450s scored 1–2–3 in class at Le Mans in 1954–55). There were others, mostly short-lived. There were always Morgan and Aston Martin.

Triumphs had ideas about taking over the Morgan Plus Four for mass production, but Morgans preferred to go their own modest way, and have done so ever since. The 4/4 and Plus Four just went on and on, light yet powerful cars with engines from Triumph, Ford and most recently a Rover V-8. Production has always been maintained at Morgan's chosen level, and the demand has happily always held up, and construction retains a high degree of craftsmanship. Morgans have always been uncompromisingly 'hard'; to addicts, this equals 'fun', and to many that is what sports cars should be all about. . . .

Aston Martin has had an up and down career, never quite reaching the heights. Taken over by the David Brown organization in 1947, the company launched the first of the DB series, the 2-litre DB1, of which a sports-racing version won the 1948 Spa 24-hour race. Most subsequent Astons have been of the two-door GT configuration, save for the open sports-racing DB3S and DBRs. These space-framed, disc-braked cars were successful in one of those uncertain periods of sports car racing. Most notably, in 1959 the team satisfied David Brown's ambitions for them by placing first and second at Le Mans, and winning the Sports Car Championship; equally meritoriously, they scored a 1957-59 hat trick in the Nürburgring 1,000 km.

The company withdrew from racing, and went through some difficult economic times, while producing cars which somehow lacked the abstract quality of exhileration in an age of Lamborghini, Euro-American hybrids, Jaguar V-12 and Ferrari 365GTB. A slight change came with the DB6/DBS of 1967, for these cars had the de Dion rear end developed on the sports-racing models, and a home-designed body in place of the Touring-styled DB4. Six-cylinder engines continued, in 'Vantage' form, and the 5·3 litre V-8 developed by 1967 later became available, to propel this heavy car to a competitive 160 mph maximum speed.

Jaguar and Ferrari

Sports car competition is road competition; the reborn road racing in the North American continent was sports car racing. The SCCA had its beginnings on the East Coast before the end of the war, the first Watkins Glen races were run on a circuit of real roads in 1948. The cars in those early races were mixed collections of pre- and post-war machines, some barely 'sports'. Very soon, however, marques began to stand out: MG, of course, Allard, Jaguar, Ferrari.

Sydney Allard started building sports cars, largely with trials in mind, around American engines in the mid-1930s, and after the war picked-up the Anglo-

Top: minor affair—Reg Parnell leading the 1953 British Empire Trophy, the last to be run over the Douglas circuit in the Isle of Man. His winning Aston Martin DB3S is followed by the C-type Jaguars driven by Stirling Moss and Ian Stewart
Below: international honours—Carroll Shelby takes the winning Aston Martin DBR1 past the flag at Le Mans in 1959.

The class-winning Lotus Elites driven by Lumsden and Riley, and Clark and Whitmore, follow. Shelby's co-driver was Roy Salvadori.
Following pages: quintet of splendid Ferraris in French enthusiast Pierre Bardinon's private collection. *Left:* a 330 LM (with blue stripe) and a 375 *spyder*. *Right:* a GTO (behind Bardinon and Jackie Ickx), a 330P4 and a 250TR

Above: Allards in very different events. Sydney Allard outside the palace at Monaco with his 1952 Monte Carlo Rally-winning P-type saloon, and *(right)* the J2 which Allard and Cole placed third at Le Mans in 1950.
Right: the sleek Jaguar XK140.
Below: one of Briggs Cunningham's lightweight E-type Jaguars at Le Mans in 1963, passing a burnt-out Ferrari 250P

American hybrid threads again, aiming at a wider market. For a few years Allards, especially the J series, were familiar road and competition cars; a J2 was third at Le Mans in 1950, and versions scored innumerable successes in the USA, where most were sold (a saloon variant won the 1951 Monte Carlo Rally, too). By 1956 Allard had turned to the Ford and Jaguar six-cylinder engines; his Palm Beach with the Jaguar unit offered no performance advantage over the Jaguar XKs, and the Jaguars were considerably cheaper. The Allard marque ceased to exist; within a few years, European chassis with American engines were to be very much in vogue again.

That Jaguar engine is one of the classics of all time, as have been many of the Jaguars it has powered. The outline of four- and six-cylinder twin-ohc units was defined by Williams Lyons, William Heynes, Claude Baily and Walter Hassan before the war ended (and while the company was still SS Cars Ltd.). The fours, XF and XJ, were dropped after prototypes had been built; the XK which went ahead was a fairly long-stroke (83 × 106 mm) 3,442 cc seven main bearing six.

It was intended to power the big Jaguar saloons, and its sports car use was almost incidental – the XK series of sports cars came about because Jaguar

thought a small run of sports cars would publicize the engine. Hence the XK120. How a car with such obvious performance potential and striking good looks could be launched without stimulating an enormous demand it is difficult to imagine, but the original production run was to be 200! More than 12,000 were built before it was succeeded by the XK140 in 1954; the XK150 followed in 1957, at last with the disc brakes Jaguar had amply proved in racing, and this model continued until 1961, when the E-type arrived.

Those production XKs were raced and rallied extensively and successfully, but generally the competition spotlight was on the C- and D-types. Lyons and Heynes watched private XK120s racing at Le Mans in 1950, and realized that a competition version of the car could win the race. A new triangulated tubular frame, revised suspension, low-drag body and 200 bhp engine made up the XK120C, or C-type; at Le Mans in 1951 Peter Whitehead and Peter Walker drove the car to an impressive debut victory at 93·50 mph.

Lighter XK120s placed 1–2–4 in 1953, when the winning car was the first to cover 2,400 miles in the history of Le Mans (actually averaging 105·85 mph). The D-type appeared at Le Mans in 1954, when the team had

problems with fuel, and one car survived the 24 hours, narrowly beaten into second place. However, the D-types won the race in 1955, 1956, and 1957, when in an Ecurie Ecosse 3·8 litre car Flockhart and Bueb averaged 113·85 mph.

The relatively unsophisticated suspension of these Jaguars meant that they were not cars for all circuits, although they performed creditably on many far removed from the billiard-table smoothness of Le Mans. For example, the first Jaguar which raced with disc brakes was lying third in the 1952 Mille Miglia, when it retired with deranged steering.

No competition successors were raced, although lightweight E-types were seen on the circuits. The out-and-out sports-racing XJ13, with a rear-mounted V-12 engine was built, but never raced (happily, the company restored it after a test accident), and Jaguar held out against even homologating the later E-types for competition purposes. The E-type was another Jaguar masterpiece when it was introduced in 1961, with a sleek body which promised to 'date' very slowly, and it was a revived masterpiece when it gained a V-12 engine in 1971. The engine was in a very low state of tune, giving a mere 272 bhp, to cause absolutely no offence against emission legis-

lation. Hence the car was no faster than in its six-cylinder form, and it was not a rasping sports car to delight the ear of a died-in-the-wool enthusiast; very real high performance here went hand in hand with turbine smoothness, and flexibility which made the sometimes awkward Jaguar gearbox almost superfluous in the 'manual' version.

Ferrari is one of the most evocative names in motoring, and in motor sport. Cars bearing the name Ferrari did not appear until 1946, although the two Fiat-based sports cars which were entered in the 1940 Mille Miglia by Scuderia Ferrari were effectively the first Ferraris (because of the contract Ferrari had with Alfa Romeo, his first 'independent' cars had to carry the name of his Auto Avio Costruzione company). The first sports car of the true line of often closely related sports, GT, and racing cars was the Ferrari Tipo 125, which appeared late in 1946. This was designed by Colombo around a V-12 engine, and like so many first-decade Ferraris was a combination of a superb engine with sometimes mediocre chassis, transmission and running gear; when resources are limited, something has to be skimped, but slowly through the years all the other parts which go to make up a Ferrari were brought up to the standard of the power units. But the engine plus the name ensured that the marque was firmly founded, and to these assets was soon added a list of competition successes. The 2 litre 166 *spyder corsa* with its archaic cycle wings was the first Ferrari to become widely familiar, and the later 166 with a more elegant *touring barchetta* body won the first post-war Le Mans 24-hour race, in 1949, driven by Chinetti and Lord Selsdon at an average of 82·27 mph.

From this car came the 2·6- and 2·7-litre 212 and 225, and then under Aurelio Lampredi came the first large-engined Ferraris, with engines between four and five litres, and bodywork from purely practical competition types to superb cabriolets and berlinetta coupés, most notably by Vignale and Pinin Farina. In racing, the 340 won the Mille Miglia twice, but gained a reputation for poor road-holding and nasty accidents. With the 4·9 litre 410, the Scuderia won at Le Mans in 1954.

Around 1955 Ferrari flirted with four- and six-cylinder engines, but in 1956 produced a new V-12, which by late 1957 (and like an earlier four) had its cylinder heads painted red. Soon Testa Rossa was adopted in a model designation, in the 250TR. Developed year by year until rear engine mounting became imperative in the early 1960s, the TRs won race after race (ironically, in the year that Ferrari at last adopted disc brakes, 1959, his cars failed to take the sports car championship). For road use and GT competition a touring version of the TR was developed, the classic 250GT.

From the GTO ('O' standing for *omologato*, and hence compliance with the GT regulations), came the 4·4 litre 330GT and the 3·3 litre 275 GTB. This

American cars at Le Mans. *Below:* a diminutive Crosley Hotshot follows an Aston Martin DB2 in 1951, and *(right)* Briggs Cunningham's own C2R leads a Talbot in the same race. *Bottom:* the Cunningham C5R which placed third in 1953; behind it is the race-winning Jaguar XK120C

survived through the 1960s, while the racing Ferraris became increasingly divorced from the road cars. However, in the Berlinetta Boxer which was unveiled in 1971 (although not on sale until 1973), the relationship to the 312P sports-racing car was obvious, for this car had an horizontally-opposed 'boxer' 4·4 litre engine mounted behind the driver. The BB had a claimed maximum speed of 195 mph, and when introduced into England in 1973 it carried a cool pre-tax price label of £13,000.

For some £3,700 less one could buy the 365GTB Daytona. With an engine of the same capacity, but in the classic V-12 format and mounted at the front, this was a 180 mph car which exuded high-performance in every one of its Pininfarina lines. As a road car it was as practical as the more svelte 365 GTB 2 plus 2 (for which a mere 160 mph was claimed), and like its 250GT predecessor gained an excellent competition record. It was thus wholly a sports car in the tradition going back to the 1920s.

Equally a sports car was the pretty little Dino. Introduced in 1965, this

had a mid-mounted V-6 which by the early 1970s had grown to 2·4 litres and 195 bhp. It sprang directly from the sports-racing line, but had the same incredibly responsive road manners as the larger 'conventional' cars.

America's Way

MG, Allard, Jaguar, Ferrari, and many lesser sporting manufacturers found a ready, and sometimes little discerning, market in the USA in that post-war decade when the dollar was the most sought-after of all currencies. But although American interest in sports cars was abundant as the 1950s opened, there was only one American sports in limited production, and that was the somewhat unlikely Crosley Hotshot. Far removed from the contemporary Detroit bulboid, this rather endearing little 726 cc two-seater was popular in local races, and one even appeared among predominantly French small fry at Le Mans in 1951 (it retired).

That entry was under the wing of the Briggs Cunningham team, which was making its first appearance in the 24 hour race with Cunningham sports

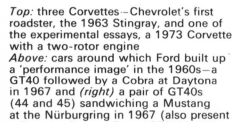

Top: three Corvettes—Chevrolet's first roadster, the 1963 Stingray, and one of the experimental essays, a 1973 Corvette with a two-rotor engine
Above: cars around which Ford built up a 'performance image' in the 1960s—a GT40 followed by a Cobra at Daytona in 1967 and *(right)* a pair of GT40s (44 and 45) sandwiching a Mustang at the Nürburgring in 1967 (also present a Porsche Carrera, Ferrari 250LM, Alfa Romeo Guilia GTZ and another GT40)

cars (having run a pair of Cadillacs in 1950). In 1951 a Cunningham C2 held second place for many hours. This was a bluntly purposeful car, powered by a 220 bhp 5·4 litre Chrysler Firepower V-8. It was followed by the C-4R (fourth at Le Mans in 1952), and the C-5R, third at the end of the 24 hours in 1953, 42 miles behind the winning Jaguar. Said Cunningham: 'we competed to the limit of the brakes . . . if Jags hadn't come that year with discs, I feel we might have won the race.' He tried again with the C-6R (which had an Offenhauser engine) and then raced European cars for a few years. Meanwhile, a few elegant road-going Cunningham C-3s were produced for sale in 1953.

That was the year the Chevrolet Corvette appeared, and American enthusiasts rejoiced that Detroit was getting the message. Not that the first 3·7 litre Corvette was really anything more than a two-seater roadster, and

certainly it was no Jaguar-eater (in the market place the two were closely comparable, at $3,400 for the Corvette, $3,345 for an XK120). But it was a positive move in the right direction, and progress was encouraging: a 4·3 litre V-8 was specified in 1956, a racing derivative appeared in 1957 (and disappeared as GM policy changed), a complete redesign came in the 5·3 litre Stingray in 1963, disc brakes in 1965, another restyling in 1965 with a 7 litre engine option, even a mid-engined show car version in 1969.

The challenger to the Corvette seemed to be Ford's Thunderbird, but this developed the wrong way, into a rather gross roadster. 1962 saw a turning point in the up and down history of Anglo-American hybrids, when Carroll Shelby married the dainty little AC Ace to a Ford V-8. V-8 power found the weaknesses in the original running gear, enforcing the immediate use of large-section tyres and starting the AC on the road to brute-power good looks. The Cobra was blessed by Ford, for it helped convey the 'sporty' image they were seeking. As the power was increased (eventually to 7 litres and 490 bhp), and looks became ever more beefy, the Cobras racked up a lot of competition successes, including the GT championship in 1965, before in Ford minds it was overshadowed by the GT40.

Meanwhile, in the Fall of 1962 Ford tantalized with a Mustang, an attractive little 1·5 litre mid-engined coupe. Reactions tested, it was put away. The name was applied in 1964 to a model which certainly wasn't a sports car (although it was dubbed 'sporty'); this projected the performance image, outsold the most optimistic sales forecast (reaching 420,000 in the first year), and was followed by a string of similar cars from the rest of the US industry. Versions of the earlier Mustangs became familiar in competitions, notably TransAm and European saloon car racing, and Carroll Shelby made the model the basis of an American GT car, in the GT350 and the 7 litre GT500. Ford lost sight of their original objective, and the basic Mustang followed a well-worn path, growing larger and larger and to the discerning, less and less desirable: bulk, standard American imprecise handling, brakes too prone to fade, negligible visibility in some directions—these were not sporty attributes. In 1973 it was dropped, when the much smaller Mustang II in the Capri idiom was introduced.

The Rear-engined Breed

Porsche is one of the oldest names in motoring, where Dr Ferdinand had been producing original designs since the beginning of the century. A car bearing the name did not appear until

Top: Porsche progress—the smooth 1948 prototype, a 356B hardtop, and the 1974 911S, complete with unlovely 'safety' bumpers
Above: famous Mercedes—a gull-wing 300SL at a service point in the 1952 Carrera Panamericana, when the team took first and second places, and *(right)* the production derivative introduced two years later

after the Second World War, however, when his son Ferry launched Porsche as a car-building company. Quite naturally, these followed the Volkswagen concept, with rear-mounted air-cooled engines; less naturally, this has been the basis of every subsequent Porsche.

The first 356 was an 1,100 cc open two-seater, completed in 1948 and in production at Stuttgart by Easter 1950. The coupé version became more familiar, bulbous to modern eyes but smooth and aerodynamically efficient (which went some way to compensate for the modest 40 bhp of its VW engine). A swing axle arrangement was used at the rear, and on all Porsches until the 911 of the mid-1960s, which endowed them with a degree of oversteer which even aficionados conceded was excessive, and which in the early cars caused the unconverted to wonder how soon they would lose it in a corner. . . .

Gradually the handling was improved until in the 356C which came in 1963 the tail-happy trait had almost

been ironed out. Engine sizes and power outputs had gone up, too, through 1,500 cc and 60 bhp in 1951 to 1,600 cc and 90 bhp by 1960. The 911 did not look so very different but it had a 2 litre horizontally opposed six-cylinder engine, which in its most modest form produced 130 good German DIN horsepower. Road manners were vastly better, and have been improved year by year. The engine was enlarged to 2·4 litres by 1971, and then to 2·7 litres in 1973, when the Carrera RS version was a deliberate step towards the RSR neo-competition variant ('Carrera' has been applied to more than one Porsche model, since their successes in the Carrera Pan American). This was a racing GT car, which soon had a 3 litre engine giving over 300 bhp in racing trim (which included such un-street-like equipment as 11 inch rear wheels); it proved capable of living with the out-and-out sports racing cars on the circuits, while the 'standard' RS dominated GT racing.

Porsches had appeared in competition almost as soon as the marque was born. In 1951 the first Porsche ran at Le Mans, and took the 1,100 cc class. Soon the open spyders were in competition, notching up class victories in race after race. Then in 1956 came the first overall victory in a 'classic', when Umberto Maglioli and Huschke von

Hanstein drove an RS version of the 550 to win the Targa Florio. This Sicilian event was to become a happy hunting ground for Porsche teams, which won 11 of the next 17 Targas! By the late 1950s RS and RSK were challenging for the lead on other less sinuous circuits, and a 1·6 litre RSK was third at Le Mans in 1958. This made Porsche hungry for outright wins, too, hungry perhaps, for their efforts to extract more power from their engines were for a while self-defeating. Eight-cylinder engines came in the early 1960s, and by 1968 Porsche were racing 3 litre 908s, and then clinched their superiority in sports car racing with the 917 (see chapter 32). This was a vastly expensive undertaking, in part at least justifiable as advanced design exercises, for the tradition of the old Porsche Büro lingered (and there was always that royalty from Volkswagen, on Beetle sales, to help balance the budget).

Meanwhile, less ferocious Porsches were being raced in events at lower levels, rallied with increasing success (including victories by 911s in the Monte Carlo Rally in 1969–70) and sold for road use for what they were—practical everyday sports cars. By 1967, 100,000 Porsches had been sold, and at that time over half the output was going to the USA, a quarter of it to California!

A sporting image still clings to the greatest of German car manufacturers, Mercedes-Benz, yet they have contested racing only spasmodically and over the years have built very few sports cars. Recently some of their models, in the 230SL/250SL/280SL 'family', have sometimes been considered sports cars, perhaps because they were effectively two-seaters which had roughly the same outward proportions as the traditional sports car; in fact they were luxury tourers – GT cars – admittedly with road behaviour and performance characteristics which shamed many sports types.

The last production Mercedes sports car, the 300SL, was properly a GT car. It derived from the 300S coupe of 1952, and the sensational gull wing 300SL which appeared at Le Mans that year, and won. A production version was built two years later, and built in limited numbers until 1956, and then through to 1963 with conventional doors and rear suspension in place of the original swing axle system. In 1954

the 240 bhp 150 mph 300SL was the fastest road car available, and surviving gull wing cars are nowadays collectors' items. In the 1950s much of the glory of the 300SLR rubbed off on the 300SL, although the two types had little in common. The 300SLR was an out-and-out sports-racing car derived directly from the W196 GP car, which scored 1–2 victories in the Mille Miglia, TT and Targa Florio. At the end of the year, Mercedes retired from racing, and so were these superb straight-eight 3-litre 300 bhp cars, save for an example 'civilized' for road use in gull wing coupé form by chief engineer Rudi Uhlenhaut.

For many years, France had few sports cars; small devices such as the DB which were based on mass-production parts and a few competition Talbots and Gordinis were about the sum total. In the 1960s, however, Alpine and Matra began to make an impression, both building 'specials', and both primarily with sporting ambitions. Alpine had little success in racing, and tended increasingly to concentrate on rallies, collecting considerable prestige benefits for their parent company, Renault – the petit glass-fibre-bodied coupés belied their appearance of fragility in some of the roughest events and took the championship in 1973. That same year saw Matra triumph on the circuits in the sports car championship, with the MS670, to the prestige benefit of

Chrysler, under whose wing Matra lived. René Bonnet had been one of the first constructors to introduce a more or less practical mid-engined road car, the DB Djet; when Bonnet was taken over by the Matra aero-space company, the Djet was succeeded by the M530, aesthetically one of the least pleasing cars of the decade.

In recent years Italy has produced a wide range of high-performance cars, but surprisingly few true sports cars. Ferrari is of course an exception, and one would like to think that companies with a long sporting heritage, like Maserati, built sports cars rather than high-speed luxury cars. . . . There have been innumerable small-run cars based on mass-production cars, many of which in any case have been wholly in the splendid Italian tradition with distinctly sporting characteristics – one has only to think of almost any Alfa Romeo or Lancia produced since the Second World War.

Alfa Romeo have built some competition sports cars. There was the 2500 Competizione of the late 1940s, and the Dicso Volante of the early 1950s, which showed considerable promise but were not fully developed, largely because funds were not available. More than a decade later, in 1967, came the first T33 sports-racing car, initially with a 2 litre V-8. Alfa did persevere with this one, but had to wait until 1971 before the 3 litre version scored a major success, when de Adamich and

Italian variety. *Below:* Abarth have produced many small sports-racing cars and competition coupes since Carlo Abarth set up shop in 1950; one of the latter races past typical Targa *graffiti* in 1967. *Below right:* Lancia's handsome Aurelia GT coupe of the early 1950s. *Bottom:* a pair of Alfa Romeo sports-racing cars sandwich an incongruous 4CV Renault at Le Mans in 1953; this Disco Volante-based Alfa was not successful

Lotus Europa *(left)* was a practical road-going GT car with a 'racing' mid-engined configuration. In 1974 Lotus revived the name Elite for this 125 mph four-seater *(below)* which was powered by their own 907 2-litre 16-valve engine. A backbone chassis and reinforced glass-fibre body was retained, with chassis side members and roll-over bar to ensure the car passed all impact tests.

Right: Fiat's X1/9 is more nearly a sports car than the Lotus models. It was conceived around some components from the 1,300 cc front-wheel drive 128 series, but with the engine mounted behind the cockpit. Glassfibre roof is detachable, designed to be stowed in the front luggage compartment.

Second car is a Fiat 124 Abarth Rally, a front-engined sports car in the old tradition

Top: a late Lotus 7. *Above:* a 1970 Lotus Elan, and *(right)* the backbone chassis of this model. The Elan was in production from 1962 until 1973, was renowned for its handling qualities

Pescarolo won the BOAC 1000 at Brands Hatch, Alfa's first international championship success since the grand prix 158 last raced, 20 years earlier. In 1971, too, Alfa Romeo were runners-up in the sports car championship, scoring almost twice as many points as Ferrari.

Lancia, too, had their competition sports car in the early 1950s, the D24, and also produced some notable GT cars, the Aurelia and the GT version of the Flaminia. Much later came the Fulvia, which built up a formidable rally record. It looked too fragile for some events, but Harry Kallstrom twice won one of the toughest, the RAC, with Fulvias, and in 1972 Lancia took the rally championship. By that time the 'smooth-road' Stratos was under development, and in 1973 proved as fast as it looked futuristic.

Abarth produced numerous Fiat-derived sports cars, and Fiat themselves took whole-heartedly to sports cars in the 1960s (earlier efforts such as the

under-developed 8V were sidelines, soon dropped). The 124 coupe was an extremely elegant car, the 124 Sport Spyder was developed by Abarth into a rugged and highly competitive rally car. There was nothing half-hearted about it, either, although traditionally the company had been disenchanted with the sport since Agnelli pulled them out of racing in the 1920s. Now Fiat ran a works team again, finished second to Lancia in the 1972 championship, and were the closest challengers to Alpine in 1973.

Combining all-round practicability with desirable handling following in train from mid-engine mounting (i.e., between driver and rear wheels) posed enormous problems for designers. Gradually, cars on these lines were catalogued, some of them expensive creations with no sporting pretensions beyond high performance, some of them sports cars in the recognizable tradition, albeit in the new 'soft' vogue – it was a long time before some diehards would accept that a sports car could have a comfortable ride and good handling qualities!

'Vintage' attributes were still to be found in Morgans, and in cars such as

the Lotus Seven. This was a very stark device, which succeeded the 6 in 1957, and confounded Colin Chapman by going on, and on, and on. Eventually he despaired of the demand for it drying up, but at least did not kill it when it was hopelessly at variance with the rest of the Lotus range – the manufacturing rights were handed over to its main distributor in 1973, when it was dubbed the Super Seven.

New standards in sports car ride were set by the Lotus Elite in 1957, in which Chapman used the strut and hub carrier rear suspension already proved on his circuit sports cars. The Elite in fact turned out to be a better circuit car than an everyday road sports model. A very pretty little coupé, it was the first production car to use glass fibre in a structural role, in an ultra-light body/chassis. This lacked rigidity, and in later road cars Chapman was to use a seperate chassis. The Elite had a maximum speed of over 110 mph (from a mere 75 bhp), but it was noisy and the owner who did not experience maintenance problems was rare. . . .

In 1963 the Elan succeeded the Elite. It had a backbone chassis, glass fibre body, and a twin-ohc version of the

1,500 cc Ford engine. It handled superbly, and had a 115 mph maximum speed, which was increased to over 120 mph in the 1,600 cc version which followed two years later; in 1967 the elegant Elan +2 was introduced, and after a few years was the only version catalogued.

Meanwhile, Chapman had put a true mid-engined sports car into production, the Europa. This again had outstanding handling, against which it was under-powered with a Renault 16 engine (used with its gearbox, both at the 'opposite end' to the French car), and the handicap of poor visibility, especially to the rear, from the reclining racing style seats. After two years, a Ford-Lotus twin-cam engine was installed, to give performance more in keeping with handling, and the rear fins were cut down.

Other cars on similar lines were the Porsche 914 (or VW-Porsche), the Matra 530, and the Fiat X1/9. The Italian car is perhaps the most practical

One of the fast but unreliable 4-litre Tipo 151 Maseratis at Le Mans in 1962; like most Maseratis entered in this race, it retired. It is followed by a Ferrari classic, a 3-litre 250GTO

mid-engined small sports car which has yet appeared. Most other mid-engined cars to actually see production have been larger, and some of the most interesting, the Rover BS, the Mercedes-Benz C111, the various Chevrolet Corvette essays, have not advanced beyond the project stage. All of them perhaps show that the mid-engined sports car can never be wholly practical, that in the interests of, for example, luggage accommodation, the racing ideal cannot be tomorrow's road car.

While the classic sports car races were increasingly contested by highly-specialized racing machines (see Chapter 32), a parallel championship for GT cars was introduced in 1962. It was hoped that the GT cars would act as a counter to the sports-racers, and a basic requirement was that 100 GT cars had to be built before a model qualified (this was later reduced to 50, and the two championships were combined in 1968).

The initials GT have been debased by their widespread application to 'improved-performance' versions of stock saloons; genuine high performance is implicit in a true *gran turismo* or grand touring car, which is normally

assumed to be a closed coupe with sporting qualities. The only precise definition is to be found in the international sporting regulations – outside those, GT is often indistinguishable from sports. Among recent GT cars which might also be termed sports cars in most respects have been almost any Aston Martin, road-going Lotus models such as the Europa, Jaguar E-types, and some classic Ferrari *berlinettas*. The outstanding competition GT cars of the 1960s were Ferraris, the 250GT and the GTO.

The costly products of some small specialist companies are sometimes too easily categorized as sports cars. They range from the business man's express (for example the Jensen) to the very refined, very luxurious machines from constructors such as Lamborghini, in which elegance is combined with very high performance. Most are built in Italy, for the *haute couture* of the motor industry is still centred around a relatively small number of Italian specialist manufacturers and coachbuilders. They combine to produce dream cars, or motor show specials; some are far from practical, some eventually see limited (very limited) production.

The Sports Racers

The sports-racing car, aimed at competition use rather than all-round practicability, has been around for a long time: there were the oddly-streamlined little French devices in the 1920s, some Alfas and Bugattis, Lago-Talbot GP cars with lights. Most of them through to quite recent years could be driven on normal roads, with exhausts suitably muffled, and occasionally a pair of heroes will demonstrate this – by taking, say, a Jaguar D-type from London to Le Mans – but these exercises usually serve only to underline the real point, that there is a wide gulf between the cars which won top races and those with 'sporting'

qualities appropriate to a holiday tour.

Over-generalizing, the acceptance of the mid-engined configuration served to widen the gap – but in the way of generalizations, this one does tempt a lot of exemption clauses. The Ford GT40 was racer enough to win twice at Le Mans, but closely similar road versions were tractable and could be used for touring (if a modest overnight bag was sufficient luggage); the Porsche Carrera RSR is racer enough to win the Daytona 24 hours, while the RS swamped the 1973 European GT championship, and is an acceptable 'civilized' road car.

In 1949, the Automobile Club de

l'Ouest faced a problem in reviving their Le Mans 24-hour Race – the shortage of new production sports cars. So they admitted production cars on a simple declaration that 10 examples had been built, and they admitted 'prototypes'. For a while all was well. The Ferrari 166 which won that race was

Right, top: a Ford GT40, driven by Jackie Ickx and Brian Redman, on its way to victory in the 1968 Spa 1,000 km.
Right below: swansong for the Ford sports programme in the 1960s came when Gurney and Foyt won at Le Mans in this Mk 4
Below: road-going Ferrari 365GTB being passed by a sports-racing 312P at Le Mans in 1973

Sports racers of the mid 1950s. *Top:* a 1.1-litre rear-engined Cooper kept out of the way of Fangio and Hawthorn at Le Mans in 1955. *Above:* Colin Chapman racing a pretty little Lotus 8 at Silverstone in 1954

the forerunner of a road series, Jaguar C-types were built for sale, so were Mercedes 300SLs. These cars met the 'spirit of the regulations' – indeed, the prototype rule stimulated the production of high-performance cars.

However, in 1955 Mercedes spared little in their effort to bring off a great double – the world grand prix and sports car championships. Earlier grand prix car adaptations such as the Lago Talbots appeared bumbling once Mercedes unveiled their thinly-disguised version of a GP car, the 300SLR.

The Le Mans accident involving one of these led the ACO to severely restrict Le Mans entries, but the prototypes were soon back. A 3 litre capacity limit followed, then international rules attempting to impose practical conditions governing areas such as windscreens and luggage space – an open invitation to meet and beat the regulations. The international gov-

erning body tried again in 1962, with a championship for production GT cars. These, the ACO felt, would not draw the usual crowd of several hundred thousand to Le Mans, so with the organizers of the Sebring, Targa Florio and Nürburgring sports car events, they devised a championship for prototype or experimental cars of up to 4 litres. As so often, the international rules soon followed the Le Mans lead, and went further, in removing the engine capacity limit (the GT championship was retained as a parallel class).

Coopers had proved the case for mounting an engine behind a driver in a competition car, but their sports car essays were limited. Porsche got the recipe right once they moved away from Type 356 derivatives with the 904, even Ferrari had come up with a rear-engined sports car by 1961. Just how efficient a car on these lines could be was shown by Colin Chapman, whose sports models since the Lotus 8 in 1955 had combined aerodynamic efficiency with above-average road-holding; in 1962 Jim Clark drove a 1·5 litre 100 bhp rear-engined Lotus 23 out of sight of the Ferrari and Porsche heavy metal at the Nürburgring.

At that time Ferrari held a dominant position in sports car racing, for the Scuderia could produce appropriate cars on a horses for courses basis – elegant little Dinos for the Targa Florio, 250P, 275P, 275LM, 330LM and the beautiful 330Ps for the faster circuits. Ferrari ruled at Le Mans year after year. By 1964 the cars from Maranello had won eight times, taking

their fifth successive win that year. But it was in 1964 that the make which was to topple them made its Sarthe debut.

Ford of America had begun to get involved in motor sport in the mid 1950s, then withdrawn in compliance with an AMA 'no racing' agreement. They backed out of this in 1962, setting their sights ambitiously on NASCAR, USAC, drag racing and international sports car racing (for which read Le Mans, for although a lot more was to follow in train, that was the race where victory was going to generate world-wide publicity which would justify the enormous costs).

As with their Indianapolis programme, Ford had no hesitation about buying in expertise. They tried to buy Ferrari, lock, stock and Commendatore Enzo, but negotiations broke down when near to conclusion (and Fiat took steps to ensure that the jewel in the Italian motor industry's crown remained firmly Italian; thereby they also opened the Maranello gates to trade unions, with the inevitable stultifying effect on flair, extemporization, flexibility and so on – the qualities essential to a competition-orientated factory).

Ford looked around, inevitably to England where the racing car innovation and production pace was being set, and whence came the ACs into which Carroll Shelby had started dropping Ford V-8s, to produce the Cobras which had reflected much credit on Ford. They lit upon Eric Broadley, and his pretty little Ford-engined Lola GT. There was the basis of a car to beat Ferrari, for winning Le Mans through most of the 1960s simply meant beating Ferrari.

Lola was in effect taken over, and out of the new Ford Advanced Vehicles firm came the 4·2 litre GT40. It didn't beat Ferrari at Le Mans in 1964, or 1965. The contest took on David and Goliath proportions, Ford threw giant resources into the Mk 2 and Mk 4 sports racers, which were built in America, and won at Le Mans in 1966 and 1967. That achieved, Ford presented the Le Mans organizers with a chicane, which seemed an insurance against the lap record of 147·89 mph set by Hulme and Andretti in Mk 4s being broken too soon, and departed the sports car scene. In the year before

the GT40s came to Le Mans, the lap record had stood at 129·07 mph, so as at Indianapolis Ford's very entry into the field had forced things along.

That should have ended the GT40 story. But the basic machine had meanwhile been developed into a very good sports car, which was in limited production until Ford decided that competition had well and truly changed their image, but that it was a skin to be sloughed off as the safety lobby began to get the upper hand in the USA.

John Wyer, a very wily old racing campaigner, had been in charge of the 'normal' GT40 programme, and had Gulf sponsorship to go on winning races like Le Mans. Which his blue and orange GT40s did in 1968 and 1969,

when Ickx and Oliver brought the car which had also won in 1968 through to win by little more than 100 yards from the Porsche with which Ickx had duelled through the final hours. That was the end of the GT40's illustrious racing career.

The white Chaparrals which appeared in the second half of the 1960s were either ugly, or were the ultimate expression of automotive science applied to racing. Jim Hall's first Chaparrals were built for American sports car races, and the line ended when the 2J 'sucker car' was outlawed in 1970. In 1966 and 1967 the 2D and 2F were raced in world championship events, each model winning one.

The 2D was a big, but outwardly not

Le Mans again. This Camoradi pair in 1960 *(right)* are a Tipo 61 Maserati, with an extraordinary low-drag screen which in vertical measurement met the 10-inch requirement of the regulations (and also serves to reveal the multitudinous small tubes of the chassis which earned the model its 'birdcage' nickname), and a Chevrolet Corvette. The 1963 group *(below)* is led by the one-off Aston Martin 215. Close behind is the 5 litre Maserati-France Tipo 151, Ferrari 250P and 330LM, an Aston Martin DB4GT, and two more Ferraris. The Aston Martin lead was short-lived and Ferraris took the first six places, headed by the car driven by Scarfiotti and Bandini (last in this group)

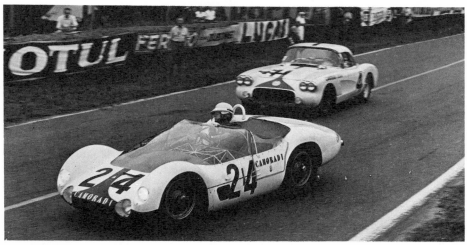

Into the middle 1960s, the best of sports-racing cars were smooth and elegant, as evidenced by this Ferrari P3 driven by John Surtees at the Nürburgring *(left)*, although even that car has small aerodynamic excrescences front and rear to aid its road holding. These are abundantly obvious on the pair of Porsche 917s at Le Mans *(right)*—these cars might have been functionally handsome in a brutal sense, but were among the most inelegant ever raced. Following the 917s are a Ferrari Daytona and a pair of Porsche 911s—cars which would not look out of place on an everyday road, and indeed are normally used on public roads. With their T33, Alfa Romeo won top international races—and one of these 3-litre cars won the last championship race for which 5-litre cars were eligible, at Watkins Glen in 1971 *(below,* Andrea de Adamich in the famous Karussel 'ditch' at the Nürburgring).

Bottom: 5 litre cars in the Spa 1000 km in 1970—*left and p 255 left* are normal Porsche 917s, the other two are Ferrari 512S, a model which enjoyed little success (race was won by Porsche 24 driven by Siffert and Redman, second was the Ferrari number 20 driven by Ickx and Surtees; the yellow Ferrari was driven by Bell and de Fierland and the yellow Porsche by Laine and van Lennep)

Left: the Ford Mk 4 in its first race, at Sebring in 1967, when it was the only one of the new type entered and won by a wide margin. A Chaparral 2D swings wide behind it. 'Half-tyre' corner markers were universally disliked by drivers.
Below: most distinctive of the Chaparrals was the high-winged 2F; headlamps blazing, a 2F chases a Porsche 908 into Tertre Rouge corner at Le Mans in 1967. A special-bodied Ferrari follows—this car ended its race in the sand banks at the other end of the long Mulsanne straight (see page 261) —a stretch detested by most drivers

too unconventional coupe. But it had many novel features, most notably a GM fluid clutch transmission, so when Jo Bonnier and Phil Hill drove it to win the 1966 Nürburgring 1,000 km they were the first to win a major road race with, to all intents and purposes, an 'automatic' car. The 1967 2F used this transmission, and exploited airflow to an unprecedented degree – every air intake and outlet played a role, from the nose (where an apparently normal inlet in fact fed an aerofoil and not a radiator) to the rear (where the air which had passed through the Chevrolet V-8's twin side radiators was exhausted above the wheel arches); to top it all there was an enormous strut-mounted rear 'wing', which was controlled by the driver through a pedal (he didn't have a clutch pedal to worry about). The team contested the 1967 sports car series, but failed to win until the last race of the season, when in the BOAC 500 miles at Brands Hatch, Phil Hill and Mike Spence drove it to victory. Then a change of regulations ruled out these splendid 7 litre cars.

Much of the GT40's opposition in its last two years had come not from Ferrari but from Porsche. For years the German company had been winning races to which their nimble cars were suited, such as the Targa Florio, and gaining class victories in virtually every other major race. Now they wanted top honours.

A change in the international regulations was aimed at restricting out and out sports-racing cars to 3 litres, with the ever-laudable but ever-failing intention of curbing excesses of speed and cost. But 5 litre cars were to be admitted, provided minimum production was 25 (largely to allow existing cars with American V-8s, such as the Lola T70s, to continue to compete). Porsche had the fleet 3 litre 908s, but there was always a threat from Ferrari's near-GP cars, the Alfas, and perhaps the Mirage, and to counter this Porsche decided to take advantage of the 5 litre loophole, and incidentally thereby blandly flaunt the spirit in which it had been written into the regulations. In these it was assumed, reasonably, that no specialist manufacturers would

go to the lengths of building 25 racing machines. Porsche did, and thus forced Ferrari to follow suit.

Porsche stuck to air cooling as a matter of faith, applying it to a flat 12 engine in the rear of a car which appeared purposeful, if ugly. At first the beast proved difficult to drive, and unreliable. But in 1970 two leading teams raced them semi-independently (one of them John Wyer's Gulf team), and from the BOAC 1,000 km at Brands Hatch they took over sports car racing. At Le Mans, Attwood and Herrmann drove a 4·5 litre version to gain the coveted victory for Porsche. The 917s won all but three of the 1971 championships races (those fell to Alfa Romeo) and Le Mans winners Marko and van Lennep averaged 138·128 mph for the 24 hours. Ford's chicane had not slowed the race for long. Then the 917s, and the unsuccessful Ferrari 512s, became ineligible for the sports car championship, as 5 litre cars were ruled out.

Fortune, which had dealt Ferrari some harsh blows, now swung – not that the Italian team needed much outside help with their superb team of 3 litre 312Ps in 1972. They won all ten races they entered. They did not contest Le Mans, and that was the only race the French Matra team did enter. It was desperately important to French national pride that a French car should win this race again after 22 years, and against rather weak opposition it would have been remarkable if the powerful Matra team had not won; Graham Hill and Henri Pescarolo did the job for them, at 121·39 mph on a revised circuit – a quite remarkable achievement, incidentally, for Hill, for he thus became the only man to win the Indianapolis 500, the Le Mans 24-hour race, and the world championship. Matra became more ambitious in 1973, and were rewarded when they took the sports car

Below: a 5-litre Porsche 917 in Gulf colours and a 3-litre Alfa Romeo T33 racing side-by-side into the Parabolica corner at Monza in 1967
Centre: the Lola T70 was familiar in sports car racing throughout the late 1960s. This car, at Brands Hatch in 1969, was part-sponsored by the publishers of this book!
Bottom: even while the big 917s reigned, smaller Porsches were by no means outclassed. Peter Revson and Steve McQueen drove this 3-litre 908 spyder into second place at Sebring in 1970. Film star McQueen drove through this race with a foot in plaster!

championship from Ferrari.

Events like the Le Mans classic are contested by cars from other classes, notably GT cars, while saloons made an appearance to surprisingly good effect in some races. Both categories included the last front-engined cars to be seen in front-line racing, notably the Ferrari 365GTB Daytona in the former, and the BMWs and Ford Capris in the latter. These foreshadowed a trend back towards something more closely resembling what Le Mans was once

all about – touring car racing. But they were as far removed from over-the-counter basic cars as NASCAR machines in America (the Capris were capable of 170 mph down the Mulsanne straight at Le Mans), and they were of course not sports cars in the accepted 'classic' sense, rather extreme examples of the proliferating breed of high-performance saloons which had partly supplanted the traditional sports car.

The sports car extreme was to found in cars categorized in 'Group 7' in the

international regulations, which meant two-seater racing cars with no restrictions on engines and precious few on anything else. In turn this largely meant CanAm racing, for the prohibitive cost of a front-line car meant that the European equivalent, Interseries, received little support.

It is therefore a little paradoxical that European machines made the CanAm running from 1966, and that the most original car was American and was protested out of the class in 1970. (This was the Chaparral 2J 'Ground Effects Vehicle', which had an auxiliary engine to exhaust under-body air, with flexible skirts to part-seal this area; thus a degree of negative lift was achieved – and was shown by rival teams to offend a detail of the regulations). The orange McLaren M8s were dominant from 1968 until 1971, then Porsches took over. These were 917s, but not the coupes which had ruled in the sports car championship; they were open cars with turbocharged engines of up to 5·4 litres, which gave up to, depending on boost even over, 1,000 bhp (at the time when the best Indianapolis engines produced 900–950 bhp).

In themselves, these Porsche 917s were complex, expensive and vastly impressive pieces of machinery, although from trackside enclosures their handling appeared so refined and they sounded so far from ferocious that they did not seem so terribly impressive. Nor, usually, did they make for exciting racing – from the days of the McLaren M8s through to the time of the Penske Porsche 917/30 there was usually one team so superior that it led races unchallenged. Nevertheless, these extreme 'sports cars' were the ultimate in road-racing machinery.

Top: Bruce McLaren in his first sports-racing model, the M1A, after winning at Canada's Ste Jovite circuit
Centre: the orange McLaren M8s were supreme in CanAm racing from 1968 until 1971. The winged M8Bs at Laguna Seca in 1969 are driven by a trio of New Zealanders, Amon, McLaren and Hulme. The M8F is being raced at Watkins Glen in 1971 by Peter Revson, first American to win the CanAm championship
Left: challenge that was ruled out. The novel Chaparral 2J 'Ground Effects Vehicle', here being driven by Vic Elford

Opposite: a typical CanAm field, and the dominant car of 1973, the Penske Porsche 917/30 at Laguna Seca

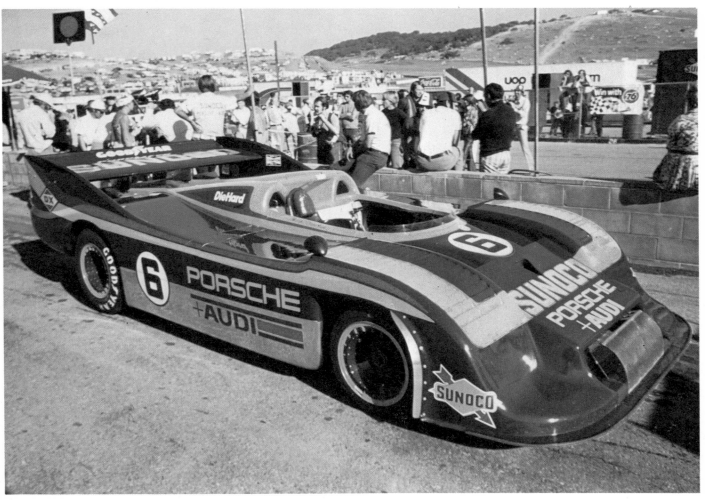

The Sports Car Classics

The Le Mans 24-hour Race has held its place as the centre-piece of sports car racing. Many teams dislike it, most top drivers do not race in it. The race retains its world-wide fascination, it attracts enormous crowds (many for a high-priced week-end fête against the backdrop of an occasionally-glimpsed motor race), the regional club which organizes it has sometimes had more influence on sports car racing than the international governing body of the sport. Just occasionally, 'Le Mans' is a good motor race.

Ferrari took the first post-war race, in 1949, Talbot the second, and France then had to wait until 1972 for another French victory (it is often difficult for the English-speaking world to comprehend the prestige importance which some countries attach to success in motor sport). Then came the years of Jaguar, Mercedes, Jaguar and Ferrari. Then 1955. After two and a half hours of what promised to be a titanic struggle between Jaguar and Mercedes, Pierre Levegh's Mercedes 300SLR hit the tail of an Austin Healey, and was launched up onto a safety bank, and into the crowded public enclosure opposite the pits. More than 80 people died, including 'Levegh' (racing pseudonym used by the French driver Bouillon, who earned his Mercedes drive after leading the race single-handed for almost 22 hours in 1952). Sensibly the race was allowed to run its course, for this meant that the approaches to the scene of the accident were not chaotically clogged (Mercedes withdrew, Jaguar won).

The world of racing shuddered. Many races were abandoned, some for ever. Motor racing was banned by the Swiss government, and ever since, there has been an awareness that a similarly disastrous accident could have more far-reaching effects. As the emotional reaction, and the hysterical witch hunt by the French Press died down, the accident was recognized for the fluke it was. (The French for a while tried to pin responsibility on Mike Hawthorn, for making a late decision to stop at the Jaguar pits, which caused Austin Healey driver Lance Macklin to swerve into the path of Levegh's much faster Mercedes; if there was any failing, it was in the race itself, which mixed cars and drivers of widely varying capabilities, which meant that the possibility of accidents was, and is, ever-present; however, the Le Mans 24-hour Race was too important a French institution to be radically changed, let alone abandoned).

For a while half-hearted attempts were made to slow the race. 'Proper' windscreens were required, for example, then came a 3 litre capacity limit (and the inevitable loophole, when unlimited GT cars were admitted in 1960; they were followed by unlimited 'experimental GT cars' in 1962). Inevitably, the 'ultimate' sports cars came back, for the spectator-drawing power of the race had to be preserved. So did French supremacy in the Index of Performance, a handicap contest for many years promoted as equal in importance to the outright race, which was decided on a formula taking into account distance covered and engine capacity.

Invariably this favoured small cars – while through the 1950s and 1960s there were no French cars capable of winning outright, there were plenty of French tiddlers which could be relied on to last 24 hours. Victory on Index could not be guaranteed: Porsche took it in 1955, Lotus in 1957 and Osca in 1958. But in 1962 the Panhard CD was going into production, and it was important that Panhard had a victory to advertise. Problem was, a pair of Lotus 23s were clear favourites to win on Index, so they had to be ruled out. Attempts to do this by the letter of the regulations failed, so the organizers resorted to exclusion on the grounds that the 23 was 'contrary to the spirit' of the race. A Panhard won the Index, Colin Chapman never contemplated entering the race again, and the cynics were confirmed in their view of Le Mans. The Index declined in importance in the late 1960s, and was discarded completely in the early 1970s. By that time, the French had a contender for outright victory again. . . .

Through the unlimited years of the late 1960s, Le Mans saw some great contests between outstanding cars built almost regardless of cost. Then came another 3 litre limit on prototypes, and 'sports cars' even further removed from sports motoring reality.

Meanwhile, at a cost of millions of francs the Le Mans circuit was changed, inevitably towards becoming an autodrome. The run and jump Le Mans start had been abandoned by 1971. Ironically, in 1972 touring cars were admitted (and a Ford Capri placed tenth), and in that respect at least the race began to move back towards its original conception.

The Mille Miglia survived longer than might have been expected – enormous disruption was caused to the everyday traffic of Italy as its hundreds of competitors raced from Brescia down to Rome and back (in 1950, 743 cars were entered, the bulk of them admittedly by local heroes out for an adrenalin-pumping ride in anything from a mildly-tuned Fiat up).

Left: first post-war start at Le Mans, in 1949. A DB Aston Martin on the left, a Delage slower to move away, then come the two Ferraris side by side—one was first, the other crashed. *Below:* confusion at Mulsanne, the slow corner at the end of the very fast Le Mans straight. A little French CD exits backwards, a Porsche 911 driver gets crossed up, a Ford Mk 4 driver surveys the situation, driver of the Drogo Ferrari looks up from his digging chore. Year is 1967. *Bottom:* sports-racers lead the 1973 field away, a pair of Ferraris leading a pair of Matras *Following pages:* a Ford GT40 at dusk at Le Mans in 1966, and (insets) the Stingray driven by Greder and Beaumont and the Pescarolo-Larrousse Matra 670 in 1973

Mille Miglia specialist Clement Biondetti won the revived race for Alfa Romeo in 1947, completed a personal hat-trick with Ferraris in 1948–49. Ferrari took the next four races, then Ascari won in a 3·3 litre D24 Lancia in 1954, when all five 4·9 litre works Ferraris retired.

The next year saw the second 'foreign' win in the history of the race (see page 131), when Mercedes spared little effort to win it, and Stirling Moss did so for them at 97·98 mph in a 300-SLR. This speed stood as an all-time record for the race.

In 1956 headstrong Eugenio Castellotti drove an amazing race in continuous rain to lead a Ferrari 1–2–3–4–5, and in 1957 veteran Piero Taruffi at last achieved his greatest ambition, winning in a Ferrari at 94·8 mph. During that race, the Marquis de Portago crashed into a crowd, and died, together with his co-driver Ed Nelson and 11 spectators. This tragedy damned the race in the eyes of clergy and government, providing an argument for ending it which was far too strong to resist.

The Carrera Pan Americana outshone even the Mille Miglia in conception, but it had a life of only five years. It was a stage event run over varying courses or around 2,000 miles. European teams contested it seriously from 1951 until 1954, victories going to Ferrari (driven by Taruffi), Mercedes (Kling), Lancia (Fangio) and Ferrari again, for whom Maglioli won the last four-stage event at an average of 107·96 mph. The event could never be properly marshalled, and the five races cost more than 20 lives, a fearful price to pay in establishing an event which to all intents and purposes was a throwback to the earliest days of racing in Europe, however desirable such an achievement might have been in other respects.

The Targa Florio had a remarkable safety record, but somehow became too unorthodox to survive. In a safety-conscious age, the very idea of letting widely-assorted cars loose through the mountains of Sicily, on roads that were virtually unguarded and inadequately policed, through village streets and masses of undisciplined spectators, was anathemic to many in Authority (never mind that the possibilities latent in certain types of accident on tight-

hemmed circuits such as Monaco are appalling – everybody in racing likes going to Monaco; it is an ironic reflection on the recent obsession with 'safe' circuits that however much the Targa may have cost in mechanical damage, it has never gained notoriety on the grounds of human casualties). But the Sicilians fought for their race . . . and for a while kept it alive.

The Targa was revived on the Madonie circuit in 1951, still controlled by its 1906 founder Vincenzo Florio (that race saw the only Targa victory for a British car, a Frazer Nash driven by Cortese). Although it became a sports car championship round, it has never been contested by all the major teams – even Ferrari has seen fit to ignore it several times.

The Targa became something of a Porsche speciality – the German cars won it seven times in the 1960s – but the fervent local crowds reserved their most hysterical joy for victorious red cars, especially when driven by Sicilian Nino Vaccarella (he won for Ferrari in 1965 and for Alfa Romeo in 1971).

This was always the slowest of championship races, speeds over the sinuous and demanding 44·74 mile circuit increasing very slowly year by year, until in 1972 Merzario and Munari scored an all-Italian win in a Ferrari 312P at 76·09 mph over 11 laps. By that time, officialdom seemed more than ever determined to put an end to this longest-lived of all great public road races, in part it appeared for no better reason than that it did not fit into the pattern of 1,000 km events. Prevarication gained a stay of execution for 1973, by which time Sicily could begin to accept the possibility of losing one championship status as the possibility grew of a GT championship Targa Florio – it was nicely appropriate therefore that the 1973 race was won by a Porsche Carrera RSR. . . .

The Tourist Trophy remained true to its fickle history, at times being run as a sports car race, sometimes for GT cars, most recently getting back towards its original conception as a race for saloons, albeit the touring car by international definition often turned out to be a pretty fierce racing device!

The greatest sports car TTs were run on a narrow, winding circuit at Dundrod, west of Belfast. Here in 1950 Stirling Moss drove his first race in a

Jaguar, and won; here in 1954 the TT became a great international event again; here in the black year 1955 three drivers died in crashes, and Moss' win in a Mercedes at 88·3 mph was the last at Dundrod.

The race moved to Goodwood, for sports cars then GT cars, the former won by Aston Martin, the latter year after year by Ferrari. It went to Oulton Park, until 1969 when it was prematurely stopped as Australian Paul Hawkins died in the blazing wreck of his Lola T70. It was moved to Silverstone as a saloon car race. Throughout its wanderings, the glory of the races at Dundrod was never recaptured.

It is odd that in recent years three of the sports car championship races should have been run in the USA, as production of road circuit machinery has never been prolific in that country. More remarkably, the first-ever world sports car championship race was run in America, at Sebring in 1953, and was won by an American car, the Cunningham C4 driven by Phil Walters and John Fitch (at 74·9 mph for the 12 hours). Not until 1965 was there another similar championship race result, when Miles and Ruby drove an 'Anglo-American' Ford GT40 to win the Daytona 24 hours.

Sebring used two runways of an airfield, and some characterless linking stretches to host the 12 hours until the early 1970s (in 1972 it was second only to Le Mans in terms of duration), and 20 years after the Cunningham victory, Ickx and Andretti won for Ferrari at 111·51 mph.

The Daytona combination of banked track and infield road circuit was first used for an international championship race in 1964, when Phil Hill and Pedro Rodriguez headed a Ferrari trio at 98·23 mph, over 2,000 km. In 1966 the race was a 24-hour event, won by Miles and Ruby in a 7 litre Ford Mk 2 at 108·02 mph, and this duration was retained until 1972. Then it was cut back to six hours, partly in deference to the fragility of 3 litre sports-racing cars – an example of the malaise of suiting races and circuits to cars, rather than the traditional and reasonable assumption that teams would race cars suitable to events! That race was run in a season when Ferrari dominated as no team had ever before in sports car racing, and Andretti and Ickx duly romped home in a 312P at 124·16 mph.

Watkins Glen in New York State is where road racing was reborn in the USA, in 1948 when an assortment of sports and sporting cars raced over a true road circuit, along streets and country roads. By 1956 a permanent circuit was in use, to become the home of the US Grand Prix in 1961, and the Six Hours championship sports car race from 1968. Ford GT40s finished first and second in that race; third was a Howmet TX, which thus became the only gas turbine powered car ever to score championship points. It was also the scene of the last 5 litre championship race, in 1971; de Adamich and Peterson beat the 5 litre cars in a 3 litre Alfa Romeo T33/3!

Six hours or 1,000 kilometres had become established as the normal desirable length for championship races by the early 1970s, Le Mans and the Targa Florio being notable exceptions. The pattern has not been consistent year by year, 1,000 km events being run at Monza, the Nürburgring and Spa, as well as at those already mentioned. The splendid Osterriechring circuit has been the venue of the Aust-

Above: a very mixed field setting off at Sebring, in the 1967 12-hour race. An Alfa Romeo heads the cars already on the move, including GT40s, Porsches and a Mustang. The Ford Mk 4 (left) at the head of the line up is just moving, the drivers of the Chaparrals next to it have yet to close their doors. *Right:* the two JWA-Gulf Porsche 917s sweep off the Daytona banking during the 1970 24-hour race; the car shared by Siffert and Redman leads here; Rodriguez and Kinnunen in the following car won the race, at 114.86 mph

Through streets and mountains—into the 1970s the Madonie circuit used for the Targa Florio was almost a survival from the early days of racing. *Top:* Brian Redman hurries the winning Porsche 908/3 between the doorsteps and citizens of Campofelice, in 1970.

Above: two gentlemen of Collesano ignore a Ferrari 330P blasting through their main street, in 1967. *Right:* GT winner—the 1973 Targa fell to this Porsche Carrera RSR, driven by van Lennep and Muller, at 71.27 mph for the 492 gruelling miles

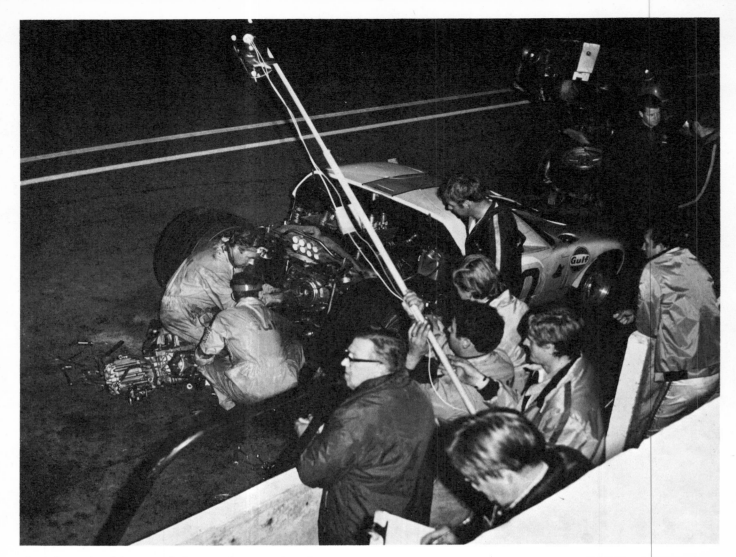

rian championship round since 1969,
an Argentine race featured in the
championship round since 1969, an
Argentine race featured in the championship again in 1971, the Buenos
Aires 1,000 km. The British round
since 1967 has been run at Brands Hatch,
as the BOAC 500, which became the
BOAC 1,000 km in 1970.

Odd events apart, sports car races
have seldom attracted the same wide
attention as the grands prix. In the
1970s the cars have been too similar to
GP cars, and too few top-flight teams
have contested the races. The appeal of
long-distance events (even though the
distance has too often been a mere
1,000 km) varies widely, too, spectator
attendances ranging from Le Mans
quarter of a million down to fewer
than 20,000 at Brands Hatch. These
factors all tended to favour the swing
towards touring car races, which in any
case was encouraged by the prospect of
the championship being run for cars
'with roofs and doors'.

Pit work has always been a vital part of
long-distance racing, although seldom
as ambitious as this attempt to rebuild
the clutch of this GT40 during the night
of the 1968 Le Mans race *(top)*. The
Ferrari stop during the 1972 BOAC
1,000 km at Brands Hatch *(above)* is
more typical. The driver taking over
listens to odd snatches of advice from
his partner, fuel is put in (the tanks are
in both sides of the car), mechanics
change a wheel, using a hydraulic tool
(its airline in the foreground). Car was at
rest for perhaps half a minute

Races for saloons ('touring cars' in the CSI regulations) became increasingly popular through the 1960s, partly because crowds enjoyed watching cars resembling those they could buy. Few people, however, could race a Lotus-Cortina as Jim Clark used to (*above*, at Oulton Park, in 1966). For a time Jaguars ruled in British saloon races, then in the mid-1960s big American cars took over (*top,* Sears' 7-litre Ford between Jaguars at Silverstone). In the 1970s Group 1 racing, for cars with few modifications, gained favour (*centre,* Ford Capri, BMW, Alfa Romeo, BMW). Sales can follow circuit success, hence this class-winning trio of Vauxhall Vivas in the Australian Armstrong 500 *(left)* which brought joy to Vauxhall, despite GM 'no-racing' policy

'Group 2' cars are subject to fewer restrictions, and while they may appear not far removed from road-going counterparts, have become highly-specialized racing devices. Some manufacturers have gone to great lengths to homologate high-performance components (ie, build sufficient to qualify them). Group 2 reached a peak in 1973, when BMW and Ford battled for top honours in the European Touring Car Championship; highlight of the season was this TT duel at Silverstone between Mass (Capri) and Quester (BMW)

The nearest American equivalent to European saloon racing has been in the SCCA TransAm series; most spectacular saloons have been raced in the NASCAR Grand National Championship, which on the super speedways has been one of the fastest of all types of racing. (SCCA, the Sports Car Club of America, is the principal US road-racing organization, founded in 1944; NASCAR, the National Association for Stock Car Auto Racing, was created by Bill France in the late 1940s).

The 1970 TransAm group *(left)* is led by

Mark Donohue in one of Penske's Javelins. He is followed by Parnelli Jones (Ford Mustang), Dan Gurney (Plymouth Barracuda prepared by his own team), Sam Posey (Dodge Charger), Jim Hall (Chevrolet Camaro prepared by his Chaparral team), Jerry Titus (Pontiac Firebird) and Milt Mintner (Camaro); out of the line on the left are Swede Savage (Gurney Barracuda) and Vic Elford (Chaparral Camaro).

The colourful NASCAR group *(above)* are slip-streaming on the Daytona banking. The Daytona race is fastest

of the 'late-stock' 500s, won by Richard Petty (Dodge) at 157.21 mph in 1973. That year the prize fund for the 28-race Winston series was $2 million —a generous inducement to hard-fought racing. In the early 1960s Chrysler and Ford allocated vast budgets to NASCAR racing, and dominated it; later Chevrolet cars became a force. Down the years, cheating the rules has been part of the NASCAR way of life, and the fund of ingenuity applied to it appears to have been bottomless! Lesser stock events are run by other US organizers

Straight Line Specialists
projectiles and dragsters

After the Second World War the story of the Land Speed Record briefly resumed where it had been left in 1939, at Bonneville. John Cobb's Railton was taken back to the Salt Flats in 1947, as the Railton-Mobil Special, and on a rough course, Cobb raised the record to 394·196 mph, comfortably exceeding 400 mph on one run.

This record stood for 16 years, and while lesser records fell to machines in the honoured tradition of record breakers – MGs again being outstanding – a whole new type of competition against the clock evolved out of the 'hot rod' movement. This had its origins in California in the 1920s, centred on Muroc, another lake bed, and by the late 1930s was becoming an organized sport. After 1945 it became a booming sport, spreading to other dry lakes and soon to the hallowed flats of Bonneville.

Hot rodding owed nothing to tradition, and little to sophistication, but a great deal to meticulous mechanical preparation and to Ford products, from the venerable Model T to the V-8, until Chrysler and Chevrolet introduced suitable V-8s into their production ranges in the early 1950s. Streamline devices built around jettisonable aircraft fuel tanks appeared alongside the basically sedan or roadster type hot rods. Out of these came more sophisticated machines, capable of challenging international records. Out of the demand for places to run straight-line competitions came drag strips, and soon another dimension. Out of the drag movement came the first man to exceed 600 mph on land.

In 1956 the last record-breaker in the tradition of the inter-war rivalry was conceived, by Sir Malcolm Campbell's son, Donald. His enterprise was dogged by the shadow of his great father and by

misfortune, and overtaken by developments in America. A new *Bluebird* was created, around a Bristol Proteus gas turbine which drove all four wheels. In 1960 it was taken to Bonneville, where several American machines of considerable potential were gathered. None broke the record; Atholl Graham was killed when he crashed, and *Bluebird* was seriously damaged when Campbell lost control.

Four years later, Campbell improved on Cobb's speed at Lake Eyre in Southern Australia, where his expedition came near to disaster, as rain persisted in falling on the normally dry lake bed. Eventually, he set a two-way mean of 403·10 mph – which was a 'car' record, but by that time was not an outright Land Speed Record.

That belonged to a vehicle which fell under the authority of the Fédération Internationale Motocycliste, for it was a three-wheeler. Craig Breedlove's *Spirit of America* was also powered by a pure jet engine, another hair-splitting facet which did not worry the Americans (or indeed the USAC). By 1964 the FIA accepted that speed was speed, whether the vehicle was squirted along or propelled through its wheels, and recognized Tom Green's 415·09 mph in the jet-propelled *Wingfoot Express* (what amounted to a subsidiary category was created for wheel-driven vehicles).

The door was open to a variety of enterprising devices far removed from cars, and in an age when men were venturing into space, public interest in mere subsonic achievements on land waned. In the context of the land speed record, however, progress was remarkable. The 500 mph and 600 mph marks were passed in one month in 1965: Art Arfons set the record at 536·71 mph, in

Green Monster; eight days later Craig Breedlove lifted it to 600·601 mph in *Spirit of America – Sonic I. Green Monster* cost a fraction of the £1 million spent on the 1956 *Bluebird*. . . .

Inevitably, rocketry attracted the straight-line experts. After proving principles with their X-1 dragster, Reaction Dynamics built *Blue Flame*, a 38 foot long three-wheeler with a 13,000 lb thrust, liquid-fuel rocket engine. One-time hot rod and dragster driver Gary Gabelich piloted *Blue Flame* to a new 630·388 mph record in October 1970.

Quite overshadowed by the pure jet machines, Bob Summers drove the four-engined *Goldenrod* to deprive Campbell of his wheel-driven record in 1965, setting it at 409·277 mph.

Class record-breaking resumed soon after the end of the Second World War. Goldie Gardner collected ten 500 cc, 750 cc and 2 litre records for MG in 1946–48, and in 1950 put the 350 cc sprint record above 120 mph. The name Ferrari entered the record lists in 1948, when Luigi Chinetti set standing-start 100 mile and 100 km records, and in 1951 a dozen long-distance records in the 1,100 cc and 1,500 cc classes fell to another new make, Porsche. Piero Taruffi set short-distance 500 cc records in 1948 with his twin-boom machine, then moved on to conquer other capacity classes. At the other end of the scale, Ab Jenkins broke four unlimited class records at Bonneville with a 25 litre Mormon Meteor in 1950.

In 1952 official records for a gas turbine car were set on the Jabbeke motorway in Belgium, the first turbine Rover achieving 151·9 mph for the flying kilometre and 82·4 mph for the standing start kilometre. In another

Above: the last conventional record-breaking cars were beautiful machines, and Cobb's Railton-Mobil (*left,* at Bonneville, in 1947) set a speed record which stood for 16 years. Donald Campbell's efforts with *Bluebird* (*right,* during a trial run at Lake Eyre) were less successful. *Left:* sheer power— Craig Breedlove's *Spirit of America Sonic I,* with which he lifted the record above 600 mph. *Below:* Gary Gabelich braking his needle-nosed tricycle *The Blue Flame* from over 600 mph at Bonneville in 1970

public demonstration Jaguar took long distance records at Montlhéry with an XK120 coupe, the slowest being 100·66 mph for 10,000 miles.

Both MG and Austin Healey sent cars to Bonneville in August 1954, when George Eyston, Ken Miles, Donald Healey, Carroll Shelby and others, collected 16 international records between them. In 1955 Bettenhausen and Lewis improved on this with 17 1,500 cc records in an Osca, from 10 miles to

12 hours; Lockett and Miles retrieved 16 of these for MG in the following year. In 1956 international records were broken in England for the first time since the war, when F. Sowery took two 1,100 cc standing-start records on an airfield, in a supercharged Cooper-JAP.

In 1959 a works MG was sent to Bonneville for the last time. In 2 litre form, EX181 was driven by Phil Hill to break half a dozen class records, the

fastest at 254·91 mph.

Many other records were broken through the 1950s and 1960s, but— ignoring the graduations of duration and distance—the public increasingly equated straight-line speed with the spectacle and obvious competition supplied in abundance by drag racing. The National Hot Rod Association was established in 1951, and the movement edged towards respectability, and once that was established, towards full works

Left: an old car in the old tradition. Goldie Gardner with his MG at Jabbeke, Ostend, where between 1946 and 1950 he broke 13 350–750 cc class records. The car had started life as EX135 in 1934, had a sleek Reid Railton body added in 1937 at one time held records in five of the ten capacity classes!

Below: in its general lines, Tony Nancy's dragster is typical of the rear-engined machines which increasingly supplanted the engine-ahead-of-driver types in the 1970s

participation by major American companies. By the mid-1950s the first 'rails' were racing, and by the mid-1960s terminal speeds were past the 200 mph mark. The stock and 'funny' categories for a while attracted manufacturers' support, and survived healthily when this was withdrawn. A slickly-run meeting offered extraordinary visual and audible appeal as the Christmas Tree lights started cars at perhaps two pairs a minute, and this appeal proved to be lasting.

Elapsed time over the quarter-mile is what matters on a drag strip, and through most of the 1960s seven seconds was the target. This was broken by Don Prudhomme in 1967, and late that year he put in three successive runs in the US national finals below this figure, in 6·99, 6·97 and 6·92 seconds (with a terminal speed of 222·76 mph). So the target became six seconds, reached right at the end of 1972, at the NHRA Supernationals meeting at the Ontario Motor Speedway in southern California, when Mike Snively clocked 5·97 seconds in a rear-engined car (later in the meeting, Don Moody turned in a 5·91 second run). At the 1973 Supernationals, Garlits completed every one of his runs in under 6 seconds.

The times achieved by 'top fuel' eliminators, the most potent dragsters, were of course well within international class record times, but the elapsed time on strips was so much of an end in itself that no great effort was made to break records. Oddly, one of few occasions when the potential of a 'top fuel' dragster has been exploited in this sphere was in Britain (where there is only one permanent strip) at a national records week-end at Elvington in 1972, when Clive Skilton broke the standing-start 500 metre record, covering the distance in 8·7 seconds (a speed of 128·55 mph). The drag movement was established slowly in Britain, and grew very slowly, although quite respectable times were returned – by 1972 Dennis Priddle had got down to 6·69 seconds (comparisons misled until 1974, when the same timing system was used in Britain and the USA).

As the 1970s opened there was a swing towards rear-engined machines – earlier efforts on these lines had been difficult to handle – and the whole drag technique was changing. Tyre development, for example, led to tyres with very flexible side walls which put a large area of rubber on the ground at low speeds, but at high speeds were deformed in a desirable fore and aft plane. Coupled with these came the bleach burn out, a pre-start wheelspin on a pool of household bleach which reacts chemically with the tyre compound to form a sticky patch on the start area, making a more efficient getaway once the Christmas Tree lights flicker to green, or the more instantaneous 'pro-start' releases a blur of sound and acceleration. In extreme cases, the track has been sprayed from a helicopter to obtain this desirable state of adhesion.

Supercharged Chrysler Hemi engines of up to 7 litres became almost universal in the later 1960s. Racing on a fuel mixture containing up to 80 per cent of nitro-methane, these units produce over 1,500 bhp – and are naturally temperamental! Stopping from terminal speeds which often exceed 230 mph is aided by parachutes.

Thus, as the appeal of traditional speed achievements was devalued by those in fields outside motoring, spectacle brought to straight-line speed more enthusiasts than it had ever known when the Land Speed Record was the most coveted title in motoring.

The Fastest Races

Only one real effort to revive track racing has been made in Europe since the end of the Second World War, and that was short-lived, so most of Europe's track energies have been expended in America, to remarkably good effect. Montlhéry gently mouldered on after the war, its banked piste de vitesse

The pace car leading the field away at Indianapolis, in 1961. Four rows of roadsters lead; Brabham's Cooper is on the inside of row 5 – as well as being rear-engined, it offended ingrained Indianapolis superstitions about green cars

being used for record attempts and that part of it incorporated in the road circuits for secondary events, until in 1973 it failed to meet safety requirements. The one new track was opened at Monza in 1955.

This was used in conjunction with the road circuit for three Italian GPs and sundry sports car races, and as a simple high-speed oval, for numerous class record attempts and for two races. These were for the Two Worlds Trophy, which was to bring together the best of US track and European road

racing. Neither was particularly successful. Top-line Europeans shunned the first, in 1957, so that the ten invited American drivers were opposed by only three Ecurie Ecosse D-type Jaguars. Only? They finished 4–5–6. Jimmy Bryan won at 166·06 mph in a Belond AP Special, one of George Salih's shapely roadsters (that year the Indianapolis 500 was won at 135·6 mph).

Some Europeans bravely came out to play in the 1958 race, when Moss and Musso showed that specially (but not

275

lavishly) prepared Maserati and Ferrari respectively were almost competitive. But victory went to Jim Rathman's Watson roadster, at 166·72 mph, which meant that the race was then the fastest ever run. The Two Worlds Trophy was not run again, and effectively closes the spasmodic chapter of speed bowl racing in Europe.

For a while the only track event left which gained international attention was the Indianapolis 500. The genuine track cars at Monza had been 'roadsters', a breed which was wholly representative of contemporary Indianapolis practice and seemed set to go on for ever.

Increasingly, they followed a rigid pattern, evolving at a pace so slow that at times it seemed that complete sterility had arrived, and cars could be raced year after year, and remain competitive year after year. Fairly constant-radius turns were thought to call for only the simplest suspension systems, and for a biased weight distribution; a complicated transmission was felt unneccesary when rolling starts were used, so two-speed gearboxes and live rear axles without differential were the order of the day; brakes were minimal by road-race standards; the twin-ohc Offenhauser four was the only engine that got anybody anywhere, and so was almost universal, normally installed offset to the left in chassis, while cockpits were to the right of the centre line with driveshafts running alongside.

Nevertheless, in their natural habitat, they seemed to go well enough. There had been the Novis, true, screaming eight-cylinder cars which were fast, but seldom held together for long, and there had been Lou Moore's front-wheel drive Blue Crown Specials. Nothing much had come out of Europe since the Maserati eight (all of those built ran at the Brickyard as something or other specials in the years after the war); there had been a highly-rated driver called Ascari with a Ferrari, but he did not last through the 1952 race; there had been quiet bow-legged little Fangio, but he had not been able to show his ability in the 1956 Kurtis roadster put at his disposal in 1958.

Then in the Autumn of 1960 an Australian, Jack Brabham, visited Indianapolis to run some trial laps with a funny little car, a Cooper. From that moment the fate of the roadster, a whole heap of cherished tradition, and the complacent myth that Indy was naturally the greatest, was doomed. In the wake of that exploratory Cooper outing was to come an avalanche of European expertise which was to demonstrate that on the international racing scale Indianapolis had become a back water.

The 500 was run again in 1946, after an uncertain period when it seemed that the Speedway might disappear. However, it was saved and over the years was largely reconstructed, under new president and general manager Wilbur Shaw. The basic track plan remained unaltered.

The old 4½ litre unsupercharged/3 litre supercharged (274 and 183 cubic inches) regulations remained in force until 1956, and in 11 races the winning speed slowly rose from 114·82 mph to a 1954 peak of 130·84 mph. Initially, some unusual cars were well-placed. Robson won with a supercharged Thorne Sparks Special in 1946, then came three victories for the Offenhauser-powered front-wheel drive Blue Crown Specials; Horn took third with a Maserati in 1946–47, while Nalon was third with a Novi in 1948. The 1950s were the Offie roadster era.

The engine limit was lowered to 4·2 litre unsupercharged/2·8 litres supercharged (256 and 170 cubic inches) in 1957, and speeds continued to rise. In 1959 all the starters were roadsters with Offenhauser engines, and it seemed that under the bright paint and glittering chrome the point of stagnation had been reached. Roger Ward won in a Watson (Leader Card Special) at 135·86 mph, and in 1960 Rathman pushed the average up to 138·77 mph.

After the American GP that year, Jack Brabham spent a couple of days at the track with a 2½ litre Formula 1 Cooper. He upset Authority by ignoring the time-honoured rule whereby a rookie was supposed to work up his lap speeds by stages, and eventually lapped at 144·8 mph – which would have put his funny little rear-engined car on the third row of the 1960 grid. Some people stopped thinking patronizingly. Roger Ward drove the Cooper, so that one leading Indianapolis personality was able to say loud and clear where the future lay....

Coopers went home and built a slightly modified version of their GP car for Indianapolis, using a Coventry Climax FPF engine bored out to 2·7 litres. Brabham qualified it to start from the fifth row, before going off to the Monaco GP (this was akin to blowing a raspberry at a sacred cow; to the American track brigade, the 500 was – and is – the race of the year to which all else is subordinated, but Indianapolis was going to have to get used to people from the grand prix world who regarded it as just another race, albeit an unusual and well-endowed one, and who found the long-drawn-out ritual of qualifying a boring nuisance).

Jack took ninth place in the 1961 race, running as high as sixth before a muffed pit stop. That was enough to keep some people thinking, not enough to spark a revolution. In 1962 Mickey Thompson produced some oddly-proportional rear-engined cars, underpowered with tuned Buick V-8s, which made no impression at all as Roger Ward won again, at 140·29 mph. But Dan Gurney, driver of one of the Thompson cars, had a guest among the spectators, Colin Chapman. There were also some slightly out of their depth Ford personnel watching, for the Ford Division of the Ford Motor Co. was thinking of going racing at Indianapolis again.

Later the two parties came together. After the American GP, an F1 Lotus was taken to the track, and with 1·5 litres and 175 bhp Clark lapped at 143 mph (he later recalled that 'it was all a bit dull'). More to the point, he got through the turns at 140 mph – and that had not been achieved by a driver with a 430 bhp roadster. Chapman told the Ford technicians what power he would need to win the race, and they were hardly convinced – after all the brain washing with superlatives, it seemed almost insolent that this outsider should specify anything less than near-unattainable power, let along propose to win with a power deficit of over 50 bhp.

But Chapman, the Ford engine men, and Jim Clark came within 34 seconds of winning the 1963 500. Those seconds were not accounted for by the power of the Offenhauser engine, but by slightly sluggish Lotus pit work, by Clark's ignorance of the Indianapolis yellow signals rules (in road racing at that time, a yellow flag was simply a

warning, whereas on the USAC tracks, as later in road racing, a yellow signal also meant 'no overtaking'; what Jimmy didn't realize was that even under the yellows back markers were considered fair game), and above all the power of the Indianapolis Establishment. Chief steward Harlan Fengler had emphatically let it be known before the race that he would black flag (i.e. order to stop) any driver whose car was losing oil, a considerable hazard on a track where the right line ('the groove') through corners is all-important. He did call in lesser lights for this reason, then in the closing stages Parnelli Jones' car started losing oil, copiously. Jones led Clark by a mere six seconds, but his car belonged to a very powerful member of the Establishment, J. C. Agajanian. The stewards were not prepared to black-flag his car, and Jones was allowed to race on, to win at 143·14 mph.

More than a third of the cars in the 1964 field were rear-engined, but again a roadster won, A. J. Foyt's Sheraton Thompson. Clark led the race in its early stages, retiring dramatically when a tyre threw its tread and the left rear suspension of his Lotus 34 collapsed.

The inevitable rear-engined victory came in 1965. The Ford racing V-8s, now taken over by Louis Meyer, one-time partner in the Meyer and Drake company which built the Offenhausers, gave some 500 bhp. Chapman had the hang of oval racing, and took care of his team's one weak point by calling in the Woods crew from Virginia stock car country (they performed astonishingly – at Clark's first stop the Lotus was at a standstill for 19·8 seconds, and 50 gallons of fuel were put in the tanks). Clark had been the first man to qualify at over 160 mph, he led the race almost as he pleased, and he became the first man to win at over 150 mph (150·686 mph).

In 1966 Clark was second to Graham Hill in a Lola, after the race had been led through much of its later stages by Jackie Stewart in another Lola. That was the high point of the grand prix invasion of Indianapolis, and by the time the 1970s opened McLaren was the only European constructor to contest the race regularly. But those four races in the mid-1960s swept aside a whole predictable order in track history. Mechanically, only the Offy survived. The Ford engine quickly passed its peak, while the venerable four-cylinder unit gained a new lease of life in turbocharged form. At first, American constructors were content to copy, so that for example it was difficult to distinguish a Brawner from the Brabham on which it was based. McLaren for a while set the pace with the M16 series, while original American designs began to appear. Most notable among these, perhaps, were Dan Gurney's Eagles – no fewer than 20 of the 33 starters in the ill-fated 1973 race were Eagles.

Speeds rose rapidly – alarmingly when the limitations of the Indiana track are considered. High speeds were also being attained on later tracks such as Ontario and Pocono, but these were an oval and a tri-oval built for the speeds of the 1970s rather than Edwardian years ('oblong' would be a more accurate description of the traditional oval, while a tri-oval has three turns linked by straights). Recently the Indianapolis 500 has been one of the 'big three' 500s in the USAC Championship series, but it remains the one on which most attention is focussed.

The recent history of Indianapolis has been punctuated with more and more accidents, a few novel cars and not a few squabbles (the two often interlinked), while the organizers cling to traditions which have become meaningless – from a distance, one senses that they would have liked the roadster to go on eternally.

The rear-engined car had hardly been accepted as the thing to race on tracks as well as roads, when the turbine arrived. And it proved to be no more welcome at the Brickyard than the Ford Motor Co. Odd turbine cars had been essayed in track racing before, but like the Miller-designed rear-engined Gulf cars of 1939–41 they hadn't worked, so nobody worried. Andy Granatelli's STP Oil Treatment Special did work in 1967, and a lot of entrants and drivers did worry. This device had a 550 shaft horsepower Pratt and Whitney turbine, mounted to the left of the centre line (with the cockpit correspondingly bulging out on the right). Pole that year was taken by Andretti at 168·982 mph, Parnelli Jones placed the turbine car on row 2, with a 166·075 mph average over the four qualifying laps. He led until the race was stopped because of rain, led again after the restart and to within three laps of the end when a bearing failed. A. J. Foyt won, but the USAC made a dead set at the turbine.

Granatelli tried everything he could (quite a lot) to restrain them, but the rules limiting the turbine air intake area (the only effective way to restrain its output) were changed. New and more sophisticated STP cars appeared in 1968, Lotus 56s. Like the 1967 car, they had four-wheel drive; unlike it, they had sleek 'wedge' bodies with the engine mounted at the rear. Practice was beset with problems; nevertheless, Joe Leonard took pole with a 56, at 171·559 mph, and Graham Hill was alongside him in another; the row was completed by Bobby Unser's turbocharged Offy Eagle. Somewhere down at the back lurked the last of the roadsters, Hurtubise' lightweight Mallard. . . .

In a repeat of the 1967 situation, Leonard was leading in an STP turbine car as the race moved into its closing stages, when the engine failed. Unser headed Gurney in an Eagle 1–2, Offenhauser and Ford powered respectively.

The USAC stifled the turbine, Granatelli stuck with Chapman, who came up with the four-wheel drive 700 bhp turbocharged Ford-powered Lotus 64s, which were withdrawn after a practice accident (Andretti went on to win the race in one of Granatelli's back-up cars, a brutal-looking Hawk). A four-wheel drive Lola T152 was third – and the USAC started to think negative thoughts about four-wheel drive. . . .

Al Unser won in 1970 to crown his triumphant USAC season (the last in which 'dirt' races counted for points) and he won again in a Colt in 1971.

Top: Graham Hill driving a Lola towards Victory Lane at Indianapolis, in 1966
Right: controversial car. Parnelli Jones with the ungainly STP gas turbine car at Indianapolis, in 1967

forms of racing on the outside, and keep its own members faithful to its own rather shaky championship trail. Happily, by early 1974, there was a new spirit of cooperation between the USAC and the SCCA, the principal US road-racing body.

Against this background, and the economic difficulties which some other tracks had been facing, it was doubly unfortunate that the 1973 Indianapolis 500 should be memorable above all for tragic and widely-reported accidents, and that the race itself was a near fiasco. There was another multiple accident at the start, and this time some spectators were injured. The race was stopped, then postponed for a day as rain fell. Then it got no further than the pace lap, as rain fell again. It was started on the following day, slowed by a fatal accident at 140 miles, then stopped at 332·5 miles (133 laps) when rain started to fall again. As more than half-distance had been covered, those 332·5 miles were the 1973 500. . . .

The USAC took measures intended to reduce speeds and increase safety, which were so faint-hearted as to seem ineffectual – this seemed to be born out when qualifying speeds at Pocono under the new rules were higher than in 1972. Then at the Texas World Speedway, Mario Andretti qualified his Viceroy Special for the Texas 200 at a shattering 214·151 mph, and the race was won by Bettenhausen in a McLaren at 181·918 mph! At the end of the year, the USAC took their fuel restrictions a stage further, allowing only 280 gallons for a 500 mile race – a stopgap meaning that during races (but not qualifying) engines are run at lower turbocharger pressures, and thus power reduced by almost a quarter, with a corresponding theoretical speed reduction (the first 500 of 1974, at Ontario in California, was won at 157·02 mph).

Despite its shortcomings the Indianapolis 500 remains the goal for every professional American driver.

That year, the McLaren M16s set new technical standards on the tracks, their best actual race placings being Revson's second at Indianapolis and Donohue's victory at Pocono. In 1972 Donohue won the 'big one' in a Penske McLaren M16B, while Unser was second in a Parnelli, a new car from the drawing board of ex-Lotus designer Maurice Phillippe.

That race was won at 162·96 mph, an increase of almost 20 mph in the 10 races since the rear-engined Lotus arrived at the Brickyard. The increase in qualifying speeds was even more dramatic. In 1963 Parnelli Jones was the last driver to put a roadster on pole, at 151·153 mph; ten years later, Rutherford was fastest in a McLaren, at 198·413 mph. Engines were more powerful, tyres were vastly improved, but above all advances in aerodynamics meant that a lap could be run almost flat out.

Thus the safety margins were very very narrow, on a track notorious for its many lurid accidents, which the sport could ill-afford because of their effect on sponsors. This relationship was further damaged by a schism in US racing, when the USAC moved to 'go it alone,' to keep outsiders from other

Changing Scene in the Sixties

The 1960s opened with a curious mixture of gloom and boom, caused, it seems, by the success of the American compacts, 'which surpassed the most optimistic forecasts.'

As soon as smaller vehicles were available from the home industry, many Americans not unnaturally preferred them to the imported vehicles; many dealers, too, lost interest in the imports as soon as they had a comparable domestic product to offer. The combination of these swings in market preference proved a blessing to Volkswagen, who increased their share of the American market at just about every other European manufacturer's expense; Renault managed to hold on to second place, but for many makers, the collapse in the market resulted in production cuts.

But it didn't end there – the American industry now began making a concentrated attack on export markets. Already the US manufacturers had well-established bridgeheads – Ford and Vauxhall in England, Ford and Opel in Germany, a Chrysler share in Simca in France and a fully-owned General Motors subsidiary – Holden – in Australia. 'An immense cash bid' brought Ford's Dagenham operation entirely under American control, a move which, as Vauxhall had been owned by General Motors, since the mid-1920s, brought half Britain's motor industry under American control; in 1964 Chrysler, too, moved into Britain, by acquiring a majority holding in the Rootes Group, who pro-

duced Humber, Hillman, Singer and Sunbeam.

In 1960, Standard-Triumph, who lacked the capacity for expansion, joined forces with the Leyland Group, famous as commercial vehicle manufacturers, forming a combine capable of building everything from light family saloons to giant trucks.

In 1966 the British Motor Corporation, which had been formed by the 1952 merger between Austin and Morris, acquired Jaguar (who had merged with Daimler in 1960). However, the new group was not as financially strong as it could or should have been, and Leyland suggested a merger, which was finally agreed after much hard

Two medium-size cars with advanced engines—Triumph's 2.5 PI Mk II *(top)* has fuel injection (a carburetter version came in 1974), while the Audi 100LS *(right)* has a power unit with a compression ratio almost as high as a diesel

Last of the Studebakers, the 1962 Avanti *(top)*. There have been two attempts to revive this model since Studebaker closed down in 1964. Contrasting with the Avanti's restrained lines was the 1966 Buick Wildcat Gran Sport convertible.
Following pages: America's prestige automobile, the immense and luxurious Cadillac Fleetwood limousine

Motors produced 'one of the world's most technically-advanced cars' in the shape of the Pontiac Tempest, with its slant-four (half a V-8) engine and automatic or manual transaxle (the combination of gearbox and final drive in one unit in fact dated back to the 1914 AC) plus a curved propellor shaft, which was claimed to revolve 'with a constant sag.'

Closely related were the Buick Special and Oldsmobile F-85; just $52\frac{1}{2}$ inches high, the trio were America's lowest cars.

Technical novelty was not, however, the exclusive preserve of the Big Three – Studebaker's swansong, the Avanti of 1962 had 'coke-bottle' styling by Raymond Loewy and the option of a Paxton centrifugal supercharger with automatic variable ratio belt-drive. However, by 1964 Studebaker's plant at South Bend, Indiana, had ceased production, bringing the company's 112 year history to a virtual close, save for a couple more years' limited activity at their Canadian plant.

Another long history to end in the 1960s was that of Panhard, acquired by Citroen in 1965 and closed down in 1967: but their latter products were ugly machines of dated appearance, and the marque's passing came as little surprise.

Citroen themselves consolidated the position of the DS19 (and its simplified ID version) during the 1960s; the model had been so far ahead of its time that a new power unit was the major modification to these cars during the decade.

Citroen's complex self-levelling hydropneumatic suspension was in a class by itself, but the British Motor Corporation introduced a simpler interlinked fluid suspension system under the name Hydrolastic at the end of 1962. The idea wasn't new, but this version, designed by Alec Moulton, was a pioneering installation for a popular family saloon. The BMC transverse-engine front-wheel drive

bargaining. It was not long before Rover (which had also taken over Alvis), also joined this new British Leyland Motor Corporation, which now combined most of the British car (and truck) makers.

Mergers were not a British prerogative, however: Mercedes and Auto-Union, rivals in the pre-war grands prix, combined at the end of the 1950s to produce touring cars, with the old established DKW company part of the set-up. Auto-Union/DKW's first offering was the Junior 1,000 cc two-stroke – 'only seven moving parts' was their slogan, but it had already been applied to the Trojan of the 1920s – which was replaced in 1965 by the advanced Audi. This had only front-wheel drive in common with its predecessor, offering 100 mph road performance from an engine with a compression ratio worthy of a diesel, by courtesy of the Mercedes engine research facilities. Volkswagen, too,

came into the Mercedes fold in the 1960s.

But though major changes in the American industry had caused these mergers and shifts of policy in Europe, all was not well in the USA.

Compacts were certainly well, but the bigger cars were an embarrasment to the dealers, who started the decade with nearly a million unsold cars on their forecourts. As a result, tooling costs on new models were trimmed, while Chrysler were forced to drop their lower-priced De Soto line altogether.

However, the compacts made up for the shortcomings of their larger contemporaries: American Motors came out with a diecast light alloy six-cylinder engine, while Oldsmobile and Buick introduced light-alloy V-8s (the Buick V-8 was later adapted by Rover). From the Chrysler group came the Dodge Lancer, a stretched version of the Plymouth Valiant, while General

The Citroen 2CV *(top)* was conceived before the Second World War; its appearance has changed little (see page 187) and this ugly duckling has become a vital part of the French motoring scene.
Centre: two Renaults aimed at different markets—the R4, introduced as a rival to the 2CV in 1962, and the 16, successful in the middle price bracket. Different approaches by two major British manufacturers are represented in the Austin 1100 *(above left)*, a variation on the Mini-inspired front-wheel drive theme, and the Hillman Imp *(above right)*, which is built in Scotland and has a rear-mounted light-alloy engine

theme was developed still further with the 1100, and in 1964 with the 1800, a luxury model far removed from the basic Mini concept. Minis, too, gained the new Hydrolastic suspension, but it did not seem to suit them as well as the old rubber springing, which was eventually reinstated.

While BLMC were ploughing a path of technical adventurousness, their chief rival, Ford, was pursuing a policy of refining a basically conventional package. In 1962 they announced a new light car, the Cortina, which the

Press described as 'comfortable and roomy yet light and inexpensive.' The original Cortina proved so popular that over a million were sold; similar sales were enjoyed by the Mark II version of 1966–69 and the Mark III which came in 1969. It was a convincing demonstration of the continued development and refinement of a theme. Other British companies, too, like Vauxhall and Rootes, followed the front-engine rear drive theme, though the 1963 Hillman Imp had a complex and efficient light alloy engine designed by Coventry Climax. Developed under great secrecy as Project Ajax, the Imp was intended to be produced in Roote's new factory at Linwood, Paisley, the first new model to be built in Scotland since the days of Arrol-Johnstone, Argyll, Beardmore and Galloway. Chrysler were not exactly enamoured of the Imp, and made little effort to promote it in the 1970s, but the fuel crisis at the end of 1973 served to prolong its production life.

Most British manufacturers had clearcut ideas on car layout but Fiat, with 75 per cent of the Italian market, offered a bewildering variety of concepts: in the mid-1960s their range covered two-, four- or six-cylinder engines in eight sizes, air- or water-cooled, leaf, coil or torsion bar springing and solid or independent rear axles.

Under the stiffer competition of the Common Market such profligacy of outlook was uneconomical, and it was noticeable as the decade wore on that cars were gaining a similarity of appearance and specification across Europe, partly due to the fact that makes were becoming increasingly interrelated, either as a result of mergers or through technical exchanges of specialist licences to manufacture. It was the latter course which made the adoption of Ford of Britain's Aeroflow ventilation system so common on European production cars.

The number of cars in use grew tremendously over the period. Typical was the case of the City of Rome, which took from March 1927 to January 1962 to record its first half-million car registrations, yet reached the million mark in November 1966.

In America, the most motorised society on earth, nearly 8 million cars were being produced annually in the mid-1960s: in 1963 there were $68\frac{1}{2}$ million cars in use, more than 18 million more than in 1950.

In Britain, too, growth was rapid: from 5 million cars in 1949, registrations soared to 11·2 million in 1969; total registrations of 14·7 million in 1973 meant that there were 72 vehicles to every mile of road. Even Britain's motorway building programme, which proceeded with increasing momentum through the 1960s was unable to keep up with the growth of motor vehicle usage.

However, despite every outward sign of increasing prosperity, the motor industry of the world could not afford to become complacent. Quite apart from competition between major parts of the industry, in America, Europe and Japan, there were mounting outside pressures to resist, or to comply with. 'Safety' became a factor which was vastly expensive in terms of research, development and manufacturing costs.

This preoccupation with safety had been engendered by the activities of self-appointed environmentalists, crusading against the perils – some genuine, many imaginary – of the motor industry with the fervour of fire-and-brimstone evangelists.

Heading the crusade was Ralph Nader, a lawyer, who published a much-publicised book claiming that the rear-engined Chevrolet Corsair and the Volkswagen Beetle were 'unsafe at any speed.' Whatever the merits of Nader's arguments, they provoked a lobby strong enough to persuade General Motors to withdraw the Corvair from production. Like an elephant frightened by a mouse, the motor industry over-reacted, and, sensing its vulnerability, the environmentalists moved in to the attack. They issued figures that claimed that cars emitted 60 million tons of carbon monoxide every year, 12 million tons of hydrocarbons, 6 million tons of nitrous oxide, a million tons of sulphur oxide and a million tons of miscellaneous 'smoke';

Top: an Alfa Romeo Giulia GTV, representative of the high-performance saloons built by this company
Right: Fiats are assembled or built under licence in a score of countries, and in sometimes confusing permutations, Chilean Fiats for example being derived from Spanish SEAT versions of Fiats. This is a 1.2-litre VAZ 2101, or Lada, the Russian version of the 124

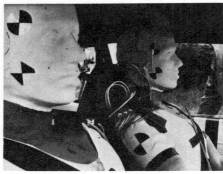

Safety engineering is a major consideration in modern car design and development, and every year manufacturers deliberately crash examples of their latest models in order to ensure that occupants are protected in accidents. Moreover, it is a requirement that all cars meet certain minimum head-on impact standards before they can be marketed in certain countries, so examples of even the most expensive cars built by companies such as Lamborghini are destroyed in controlled 'crashes' into concrete blocks.
Major companies such as Ford of Britain crash dozens of cars each year—

this sequence shows how a Capri is launched at a concrete block, and that its passenger compartment stays intact during impact

aided by the curious climate of Los Angeles, which concentrates exhaust fumes into a noxious 'smog', they called for exhausts to be cleaned up. Senator Ed Muskie promoted a bill in Congress that required exhaust pollutants to be reduced by 95 per cent, and in an effort to meet such impossible demands, engines were 'de-toxed' to such an extent that performance and efficiency suffered.

One effect of this was to encourage development of the Wankel rotary engine, which was said to have a 'cleaner' exhaust; other 'clean-exhaust' engines were proposed, too. Japanese manufacturer Honda claimed to have developed a near fume-free engine after long development. An egg-cup shaped chamber on top of each cylinder was said to act as an auxiliary combustion chamber, controlling combustion temperature and fuel mixture.

The environment lobby pressed for cars that were safe to crash, too, for that was much easier than insisting on better driving standards. Many hundreds of controlled crashes were staged every year by companies in the industry, in research programmes to improve the safety of their products, as well as to meet US Federal requirements for any who intended to sell cars in America.

Safety belts had been introduced at the end of the 1960s, and their fitment became compulsory in most countries; few governments insisted that they were actually worn. . . .

Because of the reluctance of many motorists to wear seat belts, the American lobbyists became obsessed with the air bag, which would inflate automatically in a crash, cushioning the passengers from impact. It was potentially as dangerous as the impact itself: but it took several years to persuade the airbag's protagonists of its disadvantages.

But standards were enforced for control layouts, angles of vision, tyres: the American obsession with safety meant that many European cars of perfectly sound design became difficult – or impossible – to import into the USA.

The European Economic Community, too, had decided ideas on vehicle safety: and like the Americans, one of the concepts they embraced was that of the 'safety vehicle', a sort of motorised tank that would certainly protect its

Two approaches to safety. The Volvo Experimental Safety Vehicle *(above)* protects its occupants by cocooning them in steel.

The Rover 3500 *(left)* is running at speed on a deflated Dunlop 'Denovo' tyre (right front). This safeguards against loss of control in a blow-out, and as a 'fail-safe' device is thus a very positive contribution to safety

NSU were first in the field with Wankel rotary-engined cars, and introduced the sophisticated Ro 80 *(above)* at the end of 1967, after three years of experience with a smaller Spyder. Engine had many teething troubles, and because it gained a reputation for a high fuel consumption sales lagged in 1973–74

occupants in a crash, but which would be too heavy, complex and expensive to produce. Much time and money was wasted on these futile machines, for the car makers were quite capable of making cars safer without making them impracticable: the introduction of energy-absorbing steering columns to reduce the risk of chest injuries to drivers was just one example.

In late 1972, European car manufacturers set up a committee seeking a joint solution to the problems of car safety and pollution. One of its aims was to seek and obtain greater uniformity of international regulations governing both topics.

Putting the problems in perspective, Ken Teesdale, the Tasmanian-born engineer who headed Ford's vehicle safety research programme, commented: 'It is unrealistic to expect vehicle safety design on its own to work miracles on the accident statistics. The real need is for a comprehensive approach which inter-relates the driver with his vehicle and the laws of the road.

'Everybody has the same objective,' he pointed out. 'We all want to reduce the accident and injury rate. But from the manufacturers' point of view we have only one starting point: we must design vehicles for *today's* road conditions, and they must be vehicles which people *want* to buy.

'It is time for a long, hard look to be taken at the driver's own responsibilities in the total safety picture.

'I have long advocated the introduction of a probationary period for new drivers, during which they would be limited to a top speed of, say, 50 mph. Further and more stringent driving tests would have to be taken before motorists qualify for an all groups driving licence.'

Teesdale deplored the lack of instruction for new drivers in motorway and night-driving techniques, as well as car-handling during skid conditions, also proposing compulsory annual medical tests for motorists over the age of 60.

In fact, concluded Teesdale, the growing tide of motoring legislation could prove harmful by its sheer complexity:

'There is an immediate need for simpler – and therefore more enforceable – road laws than exist at present. Their confusion hampers the level of sympathy which people normally exhibit when they recognise a concept as useful and good.'

From Revolution to Evolution
rear-engined racing

While leading constructors gave little thought to anything but the 'conventional' front-engined layout after the Second World War, the rear-engined concept was adopted whole-heartedly in the half-litre class. True, Alfa Romeo had built a rear-engined car, but it had proved to be an ill-mannered beast in tests and in any case was not needed, and there had been the ambitious four-wheel drive Cisitalia-commissioned Porsche 360, a project which ran out of money before the car was really tried. It was therefore in England that the trend towards the rear-engined layout, which now seems so obvious, really got under way.

It did not spring from high-flown design ideology, but working practicability. The half-litre movement started in England in the mid-1940s, and in June 1946, Charles and John Cooper built their first 500 cc car. To a simple box-section and tubular frame they added suspension units from Fiat 500s, a JAP single-cylinder speedway engine, and a Triumph gearbox and chain drive to the rear wheels.

In 1950, when 500 cc racing became the FIA Formula 3, it was proliferating in England, and far from being an end in itself was proving an invaluable *ab initio* class for a new generation of drivers. Coopers were the predominant cars, slowly evolving (although never becoming sophisticated), by 1951 almost invariably powered by the famous twin-ohc 'double-knocker' Norton single, giving up to 48 bhp (or over 150 bhp/ton in a Cooper). They were being produced in extraordinary numbers – little recognized at the time, a British motor racing industry was growing fast.

By the late 1950s, 500 cc racing had virtually become Cooper one-make racing, and lost much of its appeal. After a modestly successful venture into the 2 litre grands prix in 1952–53 with front-engined cars, Coopers returned to prominence under the $1\frac{1}{2}$ litre Formula 2 which came into effect in 1957, with the rear-engined T41. The car proved significant, and so was the engine usually fitted, the Coventry Climax FPF.

In 1958 and 1959 Coopers won the F2 championship, in 1960 they shared it with Porsche. Thus another constructor wedded to the rear-engined format came into single-seater racing, first with adapted RSK sports cars, then in 1959 with a from-scratch open-wheel racing car. The one outstanding feature of this $1\frac{1}{2}$ litre Formula 2 was that front-engined cars hardly featured. Lotus gained two good placings with Colin Chapman's first single-seater, the 16, but by the end of 1959 he perforce followed the Cooper example, and began to transform it with the 18; Ferrari produced the 156, with a powerful front-mounted V-6, which was raced occasionally and scored a major victory at Rheims in 1957, but in 1960 even the Scuderia turned to rear-engined cars.

By 1960 the concept had been well and truly proved in GP racing, by Cooper. Typically, an F1 Cooper 'just growed' out of the F2 car, by easy stages. At the instigation of the Coopers and Rob Walker, Coventry Climax built a 1·96 litre 175 bhp version of the FPF in 1957, and Jack Brabham drove an F2 car fitted with one of these to win a minor *formule libre* race at the end of the year. Early in 1958, Walker ran his car in the Argentine GP, a world championship race. Stirling Moss drove it, and pulled off a brilliant tactical victory – which at the time was interpreted as no more than that. Nor

was much more read into Maurice Trintignant's victory in the same car in the Monaco GP.

The Cooper single-seaters evolved from the rather spindly 1957 F2 cars, until in 1959–60 they became almost suddenly low, lithe, purposeful grand prix cars. In parallel, the Coventry Climax four-cylinder engines grew up to full 2·5 litre units, to produce 245 bhp at 6,750 rpm. And through this period, the Cooper team had an invaluable asset: Jack Brabham, then 'the quiet Australian'. With Coopers, he really fathered the modern approach to car tuning for circuits, advancing this well beyond its previous stage of concentrating preparation on the mechanicals, to patient work with suspension settings and so on – in 1960, he even won a battle with Charles Cooper, and persuaded him to adopt coil suspension 'all round'.

Brabham gained his reward in 1959, when he took the world championship, and in 1960 when he won it even more impressively, with five GP victories in succession (in the Dutch, Belgian, French, British and Portugese GPs). Jack was to attain a stature in racing which nobody would have forecast for him when he first came to Europe as a good driver with mechanical aptitude. . . .

In his championship years, Brabham was ably backed up by the Cooper number two driver, New Zealander, Bruce McLaren. At Sebring in 1959, he became the youngest driver ever to win a championship race, when he won the US Grand Prix, from Trintignant in another Cooper while Brabham pushed his car across the line to finish fourth. McLaren, too, was to become one of the outstanding men of recent motor racing.

These successes could not be ignored, and by 1960 virtually every constructor was endeavouring to emulate the Cooper T53. BRM and Ferrari conversions to the new thinking were somewhat hasty (indeed, BRM simply cut up and otherwise adapted front-engined cars). Colin Chapman, on the other hand, gave more fundamental thought to the matter; his Lotus 18 may have looked square-cut and almost primitive, but it was very light and its utilitarian body was supported on an advanced suspension.

None of this was to the liking of motor racing's traditionalists, who spilled quantities of ink lamenting the then-recent past. They really had a field day when a formula restricting GP engines to $1\frac{1}{2}$ litres was announced, to come into effect in 1961. The protests were loudest in that newly-emergent GP power, England. And unfortunately they fell on receptive ears, which meant that a great deal of time and effort was wasted in attempts to get the formula revoked, and a 'rival' Intercontinental Formula off the ground.

Ferrari got down to building $1\frac{1}{2}$ litre GP cars, based on the F2 Dino 156, and with alternative V-6 engines (the 65 degree 156 unit and a new 120 degree V-6). These cars were beaten only twice during 1961, and then by Stirling Moss rather than by other cars. Moss drove two supreme virtuoso races at Monaco and the Nürburgring, in Rob Walker's Lotus 18. That German GP drew wide attention to a trend in tyre technology; Moss used 'high-hysteresis' Dunlop tyres, and increasingly thereafter the sometimes finicky matters of compound began to demand more attention than the more obvious aspects of tread patterns.

Ferrari driver Phil Hill took the championship in 1961, the first American to do so; he secured it at the Italian GP, a tragic race where his team mate Wolfgang von Trips tangled with Jim Clark, and crashed into the crowd.

Several significant things happened in the second half of the year. Team Lotus gained its first GP victory, albeit in the absence of Ferrari, when Innes Ireland won the American race. The first Coventry Climax V-8 appeared in the back of Brabham's Cooper in the German GP, the first BRM V-8 appeared at Monza. An MRD was driven into second place in a Formula Junior race at Goodwood by Gavin Youl. The MRD was in fact the first Brabham car, for Jack had tired of the conservatism of Charles Cooper (that perhaps sounds odd, as the Coopers had so recently sparked off the GP revolution, but having done so Cooper senior was stubbornly content to rest on his laurels); in the summer of 1962 Jack was to race the first GP Brabham, designed by Ron Tauranac.

Ferrari was eclipsed in 1962, when BRM at last gained the constructors' championship after 12 years of frustration. Graham Hill was champion driver, his challenger through the season was Jim Clark. The last really great driver from the front-engined era still active, Stirling Moss, had retired after a near-fatal accident at Goodwood, when the space frame of his Lotus 18 had folded as he hit a bank.

Because of the need to accommodate a driver, a pure space frame is necessarily weak at the cockpit, but Colin Chapman had a partial solution to that almost ready in the metal, albeit driver safety was a side advantage to gaining unprecedented body rigidity, and a saving in weight. His Lotus 25 had a monocoque hull of stressed aluminium sheet, transversely braced by steel bulkheads. This hull weighed 70 lb, compared with the 84 lb of its immediate space-frame predecessor, the Lotus 24. Moreover, the whole car was sleek and low, with its driver 'sitting' in a semi-prone position. Another trend had been started. . . .

Thereafter, Jim Clark and Lotus – to which should by hyphenated Coventry Climax, Dunlop, Hewland and other suppliers whose importance was so much greater in the new 'kit-car' period – set the pace in the 1½ litre formula. Clark took the championship in 1963 and 1965, went to the last race of 1964, in Mexico, needing a victory to win the title, and was leading handsomely when his engine failed on the penultimate lap.

Graham Hill could have gained the championship at that race, too, but he was put out early after an incident with Ferrari driver Lorenzo Bandini. When Clark dropped out, Bandini let his team leader John Surtees through into second place behind Dan Gurney, and the points John scored clinched the championship for him.

This was success in the face of probability for Ferrari, whose cars in fact won only three championship races. Generally, Lotus or BRM came out on top from 1962 until 1965. Porsche came and went, with only one lucky championship victory to the credit of their air-cooled four- and eight-cylinder cars, scored by Gurney in one of the latter cars in the 1962 French GP. Lola came and went, with only a non-championship race to their credit. Cooper faded, and although Bruce McLaren persevered he gained only one championship victory in five years, at Monaco in 1962. Brabham came, and began to see rewards when Gurney won the 1964 French and Mexican GPs. Honda came, everybody feared an onslaught of motor cycle proportions, until it became obvious that the Japanese car would not quickly be made competitive (the RA-270 was a dumpy little car, with a tubular frame and a transversely-mounted V-12 for which 225 bhp at 12,500 rpm was claimed, although the reality was more modest).

The ultimate 1½ litre engine was built by Coventry Climax, and never raced. This FWMW was a flat 16 – 'flat' in the interests of compactness, 16 cylinders to gain greater piston area. It had a theoretical output of 250 bhp, but it was never needed as the revised Coventry Climax FWMV V-8 produced 215 bhp at 10,500 rpm in 1965, and this was adequate to power Jim Clark's Lotus 33 (a slightly revised 25) to six GP victories and the championship.

Runner-up was Graham Hill, and third in the championship was his new BRM team mate Jackie Stewart, who scored his first championship victory in the Italian GP at Monza. Dan Gurney was fourth in the table; in a foretaste of the coming 'tyre war' his Brabham wore Goodyear tyres. So did the Honda RA-272 which Richie Ginther drove to win the Mexican GP, and incidentally thus spoil Dunlop's record,

Above: Formula 3 cars at Silverstone in 1953, most of them Coopers powered by Norton single-cylinder engines, which brought a rather unlikely and unlovely sound to motor racing

Below: grown-up Cooper. Jack Brabham in a 2.5 litre Grand Prix Cooper-Climax in 1960, when he won his second world championship, and Coopers gained the constructors championship

for their tyres had been on every other 1½ litre winner. In the championship table Ginther placed seventh behind Ferrari drivers Surtees and Bandini, who used cars with the well-tried V-8 favoured by Ferrari since 1962 and a flat-12, for which 220 bhp at 12,000 rpm was claimed – some 20 bhp less than the output of the 1965 Honda V-12, which must therefore have been less efficiently used!

Despite early misgivings, the 1½ litre formula was successful. The smallest grand prix cars in history were by 1965 also the fastest of all time round any given road circuit where direct comparisons were possible. Unprecedented progress was made in chassis design, and in road holding; the races had been hard-fought, the pre-assumed 'lack of power' in 'roller skate cars' had not led to mediocrity, and the genius of drivers like Jim Clark had not been stunted.

Nevertheless, there was relief when the grand prix engine size was doubled for 1966: 3 litres was seen as 'the return of power.' Contrary to some expectations, however, this did not mean a return to too much power, because of the enormous progress made in aspects such as suspension design. It led only briefly to the complication pundits predicted – vastly complex multi-cylinder engines were built, were self-defeating and were in any case soon to be ruled out when a ruling restricted cylinders to 12, while four-wheel drive produced no benefits in racing. One very straightforward engine came to dominate the 3 litre GPs, year after year, while the chassis and impedimenta it propelled became increasingly sophisticated, and ever safer.

However widely it may have been welcomed, the 3 litre formula found many constructors unprepared; the withdrawal of Coventry Climax could well have been a body-blow to some British teams. Ferrari always used to have the facility to turn out an engine for any occasion, and came up with a 265 bhp 2·4 litre six, based on the 2½ litre GP engine, and the 312 V-12 derived from a sports car unit and capable of some 330 bhp. BRM stretched their V-8 to 2 litres and 260 bhp, and set about an H-16. This in effect was two flat eights, one atop the other, driving through connected crankshafts. On the bench it gave 400 bhp when it appeared halfway through 1966; in cars it seldom gave anything but trouble (although to the surprise of many Jim Clark did win the 1966 American GP with a BRM H-16-powered Lotus 43).

Through a distributorship, Cooper had connections with Maserati, and Maserati had a 3 litre racing V-12. A rather aged V-12, mark you – it dated back to 2½ litre 250F days – but the cobwebs were blown out and the bulky lump squeezed into the unlovely T81. From mid-season, Coopers had the services of John Surtees, too, for personality clashes at Ferrari meant that he left the Italian team (he snatched a victory for Coopers in the Mexican GP, before leaving to spend a generally frustrating period with Honda).

Bruce McLaren sought engines for his first GP car, the M2B designed by Robin Herd with a novel Mallite hull skin; he tried a modified Indianapolis Ford V-8, which produced an incredible amount of noise, but little power; he tried a Serenissima V-8, which at least was less noisy.

Dan Gurney arranged for Harry Weslake to produce a V-12 for his AAR Eagle, until it was ready running these superbly built cars with 2·7 litre Coventry Climax 'fours'. Late in the year, Honda came up with a V-12, this time mounted fore and aft in the RA-273; this, too, made a great noise, but at least it signified real power – unhappily, the chassis was inept. . . .

Jack Brabham and Ron Tauranac found their engine in Melbourne, Australia, where Frank Hallam and Phil Irving had designed a simple single-ohc Repco V-8 on the basis of the Oldsmobile F85 block. This Repco 620 gave a scant 300 bhp, and was mounted in the deceptively simple space-frame Brabham BT19 and BT20 – a down to earth combination which was to triumph over 'advanced technology'.

On July 3 1966 at the classic Rheims circuit – being used for the French GP for the last time – Jack Brabham became the first driver to win a world championship race in a car bearing his own name. He covered the 246 miles at 136·90 mph, which meant that his historic victory was also the fastest-ever in a grand prix on a true road circuit. Brabham went on to win the British, Dutch and German GPs, and the world championship.

The Brabham team took the 1967 championship, too, with Denny Hulme finishing ahead of Jack Brabham in the drivers' championship, in what was to be the last successful year for the Repco engine. In an effort to match the power of other engines in 1968, Repco developed the four-ohc 860 V-8, which proved extremely troublesome.

There were victories for V-12s in 1967. Pedro Rodriguez drove a Cooper to win in South Africa; this was the last GP victory for the marque. Dan Gurney achieved an immensely satisfying result in winning the Belgian GP in one of his Eagles; this was the only GP to be won by the first hatching of GP Eagles. John Surtees won the Italian GP for Honda, out-foxing Jack Brabham out of the last corner; despairing of the earlier Honda, Surtees had a lighter new chassis made in England, by Lola, but the car seldom looked competitive again, and Honda withdrew from racing after the next season.

While the championship was falling to Repco-Brabhams, and assorted V-12s were winning occasional races, a new combination was setting the real 3 litre standard: Lotus and Cosworth.

After Coventry Climax withdrew from racing, Colin Chapman approached Ford for an engine, and that company agreed to commission Keith Duckworth of Cosworth. An F2 engine was built first, the FVA based on the Ford 116E, and the DFV followed to complete the £100,000 commission. It was a straightforward V-8, compact, neat and intended from the outset to be a load-bearing member of the chassis. It met the 400 bhp target immediately, and by the end of 1967 was producing a reliable 410 bhp at 9,000 rpm.

Harley Copp and Walter Hayes, the Ford executives chiefly responsible for their company's involvement in GP racing, stood by a fence at a corner on the Zandvoort circuit when the engine was first raced. By half-distance they knew that the investment which outwardly meant the name 'Ford' cast into the rocker covers of the DFV was justified. But certainly none of us at that Dutch GP could have imagined that six years later the DFV would power a car to a championship race victory

Below left: Brabham making the first race start in a Climax V-8-powered car—his Cooper heads the field into the first turn in the 1961 German GP. Bonnier follows in a Porsche, race-winner Moss is on the left (Lotus No 1). *Below right:* Brabham (Brabham) heads Clark (Lotus) in the 1964 Aintree 200. *Bottom left:* BRM drivers Hill and Stewart lead Bandini (Ferrari) at Monaco in 1965. *Bottom right:* paper tigers—Hondas at the French GP pits in 1965

for the 66th time. Year after year in the most competitive formula in history engine constructors attempted to match it; in 1973 only car constructors who used it stood a real chance of winning. . . .

In 1967 it was used in the Lotus 49s driven by Jim Clark and Graham Hill. The 49 matched the engine in being straightforward, and neat. Its stiff sheet-aluminium monocoque hull terminated at the engine bulkhead, to which the engine was attached. The rear suspension was attached to the back of the engine through triangulated sub frames.

Jim Clark drove the 49 to a debut victory at Zandvoort, and won the British, American and Mexican GPs (as well as the revived Spanish GP, run to qualify the event for championship status in 1968). Teething troubles meant that the championship eluded Team Lotus in 1967; in 1968 it was to fall to Gold Leaf Team Lotus.

The Changing Scene
The whole grand prix scene changed rapidly in the late 1960s and early 1970s. Sponsorship from outside the motor industry became essential; the establishment's initial reaction had been to restrain tainting brashness within stipulated square centimetres on cars; under the Players arrangement with Lotus, the team became Gold Leaf Team Lotus, and the cars were painted

in the colours of the Gold Leaf cigarette brand. In a logical, although to some distasteful, extension, the Lotus 72s became 'John Player Specials' in 1972 (when the British Grand Prix was the John Player Grand Prix).

Meanwhile, other sponsors and teams had followed suit. BRMs—of all cars!—became Yardley-BRMs, and then when Yardley transferred their affiliations to the more rewarding McLaren team, they became Marlboro-BRMs—until that cigarette company tired of ineffectiveness. Cars which might have been Frank Williams Specials appeared in the guise of Politoys and Iso-Marlboro. And so on, to the point where seasonal sponsorship changes became as much a centre of interest as driver changes.

On the technical side, four-wheel drive came in 1969, as most pundits had insisted it would if the power of 3 litre engines was to be fully exploited. Lotus, Matra and McLaren all built four-wheel drive cars, and so did Cosworth, although that car was never raced. Advances in chassis, suspension and tyre design meant that the weight and complication of the arrangement were positive handicaps. Most of the four-wheel drive cars built are now curiosities to be gazed at in the Donington Collection.

Quite suddenly in 1968 aerodynamics as aids to road holding and 'putting the power on the road' became a

centre of interest. Modest nose spoilers, little more than tabs, were not unknown in the GP world, and there had been sports car experiments with larger aerofoils. At the Belgian GP, Ferrari, and Brabham and McLaren all added small rear aerofoils to their cars, mounted above the rear wheels, in the very 'dirty' airflow from the engine intakes. Characteristically, once he adopted the idea Colin Chapman carried it through logically, and very soon his Lotus 49s were carrying large 'wings' mounted directly to the rear suspension and high enough to be clear of turbulence. Their downthrust (calculated to be 400 lb at 150 mph) was effective, for a time in causing transmission failures! By the end of the year, adjustable aerofoils had appeared,

and so had outlandish 'biplane' arrangements, with high-mounted nose aerofoils on some cars.

Within a year from that Belgian GP, these strut-mounted aerofoils were banned, following two dramatic Lotus 49B crashes in the Spanish GP at Barcelona. Thereafter, aerodynamic aids were restrained within sensible limits; aerofoils remained distinctive elements of cars, at the rear often being mounted well behind gearboxes in a continuing search for the elusive 'clean' airflow in which they could function efficiently (until, in 1974, this extension to overall car length was restricted).

In a similar quest for aerodynamic efficiency came wedge noses, and side-mounted radiators, first and most notably on the Lotus 72, which suc-

Above: Stirling Moss during his great virtuoso race in Walker's Lotus at Monaco in 1961. *Right:* greatest driver of the modern era, Jim Clark
Below left: Surtees' Cooper flanked by the Ferraris of Bandini and Parkes at the start of the 1966 French GP, the last to be run at Rheims. *Right:* lumps—an H-16 BRM (Stewart) a Cooper-Maserati (Rindt) and a Honda (Ginther) in the 1966 Mexican GP

ceeded the 49 in 1970. Air boxes, to feed cold air effectively to engines, added another distinctive feature to cars in the early 1970s. By 1973, crash-resistant 'deformable' hulls were required by regulation.

The tyres on the 1966 Brabham were made to look positively skinny, as a battle developed between three companies (Dunlop backed out of this expensive contest at the end of 1970,

and Firestone tried to two years later). The right choice of tyres could be crucial, and extensive testing accounted for as many circuit miles as racing. The degree of 'stickiness' in the treads could be upset by variations in temperature, caused by changing weather or the weight of a car as fuel was used, so that tyres could 'go off' and cost race places. Tyres also became increasingly puncture-prone, although at the low pressures used (15 psi or less), a slow deflation was no longer the handicap it would once have been (the 1973 Spanish GP, for example, was won by a car with a tyre that once would have been considered 'flat'). A big step toward safety was made when methods of securing deflated tyres to wheels was introduced, for this gave drivers a chance of retaining control in a sudden blow-out.

In spite of the fact that there was one proven way to build a race winner by 1973, starting with a Cosworth DFV and a Hewland gearbox, there was more individuality among the two dozen or so cars on a GP grid than there had been for decades.

By that time, the pattern of racing

Below: Jack Brabham in a Brabham on his way to a clear victory in the 1966 British GP, and Dan Gurney in an Eagle at Monaco in 1968, both cars innocent of aerodynamic aids. Between them, Bruce McLaren has a full complement of wings on the M7 he is testing at Silverstone in 1969. *Bottom:* first aerofoils, on Amon's Ferrari in the 1968 Belgian GP; end of wings (Rindt's wing buckling just before he crashed in the 1969 Spanish GP); cars still flew at the Nürburgring (Beltoise in a Matra)

had changed vastly. The world championship series embraced North and South America, and South Africa, as well as Europe. Just as the costs of competing had escalated wildly, so had the expense of mounting races. A widespread safety campaign made heavy demands on circuit owners, although apparent compliance with the letter of regulations did not necessarily buy safety.

Costs plus the safety requirements spelled the end of some races. Of the once-numerous non-championship events for GP cars, only two British events continued to be run regularly, the Race of Champions at Brands Hatch and the International Trophy at Silverstone, and both admitted F5000 cars to make up full grids. By this time, only Silverstone of all the GP circuits in use 20 years earlier was substantially unchanged, and ironically this once despised airfield circuit had become one of the most testing for drivers. The Nürburgring had been eased, Monaco had been extended, although both retained their unique characteristics; Rheims lay abandoned, and its old equal in the speed table, Spa, was abandoned by GP cars after the 1970 race. The superb Osterreichring at Zeltweg was used for the Austrian GP from 1970, when the German race was run at the potentially dangerous Hockenheim circuit while the Nürburgring was made 'safe'. In its eternally nomadic progress around France, the oldest of all GPs went to the near-natural circuit of Clermont-Ferrand and to the wholly artificial racing

facility created by Paul Ricard near Bandol. The Spanish race alternated between Jarama and Barcelona, after deserting Spa the Belgians for political reasons ran their race at the artificial Nivelles and Zolder tracks (the latter being the setting for a notably unworthy event in 1973).

The Championships
The period of Cosworth domination started in 1968, when the engine became available to other constructors. Happily, however, Graham Hill took the championship, for the first half of the season had been tragic for Lotus. After winning the first championship race, in South Africa, and clinching the Tasman championship in a 2·5 litre Lotus 49, the greatest driver of the rear-engined era, Jim Clark, was killed in a mysterious accident in a Hockenheim F2 race. Then Mike Spence was killed in a Lotus at Indianapolis.

The team pulled itself together, Hill doing a sterling job (although Chapman was not to establish the sort of rapport he had with Clark until Emerson Fittipaldi blossomed two years later).

Championship runner-up was Hill's one-time team-mate Jackie Stewart, driving a Matra. This French company moved into Formula I with the MS-11, powered by their own V-12 (which in its first F1 guise produced a lot of noise and a second place to justify the small fortune in French taxpayers' money invested in it), and the DFV-powered MS-10 and MS-80 which were entrusted to Ken Tyrrell to race (he had ordered DFVs before he knew which

Top: Colin Chapman driving the clean and functional Lotus 49 before it was first raced in the 1967 Dutch GP which Clark *(right)* won. *Centre:* less successful Lotus essays were the 4-wd 63 of 1969 (Rindt at Oulton Park) and the 4-wd gas turbine 56B of 1971 (Wisell in the British GP). *Above:* the 72 in its John Player Special guise — Fittipaldi about to retire in the US GP with a deflated rear tyre and *(right)* a pair of JPS in the Kendall Centre at Watkins Glen; inboard mounting of front brakes and monocoque hull show clearly on nearest car

Following pages: Jackie Stewart, supreme driver of 1973, in a Tyrrell. *Inset, left to right:* also present in 1973 were JPS, McLaren, March, Ferrari and Shadow

chassis he would be using!). In Tyrrell's cars, Stewart won the Dutch, German and American GPs. Denny Hulme won the Italian and Canadian GPs in McLarens; earlier in the year Bruce McLaren had won at Spa, to become the second man to win a GP in a car bearing his name.

The following year was Stewart's, for he drove a Tyrrell Matra to victory in South Africa, Spain, Holland, France, Britain and Italy. Hill gained a remarkable fifth victory at Monaco, and his new Lotus team mate Jochen Rindt won in the USA.

Rindt became racing's first posthumous champion in 1970, when he led the Lotus team. Their car was the 72, a handsome 'wedge' bodied machine, with side radiators, torsion bar suspension and inboard brakes at the front as well as the rear (customary by this time). It suffered teething problems, but in the Dutch GP Rindt scored a runaway victory, following this with wins in France, Britain and Germany. Then in practice for the Italian GP he crashed fatally in the braking area for the fast Parabolica at Monza. In the rest of the season, his points score was not surpassed, in part because his young team mate Brazilian Emerson Fittipaldi, won the American GP.

Jack Brabham scored his last GP victory in South Africa, and at the end of the season he retired. His company was run for a while by his partner Ron Tauranac, who then rather surprisingly sold it to Bernie Ecclestone.

In Spain, Stewart had scored the first championship victory for a new marque, March, which arrived rather abruptly and brashly on the GP scene — at all events that victory for a 701 had to suffice them for some time. Ken Tyrrell admitted that he ran a March

Varied circuits. *Top:* Peter Gethin (BRM) 'towing' Peterson (March) and Hailwood (Surtees) past the Monza pits in 1971, last year when the end-of-European-season Italian GP was a glorious flat-out blind; chicanes to break up this sort of racing were introduced in 1972
Centre: Brazilian national hero Emerson Fittipaldi leading the 1973 Brazilian

GP field at Interlagos. Purpose-built circuit squeezes 4.94 miles of track in a very small area.
Above: Barcelona's Montjuich Park, in the centre of the city. Peterson (JPS) and Hulme (McLaren) leading the packed 1973 Spanish GP field away from the grid. Cevert and Stewart in Tyrrells follow, Reutemann takes his Brabham wide on the left

simply as a stand in, for during the season he unveiled his own Tyrrell-Ford.

John Surtees also emerged as a constructor, winning the Oulton Park Gold Cup in his TS7. A great driver-constructor, Bruce McLaren, died in a CanAm car test accident at Goodwood; under strong management his company and racing teams continued.

In both 1970 and 1971 there was the promise of a V-12 challenge. Ferrari won the 1970 Austrian, Italian, Canadian and Mexican GPs, and the first of 1971, when Ickx also won the Dutch GP. Jo Siffert and Peter Gethin, respectively, took the Austrian and Italian GPs for BRM. The BRM V-12 had been slow to mature, since the team had started from what was intended to be a second-string unit – until they threw away their cumbersome H-16. During 1971 BRM's two best drivers, around whom a sound team might have been built, died in crashes – Pedro Rodriguez in a minor German sports car event, Jo Siffert in a secondary F1 race at Brands Hatch at the end of the season.

In the following year BRM collected one lucky victory, at Monaco. Ferrari did little better, *Ringmeister* Ickx gaining their only victory, in the German GP.

The Tyrrell team completely dominated 1971, Stewart winning six GPs, Francois Cevert one. This state might have been expected to continue in 1972, but there was a strong resurgence of Lotus fortunes. In 1971 the team was unsettled; Fittipaldi was off-form for much of the season after a road accident, Wisell suffered the misfortunes of his predecessors in the Lotus number two seat; much time was spent on the turbine-powered four-wheel drive 56B which was never competitive. Slightly refined in 1972, the 72s appeared as John Player Specials, and there was a new sense of purpose in the team under Peter Warr. Emerson Fittipaldi matured, and clinched the championship by winning the Italian GP.

Jackie Stewart had been unwell during 1972, but he was most decidedly on top form in 1973, when he demonstrated that in single-seater racing he had no peer. He quite clearly took his third world championship, and at the end of the season announced his retire-

Grand Prix variety in 1973—McLaren, Surtees, Iso-Marlboro and Brabham cars, with Cosworth engines and Hewland gearboxes as common factors.

Above: the 1974 season was more open, and saw a resurgence of V-12 engines. This group braking for the first corner at Kyalami is headed by the Ferraris driven by Regazzoni and Lauda, flanking Carlos Reuteman's Brabham BT44. Reuteman won this South African GP, the first Argentinian driver to win a world championship event since Fangio; it was also the first championship victory for the Brabham marque since Jack Brabham won the race four years earlier. Following are Scheckter's Tyrrell, Merzario's Iso-Marlboro, and Fittipaldi's McLaren. Under the varied 'cold-air boxes' further back are BRMs and an assortment of Cosworth-engined cars—Surtees, March, JPS, Lola and Hesketh (during the year more than a dozen constructors built cars around the Cosworth V-8).

Lauda and Regazzoni took the first two places in the Spanish GP at Jarama, to confirm the revival in Ferrari's fortunes, which was in part due to their concentration on GP racing.

ment. This closed an era, for not only was there no immediately apparent British driver of similar stature, for the first time in some 20 years, there was no other driver with quite his combination of outstanding qualities – off the tracks as well as on them. In nine years, Stewart raced in 99 world championship events, and won 27, more than any other driver in the history of the championship.

Stewart retired when he was on top, and from an unsettled grand prix world; fortunately, the quality of racing in 1973 more than offset the season-long bickering around too many aspects of racing. The only teams to win in 1973 were Lotus, Tyrrell, and McLaren. Their cars were powered by the Cosworth DFV engine; on one hand this was an outstanding achievement, but also undermined the old premise that racing was a forcing ground for technical advances!

Lotus ran Emerson Fittipaldi and the Swede Ronnie Peterson as well-publicized 'joint number one drivers,' and they gained second and third places in the world championship, and secured for Chapman the constructors' championship. Ken Tyrrell's efficient team, where the old number one and number two idea was regarded as obsolete, at least insofar as car preparation was concerned, might well have taken the constructors' title, if he had not withdrawn it from the American GP after François Cevert had been killed in a practice accident. McLaren drivers Hulme and Revson won three GPs, with the efficient M23. The other teams did little more than bulk out grids, and the gulf was largely accounted for by resources. In the GPs of the 1970s there was little chance for the less well-endowed, the badly-managed, those with inadequate technical resources, or even those enjoying passing bad luck. The world of grand prix racing had changed vastly even during the span of the 3 litre formula; it seemed light years removed from the last classic era of the 1950s.

Secondary classes. March *(top)* and Surtees *(centre)* took the European Formula 2 championship in 1973 and 1972 respectively. Formula 5000 is a predominantly Anglo-American class, for cars built around stock-block 5 litre engines. Past Rothmans F5000 champion Peter Gethin with a Chevron B24 at Brands Hatch in 1973

Uncertain Seventies

The Motor Age reached its 75th birthday in 1970; whether it will reach its centenary in a form recognisable to today's motorists is anybody's guess. Certainly the growth rate of the late 1960s was maintained into the first years of the new decade, but it was equally obvious that things could not go on in the same way for ever.

For one thing, the number of cars in use had increased so greatly that, es-

The Holden, 'Australia's own car', has broken from its one-time Vauxhall image with models such as this Monaro LS, which has a positive identity of its own

pecially in city centres, congestion was eroding the car's great advantage, that of rapid door-to-door transportation. Then came the first signs of a real awareness that the world's fuel and raw materials reserves were not infinite, albeit this was forced by a Middle East conflict.

But at first things continued as usual. Britain's car industry, which produced 1,900,000 cars in 1972 was all set to produce 2,500,000 in 1973, targets that had not been seen since the boom years of the 'never had it so good' early 1960s.

Setting the pace was Ford, whose policy of providing the most car for

the money was a carefully planned marketing strategy that gave the company a quarter of the British market; for almost two years the Mark III Cortina topped the sales charts. In an attempt to 'out-Ford Ford', British Leyland hired ex-Ford personnel, to develop and market a new model, the Morris Marina, which was the exact antithesis of the group's complex, expensive to produce, front-wheel drive models, and when industrial troubles briefly slowed up Cortina production, it was the Marina which replaced it at the top of the sales charts.

By announcing the front-wheel

Left: the carriage trade, 1970s style. Mercedes-Benz offer both limousines and sporting roadsters *(top),* including the 2.7-litre 280SE, and the 4.5-litre 450SL roadster and long wheelbase 450SEL luxury model.
Centre and bottom: the Rolls-Royce Corniche saloon and the Bentley Corniche convertible are basically identical cars

drive Austin Allegro in mid-1973 as a replacement for part of the 1100–1300 range dating from 1962, BLMC seemed to be hedging their bets: the announcement also gave them a confusingly large range, with many models which seemed to be in direct competition with each other.

Competing for a share of the British market with these two giants were the two other American-owned companies, Vauxhall and Chrysler, who both account for about 10 per cent of sales.

Vauxhall, unlike Ford, did not rationalise their product range with their European counterpart, Opel, though the two ranges are roughly similar in style and content. Chrysler made only token attempts at product integration with Simca (the 160/180 range was largely designed in England, is built in France and marketed in England); indeed, the parent company almost withdrew from Britain entirely in the aftermath of a crippling strike in mid-1973.

Apart from the three giants, the British industry is made up of small specialists, from Rolls-Royce, who survived the liquidation of their parent company, through relatively large companies like Lotus and Reliant, to companies like Panther, which builds a strictly limited edition replica Jaguar SS100 powered by the current Jaguar engine.

Top right: the Hillman Avenger GLS, once marketed in the USA as the Plymouth Cricket. Later Chrysler replaced it in their US line with the five-model Dodge Colt range—cars which were built in Japan by Mitsubishi. *Bottom:* BMW's 2002 Turbo was the first turbo-supercharged model to be marketed by the German company; it had a claimed maximum speed of over 130 mph. *Following pages:* varied British cars of the early 1970s. The front-wheel drive Austin Allegro *(bottom left)* and the Jaguar XJ12 *(top right),* which boasted the only mass-production V-12 engine of the period, are two of the diverse British Leyland range. The Vauxhall Victor FE *(top left)* has 'Transcontinental' styling, very different to Ford's smooth 1974 Capri II *(bottom right)*

Products of two of Europe's largest companies. *Top to bottom:* the Ford Cortina Mk III, announced in 1970, was the latest car in a Cortina line dating back to 1962. Ford's moderately successful large cars of the 1960s, Zephyr and Zodiac, were replaced by the Consul (shown here) with V-4 and V-6 engines, and the more luxurious V-6 Granada, which used the same body shell.

Volkswagen's front-wheel drive 1.6-litre K70 was a determined effort by the German company to show that they could break away from the Beetle image. It was followed by the 1.5 litre Passat, and then the more compact 1.1 and 1.5 litre Golf. By the 1970s, the VW range was extensive, and far-removed from its one-model origins

The French industry, once one of the most diverse in Europe, has become one of the most closely-knit: there are now only four major companies – Renault, Citroen, Peugeot and Chrysler-France – plus a couple of specialists, Alpine-Renault and Matra-Simca, and a few ultra-specialised, ultra-tiny companies whose products have been aimed primarily at home market enthusiast motorists.

But this close grouping seems to work, for France's car industry has enjoyed a growth rate faster than that of any other country than Japan, more than doubling its output from 1965 to 1972, from 1·5 million to 3·3 million. This, too, in the wake of a whole series of groupings (and 'ungroupings') of international proportions. Citroen at one stage made overtures to Peugeot. This broke up, and Volkswagen were approached. There was talk that Citroen would develop a replacement for the VW Beetle, but this came to nothing. However, a tenuous link remained, in the shape of the Comotor Company, jointly owned by Citroen and Audi-NSU, a Volkswagen subsidiary. This company, which operates from a new factory in the Saarland, produces Wankel rotary engines, involvement with which proved so expensive that it cost NSU their independence. The engine, however, appeared in Citroen prototypes.

Citroen itself is controlled by Pardevi, a Swiss company of which Michelin has the majority holding (51 per cent) with Fiat owning 49 per cent.

But the relationship between Citroen and Fiat seems to have been one of cautious cooperation, with the French company proudly retaining its independence. In fact, there have been signs that the state-owned Renault company and the staunchly private Peugeot group, who have operated joint research, development and investment programmes since 1966, would be interested in taking over from Fiat (but it seems unlikely that Michelin would agree to such a move).

Meanwhile Citroen produced a 'baby DS', the 1 litre GS, which has won many design awards and slots neatly between the more agricultural small models and the larger DS and ID.

The Volkswagen range became increasingly diversified. The familiar Beetle lived on, while the rear-engined format became demode – Fiat's little 126 was the only rear-engined, aircooled mass-production car to be introduced by a major manufacturer in a decade – and VW turned to front-wheel drive and water-cooled engines, in the K70, the Passat and the Scirocco. In this small car the engine was not only watercooled, it was mounted transversely in the fashion set by the Mini in 1959. The body of the Scirocco followed the rather stubby lines fashionable on small cars of the period.

The 1970s, then, have seen the motor car become more refined, with items like servo-assisted disc brakes, heated rear windows and fuel injection common features of production cars – Rover even brought four-wheel drive within the reach of the middle-class motorist with the Range Rover.

As cars increased in sophistication, however, so the restrictions on their use increased. In 1965 Britain's motorists were faced with a blanket speed limit of 70 mph, even on the new motorways – 'For four months, just as an experiment,' said the Minister of Transport – which has remained in force ever since. And the regular increases in vehicle and

More cars in the British Leyland multi-model range. *Top to bottom:* the front-wheel drive Austin Maxi; the four-wheel drive 'luxury-utility' Range Rover, which has a 3.5 litre V-8 engine; the Triumph Stag, a roadster powered by a 3-litre V-8. The Leyland P76 was developed in Australia, primarily for the Australian market as a counter to cars in a similar class marketed by American-owned companies. It was introduced in 1973, with alternative engines—a 2.6-litre straight six, or a 4.4-litre V-8. The V-8 in the Range Rover and the Leyland P76 have a common background in a General Motors engine, whereas the Triumph V-8 has been seen only in the Stag

fuel tax, which date back to Winston Churchill's raids on the Road Fund in the 1920s, show that Government regards motoring as a sure-fire fund-raiser.

Even more restrictions resulted from circumstances caused by the Arab-Israeli War of late 1973 and the resultant Arab embargo on oil exports. Governments all over the world had to take positive measures to restrict oil consumption. In many European countries a total ban was placed on Sunday driving; in others formal rationing was introduced for short periods, while rocketing fuel prices proved another effective restriction. Severe speed limits aimed at fuel conservation became commonplace, although these were relaxed as the immediate crisis passed. Supply problems led to acute shortages in many American states, to a general reaction against wastefully thirsty cars, and to some second thoughts about proposed pollution-reducing legislation, which would not lead to improvements in engine fuel consumption.

In Italy, the first carless Sunday emptied the street of everything but taxis and buses, and on-the-spot fines of £67 were imposed on drivers breaking the ban. A man rode through Rome in a chariot drawn by two white horses, while another man trotted round the city shouting that the end of the world was in sight.

A French writer, faced with curbs on speed, exploded: 'To limit the speed of a French driver is like cutting off a rooster's coxcomb.' But the ban stayed, and all racing and rallying was suspended, for a short period (long enough to cause the 1974 Monte Carlo Rally to be cancelled, though). Motor sport in

Left, top to bottom: Citroen's GS is virtually a miniature DS, mechanically complex but delightful to drive. Alfa Romeo revived a famous racing name in the 1779 cc Alfetta. The same company's front-wheel drive Alfasud is a 1.2 litre car developed for production in a new factory built to relieve unemployment in southern Italy. Lancia revived an Edwardian model name in their Beta, made with 1.4, 1.6 or 1.8-litre engines, with saloon or coupe bodies.
Opposite: Fiat's 126 is the latest in a line of miniature cars stretching back to the 1936 570 cc Topolino. The 126 has an air-cooled twin-cylinder 593 cc engine mounted at the rear. It is a practical and economical town runabout, but cramped for long-distance motoring

most countries was restricted to varying degrees, some following the French
example, others being selective – Finland's major winter rally was made an
exception to a total ban, for example,

and so were the Tasman Championship
races in New Zealand.

The crisis hit makers of big cars
hardest. In some American plants,
workers were laid off while production

lines for 'gas guzzlers' were torn out
to make way for smaller models – the
demand for Pintos and Vegas exceeded
supply, and economical imports enjoyed a new boom. In Germany,

Daimler-Benz experienced a slump in orders for Mercedes limousines, at one time Opel was reported to have 30,000 big cars 'unsaleable', and BMW closed down for a short period. Italian high-performance specialists, such as Ferrari, Lamborghini and Maserati, laid off workers as stocks of unsold cars built up. Japan's industry, too, was forced to cut back production, after a record year in 1973, when over seven million vehicles of all types were produced.

Manufacturers were investigating alternate power sources, too. In the spring of 1974 Ford began trials of a Pinto compact fitted with a Stirling 'hot-air' engine which, it was claimed, could run on anything from peanut oil to atomic energy, while General Motors continued development of the Wankel rotary engine. Fresh appraisals were being made of steam and electric cars, too.

In fact, the world wide situation at the beginning of 1974 posed a number of major questions: provided that you could get the fuel to operate it, would you still be able to take your car where you wanted when you wanted?

Was the three-quarters of a century of glorious personal freedom that the car had brought about to end, would a new form of personal transportation take over – or could the governments and motor industries of the world find a joint solution?

Time alone, as they say, would tell....

Motoring could still be fun in the gloomy winter of 1973! One of the authors enjoying himself in a pair of economical sporting saloons, a Triumph Dolomite Sprint *(top)* and a Ford Escort RS2000 *(right)*. This type of car took over part of the market once considered the preserve of open two-seaters, fulfilling the same roles in having above-average handling and performance for open-road driving, and being suitable for competition use in racing and rallies

The Preserved Past

Motoring is so much a part of our everyday life that it sometimes is difficult to realise that there are still people living who can remember when there were no more than a couple of hundred cars in the whole of Britain. In the early 1970s I had a long conversation with an 89-year-old sur- vivor of the 1896 London–Brighton Run, who when a teenager had co- driven his father's electric car as an unofficial entry in Mr Lawson's Motor Car Club run; another octogenarian I met around this time could remember clearly his boyhood when there were no cars, and he walked in front of a traction engine with a red flag to warn owners of restive horses.

Paradoxically, though the develop- ment of motoring has been so very rapid, there has always been an interest in its early history. Books on automo- tive development started appearing in the late 1890s, and as early as 1903 the

Hon C. S. Rolls attracted visitors to his stand in the Crystal Palace Automobile Show with a 'relic of the past', a Panhard which had run in the 1895 Paris-Bordeaux race; alongside Roll's new 60 hp racing Mors, the little Panhard must have looked incredibly quaint.

The earliest exhibition of a collection of early cars took place at the 1908 Paris Motor Show, where a 'retrospective exhibition' of several dozen early vehicles, from Cugnot's 1770 *fardier* to cars only four or five years old, was organised.

Four years later, in Britain, Edmund Dangerfield, publisher of *The Motor*, set up a permanent museum of early cars; unhappily this was dispersed during the First World War and several of the exhibits destroyed.

There was, however, sufficient interest in early vehicles to inspire the Daily Sketch to organise an 'Old Crocks Race' from London to Brighton in 1927; some really early vehicles turned up, with drivers garbed in what they fondly thought was period costume, and the event proved so popular that it became an annual occurrence, organised by *The Autocar* until the RAC took it over.

In 1930, three of the old car owners, including S. C. H. Davis, Sports Editor of *The Autocar*, who owned an early Leon Bollée tricar, proposed the formation of a club to encourage the preservation and use of these early vehicles. And the Veteran Car Club, which they set up, is still active today, the world's premier antique vehicle organisation, with around 2,000 members. Originally restricted to owners of pre-1905 machinery, it has latterly extended its terms of reference to take in cars up to 1918.

A few years later, in 1934, another group of enthusiasts, who believed that cars such as the 'old school' Bentleys and the 30/98 Vauxhalls were vastly superior to the models contemporary manufacturers were offering as sporting machinery, formed the Vintage Sports Car Club. After the war it recognised the humbler vintage vehicles, and certain approved 'Post-Vintage Thoroughbreds', too; today it has over 6,000 members.

In America, interest in old cars had developed at an early date, too. In the late 1920s Henry Ford had assembled a representative collection of early vehicles in his mammoth museum at

This 1907 Grand Prix Fiat outside the Biscaretti Museum at Turin is a relic of one of the most remarkable seasons in racing history, when Felice Nazzaro won the three major races—Targa Florio, Kaiserpreis, and French Grand Prix. This is the 16-litre French Grand Prix car

The old car movement has come a long way from the London–Brighton runs of the 1920s (prize-winning Clément-Bayard, *left*) to modern British races for historic cars (two Alfa Romeos heading an ERA at Crystal Palace, *right*)

Greenfield Village, where the main building boasted an 8-acre parquet floor, and in the mid-1930s the Antique Automobile Club of America was formed in Philadelphia. Now it is the world's largest organisation of its kind, with around 100,000 members, producing a glossy magazine of professional quality.

Around the same time, the Horseless Carriage Club of America was founded on the West Coast, while in Boston the Veteran Motor Car Club of America was organised. Leading lights in the VMCCA were two wealthy young men, George Waterman and Kirkland Gibson, who between them acquired a considerable collection of desirable vehicles, eventually proposing to open a museum in an 1880s mansion and carriage house called Belcourt. But the war put an end to this project; wartime scrap drives also caused the wanton destruction of many historic vehicles for whatever brass and aluminium they contained.

Fortunately, many more old cars survived the hostilities, and when in 1946 the British and American motor industries celebrated their Golden Jubilees, drive pasts by antique cars were a prominent part of the proceedings. In the British Jubilee parades the processions were led by what was probably the oldest working road vehicle in the world, the 1875 Grenville steamer, which is now preserved in a West Country museum.

Even so, not everyone realised the historic value of these early vehicles. When in 1949 ex-Brooklands racer R. G. J. Mash applied for planning permission to build a museum at Send, on the Portsmouth Road, to house his unique collection of 105 old vehicles and aircraft, the Surrey County Planning Committee and Guildford Rural Council rejected his application. The chairman of the planning committee, one Alderman Wykeham-Price, pronounced judgment in the following terms: 'It was decided that a museum for such a dull subject in that particular situation would not have a single visitor.'

The lie was given to this aldermanic depression by the huge crowds attending the revived Brighton Run, which soon was attracting an increasing number of overseas entries, one of the most remarkable of which was the 1886 Hammel from Denmark, which had such engaging features as steering which worked 'wrong way round' – turning the steering wheel to the right made the car turn left, and vice versa.

By the 1970s the Brighton Run had established itself as the world's most popular motor sporting event, attracting over 250 entries – all built before 1905! – and two million spectators every year. Entrants came from as far afield as America, shipping their cars across the Atlantic for the 50-mile run and the chance of a finisher's medal.

It was a minor illustration of the reversal of a trend: in the post-war years American collectors had acquired quite a few historic vehicles from Europe; now European collectors were buying American cars. Some of those Brighton runners, indeed, were Ameri-

can imports, like a two-cycle Elmore; this growing international trade in early cars meant that prices inevitably rose. In fact, they soared, especially when auction sales were organised. At the beginning of the 1960s you could buy a perfectly sound vintage tourer for under £50; ten years later it was virtually impossible to find one under £500, and the humbler cars of the 1930s were beginning to acquire a collectors' cachet.

In 1972 Lord Montagu, whose old car collection at his stately home at Beaulieu, Hampshire had formed the nucleus of the National Motor Museum, paid a world record price of £34,000 for a 1908 Grand Prix Benz, which had changed hands only months earlier at an American auction.

While these increasing values have caused greater attention to be paid to authenticity of restoration, they have also priced many enthusiasts out of the old car market – and even led to isolated examples of faking which can be especially difficult to detect in these days when cars can be restored from a handful of original components plus a good measure of replica parts and bodywork.

A few years back, old vehicle enthusiasts were chuckling at the perhaps apocryphal tale of two ingenious tricksters who acquired a perfect example of a much prized American raceabout of the Edwardian era, stripped it down to the last nut and bolt, and made two replicas of every item. Then, using a combination of real and replica parts, they made three cars where one had stood before. Over a period of two or three years they unloaded the three cars at auction sales, where they dec-

Museums. Achille Philion's little 1892 steam car, driven by Joseph Cotten in *The Magnificent Ambersons,* is now part of the massive Harrah Collection at Reno, Nevada *(below).* A leading French collection, belonging to Henri Malartre, is at Rochtaillée-sur-Saône, near Lyon. Cars shown *(bottom left)* are a 1909 Rolland Pilain *(left)* Leon Bollée *berline de voyage* of 1911 and a 1913 Clément Bayard. Central feature of Britain's National Motor Museum at Beaulieu is this display of Land Speed Record cars, with *Golden Arrow* in the foreground, the '1,000 hp' Sunbeam and Donald Campbell's *Bluebird* behind it

eived the most hardened experts, and netted a handsome profit for the scheme's perpetrators.

However, it is still possible for the enthusiast to find genuine, unrestored cars, even in the legendary old barn. Cars like the rumoured 1904 Sunbeam that powers a Sussex lighting plant, like the Rolls-Royce Silver Ghost slung from a garage ceiling, like the Model T Ford that drives a sawbench in Cheshire. All have been reported in the past year or so, all *may* be genuine.

One that can be personally vouched for is the 1920 Angus Sanderson which blocks a hole in a hedge in mid-Kent. In the early 1970s, although battered and fitted with solid iron tyres on home-made rims, it looked complete. So I enquired at the nearby house whether the car was for sale.

'Dear me, no,' came the reply. 'We own a timber business, and Grandad still uses the car to pull logs up from the lower meadow. What would he use if we sold the car?'

Index